D0204138

On Course

SIXTH EDITION

On Course

Strategies for Creating Success in College and in Life

SKIP DOWNING

WADSWORTH
CENGAGE Learning™

Australia • Brazil • Japan • Korea • Mexico • Singapore • Spain • United Kingdom • United States

WADSWORTH
CENGAGE Learning

On Course: Strategies for Creating Success in College and in Life, Sixth Edition
Skip Downing

Senior Publisher: Lyn Uhl

Senior Sponsoring Editor: Shani Fisher

Development Editor: Marita Sermolins

Assistant Editor: Daisuke Yasutake

Editorial Assistant: Cat Salerno

Media Editor: Emily Ryan

Senior Marketing Manager: Kirsten Stoller

Marketing Coordinator: Ryan Ahern

Marketing Communications Manager: Martha Pfeiffer

Content Project Manager: Susan Miscio

Art Director: Linda Jurras

Print Buyer: Julio Esperas

Permissions Editor: Bob Kauser

Production Service: S4Carlisle Publishing Services

Text and Cover Designer: Carol Maglitta/ One Visual Mind

Photo Manager: John Hill

Photo Researcher: PrePress PMG

Cover Images: Compass and Map ©istock

Compositor: S4Carlisle Publishing Services

© 2011. Wadsworth, Cengage Learning

ALL RIGHTS RESERVED. No part of this work covered by the copyright herein may be reproduced, transmitted, stored, or used in any form or by any means graphic, electronic, or mechanical, including but not limited to photocopying, recording, scanning, digitizing, taping, Web distribution, information networks, or information storage and retrieval systems, except as permitted under Section 107 or 108 of the 1976 United States Copyright Act, without the prior written permission of the publisher.

For product information and technology assistance, contact us at
Cengage Learning Customer & Sales Support, 1-800-354-9706

For permission to use material from this text or product, submit all requests online at **cengage.com/permissions**. Further permissions questions can be emailed to **permissionrequest@cengage.com**

Library of Congress Control Number: 2009935402

ISBN-13: 978-1-4390-8620-9

ISBN-10: 1-4390-8620-6

Wadsworth
20 Channel Center Street
Boston, MA 02210
USA

Cengage Learning products are represented in Canada by Nelson Education, Ltd.

For your course and learning solutions, visit **www.cengage.com**.

Purchase any of our products at your local college store or at our preferred online store **www.ichapters.com**

Printed in the United States of America
1 2 3 4 5 6 7 13 12 11 10 09

To Carol, my compass

Contents

3

Discovering Self-Motivation 63

4   Mastering Self-Management   101

---

8 Developing Emotional Intelligence   243

9 **Staying On Course to Your Success**   279

Preface

On Course is intended for college students of any age who want to create success both in college and in life. Whether you are taking a student success or first-year seminar course, a composition course, or an "inward-looking" course in psychology, self-exploration, or personal growth, *On Course* is your instruction manual for dramatically improving the quality of your outcomes and experiences. In each chapter, you'll learn essential study skills—reading, note-taking, studying, memorizing, test taking, and writing—for success in college. However, that's just the beginning. Through self-assessments, articles, guided journals, case studies in critical thinking, and inspiring stories from fellow students, *On Course* will empower you with time-proven strategies for creating a great life—academic, personal, and professional. You are about to learn the techniques that have helped many thousands of students create extraordinary success! Get ready for the only course you'll probably ever take where the subject of the course is . . . YOU!

New and Proven Features of the Sixth Edition

- **Self-Assessment Questionnaires.** *On Course* begins and ends with a self-assessment questionnaire. By completing the initial questionnaire, you see areas of growth that need attention. By completing the concluding questionnaire, you see your semester's growth. You have the option of completing the questionnaire either in the text or online. An advantage of the online version is that it gives you an immediate printout of your scores. To access the self-assessment online, go to *www.cengage.com/success/Downing/OnCourse6e.*

- **Articles on Proven Success Strategies.** Thirty-two brief articles explain powerful strategies for creating success in college and in life. Each article presents a success strategy from influential figures in psychology, philosophy, business, sports, politics, and personal and professional growth. In these articles, you'll learn the "secrets" of the extraordinarily successful.

- **NEW! Expanded Coverage of Critical Thinking.** When polled, virtually every college educator agrees that critical thinking is essential for success in college and in life. Through Case Studies for Critical Thinking as well as a new essay and journal entry on critical thinking skills, you'll learn effective ways to solve challenging problems. You'll also learn valuable reasoning skills that will help you create and analyze persuasive arguments. These skills will sharpen your thinking ability and provide you with greater control over the quality of your life.

- **Guided Journal Entries.** A guided journal entry immediately follows each article, giving you an opportunity to apply the success strategy you just learned to enhance your results in college and in life. *Believing in Yourself* articles and journal activities appear in each chapter, reinforcing the importance of developing strong self-esteem for long-term success.

- **Embracing Change Activities.** These activities encourage you to experiment for a week with one of the specific success strategies you have just learned. In this way, you can assess the results that this new choice creates in your life. In many cases, you'll want to add it to your toolbox of success strategies and use it for the rest of your life.

- **One Student's Story—More Added!** A popular feature in earlier editions, these short essays are authored by students who used *On Course* strategies to improve the quality of their college outcomes and experiences. These stories show the positive and dramatic results possible when you apply what you learn in this course to overcome the multitude of challenges that can sabotage success in college, and beyond. With the addition of seven student stories, this edition now offers twenty-three inspiring student essays.

- **NEW! CORE Learning System.** Discover and apply the secrets of how effective learners learn. All good learners employ four principles that lead to deep and lasting learning. You'll learn how to use these four principles to create your own system for learning any subject or skill.

- **REVISED and EXPANDED! Wise Choices in College.** This feature helps you learn the **essential study skills** necessary to succeed in college—reading, note-taking, studying, memorizing, test taking, and writing. New strategies have been added to provide even more help for deeper learning and better grades. Additionally, you'll find sections on learning college customs and making wise choices with money, both important factors for success in college.

- **Case Studies for Critical Thinking.** Case studies help you apply the strategies you learn to a real-life situation. As such, they help prepare you to make wise choices in the kinds of challenging situations you will likely face in college. Because case studies don't have "right" answers, they also promote critical and creative thinking.

- ***On Course* Principles at Work.** These sections show how important the *On Course* success strategies are for choosing the right career, getting hired, and succeeding in the work world.

- **Quotations.** Marginal quotations express the timeless wisdom of famous and not-so-famous people regarding the success strategies under consideration in articles throughout the text.

- **NEW! Cartoons.** Created specifically for *On Course* by Rob Dunalvey, cartoons appear throughout the book and are thematically linked with the success strategies being explored. Plus, they're fun!

Support for Students

- **Premium Website at www.cengage.com/success/Downing/OnCourse6e.** This Website includes many resources that will help your understanding of the principles and ideas found in *On Course*. You will find an electronic version of the self-assessments from the text, as well as practice tests, a learning styles inventory, Success Tools that provide various activities that cover various College Success themes, discussion questions, essay topics, and many other exercises that allow for further exploration of text features such as On Course at Work and Wise Choices.

Support for Instructors

- **Additional Premium Website Content. FREE when bundled with new textbooks.** By requesting the free Printed Access Card (PAC) (0495900702) to be packaged with your new textbook order, you and your students will obtain access to new VideoSkillbuilders, interactive video and exercises that showcase real students talking about their struggles and successes in college. More than 15 topics are covered including *Taking Notes to Improve Your Grade, Keeping Your Mind and Body in Shape, Test Taking,* and *Learning Styles.* Instructors can assign viewing questions for homework and have discussions about the videos in class.

- **NEW! Online Multimedia EBook.** This Online Multimedia Ebook for *On Course* provides an interactive version of the textbook with linked videos, online journaling, and the electronic version of the self-assessment. Request the Printed Access Card (PAC) (0538792639) for an additional fee for the Premium Website with the Online Multimedia Ebook to be packaged with your new textbook order for you and your students to obtain access to the Online Mulitmedia Ebook as part of the Premium Website.

- **Updated Instructor Companion Site at www.cengage.com/success/ Downing/OnCourse6e.** This Website provides educators with many resources to offer a course that empowers students to become active, responsible, and successful learners. Download the Facilitator's Manual (which is also offered in a printed version, also explained below). Also download PowerPoint Slides, view the content from the DVD *On Course: A Comprehensive Program for Promoting Student Academic Success and Retention,* and find a useful transition guide for educators who used previous editions of *On Course*.

- **NEW! Join the New *On Course* Community Online at http://community .cengage.com/OnCourse/.** If you're a college or university educator seeking innovative ways to help students achieve *greater academic success and retention,* this online community is for you! Connect with *On Course* author Skip Downing, educators, counselors, TeamUP Faculty Program Consultants, and the editors— and stay on top of new ideas to teach your first-year students! We invite you to join the community to participate in discussions to learn and share best practices and resources for making a measurable difference in students' lives.

- **Newly Revised Facilitator's Manual.** The facilitator's manual, now offered both in a printed version (0495899461) and online on the Instructor Companion Site, offers educators specific suggestions for using *On Course* in various kinds of courses, and it endeavors to answer questions that educators might have about using the text. One of the most popular elements of this resource is the numerous in-class exercises that encourage active exploration of the success strategies presented in the text. These exercises include role playing, learning games, dialogues, demonstrations, metaphors, mind-mappings, brainstorms, questionnaires, drawings, skits, scavenger hunts, and many others.

- **NEW! PowerLecture CD-ROM for *On Course*** (0495906778). PowerLecture contains a brand new test bank in the ExamView test-generating software, enhanced instructor PowerPoint slides created by *On Course* Ambassador Carmen Eitienne of Oakland University, MI, and a PDF of the Facilitator's Guide. The test bank materials were created specifically for the Sixth Edition by *On Course* Ambassador Dana Murphy of National Park Community College, AR. Use the dynamic software to create customized exams specific to your class!

- ***On Course: A Comprehensive Program for Promoting Student Academic Success and Retention* DVD** (0547002173). This DVD provides instructors with an overview of the problems that keep today's capable students from being successful, complete with an explanation by author Skip Downing about how *On Course* differs from other student success approaches. Additional features on this DVD include a description of the extensive *On Course* learner-centered resources, videos of three students presenting their One Student's Story essays that appear in the text, and a sample *On Course* learner-centered activity, facilitated by Skip Downing. Following the activity, a group of college and university educators discuss how this same activity positively affected their students. Presented in short chapters, parts of this DVD are intended for instructors and other parts are perfect for showing to students.

- **NEW! Online Course Cartridge Materials.** If you're taking your *On Course* class online, you'll want to check out the new course cartridge materials in WebTutor, which can be used with Blackboard, WebCT and Angel platforms. The WebTutor offers a number of instructor resources to complement the main text, including discussion questions and gradebook content. Additional features include journal activities, essay topics, samples of student work, personal research assignments, workplace-related activities, technology exercises, discussion board topics, quizzes, links to the student website, and interactive reflection tasks. Instructors have the option of using the electronic gradebook, receiving assignments from students via the Internet, and tracking student use of the communication and collaboration functions. An access code is required for purchase by your students to reach this material. This resource is available for packaging with a Printed Access Code (PAC), or students can purchase an Instant Access Code (IAC) online at ichapters.com. Talk to your Cengage sales representative for more information. Need help finding your rep? Visit *http://academic.cengage.com*.

- **NEW! Ebook. An Ebook is now available for *On Course*.** Students can download the complete *On Course* textbook at a cost savings at Cengage Learning's Online Bookstore, *http://ichapters.com*.

- **Assessment Tools.** If you're looking for additional ways to assess your students, Cengage Learning has additional resources for you to consider. For more in-depth information on any of these items, talk with your sales representative, or visit the *On Course* website.

  - **College Success Factors Index:** This pre- and post-test determines student's strengths and weaknesses in areas proven to be determinants of college success.

  - **CL Assessment and Portfolio Builder:** This personal development tool engages students in self-assessment, critical-thinking, and goal-setting activities to prepare them for college and the workplace. The access code for this item also provides students with access to the Career Resource Center.

  - **Noel-Levitz College Student Inventory:** *The Retention Management System™ College Student Inventory* (CSI from Noel-Levitz) is an early-alert, early-intervention program that identifies students with tendencies that contribute to dropping out of school. Students can participate in an integrated, campus-wide program. Cengage Learning offers you three assessment options that evaluate students on nineteen different scales: Form A (194 items), Form B (100 items), or an online etoken (that provides access to either Form A, B, or C; 74 items). Advisors are sent three interpretive reports: the Student's Report, the Advisor/Counselor Report, and the College Summary and Planning Report.

  - **The *Myers-Briggs Type Indicator® (MBTI®) Instrument*[1]:** MBTI is the most widely used personality inventory in history—and it is also available for packaging with *On Course*. The standard Form M self-scorable instrument contains ninety-three items that determine preferences on four scales: Extraversion-Introversion, Sensing-Intuition, Thinking-Feeling, and Judging-Perceiving.

- **College Success Planner.** Package your *On Course* textbook with this twelve-month week-at-a-glance academic planner. The College Success Planner assists students in making the best use of their time both on and off campus, and includes additional reading about key learning strategies and life skills for success in college. Ask your Cengage Learning sales representative for more details.

- **Cengage Learning's TeamUP Faculty Program Consultants.** An additional service available with this textbook is support from **TeamUP Faculty Program Consultants.** For more than a decade, our consultants have helped faculty reach and engage

---

[1]MBTI and Myers-Briggs Type Indicator are registered trademarks of Consulting Psychologists Press, Inc.

first-year students by offering peer-to-peer consulting on curriculum and assessment, faculty training, and workshops. Our consultants are educators and higher-education professionals who provide full-time support to help educators establish and maintain effective student success programs. They are available to help you to establish or improve your student success program and provide training on the implementation of our textbooks and technology. To connect with your TeamUP Consultant, call 1-800-528-8323 or visit *www.cengage.com/teamup*.

- **On Course Workshops and Conference.** Skip Downing, author of *On Course*, offers faculty development workshops for all educators who want to learn innovative strategies for empowering students to become active, responsible, and successful learners. These highly regarded professional development workshops are offered at conference centers across North America, or you can host a one- to three-day event on your own campus. An online graduate course (3 credits) is available as a follow up to two of the workshops. Additionally, you are invited to participate in the annual On Course National Conference, where hundreds of learner-centered educators gather to share their best practices. For information about these workshops, graduate courses, and the national conference (including testimonials galore), go to *www.OnCourseWorkshop.com*. Questions? Email *info@OnCourseWorkhop.com*

- *On Course* **Newsletter.** All college educators are invited to subscribe to the free *On Course Newsletter*. More than forty thousand educator-subscribers worldwide receive biweekly emails (monthly in the summer) with innovative, learner-centered strategies for engaging students in deep and lasting learning. To subscribe, simply go to *www.oncourseworkshop.com* and follow the easy, one-click directions.

Acknowledgments

This book would not exist without the assistance of an extraordinary group of people. I can only hope that I have returned (or will return) their wonderful support in kind.

At Cengage Learning, I would like to thank Shani Fisher, Marita Sermolins, Susan Miscio, Mary Tindle, Daisuke Yasutake, and Cat Salerno, for their unflagging attention to details and encouraging guidance. Also, thanks to Rob Dunalvey for creating the new cartoons and Deborah Rodman for shepherding the cartoons through the artistic process. At Baltimore City Community College, my thanks go to my colleagues, the amazing teachers of the College Success Seminar. At *On Course* Workshops, thanks to the extraordinary support and wisdom of my colleagues and friends Jonathan Brennan, Robin Middleton, Deb Poese, Eileen Zamora, and Dick Harrington. Thanks also to the *On Course* Ambassadors, some of the greatest educators in the world who work tirelessly to introduce their students and colleagues to *On Course*. And especially Carol—your unwavering love and support keep me on course. You are my compass.

A number of wise and caring reviewers have made valuable contributions to this book, and I thank them for their guidance:

Josephine Adamo, Buffalo State College, NY

Kathryn Burns, Northwest Nazarene University, ID

Lisa Christman, University of Central Arkansas, AR

Rosie DuBose, Century College, MN

Phyllis J. Dukes, Cuyahoga Community College, OH

Michelle Farnam, Mira Costa College, CA

Rachel Gray, North Central University, MN

Patricia A. Grissom, San Jacinto College South, TX

Monica Hixson, Brevard Community College, Cocoa Campus, FL

Michele D. Kegley, Southern State Community College, OH

Lisa Marks, Ozarks Technical Community College, MO

Andrea Neptune, Sierra College, CA

Laura C. Padgett, Lees-McRae College, NC

June Pomann, Union County College, NJ

Susan Starr, Chaffey College, CA

Cora Weger, Illinois Eastern Community Colleges–Lincoln Trail, IL

Mark Williams, The Community College of Baltimore County, MD

Finally, my deep gratitude goes out to the students who over the years have had the courage to explore and change their thoughts, actions, feelings, and beliefs. I hope, as a result, you have all lived richer, more personally fulfilling lives. I know I have.

Travel with Me

On Course is the result of my own quest to live a rich, personally fulfilling life and my strong desire to pass on what I've learned to my students. As such, *On Course* is a very personal book, for me and for you. I invite you to explore in depth what success means to you. I suggest that if you want to achieve your greatest potential in college and in life, dig deep inside yourself where you already possess everything you need to make your dreams come true.

During my first two decades of teaching college courses, I consistently observed a sad and perplexing puzzle. Each semester I watched students sort themselves into two groups. One group achieved varying degrees of academic success, from those who excelled to those who just squeaked by. The other group struggled mightily; then they withdrew, disappeared, or failed. But, here's the puzzling part. The struggling students often displayed as much academic potential as their more successful classmates, and in some cases more. What, I wondered, causes the vastly different outcomes of these two groups? And what could I do to help my struggling students achieve greater success?

Somewhere around my twentieth year of teaching, I experienced a series of crises in both my personal and professional life. In a word, I was struggling. After a period of feeling sorry for myself, I embarked on a quest to improve the quality of my life. I read, I took seminars and workshops, I talked with wise friends and acquaintances, I kept an in-depth journal, I saw a counselor, I even returned to graduate school to add a master's degree in applied psychology to my doctoral degree in English. I was seriously motivated to change my life for the better.

If I were to condense all that I learned into one sentence, it would be this: **People who are successful (by their own definition) consistently make wiser choices than people who struggle**. I came to see that the quality of my life was essentially the result of all of my previous choices. I saw how the wisdom (or lack of wisdom) of my choices influenced, and often determined, the outcomes and experiences of my life. The same, of course, was true for my struggling students.

For nearly two decades, I have continued my quest to identify the inner qualities that empower a person to make consistently wise choices, the very choices that lead to success both in college and in life. As a result of what I learned (and continue to learn), I created a course at my college called the College Success Seminar. This course was a departure from traditional student success courses because instead of focusing primarily on study skills, it focused on empowering students from the inside out. I had come to realize that most students who struggle in college are perfectly capable of earning a degree and that their struggles go far deeper than not knowing study skills. I envisioned a course that would empower students to develop their natural inner strengths, the qualities that would help them make the wise choices that would create the very outcomes and experiences they wanted in college, and in life. When I couldn't find a book that did this, I wrote *On Course*. A few years later, I created a series of professional development workshops to share what I had learned with other educators who want to see their students soar. Then, to provide an opportunity for workshop graduates to continue to exchange their experiences and wisdom, I started a listserv, and this growing group of educators soon named themselves the *On Course* Ambassadors, sharing *On Course* strategies with their students and colleagues alike. Later, I created two online graduate courses that further help college educators learn cutting-edge strategies for empowering their students to be more successful in college and in life. To launch the second decade of *On Course*, the *On Course* Ambassadors hosted the first *On Course* National Conference, bringing together an overflow crowd of educators hungry for new ways to help their students achieve more of their potential in college and in life. Every one of these efforts appeals to a deep place in me because they all have the power to change people's lives for the better. But that's not the only appeal. These activities also help *me* stay conscious of the wise choices I must consistently make to live a richer, more personally fulfilling life.

Now that much of my life is back on course, I don't want to forget how I got here!

Getting On Course to Your Success

Successful Students . . .	Struggling Students . . .
accept personal responsibility, seeing themselves as the primary cause of their outcomes and experiences.	**see themselves as victims,** believing that what happens to them is determined primarily by external forces such as fate, luck, and powerful others.
discover self-motivation, finding purpose in their lives by discovering personally meaningful goals and dreams.	**have difficulty sustaining motivation,** often feeling depressed, frustrated, and/or resentful about a lack of direction in their lives.
master self-management, consistently planning and taking purposeful actions in pursuit of their goals and dreams.	**seldom identify specific actions needed to accomplish a desired outcome,** and when they do, they tend to procrastinate.
employ interdependence, building mutually supportive relationships that help them achieve their goals and dreams (while helping others do the same).	**are solitary,** seldom requesting, even rejecting, offers of assistance from those who could help.

Taking the First Step

 FOCUS QUESTIONS What does "success" mean to you? When you achieve your greatest success, what will you **have**, what will you be **doing**, and what kind of person will you **be?**

Congratulations on choosing to attend college! With this choice, you've begun a journey that can lead to great personal and professional success.

What Is Success?

I've asked many college graduates, "What did success mean to you when you were an undergraduate?" Here are some typical answers:

When I was in college, success to me was . . .

. . . getting all A's and B's while working a full-time job.
. . . making two free-throws to win the conference basketball tournament.
. . . having a great social life.
. . . parenting two great kids and still making the dean's list.
. . . being the first person in my family to earn a college degree.

> College is a place where a student ought to learn not so much how to make a living, but how to live.
>
> *Dr. William A. Nolen*

Notice that each response emphasizes *outer success:* high grades, sports victories, social popularity, and college degrees. These successes are public, visible achievements that allow the world to judge one's abilities and worth.

I've also asked college graduates, "If you could repeat your college years, what would you do differently?" Here are some typical answers:

If I had a chance to do college over, I would . . .

. . . focus on learning instead of just getting good grades.
. . . major in engineering, the career I had a passion for.
. . . constantly ask myself how I could use what I was learning to enhance my life and the lives of the people I love.
. . . discover my personal values.
. . . learn more about the world I live in and more about myself . . . especially more about myself!

Notice that the focus some years after graduation often centers on *inner success:* enjoying learning, following personal interests, focusing on personal values, and creating more fulfilling lives. These successes are private, invisible victories that offer a deep sense of personal contentment.

Only with hindsight do most college graduates realize that, to be completely satisfying, success must occur both in the visible world and in the invisible spaces within our minds and hearts. This book, then, is about how to achieve both outer and inner success in college and in life.

To that end, I suggest the following definition of success: **Success is staying on course to your desired outcomes and experiences, creating wisdom, happiness, and unconditional self-worth along the way.**

As a college instructor, I have seen thousands of students arrive on campus with dreams, then struggle, fail, and fade away. I've seen thousands more come to college with dreams, pass their courses, and graduate, having done little more than cram their brains with information that's promptly forgotten after the final exam. They've earned degrees, but in more important ways they have remained unchanged.

Our primary responsibility in life, I suggest, is to realize the incredible potential with which each of us is born. All of our experiences, especially those during college, can contribute to the creation of our best selves.

On Course shows how to use your college experience as a laboratory experiment. In this laboratory you'll learn and apply proven strategies that help you create success—academically, personally, and professionally. I'm not saying it'll be easy, but you're about to learn time-tested strategies that have made a difference in the lives of thousands of students before you. So get ready to change the outcomes of your life and the quality of your experiences along the way! Get ready to create success as *you* define it.

To begin, consider a curious puzzle: Two students enter a college class on the first day of the semester. Both appear to have similar intelligence, backgrounds, and abilities. The weeks slide by, and the semester ends. Surprisingly, one student soars and the other sinks. One fulfills his potential; the other falls short. Why do students with similar aptitudes perform so differently? More important, which of these students is you?

Teachers observe this puzzle in every class. I bet you've seen it, too, not only in school, but wherever people gather. Some people have a knack for achievement. Others wander about confused and disappointed, unable to create the success they claim they want. Clearly, having potential does not guarantee success.

What, then, are the essential ingredients of success?

The Power of Choice

The main ingredient in all success is wise choices. That's because the quality of our lives is determined by the quality of the choices we make on a daily basis. Successful people stay on course to their destinations by wisely choosing their beliefs and behaviors.

Do beliefs cause behaviors, or do behaviors lead to beliefs? Like the chicken and the egg, it's hard to say which came first. This much is clear: Once you choose a positive belief or an effective behavior, you usually find yourself in a cycle of success. Positive beliefs lead to effective behaviors. Effective behaviors lead to success. And success reinforces the positive beliefs.

Here's an example showing how the choice of beliefs and behaviors determines results. Until 1954, most track-and-field experts believed it was

> There is only one success—to be able to spend your life in your own way.
>
> *Christopher Morely*

> The deepest personal defeat suffered by human beings is constituted by the difference between what one was capable of becoming and what one has in fact become.
>
> *Ashley Montagu*

© Tee and Charles Addams Foundation.

impossible for a person to run a mile in less than four minutes. On May 6, 1954, however, Roger Bannister ran a mile in the world-record time of 3:59.4. Once Bannister had proven that running a four-minute mile was possible, within months, many other runners also broke the four-minute barrier. In other words, once runners chose a new belief (a person can run a mile less than four minutes), they pushed their physical abilities, and suddenly the impossible became possible. By the way, the present world's record, set in 1999 by Hicham El Guerrouj of Morocco, is an amazing 3:43.13. So much for limiting beliefs!

Consider another example. After a disappointing test score, a struggling student thinks, "I knew I couldn't do college math!" This belief will likely lead the student to miss classes and neglect assignments. These self-defeating behaviors will lead to even lower test scores, reinforcing the negative beliefs. This student, caught in a cycle of failure, is now in grave danger of failing math.

In that same class, however, someone with no better math ability is passing the course because this student believes she *can* pass college math. Consequently, she chooses positive behaviors such as attending every class, completing all of her assignments, getting a tutor, and asking the instructor for help. Her grades go up, confirming her empowering belief. The cycle of success has this student on course to passing math.

Someone once said, "If you keep doing what you've been doing, you'll keep getting what you've been getting." That's why if you want to improve your life (and why else would you attend college?), you'll need to change some of your beliefs and behaviors. Conscious experimentation will teach you which ones are already working well for you and which ones need revision. Once these new beliefs and behaviors become a habit, you'll find yourself in the cycle of success, on course to creating your dreams in college and in life.

> Life is a self-fulfilling prophesy . . . in the long run you usually get what you expect.
>
> *Denis Waitley*

Write a Great Life

College offers the perfect opportunity to design a life worth living. A time-tested tool for this purpose is a journal, a written record of your thoughts and feelings, hopes and dreams. Journal writing is a way to explore your life in depth and discover your best "self." This self-awareness will enable you to make wise choices about what to keep doing and what to change.

Many people who keep journals do what is called "free writing." They simply write whatever thoughts come to mind. This approach can be extremely valuable for exploring issues present in one's mind at any given moment.

In *On Course,* however, you will write a guided journal. This approach is like going on a journey with an experienced guide. Your guide takes you places and shows you sights you might never have discovered on your own.

Before writing each journal entry, you'll read an article about proven success strategies. Then you'll apply the strategies to your own life by completing the guided journal entry that follows the article. Here are five guidelines for creating a meaningful journal:

- **Copy the directions for each step into your journal (just the bold print):** When you find your journal in a drawer or computer file twenty years from now, having the directions in your journal will help you make sense of what you've written. Underline or bold the directions to distinguish them from your answers.

- **Be spontaneous:** Write whatever comes to mind in response to the directions. Imagine pouring liquid thoughts into your journal without pausing to edit or rewrite. Unlike public writings, such as an English composition or a history research paper, your journal is a private document written primarily for your own benefit.

- **Be honest:** As you write, tell yourself the absolute truth; honesty leads to your most significant discoveries about yourself and your success.

- **Be creative:** Add favorite quotations, sayings, and poems. Use color, drawings, clip art, and photographs. Express your best creative "self."

- **Dive deep:** When you think you have exhausted a topic, write more. Your most valuable thoughts will often take the longest to surface. So, most of all—DIVE DEEP!

> Journal work is an excellent approach to uncovering hidden truths about ourselves . . .
>
> *Marsha Sinetar*

For easy reference, these five important guidelines are also printed on the inside back cover of this book.

Whether you handwrite your journal or create it on a computer, I urge you to keep all of your journal entries together in one book or file. If you do, one day many years from now, you'll have the extraordinary pleasure of reading this auto-biography of your growing wisdom about succeeding in college and in life.

Assess Yourself

Before we examine the choices of successful students, take a few minutes to complete the self-assessment questionnaire on the next two pages. Your scores will identify behaviors and beliefs that support your success. They'll also point out behaviors and beliefs you may want to change to achieve more of your potential in college and in life. In the last chapter, you will have an opportunity to repeat this self-assessment and compare your two scores. I think you're going to be pleasantly surprised!

This self-assessment is not a test. There are no right or wrong answers. The questions simply give you an opportunity to create an accurate and current self-portrait. Be absolutely honest and have fun with this activity, for it is the first step on an exciting journey to a richer, more personally fulfilling life.

Self-Assessment

You can take this self-assessment on the Internet by visiting the *On Course* website at www.cengage.com/success/Downing/OnCourse6e.

Read the following statements and score each one according to how true or false you believe it is about you. To get an accurate picture of yourself, consider what **IS** true about you (not what you want to be true). Remember, there are no right or wrong answers. Assign each statement a number from 0 to 10, as follows:

Totally false   0   1   2   3   4   5   6   7   8   9   10   Totally true

1. _____   I control how successful I will be.
2. _____   I'm not sure why I'm in college.
3. _____   I spend most of my time doing important things.
4. _____   When I encounter a challenging problem, I try to solve it by myself.
5. _____   When I get off course from my goals and dreams, I realize it right away.
6. _____   I'm not sure how I learn best.
7. _____   Whether I'm happy or not depends mostly on me.
8. _____   I'll truly accept myself only after I eliminate my faults and weaknesses.
9. _____   Forces out of my control (such as poor teaching) are the cause of low grades I receive in school.
10. _____   I place great value on getting my college degree.
11. _____   I don't need to write things down because I can remember what I need to do.
12. _____   I have a network of people in my life that I can count on for help.
13. _____   If I have habits that hinder my success, I'm not sure what they are.
14. _____   When I don't like the way an instructor teaches, I know how to learn the subject anyway.
15. _____   When I get very angry, sad, or afraid, I do or say things that create a problem for me.
16. _____   When I think about performing an upcoming challenge (such as taking a test), I usually see myself doing well.
17. _____   When I have a problem, I take positive actions to find a solution.
18. _____   I don't know how to set effective short-term and long-term goals.
19. _____   I am organized.
20. _____   When I take a difficult course in school, I study alone.
21. _____   I'm aware of beliefs I have that hinder my success.
22. _____   I'm not sure how to think critically and analytically about complex topics.
23. _____   When choosing between doing an important school assignment or something really fun, I do the school assignment.
24. _____   I break promises that I make to myself or to others.
25. _____   I make poor choices that keep me from getting what I really want in life.
26. _____   I expect to do well in my college classes.
27. _____   I lack self-discipline.
28. _____   I listen carefully when other people are talking.
29. _____   I'm stuck with any habits of mine that hinder my success.

(*continued*)

30. _____ When I face a disappointment (such as failing a test), I ask myself, "What lesson can I learn here?"
31. _____ I often feel bored, anxious, or depressed.
32. _____ I feel just as worthwhile as any other person.
33. _____ Forces outside of me (such as luck or other people) control how successful I will be.
34. _____ College is an important step on the way to accomplishing my goals and dreams.
35. _____ I spend most of my time doing unimportant things.
36. _____ When I encounter a challenging problem, I ask for help.
37. _____ I can be off course from my goals and dreams for quite a while without realizing it.
38. _____ I know how I learn best.
39. _____ My happiness depends mostly on what's happened to me lately.
40. _____ I accept myself just as I am, even with my faults and weaknesses.
41. _____ I am the cause of low grades I receive in school.
42. _____ If I lose my motivation in college, I don't know how I'll get it back.
43. _____ I have a written self-management system that helps me get important things done on time.
44. _____ I know very few people whom I can count on for help.
45. _____ I'm aware of the habits I have that hinder my success.
46. _____ If I don't like the way an instructor teaches, I'll probably do poorly in the course.
47. _____ When I'm very angry, sad, or afraid, I know how to manage my emotions so I don't do anything I'll regret later.
48. _____ When I think about performing an upcoming challenge (such as taking a test), I usually see myself doing poorly.
49. _____ When I have a problem, I complain, blame others, or make excuses.
50. _____ I know how to set effective short-term and long-term goals.
51. _____ I am disorganized.
52. _____ When I take a difficult course in school, I find a study partner or join a study group.
53. _____ I'm unaware of beliefs I have that hinder my success.
54. _____ I know how to think critically and analytically about complex topics.
55. _____ I often feel happy and fully alive.
56. _____ I keep promises that I make to myself or to others.
57. _____ When I have an important choice to make, I use a decision-making process that analyzes possible options and their likely outcomes.
58. _____ I don't expect to do well in my college classes.
59. _____ I am a self-disciplined person.
60. _____ I get distracted easily when other people are talking.
61. _____ I know how to change habits of mine that hinder my success.
62. _____ When I face a disappointment (such as failing a test), I feel pretty helpless.
63. _____ When choosing between doing an important school assignment or something really fun, I usually do something fun.
64. _____ I feel less worthy than other people.

Transfer your scores to the scoring sheets on the next page. For each of the eight areas, total your scores in columns A and B. Then total your final scores as shown in the sample on the next page.

SELF-ASSESSMENT SCORING SHEET

Sample

A		B	
6. _8_		29. _3_	
14. _5_		35. _3_	
21. _6_		50. _6_	
73. _9_		56. _2_	
	_28_ + 40 −	_14_ = 54	

SCORE #1: Accepting Personal Responsibility

A	B
1. ___	9. ___
17. ___	25. ___
41. ___	33. ___
57. ___	49. ___
___ + 40 − ___ = ___	

SCORE #2: Discovering Self-Motivation

A	B
10. ___	2. ___
26. ___	18. ___
34. ___	42. ___
50. ___	58. ___
___ + 40 − ___ = ___	

SCORE #3: Mastering Self-Management

A	B
3. ___	11. ___
19. ___	27. ___
43. ___	35. ___
59. ___	51. ___
___ + 40 − ___ = ___	

SCORE #4: Employing Interdependence

A	B
12. ___	4. ___
28. ___	20. ___
36. ___	44. ___
52. ___	60. ___
___ + 40 − ___ = ___	

SCORE #5: Gaining Self-Awareness

A	B
5. ___	13. ___
21. ___	29. ___
45. ___	37. ___
61. ___	53. ___
___ + 40 − ___ = ___	

SCORE #6: Adopting Lifelong Learning

A	B
14. ___	6. ___
30. ___	22. ___
38. ___	46. ___
54. ___	62. ___
___ + 40 − ___ = ___	

SCORE #7: Developing Emotional Intelligence

A	B
7. ___	15. ___
23. ___	31. ___
47. ___	39. ___
55. ___	63. ___
___ + 40 − ___ = ___	

SCORE #8: Believing in Myself

A	B
16. ___	8. ___
32. ___	24. ___
40. ___	48. ___
56. ___	64. ___
___ + 40 − ___ = ___	

CHOICES OF SUCCESSFUL STUDENTS

Successful Students . . .	Struggling Students . . .
accept personal responsibility, seeing themselves as the primary cause of their outcomes and experiences.	**see themselves as victims,** believing that what happens to them is determined primarily by external forces such as fate, luck, and powerful others.
discover self-motivation, finding purpose in their lives by discovering personally meaningful goals and dreams.	**have difficulty sustaining motivation,** often feeling depressed, frustrated, and/or resentful about a lack of direction in their lives.
master self-management, consistently planning and taking purposeful actions in pursuit of their goals and dreams.	**seldom identify specific actions needed to accomplish a desired outcome,** and when they do, they tend to procrastinate.
employ interdependence, building mutually supportive relationships that help them achieve their goals and dreams (while helping others do the same).	**are solitary,** seldom requesting, even rejecting, offers of assistance from those who could help.
gain self-awareness, consciously employing behaviors, beliefs, and attitudes that keep them on course.	**make important choices unconsciously,** being directed by self-sabotaging habits and outdated life scripts.
adopt lifelong learning, finding valuable lessons and wisdom in nearly every experience they have.	**resist learning new ideas and skills,** viewing learning as fearful or boring rather than as mental play.
develop emotional intelligence, effectively managing their emotions in support of their goals and dreams.	**live at the mercy of strong emotions such as anger,** depression, anxiety, or a need for instant gratification.
believe in themselves, seeing themselves as capable, lovable, and unconditionally worthy human beings.	**doubt their competence and personal value,** feeling inadequate to create their desired outcomes and experiences.

INTERPRETING YOUR SCORES

A score of . . .

0–39	Indicates an area where your choices will **seldom** keep you on course.
40–63	Indicates an area where your choices will **sometimes** keep you on course.
64–80	Indicates an area where your choices will **usually** keep you on course.

Forks in the Road

Why are these eight qualities so important? Because the road of life is rich with both opportunities and obstacles. At every opportunity or obstacle, the road forks and we have to make a choice. Some of those choices are so significant they will literally change the outcomes of our lives. In college, students encounter opportunities such as work-study, lunch with an instructor, study groups, social events, sports teams, new friends, study-abroad programs, romantic relationships, academic majors, all-night conversations, diverse cultures, challenging viewpoints, and field trips, among others.

Possible obstacles include disappointing grades, homesickness, death of a loved one, conflicts with friends, loneliness, health problems, endless homework, anxiety, broken romances, self-doubt, lousy class schedules, lost motivation, difficult instructors, academic probation, confusing tests, excessive drinking, frustrating rules, mystifying textbooks, conflicting work and school schedules, paralyzing depression, jealous friends, test anxiety, learning disabilities, and financial difficulties, to name a few.

In other words, college is just like life. There are always opportunities and obstacles, and the choices we make at each of these forks in the road determine whether we sink or soar. It takes a lot more than potential to excel in college or in life. And you're about to find out how to succeed in both . . . despite inevitable challenges. You see, while life is generating a dizzying array of options, successful people are making one wise choice after another.

A Few Words of Encouragement

In this course, you'll be taking a personal journey designed to help you develop the empowering beliefs and behaviors that will help you maximize your potential and achieve the outcomes and experiences you desire. However, before we depart, let's see how you're feeling about this upcoming trip. Please choose the statement below that best describes how you feel right now:

1. I'm excited about developing the inner qualities, outer behaviors, and academic skills that have helped others achieve success in college and in life.

2. I'm feeling okay about this journey because I'll probably learn a few helpful things along the way.

3. I can't say I'm excited, but I'm willing to give it a try.

4. I'm unhappy, and I don't want to go!

In nearly every *On Course* group I've worked with, there have been some reluctant travelers. If that's you, I want to offer some personal words of encouragement.

For a long time it had seemed to me that life was about to begin—real life. But there was always some obstacle in the way. Something to be got through first, some unfinished business, time still to be served, a debt to be paid. Then life would begin. At last it dawned on me that these obstacles were my life.

Fr. Alfred D'Souza

First, I can certainly understand why you might be hesitant. Frankly, I would have been a reluctant traveler on this journey when I was a first-year college student. I can tell you, though, I sure wish I'd known then what you're about to learn. Many students after completing the course have asked, "Why didn't they teach us this stuff in high school? It sure would have helped!" Even some of the reluctant travelers have later said, "Every student should be required to take this course!"

I can't promise that you'll feel this way after finishing the course. But I can promise that if you do only the bare minimum or, worse yet, drop out, you'll never know if this course could have helped you improve your life. So, quite frankly, my goal here is to persuade you to give this course a fair chance.

Maybe you're thinking, *"I don't need this success stuff. Just give me the information and skills I need to get a good job."* If so, you're going to be pleased to discover that the skills you'll learn in this course are highly prized in the work world. In fact many companies pay corporate trainers huge fees to teach these same skills to their employees. Think of the advantage you'll have when you bring these skills with you to the job.

Or, perhaps you're thinking, *"I already know how to be successful. This is just a waste of my time."* I thought this, too, at one time. And I had three academic degrees from prestigious universities and a good job to back up my claim. Hadn't I already proven I could be a success? But when I opened myself to learning the skills that you'll discover in these pages, the quality of both my professional and personal life improved dramatically. I've also taught these skills to successful college educators (perhaps even your own instructor), and many of them have had the same experience I did. You see, there is success . . . and then there is SUCCESS!

Or, maybe you're thinking, *"I don't want to examine and write about myself. That's not what college should be about."* I understand this objection! When I was in college, self-examination was about the last thing on my to-do list (right after walking backwards to the North Pole in my bathing suit). Of course I had a "good" reason: Athletes like me didn't look inward. I labeled it "touchy feely" and dismissed self-exploration. I'm sure you have reasons for your reluctance: shyness, your cultural upbringing, or a host of other explanations that make you uncomfortable when looking within for the keys to your success. I urge you to overcome your resistance. Today, I'm sorry it took me so long to realize that success occurs from inside out, not outside in. *You* are the key to your success, and apparently your instructors agree or they wouldn't have chosen this book for you to read.

So, I hope you'll give this course your best effort. Most likely, it's the only one you'll ever take in college where the subject matter is YOU. And, believe me, if you don't master the content of this course, every other course you take (both in college and in the University of Life) will suffer. I wish you a great journey. Let the adventure begin!

> The battles that count aren't the ones for gold medals. The struggles within yourself—the invisible battles inside all of us—that's where it's at.
>
> *Jessie Owens, winner of four gold medals at the 1936 Olympics*

JOURNAL ENTRY　1

In this activity, you will take an inventory of your personal strengths and weaknesses as revealed by your self-assessment questionnaire.

1. In your journal, write the eight areas of the self-assessment and record your scores for each, as follows:

_____　1. Accepting personal responsibility

_____　2. Discovering self-motivation

_____　3. Mastering self-management

_____　4. Employing interdependence

_____　5. Gaining self-awareness

_____　6. Adopting lifelong learning

_____　7. Developing emotional intelligence

_____　8. Believing in myself

Transfer your scores from the self-assessment to the appropriate lines above.

2. **Write about the areas on the self-assessment in which you had your highest scores.** Explain why you think you scored higher in these areas than in others. Also, explore how you feel about these scores. Your entry might begin, "By doing the self-assessment, I learned that I . . . ."

3. **Write about the areas on the self-assessment in which you had your lowest scores.** Explain why you think you scored lower in these areas than in others. Also, explore how you feel about these scores. Remember the saying, "If you keep doing what you've been doing, you'll keep getting what you've been getting." With this thought in mind, write about any specific changes you'd like to make in yourself during this course. Your entry might begin, "By doing the self-assessment, I also learned that I . . . ."

The five suggestions for creating a meaningful journal are printed on the inside back cover of *On Course*. Please review these suggestions before writing. **Especially remember to copy the directions for each step (just the bold print) into your journal before writing.**

All glory comes from daring to begin.

Eugene F. Ware

My journal from this course is the most valuable possession I own. I will cherish it always.

Joseph Haskins, student

One Student's Story

Jalayna Onaga
University of Hawaii-Hilo, Hawaii

It's amazing how fast someone can go from being excited about college to flunking out. A year and a half ago, I received a letter from the University of Hawaii at Hilo informing me that I was being dismissed due to my inability to maintain a GPA of at least 2.0. I wasn't surprised because I had spent the whole semester making one bad choice after another. I hardly ever attended classes. I didn't do much homework. I didn't study for tests. And I never asked anyone for help. Mostly I just hung out with friends who told me I didn't need to go to college. But, fast-forward to today and you'll see a woman who has clear goals for her future, the motivation to reach those goals, and a plan to carry her to her dreams. However, it took a lot of learning in order for me to make such a huge change in my life.

After taking courses for a while at a community college, I got permission to re-enroll at the university. I was so nervous! I worried that I'd get dismissed again and I'd never do anything with my life. A counselor suggested that I take the University 101 course, and I'm so thankful I did. While writing the *On Course* journals, I learned so much about myself and how I can succeed. I realized that when I first enrolled at the university, I was taking nursing courses because my parents wanted me to and I couldn't get motivated. This time I got inspired because my journals helped me look inside myself to figure out my own dreams for the future and to create a plan to reach them. For the first time, the plans I made were coming from my heart, not from someone telling me what I should do. I realized that I really

love kids and *my* dream is to teach second or third graders. That's when I made a personal commitment to attend every class and learn as much as I could. In later journals I learned that making a schedule and writing everything down helped me get the important things done. I even learned to ask for help, and when I was absent because my car broke down, I met with the teacher to find out what I had missed. Before tests, I found it inspiring to read over my journal because my own words reminded me of my dreams and why I should study hard to get them.

Best of all, my new choices really paid off. When the semester ended, I had three A's and a B+ and I made the dean's list. My University 101 course and the *On Course* textbook really changed me as a student and as a person. Not long ago, I was a student without a direction. Now I can envision myself in the near future teaching a class full of eager students, watching them learn and grow, just like I was able to do.

Becoming an Active Learner

 FOCUS QUESTIONS How does the human brain learn? How can you use this knowledge to develop a highly effective system for learning?

Successful athletes understand how to get the most out of their physical abilities. Likewise, to be a successful learner, you need to know how to get the most out of your mental abilities. Much has been discovered, especially in the last few decades, about how human beings learn. To benefit from these discoveries, let's take a quick peek into our brains.

How the Human Brain Learns

The human brain weighs about three pounds and is composed of trillions of cells. About 100 billion of them are neurons, and here's where much of our learning takes place. When a potential learning experience occurs (such as reading this sentence), some neurons send out spikes of electrical activity. This activity causes nearby neurons to do the same. When a group of neurons fire together, they form what is called a "neural network." I like to picture a bunch of neurons joining hands in my brain, jumping up and down, and having a learning party. If this party happens only once, learning is weak (as when you see your instructor solve a math problem one day and can't recall how to do it the next). However, if you cause the same collection of neurons to fire repeatedly (as when you solve ten similar math problems yourself), the result is likely a long-term memory. According to David Sousa, author of *How the Brain Learns,* "Eventually, repeated firing of the pattern binds the neurons together so that if one fires, they all fire, ultimately forming a new memory trace."

In other words, if you want learning to stick, you need to create strong neural networks. In this way, learning literally changes the structure of your brain. Through autopsies, neuroscientist Robert Jacobs and his colleagues determined

> The human brain has the largest area of uncommitted cortex (no particular required function) of any species on earth. This gives humans extraordinary flexibility and capacity for learning.
>
> *Eric Jensen*

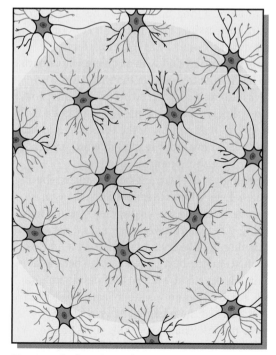

Neurons before Learning

Neurons after Learning

that graduate students actually had 40 percent more neural connections than those of high school dropouts. Jacobs's research joins many other brain studies to reveal an important fact: **To excel as a learner, you need to create as many neural connections in your brain as possible.**

Three Principles of Deep and Lasting Learning

With this brief introduction to what goes on in our brains, let's explore how highly effective learners maximize their learning. Whether they know it or not, they have figured out how to create many strong neural connections in their brain. And you can, too.

How? The short answer is: **Become an active learner.** Learning isn't a spectator sport. You don't create deep and lasting learning by passively listening to a lecture, casually skimming a textbook, or having a tutor solve math problems for you. In order to create strong neural networks, you've got to participate actively in the learning process.

Now, here's the longer answer. Good learners, consciously or unconsciously, implement three principles of deep and lasting learning:

1. **PRIOR LEARNING.** Brain research reveals that when you connect what you are learning now to previously stored information (i.e., already-formed neural networks), you learn the new information or skill faster and more deeply. For example, the first word processing program I learned was Word Perfect. It took me a long time to learn because I had no prior knowledge about word processing; thus, my brain contained few, if any, neural networks relevant to what I was learning. First, I needed to learn what word processing can do (such as delete whole paragraphs) and then I needed to learn how to perform that function with Word Perfect. Later, when I was learning another word processing program, Microsoft Word, I already knew what word processing can do, so I was able to learn this new program in a fraction of the time. Put another way, I already had neural networks in my brain related to word processing, and learning Microsoft Word got those neurons partying.

   The contribution of past learning to new learning helps explain why some learners have difficulty in college with academic skills such as math, reading, and writing. If their earlier learning was shaky, they're going to have difficulty with new learning. They don't have strong neural networks on which to attach the new learning. It's like trying to construct a house on a weak foundation. In such a situation, the best option is to go back and strengthen the foundation, which is exactly the purpose of developmental (basic skills) courses. However, there's no point trying to learn these foundational skills the same way you learned them before. After all, how you learned them before didn't make the information or skills stick. So this time you'll need to employ different, more effective learning strategies, ones that will create the needed neural networks. If that's your situation,

In a time of drastic change, it is the learners who inherit the future.

Eric Hoffer

Almost everyone has had occasion to look back upon his school days and wonder what has become of the knowledge he was supposed to have amassed during his days of schooling.

John Dewey

this time you'll have the advantage of employing the more effective strategies described here in *On Course*. And if you're a learner with a strong foundation, you'll find strategies here that will increase your effectiveness as a learner even more.

2. **QUALITY OF PROCESSING.** How you exercise affects your physical strength. Likewise, how you study affects the strength of your neural networks and therefore the quality of your learning. Some information (such as math formulas or anatomy terms) must be recalled exactly as presented. For such learning tasks, effective memorization strategies are the types of processing that work best. However, much of what you'll be asked to learn in college is too complex for mere memorization (though many struggling students try). For mastering complex information and skills, you'll want to use what learning experts call **deep processing.** These are the very strategies that successful learners use to maximize their learning and make it stick. You'll learn both effective memorization and deep-processing strategies in the "Wise Choices in College" sections in later chapters.

> Mathematics teachers ... see students using a certain formula to solve problems correctly one day, but they cannot remember how to do it the next day. If the process was not stored, the information is treated as brand new again!
>
> *David A. Sousa*

Don't just use one deep-processing strategy, however. Successful athletes know the value of cross training, so they use a variety of training strategies. Similarly, successful learners know the value of employing *varied* deep-processing strategies. That's because the more ways you deep-process new learning, the stronger your neural networks become.

When you actively study any information or skill using *numerous and varied deep-processing strategies*, you create and strengthen related neural networks and your learning soars.

3. **QUANTITY OF PROCESSING.** The quality of your learning is significantly affected by how often and how long you engage in varied deep processing. This factor is often called "time on task," and the most effective approach is *distributed practice*. The human brain learns best when learning efforts are distributed over time. No successful athlete waits until the night before a competition to begin training. Why then, do struggling students think they can start studying the night before a test? An all-night cram session may make a deposit in their short-term memory, perhaps even allowing them to pass a test the next day. However, even students who got good grades have experienced the ineffectiveness of cramming when they encounter "summer amnesia"— the inability to remember in fall-term classes what they learned during the previous school year. That's the result of not creating strong neural networks that make learning last. To create strong neural networks, you need to process the target information or skill with numerous and varied deep-processing strategies and do it *frequently*.

> ### Three Principles of Deep and Lasting Learning
>
> 1. **Prior Learning.** Relate new information to previously learned information.
> 2. **Quality of Processing.** Use numerous and varied deep-processing strategies.
> 3. **Quantity of Processing.** Use frequent practice sessions of sufficient length distributed over time.

In addition to how frequently you use deep-processing strategies, also important is the *amount of time* you spend learning. Obviously, deep processing for sixty minutes generates more learning than deep processing for five minutes. So, highly effective learners put in **sufficient time on task.** The traditional guideline for a week's studying is two hours for each hour of class time. Thus, if you have fifteen hours of classes per week, the estimate for your "sufficient time on task" is about thirty hours per week. Many struggling students neither study very often nor very long. However, some fool themselves by putting in "sufficient time," but spend little of it engaged in effective learning activities. They skim complex information in their textbooks. They attempt to memorize information they don't understand. Their minds wander to a conversation they had at lunch. They rummage through their book bag and dresser drawers and closets looking for the handout on how to write a term paper. They play a video game or two. They send a couple of text messages, and the next thing they know, it's time to go to bed.

Some students have a chemical imbalance that prevents them from focusing for long periods of time and their learning suffers. If you think this may be true for you, make an appointment with your college's disability counselor to get help. But the reason most struggling students don't live up to their potential as learners is fully within their control. You don't need a genius IQ to be a good learner and do well in college. What you do need is a learning system that employs what we now know about how the human brain learns. Billions of neurons between your ears are ready to party. Let the festival of learning begin!

> Good learners, like everyone else, are living, squirming, questioning, perceiving, fearing, loving, and languaging nervous systems, but they are good learners precisely because they believe and do certain things that less effective learners do not believe and do. And therein lies the key.
>
> *Neil Postman & Charles Weingartner*

The CORE Learning System

Four general strategies are common to good learners. To remember these strategies simply think of the word CORE (see Figure 1.1). CORE stands for **Collect, Organize, Rehearse,** and **Evaluate.** The CORE learning system is effective because it automatically guides you to implement the active learning principles discussed earlier. Thus, by applying what we know about how the human brain learns, the CORE learning system helps you create deep and lasting learning. Here's how it works:

Collect: In every waking moment, we're constantly collecting perceptions through our five senses. Without conscious effort, the brain takes in a multitude of sights, sounds, smells, tastes, and physical sensations. Most perceptions disappear within moments. Some, such as our first language, stick for a lifetime. Thus, much of what we learn in life we do without intention. In college, however, learning needs to be more conscious. That's because instructors expect you to learn specific information and skills. Then, of course, they want you to demonstrate that knowledge on quizzes, tests, exams,

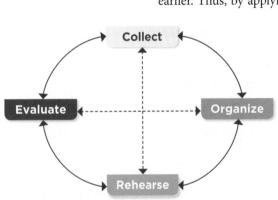

Figure 1.1 ▲ The CORE Learning System

term papers, and other forms of evaluation. In college, two of the most important ways you'll collect information and skills are through reading textbooks and attending classes. In Chapters 2 and 3 you'll learn proven strategies for maximizing the amount of high-quality information you collect in these ways.

Organize: Once we collect information, we need to make sense of it. When learning in everyday life, we tend to organize collected information in unconscious ways. We don't even realize that we're doing it. However, in a college course, you need to organize information systematically so it makes sense to you. In fact, making meaning from collected information is one of the most important outcomes of studying. In Chapters 4, 5, and 6 you'll learn proven strategies for organizing information into study materials that will lead to deep learning.

Rehearse: Once we collect and organize our target knowledge, we need to remember it for future use. Rehearsing (also called "practicing") strengthens neural networks and makes learning stick. When you solve ten challenging math problems, you're rehearsing. Over time, the process of solving becomes easier and more natural. In Chapters 4, 5, and 6, you'll learn proven ways to rehearse information and skills so you can remember them for future use, whether on a test, in your career, or in your personal life.

Evaluate: Life is great at giving us informal feedback about the quality of our learning. Maybe you tell a joke and forget the punch line. You know immediately you have more learning to do. Higher education, however, provides us with more formal feedback. Yup, those pesky tests, term papers, quizzes, lab reports, essays, classroom questions, and final exams. Evaluation, both informal and formal, is an essential component of all learning because without feedback, we could never be sure if our learning is accurate or complete. Chapters 6 and 7 provide you with proven ways to assess what you have learned in your courses. Then you'll discover how to demonstrate that learning to instructors so you can maximize your grades in college.

Learning doesn't occur in a tidy, step-by-step fashion. At any moment while learning, you may need to jump to a different component in the CORE system. For example, while **Rehearsing,** you might realize that some information doesn't make sense to you, so you **Organize** it in a different way. At times you may engage two or more components simultaneously. For instance, when **Rehearsing** study materials, you're probably **Evaluating** your mastery of that knowledge at the same time. Thus, you can expect to use the four components of the CORE Learning System in any order and in any combination.

While the CORE system is an effective blueprint for creating deep and lasting learning, not all learners prefer to **Collect, Organize, Rehearse,** and **Evaluate** in the same way. That's why you'll encounter many specific strategies in *On Course.* Your task is to experiment with and find the ones that work best for you. What you'll ultimately construct is a personalized learning system, one you can use for the rest of your life. In this way, you can be confident of your ability to learn anything you need to know on the path to achieving your goals and dreams in college and beyond.

When something is meaningful it is organized; when it is organized, it is simplified in the mind.

Robert Ornstein

Education which strengthens a person's ability to gather, organize and evaluate information, contributes to more accurate adult judgments.

Muriel James & Dorothy Joneward

JOURNAL ENTRY   2

In this activity, you'll explore how you learned something (anything) using the approach of an active learner. Then you'll plan how you could use this same approach to improve your learning outcomes and experiences in college.

1. **Identify something you have learned simply because you enjoyed learning it.** It can be something you learned in school or anywhere else. What are you good at? What do you know more about than most people? What skills have you mastered? What are your hobbies? What have you spent a lot of time doing? To complete this step, simply write the completion of this sentence in your journal: "One thing I enjoyed learning is . . . ."

2. **With a focus on the information or skill you loved learning, write answers to the following questions (and anything else that will explain how you prefer to learn):**

- How did you gather the information or skills you needed to learn this? (Collect)
- What did you do to learn the information or skills needed to learn this? (Organize)
- What else did you do to learn this? (Rehearse—Variety)
- How often did you engage in learning this? (Rehearse—Frequency)
- When you engaged in learning this, how long did you usually spend? (Rehearse—Duration)
- What feedback did you use to determine how well you had learned this? (Evaluate)
- How did you feel when you engaged in learning this? (Motivating Experiences)
- What were the rewards for learning this? (Motivating Outcomes)

3. **Write about what you have learned or relearned about learning and how you will use this knowledge to maximize your learning in college.**

For example, your journal entry might begin, *By reading and writing about learning, I have learned/relearned that . . . . I will use this knowledge to maximize my learning in college by . . . .* Be specific!

Be sure to use the five suggestions printed on the inside back cover of *On Course. Especially remember to dive deep!* Diving deep changes the neurons in your brain and leads to deep and lasting learning. As you may have already realized, writing an in-depth journal entry is a powerful way to deep-process your experiences!

I don't love studying. I hate studying. I like learning. Learning is beautiful.

Natalie Portman

Learning . . . should be a joy and full of excitement. It is life's greatest adventure; it is an illustrated excursion into the minds of noble and learned men, not a conducted tour through a jail.

Taylor Caldwell

On Course Principles
AT WORK

I think we have to appreciate that we're alive for only a limited period of time, and we'll spend most of our lives working.
Victor Kiam, Chairman, Remington Products

Applying the strategies you're going to learn in *On Course* will not only improve your results in college, it will also boost your success at work. You're about to explore dozens of proven strategies that will help you achieve your goals both in college and in your career.

Creators Wanted!

Candidates must demonstrate mastery of both the hard and soft skills necessary for carrer success.

This is no small matter. Career success (or lack of it) affects nearly every part of your life: family, income, self-esteem, whom you associate with, where you live, your level of happiness, what you learn, your energy level, your health, and maybe even the length of your life.

Some students think, "All I need for success at work is the special knowledge of my chosen career." All that nurses need, they believe, are good nursing skills. All that accountants need are good accounting skills. All that lawyers need are good legal skills. These skills are called *hard* skills, the knowledge needed to perform a particular job. Hard skills include knowing where to insert the needle for an intravenous feeding drip, how to write an effective business plan, and what the current inheritance laws are. These are the skills you'll be taught in courses in your major field of study. They are essential to qualify for a job. Without them you won't even get an interview.

But, most people who've been in the work world a while will tell you this: Hard skills are essential to get a job but often insufficient to keep it or advance. That's because nearly all employees have the hard skills necessary to do the job for which they're hired. True, some may perform these skills a little better or a little worse than others, but one estimate suggests that only 15 percent of workers lose their jobs because they can't do the work. That's why career success is often determined by *soft* skills, the same strategies you'll be learning in this book. As one career specialist put it, "Having hard skills gets you hired; lacking soft skills gets you fired."

A U.S. government report confirms that soft skills are essential to job success. The Secretary of Labor asked a blue-ribbon panel of employers to identify what it takes to be successful in the modern employment world. This panel published a report in 1992 called the Secretary's Commission on Achieving Necessary Skills (SCANS). The report presents a set of foundation skills and workplace competencies that employers consider essential for work world success, and the report's timeless recommendations continue to be a valuable source of information for employers and employees alike. No one familiar with today's work world will find many surprises in the report, especially in the foundation skills. The report calls for employees to develop the same soft skills that employers include in job descriptions, look for in reference letters, probe for in job interviews, and assess in evaluations of their workforce.

The SCANS report identifies the following soft skills as necessary for work and career success: taking responsibility, making effective decisions, setting goals, managing time, prioritizing tasks, persevering, giving strong efforts, working well in teams, communicating effectively, having empathy, knowing how to learn, exhibiting self-control, and believing in one's own self-worth. The report

identifies these necessary skills but doesn't suggest a method for developing them. *On Course* will show you how.

Learning these soft skills will help you succeed in your first career after college. And, because soft skills are portable (unlike many hard skills), you can take them with you in the likely event that you later change careers. Most career specialists say the average worker today can expect to change careers at least once during his or her lifetime. In fact, some 25 percent of workers in the United States today are in occupations that did not even exist a few decades ago. If a physical therapist decides to change careers and work for an Internet company, he needs to master a whole new set of hard skills. But the soft skills he's mastered are the same ones that will help him shine in his new career.

So, as you're learning these soft skills, keep asking yourself, "How can I use these skills to stay on course to achieving my greatest potential at work as well as in college?" Be assured that what you're about to explore can make all the difference between success and failure in your career.

▸ *Believing in Yourself*
Develop Self-Acceptance

 FOCUS QUESTIONS Why is high self-esteem so important to success? What can you do to raise your self-esteem?

The foundation of anyone's ability to cope successfully is high self-esteem. If you don't already have it, you can always develop it.

Virginia Satir

Roland was in his forties when he enrolled in my English 101 class. He made insightful contributions to class discussions, so I was perplexed when the first two writing assignments passed without an essay from Roland. Both times, he apologized profusely, promising to complete them soon. He didn't want to make excuses, he said, but he was stretched to his limit: He worked at night, and during the day he took care of his two young sons while his wife worked. "Don't worry, though," he assured me, "I'll have an essay to you by Monday. I'm going to be the first person in my family to get a college degree. Nothing's going to stop me."

But Monday came, and Roland was absent. On a hunch, I looked up his academic record and found that he had taken English 101 twice before. I contacted his previous instructors. Both of them said that Roland had made many promises but had never written an essay.

I called Roland, and we made an appointment to talk. He didn't show up. During the next class, I invited Roland into the hall while the class was working on a writing assignment.

"Sorry I missed our conference," Roland said. "I meant to call, but things have been piling up."

Self-esteem is the reputation we have with ourselves.

Nathaniel Brandon

"Roland, I talked to your other instructors, and I know you never wrote anything for them. I'd love to help you, but you need to take an action. You need to write an essay." Roland nodded silently. "I believe you can do it. But I don't know if *you* believe you can do it. It's decision time. What do you say?"

"I'll have an essay to you by Friday."

I looked him in the eye.

"Promise," he said.

I knew that what Roland actually did, not what he promised, would reveal his deepest core beliefs about himself.

Self-Esteem and Core Beliefs

So it is with us all. Our core beliefs—true or false, real or imagined—form the inner compass that guides our choices.

At the heart of our core beliefs is the statement *I AM* ___. How we complete that sentence in the quiet of our souls has a profound effect on the quality of our lives.

High self-esteem is the fuel that can propel us into the cycle of success. Do we approve of ourselves as we are, accepting our personal weaknesses along with our strengths? Do we believe ourselves capable, admirable, lovable, and fully worthy of the best life has to offer? If so, our beliefs will make it possible for us to make wise choices and stay on course to a rich, full life.

For example, imagine two students: one with high self-esteem, the other with low self-esteem. Picture them just after they get very disappointing test scores. What do they do next? The student with low self-esteem will likely choose options that protect his fragile self-image, options such as dropping the course rather than chancing failure. The student with high self-esteem, on the other hand, will likely choose options that move her toward success, options such as persisting in the course and getting additional help to be successful. Two students, same situation. One focuses on weaknesses. One focuses on strengths. The result: two different choices and two very different outcomes.

The good news is that self-esteem is learned, so anyone can learn to raise his or her self-esteem. Much of this book is about how you can do just that.

Know and Accept Yourself

People with high self-esteem know that no one is perfect, and they accept themselves with both their strengths and weaknesses. To paraphrase philosopher Reinhold Niebuhr, successful people accept the things they cannot change, have the courage to change the things they can change, and possess the wisdom to know the difference.

Successful people have the courage to take an honest self-inventory, as you began doing in Journal Entry 1. They acknowledge their strengths without false humility, and they admit their weaknesses without stubborn denial. They tell the truth about themselves and take action to improve what they can.

> Self-esteem is more than merely recognizing one's positive qualities. It is an attitude of acceptance and non-judgment toward self and others.
>
> *Matthew McKay & Patrick Fanning*

AS SMART AS HE WAS, ALBERT EINSTEIN COULD NOT FIGURE OUT HOW TO HANDLE THOSE TRICKY BOUNCES AT THIRD BASE.

© Sidney Harris/ScienceCartoonsPlus.com

Fortunately for Roland, he decided to do just that. On the Friday after our talk, he turned in his English 101 essay. His writing showed great promise, and I told him so. I also told him I appreciated that he had let go of the excuse that he was too busy to do his assignments. From then on, Roland handed in his essays on time. He met with me in conferences. He visited the writing lab, and he did grammar exercises to improve his editing skills. He easily passed the course.

A few years later, Roland called me. He had transferred to a four-year university and was graduating with a 3.8 average. He was continuing on to graduate school to study urban planning. What he most wanted me to know was that one of his instructors had asked permission to use one of his essays as a model of excellent writing. "You know," Roland said, "I'd still be avoiding writing if I hadn't accepted two things about myself: I was a little bit lazy and I was a whole lot scared. Once I admitted those things about myself, I started changing."

> We cannot change anything unless we accept it.
>
> *Carl Jung*

Each of us has a unique combination of strengths and weaknesses. When struggling people become aware of a weakness, they typically blame the problem on others or they beat themselves up for not being perfect. Successful people, however, usually make a different choice: They acknowledge the weakness, accept it without self-judgment, and, when possible, take action to create positive changes. As always, the choices we make determine both where we are headed and the quality of the journey. Developing self-acceptance helps us to make the choices wisely.

JOURNAL ENTRY 3

In this activity, you will explore your strengths and weaknesses and the reputation you have with yourself. This exploration of your self-esteem will allow you to begin revising any limiting beliefs you may hold about yourself. By doing so you will take a major step toward your success.

> Be what you is, not what you ain't, 'cause if you ain't what you is, you is what you ain't.
>
> *Luther D. Price*

1. In your journal, write a list of ten or more of your personal strengths. For example, mentally: *I'm good at math*; physically: *I'm very athletic*; emotionally: *I seldom let anger control me*; socially: *I'm a good friend*; and others: *I am almost always on time.*

2. Write a list of ten or more of your personal weaknesses. For example, mentally: *I'm a slow reader*; physically: *I am out of shape*; emotionally: *I'm easily hurt by criticism*; socially: *I don't listen very well*; and others: *I'm a terrible procrastinator.*

3. Using the information in steps 1 and 2 and score #8 on your self-assessment, write about the present state of your self-esteem. On a scale of 1 to 10 (with 10 high), how strong is your self-esteem? How do you think it got to be that way? How would you like it to be? What changes could you make to achieve your ideal self-esteem?

To create an outstanding journal, remember to use the five suggestions printed on the inside back cover of *On Course*. Especially remember to dive deep!

One Student's Story

Phyllis Honore

Cuyahoga Community College, Ohio

At the age of forty-four, I enrolled for my second attempt at college. After taking the placement tests, I was told I'd have to take Math 0850, a developmental math course. I refused to believe I was that bad in math. I argued that, as an older student, I knew what I was capable of and I should be allowed to skip Math 0850. Finally, the advisor gave in, and I took a higher-level math course than I was supposed to . . . and I failed.

I realize now that I just couldn't accept that I need a lot of help in math. I also realize that, for years, I haven't accepted many things about me. Growing up, I didn't like who I was. I had no self-esteem or self-worth. Now, don't get me wrong. My mom was a high school history teacher, and she raised me to believe in myself. But I wore thick glasses and had crooked teeth. I was tall and skinny, and I didn't feel pretty enough. Plus, I knew that a little girl from the ghetto would never be smart enough.

After high school, I went to the Fashion Institute of Design and Merchandising in California. The problem was I took *me* with me to California. That meant all of my self-criticisms came along, and I told myself that this little black girl from East Cleveland couldn't measure up to the white girls from Malibu. Even though I was raised to be proud of my heritage, I didn't know who I was. I tried the hippie culture and the world of black gangster soul. I hung out with dope dealers in the inner city of L.A. I gave in to peer pressure and got involved with alcohol and drugs. I slept all day and partied all night. I hardly ever studied because I was at the beach or shoveling something up my nose. When I *did* study for a test, I would do it at the last minute. Needless to say, I kept getting F's, and it wasn't long before I had thrown it all away.

When I came back to Cleveland, I was an addict. I was able to get a good job at General Electric, but my involvement with drugs and alcohol continued. In 2002, I joined a twelve-step program to try to change my life. The fourth step is about doing a fearless and searching moral inventory, which was a real challenge for me. Not long after, I went into a residential treatment center, and I couldn't even look at myself in the mirror. I hated myself for what I had done to myself, and I couldn't forgive myself for messing up in school and disappointing my mom and sister. My spirit was dampened like a flickering flame about to go out.

Six years later was when I got the courage to enroll in college a second time, but when I failed that first math course, I was discouraged. Still I refused to quit. In my second semester, I enrolled in Math 0850, the course I was supposed to take in my first semester. It was paired with an *On Course* class where I read that "successful people acknowledge their strengths without false humility and they admit their weakness without stubborn denial." You tell the truth about yourself, the book said, and take action to improve what you can. These ideas reinforced what I had been learning in my twelve-step program. In Journal Entry 3, I did a "fearless and searching moral inventory" of my strengths and weaknesses. It's powerful when you put yourself on paper and can go back and reread it. I had to humble myself and tell myself I had insisted on taking a math course I wasn't ready for and I failed it. Being in denial is having a weakness you don't accept. I needed help with math, but I acted like I didn't. If you have a weakness and you don't accept it, you won't do what needs to be done. Failing math forced me to look at myself, and the *On Course* class helped me learn to accept that failure and still keep moving in the right direction.

Last semester I passed Math 0850, and now I'm retaking the math course I failed in my first semester. I got an 88 on the first test. I am no longer that little girl who refused to accept her weaknesses along with her strengths. I've discovered that it's okay not to know something or not be perfect. I can honestly say that now, when I look in the mirror, I'm able to say, "I love and accept you just the way you are."

Photo: Courtesy of Phyllis Honore

Wise Choices in College COLLEGE CUSTOMS

Entering college is like crossing the border into another country. Each has new customs to learn. If you learn and heed the following college customs, your stay in higher education will be not only more successful but more enjoyable as well.

1. Read your college catalogue. This resource contains most of the factual information you'll need to plot a great journey through higher education. It explains how your college applies many of the customs discussed in this section. Keep a college catalogue on hand and refer to it often. Catalogues are usually available in the registrar's or counseling office, and many colleges post a copy of the catalogue on their website.

2. See your advisor. Colleges provide an advisor who can help you make wise choices. Sometimes this person is a counselor, sometimes an instructor. Find out who your advisor is, make an appointment, and get advice on what courses to take and how to create your best schedule. Students who avoid advisors often enroll in unnecessary courses or miss taking courses that are required for graduation. Your tuition has paid for a guide through college; use this valuable resource effectively.

3. Understand prerequisites. A "prerequisite" is a course that must be completed before you can take another course. For example, colleges require the completion of calculus before enrollment in more advanced mathematics courses. Before you register, confirm with your advisor that you have met all of the prerequisites. Otherwise you may find yourself registered for a course you aren't prepared to pass. Prerequisites usually appear within each course description in your college catalogue.

4. Complete your general education requirements. Most colleges require students to complete a minimum number of general education credits. Typically, you need to take one or more courses from broad fields of study such as communication,

natural science and technology, math, languages, humanities, and social and behavioral science. For example, to fulfill your requirement in science, you might need to complete 4 credits by taking any one of the following courses: biology, chemistry, astronomy, geology, or physics. Find a list of these required general education courses in your college catalogue, and check off each requirement as you complete it. Regardless of how many credits you earn, you can't graduate until you've completed the general education requirements. Depending on your college, general education requirements may also be called core requirements, core curriculum, or general curriculum.

5. Choose a major wisely. You'll usually choose a major area of study in your first or second year. Examples of majors include nursing, early childhood education, biology, English, mechanical engineering, and art. You'll take the greatest number of courses in your major, supplemented by your general education courses and electives. Even if you've already picked a major, visit the career counseling center to see if other majors might interest you even more or be a better steppingstone to your chosen career. Your career counseling center can provide you with assessments to help you find a career that fits your interests and personality, and you can complete career inventories prior to choosing a major to help you narrow the best major for your intended career. For example, majoring in English is great preparation for a law degree. All majors and their required courses are available in your college catalogue. Until you've entered a major, you're wise to concentrate on completing your general education requirements. And don't ignore the usually free services available to you at the career counseling center.

6. Take a realistic course load. I once taught a student who worked full-time, was married with three small children, and had signed up for six courses in her first semester. After five weeks, she was exhausted and withdrew from college. There are only 168 hours in a week. Be realistic about the number of courses you can handle given your other responsibilities. Students often register for too many credits because of their mistaken belief that this choice will get them to graduation more quickly. Too often the actual result is dropped and failed classes, pushing graduation farther into the future.

7. Attend the first day of class (on time). Of course it's wise to attend *every* day, but whatever you do, be present on the first day! On this day instructors usually provide the class assignments and rules for the entire semester. If you're absent, you may miss something that will come back to haunt you later.

8. Sit in class where you can focus on learning. Many students focus best sitting up front. Others prefer sitting on the side about halfway back where they can see all of their classmates and the instructor during a discussion. Experiment. Try different places in the room. Once you find the place that best supports your learning, sit there permanently . . . unless you find that changing seats every day helps you learn better.

9. Study the syllabus. In the first class, instructors usually provide a syllabus (sometimes called a first-day handout). The syllabus is the single most important handout you will receive all semester. Typically, it contains the course objectives, the required books and supplies, all assignments and due dates, and the method for determining grades. This handout also presents any course rules you need to know. Essentially, the course syllabus is a contract between you and your instructor, who will assume that you've read and understood this contract; be sure to ask questions about any part you don't understand.

10. Buy required course books and supplies as soon as possible. College instructors cover a lot of ground quickly. If you don't have your study

materials from the beginning of the course, you may fall too far behind to catch up. To get a head start on their classes, some students go to their college bookstore or an online bookstore weeks before the semester or quarter begins and purchase course materials. If money is tight, check with the financial aid office to see if your college provides temporary book loans. Or, as a last resort, ask your instructors if they will put copies of the course texts on reserve at your college library.

11. Introduce yourself to one or more classmates and exchange phone numbers and email addresses. After an absence, contact a classmate to learn what you missed. Few experiences in college are worse than returning to class and facing a test that was announced in your absence.

12. Inform your instructor before an absence. Think of your class as your job and your instructor as your employer. Professional courtesy dictates notifying your employer of anticipated absences. The same is true with instructors.

13. If you arrive late, slip in quietly. Don't make excuses. Just come in and sit down. If you want to explain your lateness, see the instructor after class.

14. Ask questions. If the question you don't ask shows up on a test, you're going to be upset with yourself. Your classmates are equally nervous about asking questions. Go ahead, raise your hand and ask one on the first day; after that, it'll be easier.

15. To hold an extended conversation with your instructors, make an appointment during their office hours. Most college instructors have scheduled office hours. Ask your instructor for his or her office hours and mention that you'd like to make an appointment to discuss a specific topic. Be sure to show up (or call beforehand to reschedule).

16. Get involved in campus life. Most colleges offer numerous activities that can broaden your education, add pleasure to your life, and introduce you to new friends. Consider participating in the drama club, school newspaper, intercultural counsel, student government, athletic teams, band or orchestra, literary magazine, yearbook committee, science club, or one of the many other organizations on your campus.

17. Know the importance of your grade point average (GPA). Your GPA is the average grade for all of the courses you have taken in college. At most colleges, GPAs range from 0.0 ("F") to 4.0 ("A"). Your GPA affects your future in many ways. At most colleges a minimum GPA (often 2.0, a "C") is required to graduate, regardless of how many credits you have accumulated. Students who fall below the minimum GPA are usually ineligible for financial aid and cannot play intercollegiate sports, or, in some cases, are in danger of academic dismissal, particularly for students who are already on academic probation. Academic honors (such as the dean's list) and some scholarships are based on your GPA. Finally, potential employers often note GPAs to determine if prospective employees have achieved success in college.

18. Know how to compute your grade point average (GPA). At most colleges, GPAs are printed on a student's transcript, which is a list of courses completed (with the grade earned). You can get a copy of your transcript from the registrar's office. Transcripts are usually free or available for a nominal charge. Computing your own grade point average is simple using the formula below. Or you can do it online at http://www.back2college.com/gpa.htm.

19. If you stop attending a class, withdraw officially. Students are enrolled in a course until they're *officially* withdrawn. A student who stops attending is still on the class roster at semester's end when grades are assigned, and the instructor will very likely give the nonattending student an "F." That failing grade is now a permanent part of the student's record, lowering the GPA and discouraging potential employers. If you decide (for whatever reason) to stop attending a class, go directly to the registrar's office and follow the official procedures for withdrawing from a class. Make certain that you withdraw before your college's deadline. This

---

Formula for Computing Your Grade Point Average (GPA)

$$\frac{(G1 \times C1) + (G2 \times C2) + (G3 \times C3) + (G4 \times C4) + \cdots (Gn \times Cn)}{\text{Total \# of Credits Attempted}}$$

In this formula, G = the grade in a course and C = number of credits for a course. For example, suppose you had the following grades:

"A" in Math 110 (4 Credits)	G1 ("A") = 4.0
"B" in English 101 (3 Credits)	G2 ("B") = 3.0
"C" in Sociology 101 (3 Credits)	G3 ("C") = 2.0
"D" in Music 104 (2 Credits)	G4 ("D") = 1.0
"F" in Physical Education 109 (1 Credit)	G5 ("F") = 0.0

Here's how to figure the GPA from the grades above:

$$\frac{(4.0 \times 4) + (3.0 \times 3) + (2.0 \times 3) + (1.0 \times 2) + (0.0 \times 1)}{4 + 3 + 3 + 2 + 1} = \frac{16 + 9 + 6 + 2 + 0}{13} = 2.54$$

date is often about halfway through a semester or quarter.

20. Talk to your instructor before withdrawing. If you're going to fail a course, withdraw to protect your GPA. But don't withdraw without speaking to your instructor first. Sometimes students think they are doing far worse than they really are. Discuss with your instructor what you need to do to pass the course and make a step-by-step plan. Be sure to discuss your plans with your advisor as well. He or she might have insights about what will be best for your general or major requirements and when courses are available for you to retake. If you discover that failing is inevitable, withdraw officially.

21. Keep a file of important documents. Forms get lost in large organizations such as colleges. Save everything that may affect your future: course syllabi, completed tests and assignments, approved registration forms, scholarship applications, transcripts, and paid bills. If you're exempted from a college requirement or course prerequisite, get it in writing and add the document to your files.

22. Finally, some college customs dictate what you should *not* do. Avoiding these behaviors shows respect for your classmates and instructors.

- Don't pack up your books or put on your coat until the class is over.
- After an absence, don't ask your instructor, "Did I miss anything?" (Of course you did.)
- Don't wear headphones during class.
- Don't let a pager or cellular phone disturb the class.
- Don't talk with a classmate.
- Don't read or send text messages during class.
- Don't make distracting noises in class (e.g., clicking pen, popping gum, drumming fingers, and so on).

College Customs Exercise

Ask an upperclassman, "What is the one thing you now know about college customs that you wish you had known on your first day? Explain why this college custom has been so important to you throughout your college career." Be prepared to report your findings.

Accepting Personal Responsibility

I accept responsibility for creating my life as I want it.

Successful Students . . .	Struggling Students . . .
adopt the Creator role, believing that their choices create the outcomes and experiences of their lives.	**accept the Victim role,** believing that external forces determine the outcomes and experiences of their lives.
master Creator language, accepting personal responsibility for their results.	**use Victim language,** rejecting personal responsibility by blaming, complaining, and excusing.
make wise decisions, consciously designing the future they want.	**make decisions carelessly,** letting the future happen by chance rather than by choice.

Case Study in Critical Thinking

The Late Paper

Professor Freud announced in her syllabus for Psychology 101 that final term papers had to be in her hands by noon on December 18. No student, she emphasized, would pass the course without a completed term paper turned in on time. As the semester drew to a close, **Kim** had an "A" average in Professor Freud's psychology class, and she began researching her term paper with excitement.

Arnold, Kim's husband, felt threatened that he had only a high school diploma while his wife was getting close to her college degree. Arnold worked the evening shift at a bakery, and his coworker **Philip** began teasing that Kim would soon dump Arnold for a college guy. That's when Arnold started accusing Kim of having an affair and demanding she drop out of college. She told Arnold he was being ridiculous. In fact, she said, a young man in her history class had asked her out, but she had refused. Instead of feeling better, Arnold became even more angry. With Philip continuing to provoke him, Arnold became sure Kim was having an affair, and he began telling her every day that she was stupid and would never get a degree.

Despite the tension at home, Kim finished her psychology term paper the day before it was due. Since Arnold had hidden the car keys, she decided to take the bus to the college and turn in her psychology paper a day early. While she was waiting for the bus, **Cindy,** one of Kim's psychology classmates, drove up and invited Kim to join her and some other students for an end-of-semester celebration. Kim told Cindy she was on her way to turn in her term paper, and Cindy promised she'd make sure Kim got it in on time. "I deserve some fun," Kim decided, and hopped into the car. The celebration went long into the night. Kim kept asking Cindy to take her home, but Cindy always replied, "Don't be such a bore. Have another drink." When

Cindy finally took Kim home, it was 4:30 in the morning. She sighed with relief when she found that Arnold had already fallen asleep.

When Kim woke up, it was 11:30 A.M., just thirty minutes before her term paper was due. She could make it to the college in time by car, so she shook Arnold and begged him to drive her. He just snapped, "Oh sure, you stay out all night with your college friends. Then, I'm supposed to get up on my day off and drive you all over town. Forget it." "At least give me the keys," she said, but Arnold merely rolled over and went back to sleep. Panicked, Kim called Professor Freud's office and told **Mary,** the secretary, that she was having car trouble. "Don't worry," Mary assured Kim, "I'm sure Professor Freud won't care if your paper's a little late. Just be sure to have it here before she leaves at 1:00." Relieved, Kim decided not to wake Arnold again; instead, she took the bus.

At 12:15, Kim walked into Professor Freud's office with her term paper. Professor Freud said, "Sorry, Kim, you're fifteen minutes late." She refused to accept Kim's term paper and gave Kim an "F" for the course.

Listed below are the characters in this story. Rank them in order of their *responsibility for Kim's failing grade in Psychology 101.* Give a different score to each character. Be prepared to explain your choices.

| Most responsible | ← 1 2 3 4 5 6 → | Least responsible |

____ **Professor Freud,** the teacher

____ **Philip,** Arnold's coworker

____ **Kim,** the psychology student

____ **Cindy,** Kim's classmate

____ **Arnold,** Kim's husband

____ **Mary,** Prof. Freud's secretary

DIVING DEEPER Is there someone not mentioned in the story who may also bear responsibility for Kim's failing grade?

Adopting the Creator Role

 FOCUS QUESTIONS What is self-responsibility? Why is it the key to gaining maximum control over the outcomes and experiences of your life?

When psychologist Richard Logan studied people who survived ordeals such as being imprisoned in concentration camps or lost in the frozen Arctic, he found that all of these victors shared a common belief. They saw themselves as personally responsible for the outcomes and experiences of their lives.

Ironically, responsibility has gotten a bad reputation. Some see it as a heavy burden they have to lug through life. Quite the contrary, personal responsibility is the foundation of success because without it, our lives are shaped by forces outside of us. **The essence of personal responsibility is responding wisely to life's opportunities and challenges, rather than waiting passively for luck or other people to make the choices for us.**

Whether your challenge is surviving an Arctic blizzard or excelling in college, accepting personal responsibility moves you into cooperation with yourself and with the world. As long as you resist your role in creating the outcomes and experiences in your life, you will fall far short of your potential.

I first met Deborah when she was a student in my English 101 class. Deborah wanted to be a nurse, but before she could qualify for the nursing program, she had to pass English 101. She was taking the course for the fourth time.

"Your writing shows fine potential," I told Deborah after I had read her first essay. "You'll pass English 101 as soon as you eliminate your grammar problems."

"I know," she said. "That's what my other three instructors said."

"Well, let's make this your last semester in English 101, then. After each essay, make an appointment with me to go over your grammar problems."

"Okay."

"And go to the Writing Lab as often as possible. Start by studying verb tense. Let's eliminate one problem at a time."

"I'll go this afternoon!"

But Deborah never found time: *No, really . . . . I'll go to the lab just as soon as I . . . .*

Deborah scheduled two appointments with me during the semester and missed them both: *I'm so sorry . . . . I'll come to see you just as soon as I . . . .*

To pass English 101 at our college, students must pass one of two essays written at the end of the semester in an exam setting. Each essay, identified by social security number only, is graded by two other instructors. At semester's end, Deborah once again failed English 101. "It isn't fair!" Deborah protested. "Those exam graders expect us to be professional writers. They're keeping me from becoming a nurse!"

I suggested another possibility: "What if *you* are the one keeping you from becoming a nurse?"

I am the master of my fate; I am the captain of my soul.

William E. Henley

The more we practice the habit of acting from a position of responsibility, the more effective we become as human beings, and the more successful we become as managers of our lives.

Joyce Chapman

Deborah didn't like that idea. She wanted to believe that her problem was "out there." Her only obstacle was *those* teachers. All her disappointments were *their* fault. The exam graders weren't fair. Life wasn't fair! In the face of this injustice, she was helpless.

I reminded Deborah that it was *she* who had not studied her grammar. It was *she* who had not come to conferences. It was *she* who had not accepted personal responsibility for creating her life the way she wanted it.

"Yes, but . . . ." she said.

> Every time your back is against the wall, there is only one person that can help. And that's you. It has to come from inside.
>
> *Pat Riley, professional basketball coach*

Victims and Creators

When people keep doing what they've been doing even when it doesn't work, they are acting as **Victims.** When people change their beliefs and behaviors to create the best results they can, they are acting as **Creators.**

When you accept personal responsibility, you believe that you create *everything* in your life. This idea upsets some people. Accidents happen, they say. People treat them badly. Sometimes they really are victims of outside forces.

This claim, of course, is true. At times, we *are* all affected by forces beyond our control. If a hurricane destroys my house, I am a victim (with a small "v"). But if I allow that event to ruin my life, I am a Victim (with a capital "V").

The essential issue is this: Would it improve your life to act *as if* you create all of the joys and sorrows in your life? Answer "YES!" and see that belief improve your life. After all, if you believe that someone or something out there causes all of your problems, then it's up to "them" to change. What a wait that can be! How long, for example, will Deborah have to wait for "those English teachers" to change?

If, however, you accept responsibility for creating your own results, what happens then? You will look for ways to create your desired outcomes and experiences despite obstacles. And if you look, you've just increased your chances of success immeasurably!

The benefits to students of accepting personal responsibility have been demonstrated in various studies. Researchers Robert Vallerand and Robert Bissonette, for example, asked 1,000 first-year college students to complete a questionnaire about why they were attending school. They used the students' answers to assess whether the students were "Origin-like" or "Pawn-like." The researchers defined *Origin-like* students as seeing themselves as the originators of their own behaviors, in other words, Creators. By contrast, Pawn-like students see themselves as mere puppets manipulated by others, in other words, Victims. A year later, the researchers returned to find out what had happened to the 1,000 students. They found that significantly more of the Creator-like students were still enrolled in college than the Victim-like students. If you want to succeed in college (and in life), then being a Creator gives you a big edge.

> I believe that we are solely responsible for our choices, and we have to accept the consequences of every deed, word, and thought throughout our lifetime.
>
> *Elisabeth Kübler-Ross*

Responsibility and Choice

The key ingredient of personal responsibility is **choice.** Animals respond to a stimulus because of instinct or habit. For humans, however, there is a brief, critical moment of decision available between the stimulus and the response. In this moment, we make the choices—consciously or unconsciously—that influence the outcomes of our lives.

Numerous times each day, you come to a fork in the road and must make a choice. Even not making a choice is a choice. Some choices have a small impact: Shall I get my hair cut today or tomorrow? Some have a huge impact: Shall I stay in college or drop out? The sum of the choices you make from this day forward will create the eventual outcome of your life. The Responsibility Model in Figure 2.1 shows what the moment of choice looks like.

In that brief moment between stimulus and response, we can choose to be a Victim or a Creator. When we respond as a Victim, we complain, blame, make excuses, and repeat ineffective behaviors. When we respond as a Creator, we pause at each decision point and ask, "What are my options, and which option will best help me create my desired outcomes and experiences?"

The difference between responding to life as a Victim or Creator is how we choose to use our energy. When I'm blaming, complaining, and excusing, my efforts cause little or no improvement. Sure, it may feel good in that moment to claim that I'm a poor Victim and "they" are evil persecutors, but my good feelings are fleeting because afterward my problem still exists. By contrast, when I'm seeking solutions and taking actions, my efforts often (though not always) lead to improvements. At critical forks in the road, Victims waste their energy and remain stuck, while Creators use their energy for improving their outcomes and experiences.

> I do think that the greatest lesson of life is that you are responsible for your own life.
>
> *Oprah Winfrey*

But, let's be honest. No one makes Creator choices all of the time. I've never met anyone who did, least of all me. Our inner lives feature a perpetual tug of war between the Creator part of us and the Victim part of us. My own experiences have taught me the following life lesson: The more choices I make as a Creator,

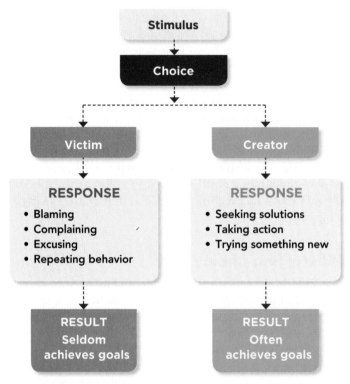

Figure 2.1 ▲ Responsibility Model

the more I improve the quality of my life. That's why I urge you to join me in an effort to choose more often as a Creator. It won't be easy, but it's worth it. You may have to take my word for it right now, but if you experiment with the strategies in this book and continue using the ones that work for you, in a few months you'll see powerful proof in your own life of the value of making Creator choices.

Here's an important choice you can make immediately. Accept, as Creators do, this belief: *I am responsible for creating my life as I want it.* Of course sometimes you won't be able to create the specific outcomes and experiences you want. The reality is that some circumstances will defy even your best efforts. But, believing that you always have a way to improve your present situation will motivate you to look for it, and by looking you'll often discover options you would never have found otherwise. For this reason, choosing to accept personal responsibility is the first step toward your success.

Here's a related choice. Set aside any thought that Creator and Victim choices have anything to do with being good or bad, right or wrong, smart or dumb, worthy or unworthy. If you make a Victim choice, you aren't bad, wrong, dumb, or unworthy. For that matter, if you make a Creator choice, you aren't good, right, smart, or worthy. These judgments will merely distract you from

When you make the shift to being the predominant creative force in your life, you move from reacting and responding to the external circumstances of your life to creating directly the life you truly want.

Robert Fritz

the real issue: Are you getting the outcomes and experiences that *you* want in *your* life? If you are, then keep making the same choices because they're working. But, if you're not creating the life you want, then you'd be wise to try something new. We benefit greatly when we shift our energy from defending ourselves from judgments and put it into improving the outcomes and experiences of our lives.

"Oh, I get what you mean!" one of my students once exclaimed as we were exploring this issue of personal responsibility, "You're saying that living my life is like traveling in my car. If I want to get where I want to go, I better be the driver and not a passenger." I appreciate her metaphor because it identifies that personal responsibility is about taking hold of the steering wheel of our lives, about taking control of where we go and how we get there.

Ultimately each of us creates the quality of our life with the wisdom or folly of our choices.

> I am a Shawnee. My forefathers were warriors. Their son is a warrior . . . . From my tribe I take nothing. I am the maker of my own fortune.
>
> *Tecumseh*

JOURNAL ENTRY　4

In this activity, you will experiment with the Creator role. By choosing to take responsibility for your life, you will immediately gain an increased power to achieve your greatest potential.

1. **Write and complete each of the ten sentence stems below.** For example, someone might complete the first sentence stem as follows: If I take full responsibility for all of my actions, *I will accomplish great things.*

　1.　If I take full responsibility for all of my actions . . .

　2.　If I take full responsibility for all of my thoughts . . .

　3.　If I take full responsibility for all of my feelings . . .

　4.　If I take full responsibility for my education . . .

　5.　If I take full responsibility for my career . . .

　6.　If I take full responsibility for my relationships . . .

　7.　If I take full responsibility for my health . . .

　8.　If I take full responsibility for all that happens to me . . .

　9.　When I am acting fully responsible for my life . . .

　10.　If I were to create my very best self . . .

2. **Write about what you have learned or relearned in this journal about personal responsibility and how you will use this knowledge to improve your life.** You might begin, *By reading and writing about personal responsibility, I have learned . . .*

> Whatever reason you had for not being somebody, there's somebody who had that same problem and overcame it.
>
> *Barbara Reynolds*

One Student's Story

Brian Moore

Glendale Community College, Arizona

During my first semester in college, I was enrolled in a first-year English class. In high school I was usually able to pull off an A on my honors English papers without much work, and I thought I was a pretty good writer. So when I turned in my first college essay, I was expecting to get an A, or at worst a B. However, I was about to get a rude awakening. When we received our papers back a week later, I was shocked to see a C+ on my paper. I went to the instructor, and she said I just needed more practice and not to worry because I was in the class to learn. However, since I have high expectations for myself, those words weren't very comforting.

About that same time in my Strategies for College Success class, we were assigned to read a chapter in

On Course about personal responsibility. The main idea is to adopt a "Creator" approach to problems, which I understood to mean basically seek solutions and not dwell on the negative. Then it clicked for me; I am responsible for my grades and I need to do whatever is necessary to get the ones I want. In high school, I could write one draft of an essay, turn it in, and I'd usually get an A, but that approach wasn't working in college. So, now I had to do something different. I started writing my papers before they were due and then meeting with my English teacher at least once a week to get her suggestions. Because I was a full-time student and also worked seventeen to twenty hours a week in the cashier's office, sometimes I had to see her during

times that were inconvenient. But I had to be flexible if I wanted her critique. During English class, we'd do peer editing, and I found that helpful, too. When I was in high school, I only spent about an hour or two writing an essay. Now I was spending at least three to five hours.

To my surprise, after some not-so-great increases in grades, I received what I had been waiting for: my first A on an essay. Although my final grade in English was a B, I learned a number of important lessons. It's really important to take your time with writing, to have your instructor or someone else read a rough draft and give you some suggestions, and then to write a final draft. I also learned that nobody can make the grade for you; you have to be responsible for yourself. I may not always get an A, but I learned to face a challenge, and no matter what grade I receive, knowing that I took responsibility as a "Creator" was the greatest lesson of all.

Mastering Creator Language

FOCUS QUESTION How can you create greater success by changing your vocabulary?

The world of self-criticism on the one side and judgment toward others on the other side represents a major part of the dance of life.

Hal Stone & Sidra Stone

Have you ever noticed that there is almost always a conversation going on in your mind? Inner voices chatter away, offering commentary about you, other people, and the world. This self-talk is important because what you say to yourself determines the choices you make at each fork in the road. Victims typically listen to the voice of their Inner Critic or their Inner Defender.

Self-Talk

THE INNER CRITIC. This is the internal voice that judges us as inadequate: *I'm so uncoordinated. I can't do math. I'm not someone she would want to date.*

I never say the right thing. My ears are too big. I'm a lousy writer. The Inner Critic blames us for whatever goes wrong in our life: *It's all my fault. I always screw up. I knew I couldn't pass biology. I ruined the project. I ought to be ashamed. I blew it again.* This judgmental inner voice can find fault with anything about us: our appearance, our intellect, our perfor-mance, our personality, our abilities, how others see us, and, in severe cases, even our value as a human being: *I'm not good enough. I'm worthless, I don't deserve to live.* (While nearly everyone has a critical inner voice at times, if you often think toxic self-judgments like these last three, don't mess around. Get to your college's counseling office immediately and get help revising these noxious messages so you don't make self-destructive choices.)

Ironically, self-judgments have a positive intention. By criticizing ourselves, we hope to eliminate our flaws and win the approval of others, thus feeling more worthy. Occasionally when we bully ourselves to be perfect, we *do* create a positive outcome, though we make ourselves miserable in the effort. Often, though, self-judgments cause us to give up, as when I tell myself, *I can't pass math,* so I drop the course. What's positive about this? Well, at least I've escaped my problem. Freed from the pressures of passing math, my anxieties float away and I feel better than I have since the semester started. Of course, I still have to pass math to get my degree, so my relief is temporary. The Inner Critic is quite content to trade success in the future for comfort in the present.

Where does an Inner Critic come from? Here's one clue: Have you noticed that its self-criticisms often sound like judgmental adults we have known? It's as if our younger self recorded their judgments and, years later, our Inner Critic replays them over and over. Sometimes you can even trace a self-judgment back to a specific comment that someone made about you years ago. Regardless of its accuracy now, that judgment can affect the choices you make every day.

THE INNER DEFENDER. The flip side of the Inner Critic is the Inner Defender. Instead of judging ourselves, the Inner Defender judges others: *What a boring teacher. My advisor screwed up my financial aid. My roommate made me late to class. No one knows what they're doing around here. It's all **their** fault!* Inner Defenders can find something to grumble about in virtually any situation. Their thoughts and conversations are full of blaming, complaining, accusing, judging, criticizing, and condemning others.

Like Inner Critics, Inner Defenders have a positive intention. They, too, want to protect us from discomfort and anxiety. They do so by blaming our problems on

> A loud, voluble critic is enormously toxic. He is more poisonous to your psychological health than almost any trauma or loss. That's because grief and pain wash away with time. But the critic is always with you—judging, blaming, finding fault.
>
> *Matthew McKay & Patrick Fanning*

© Cathy Guisewite/Universal Press Syndicate

forces that seem beyond our control, such as other people, bad luck, the government, lack of money, uncaring parents, not enough time, or even too much time. My Inner Defender might say, *I can't pass math because my instructor is terrible. She couldn't teach math to Einstein. Besides that, the textbook stinks and the tutors in the math lab are rude and unhelpful. It's obvious this college doesn't really care what happens to its students.* Now I breathe a sigh of relief because I'm covered. If I drop the course, hey, it's not my fault. If I stay in the course and fail, it's not my fault either. And, if I stay in the course and somehow get a passing grade (despite my terrible instructor, lousy textbook, worthless tutors, and uncaring college), well, then I have performed no less than a certified miracle! Regardless of how bad things may get, I can find comfort knowing that at least it's not my fault. It's *their* fault!

And where did this voice come from? Perhaps you've noticed that the Inner Defender's voice sounds suspiciously like our own voice when we were scared and defensive little kids trying to protect ourselves from criticism or punishment by powerful adults. Remember how we'd excuse ourselves from responsibility, shifting the blame for our poor choices onto someone or something else: *It's not my fault. He keeps poking me. My dog ate my homework. What else could I do? I didn't have any choice. My sister broke it. He made me do it. Why does everyone always pick on me? It's all their fault!*

We pay a high price for listening to either our Inner Critic or Inner Defender. By focusing on who's to blame, we distract ourselves from acting on what needs to be done to get back on course. To feel better in the moment, we sabotage creating a better future.

Fortunately, another voice exists within us all.

THE INNER GUIDE. This is the wise inner voice that seeks to make the best of any situation. The Inner Guide knows that judgment doesn't improve difficult situations. So instead, the Inner Guide objectively observes each situation and asks, *Am I on course or off course? If I'm off course, what can I do to get back on course?* Inner Guides tell us the impartial truth (as best they know it at that time), allowing us to be more fully aware of the world around us, other people, and especially ourselves. With this knowledge, we can take actions that will get us back on course.

> What you're supposed to do when you don't like a thing is change it. If you can't change it, change the way you think about it. Don't complain.
>
> Advice to Maya Angelou
> from her grandmother

Some people say, "But my Inner Critic (or Inner Defender) is *right*!" Yes, it's true that the Inner Critic or Inner Defender can be just as "right" as the Inner Guide. Maybe you really are a lousy writer and the tutors in the math lab actually *are* rude and unhelpful. The difference is that Victims expend all their energy in judging themselves or others, while Creators use their energy to solve the problem. The voice we choose to occupy our thoughts determines our choices, and our choices determine the outcomes and experiences of our lives. So choose your thoughts carefully.

The Language of Responsibility

Translating Victim statements into the responsible language of Creators moves you from stagnant judgments to dynamic actions. In the following chart, the left-hand column presents the Victim thoughts of a student who is taking a challenging college course. Thinking this way, the student's future in this course is easy to predict . . . and it isn't pretty.

But, if she changes her inner conversation, as shown in the right-hand column, she'll also change her behaviors. She can learn more in the course and increase her likelihood of passing. More important, she can learn to reclaim control of her life from the judgmental, self-sabotaging thoughts of her Inner Critic and Inner Defender.

As you read these translations, notice two qualities that characterize Creator language. First, Creators accept responsibility for their situation. Second, they plan and take actions to improve their situation. So, when you hear **ownership** and an **action plan,** you know you're talking to a Creator.

> You must change the way you talk to yourself about your life situations so that you no longer imply that anything outside of you is the immediate cause of your unhappiness. Instead of saying, "Joe makes me mad," say, "I make myself mad when I'm around Joe."
>
> *Ken Keyes*

Victims Focus on Their Weaknesses I'm terrible in this subject.	Creators Focus on How to Improve I find this course challenging, so I'll start a study group and ask more questions in class.
Victims Make Excuses The instructor is so boring he puts me to sleep.	Creators Seek Solutions I'm having difficulty staying awake in this class, so I'm going to ask permission to record the lectures. Then I'll listen to them a little at a time and take detailed notes.
Victims Complain This course is a stupid requirement.	Creators Turn Complaints into Requests I don't understand why this course is required, so I'm going to ask my instructor to help me see how it will benefit me in the future.
Victims Compare Themselves Unfavorably to Others I'll never do as well as John; he's a genius.	Creators Seek Help from Those More Skilled I need help in this course, so I'm going to ask John if he'll help me study for the exams.
Victims Blame The tests are ridiculous. The professor gave me an "F" on the first one.	Creators Accept Responsibility I got an "F" on the first test because I didn't read the assignments thoroughly. From now on I'll take detailed notes on everything I read.

> Excuses rob you of power and induce apathy.
>
> *Agnes Whistling Elk*

(continued)

Victims See Problems as Permanent Posting comments on our class's Internet discussion board is impossible. I'll never understand how to do it.	**Creators Treat Problems as Temporary** I've been trying to post comments on our class's Internet discussion board without carefully reading the instructor's directions. I'll read the directions again and follow them one step at a time.
Victims Repeat Ineffective Behaviors Going to the tutoring center is no help. There aren't enough tutors.	**Creators Do Something New** I've been going to the tutoring center right after lunch when it's really busy. I'll start going in the morning to see if more tutors are available then.
Victims Try I'll try to do better.	**Creators Do** To do better, I'll do the following: Attend class regularly, take good notes, ask questions in class, start a study group, and make an appointment with the teacher. If all that doesn't work, I'll think of something else.
Victims Predict Defeat and Give Up I'll probably fail. There's nothing I can do. I can't . . . I have to . . . I should . . . I quit . . .	**Creators Think Positively and Look for a Better Choice** I'll find a way. There's always something I can do. I can . . . I choose to . . . I will . . . I'll keep going . . .

> I used to want the words "She tried" on my tombstone. Now I want, "She did it."
>
> *Katherine Dunham*

When Victims complain, blame, and make excuses, they have little energy left over to solve their problems. As a result, they typically remain stuck where they are, telling their sad story over and over to any poor soul who will listen. (Ever hear of a "pity party"?) In this way, Victims exhaust not only their own energy but often drain the energy of the people around them.

By contrast, Creators use their words and thoughts to improve a bad situation. First, they accept responsibility for creating their present outcomes and experiences, and their words reflect that ownership. Next they plan and take positive actions to improve their lives. In this way, Creators energize themselves and the people around them.

> Blaming . . . is a pastime for losers. There's no leverage in blaming. Power is rooted in self-responsibility.
>
> *Nathaniel Branden*

Whenever you feel yourself slipping into Victim language, ask yourself: What do I want in my life—excuses or results? What could I think and say right now that would get me moving toward the outcomes and experiences that I want?

JOURNAL ENTRY   5

In this activity you will practice the language of personal responsibility. By learning to translate Victim statements into Creator statements, you will master the language of successful people.

1. Draw a line down the middle of a journal page. On the left side of the line, copy the ten Victim language statements found on the next page.

JOURNAL ENTRY | **5** | *continued*

2. **On the right side of the line, translate the Victim statements into the words of a Creator.** The two keys to Creator language are taking ownership of a problem and taking positive actions to solve it. When you respond as if you are responsible for a bad situation, then you are empowered to do something about it (unlike Victims, who must wait for someone else to solve their problems). Use the translations on pages 39–40 as models.

3. **Write what you have learned or relearned about how you use language: Is it your habit to speak as a Victim or as a Creator? Do you find yourself more inclined to blame yourself, blame others, or seek solutions?** Be sure to give examples. What is your goal for language usage from now on? How, specifically, will you accomplish this goal? Your paragraph might begin, *While reading about and practicing Creator language, I learned that I . . .*

Remember to DIVE DEEP!

> The way you use words has a tremendous impact on the quality of your life. Certain words are destructive; others are empowering.
>
> *Susan Jeffers*

VICTIM LANGUAGE	CREATOR LANGUAGE
1. If they'd do something about the parking on campus, I wouldn't be late so often.	1.
2. I'm failing my online class because the site is impossible to navigate.	2.
3. I'm too shy to ask questions in class even when I'm confused.	3.
4. She's a lousy instructor. That's why I failed the first test.	4.
5. I hate group projects because people are lazy and I always end up doing most of the work.	5.
6. I wish I could write better, but I just can't.	6.
7. My friend got me so angry that I can't even study for the exam.	7.
8. I'll try to do my best this semester.	8.
9. The financial aid form is too complicated to fill out.	9.
10. I work nights so I didn't have time to do the assignment.	10.

> If you are in shackles, "I can't" has relevance; otherwise, it is usually a roundabout way of saying "I don't want to," "I won't," or, "I have not learned how to." If you really mean "I don't want to," it is important to come out and say so. Saying "I can't" disowns responsibility.
>
> *Gay Hendricks & Kathlyn Hendricks*

One Student's Story

Alexsandr Kanevskiy

Lane Community College, Oregon

When I began college, I was unmotivated and chose to blame others for my problems and my shortcomings. I was so much smarter than everyone that I didn't need to do all the work that everyone else did; at least that's what I thought. My favorite pastime was staring blankly at a television, rather than attending lecture or doing assigned homework. I figured everything would take care of itself without my interference. I had carried this uninhibited laziness with me through high school and it, unfortunately, translated into my college career. It was then that the gravitas of my situation hit me; at my current rate I was going to be dismissed from school. I was placed on academic probation my sophomore year and unless I improved, I was out.

This was when I first laid my eyes and hands on the *On Course* book. I didn't think much of it at first; just another guide for the misguided, full of backwards theories and advice that wouldn't help me, or anyone else. But from the first reading, I noticed that this book was different. It used different language, language that didn't bore me or induce disinterest. What's funniest, though, was that one of the first journals that I was assigned had the most profound impact on my changing as a student. Just as *On Course* used innovative and interesting language to teach, this journal was all about changing my own language. Rather than use language that blames others or is blatantly negative, that journal taught me to use positive Creator language. I needed to think and speak in a language that searched for answers and solutions, not a language that kept me unmotivated and helpless. When I rephrased my thinking and speaking, the rest of life followed. All of a sudden, responsibility was in my own hands and the solutions that I needed, but was afraid to search out, became much clearer. Now that I knew there were, in fact, answers and solutions, I didn't look to blame those around me. I realized that it was up to me to find these solutions; that they would not magically appear before my eyes and that nobody else would find them for me. My faults and shortcomings became more apparent than ever, and my arrogance was startling. I saw that I was not smart enough to be exempt from school and from the work of my fellow students. They all searched for solutions and held themselves responsible for these solutions; I never realized this because I had never yearned for these solutions, and therefore never had responsibility.

I stopped expecting solutions to come to me naturally and started to work, rather than fall asleep at the television. Positive Creator language was only the first step, but what I took from this first lesson carried through to every other lesson in class and in life. I found that I was newly interested in my classes; homework became a pleasure because each assignment was yet another opportunity to learn. Rather than fall asleep at the television, I now fell asleep after studying. And probation? That became a thing of the past. Even in basketball (my sport of choice) I started to take more of an interest in passing, rather than scoring, and helping my teammates, instead of blaming them for mistakes. Amongst my friends I am now known as the "problem solver," which is just as surprising to me as it is to them. They've noticed a definite change, and I am glad to advise them to read my *On Course* book so that maybe they too will find a lesson that sparks their own improvement. *On Course* provided me with valuable steppingstones that have made me into a student and person who cares enough to take responsibility for his language and his actions, doing what needs to be done in order to succeed in school and in the outside world.

Making Wise Decisions

 FOCUS QUESTIONS How can you improve the quality of the decisions you make? How can you take full responsibility for the outcomes and experiences in your life?

Life is a journey with many opportunities and obstacles, and every one requires a choice. Whatever you are experiencing in your life today is the result of your past choices. More important, whatever you'll experience in the future will be fashioned by the choices you make from this moment on.

This is an exciting thought. If we can make wiser choices, we can more likely create the future we want. On the road to a college degree, you will face important choices such as these:

Shall I . . .

- major in business, science, or creative writing?
- work full-time, part-time, or not at all?
- drop a course that bores me or stick it out?
- study for my exam or go out with friends?

The sum of these choices, plus thousands of others, will determine your degree of success in college and in life. Doesn't it seem wise, then, to develop an effective strategy for choice management?

The Wise Choice Process

In the face of any challenge, you can make a responsible decision by answering the six questions of the Wise Choice Process. This process, you might be interested to know, is a variation of a decision-making model that is used in many career fields. For example, nurses learn a similar process for helping patients that is abbreviated ADPIE. These letters stand for Assess, Diagnose, Plan, Implement, and Evaluate. Counselors and therapists in training may learn a similar process for solving personal problems that was described in 1965 by William Glasser in his book *Reality Therapy.*

And the *NASA Systems Engineering Handbook* says, "Systems engineering [. . .] consists of identification and quantification of system goals, creation of alternative system design concepts, performance of design trades, selection and implementation of the best design, verification that the design is properly built and integrated, and post-implementation assessment of how well the system meets (or met) the goals." In layman's terms, this explanation simply means that systems engineers are in the business of identifying goals and then designing systems that define wise choices to overcome any problems that interfere with achieving those goals.

> The end result of your life here on earth will always be the sum total of the choices you made while you were here.
>
> *Shad Helmstetter*

> My choice; my responsibility; win or lose, only I hold the key to my destiny.
>
> *Elaine Maxwell*

You are about to learn a system that will empower you to take full responsibility for creating your life as you want it to be despite the inevitable challenges that life presents.

1. **WHAT'S MY PRESENT SITUATION?** Begin by identifying your problem or challenge, being sure to define the situation as a Creator, not as a Victim. The important information here is "What exists?" (not "Whose fault is it?"). Quiet your Inner Critic, that self-criticizing voice in your head: *I am a total loser in my history class.* Likewise, ignore your Inner Defender, that judgmental voice that blames everyone else for your problems: *My history instructor is the worst teacher on the planet.* Instead, rely on your Inner Guide, your wise, impartial inner voice that tells the truth as best it can. Consider only the objective facts of your situation, including how you feel about them. For example:

   I stayed up all night studying for my first history test. When I finished taking the test, I hoped for an A. At worst, I expected a B. When I got the test back, my grade was a D. Five other students got A's. I feel depressed and angry.

   By the way, sometimes when we accurately define a troublesome situation, we immediately know what to do. The problem wasn't so much the situation as our muddy understanding of it.

2. **HOW WOULD I LIKE MY SITUATION TO BE?** You can't change the past, but if you could create your desired outcome in the future, what would it look like?

   I would like to get A's on all of my future tests.

3. **WHAT ARE MY POSSIBLE CHOICES?** Create a list of possible choices that you *could* do, knowing you aren't obligated to do any of them. Compile your list without judgment. Don't say, "Oh, that would never work." Don't even say, "That's a great idea." Judgment during brainstorming stops the creative flow. Move from judgments to possibilities, discovering as many creative options as you can. Give yourself time to ponder, explore, consider, think, discover, conceive, invent, imagine. Then dive even deeper. If you get stuck, try one of these options. First, take a different point of view. Think of someone you admire and ask, "What would that person do in my situation?" Or, pretend your problem belongs to someone else. What advice would you give them? Third, incubate. That is, set the problem aside and let your unconscious mind work on a solution while you do other things. Sometimes a great option will pop into your mind while you are brushing your hair, doing math homework, or even sleeping. Your patience will often pay off with a helpful option that would have remained invisible had you accepted the first idea that came to mind or, worse, given up.

   - *I could complain to my history classmates and anyone else who will listen.*
   - *I could drop the class and take it next semester with another instructor.*

> I am the cause of my choices, decisions, and actions. It is I who chooses, decides, and acts. If I do so knowing my responsibility, I am more likely to proceed wisely and appropriately than if I make myself oblivious of my role as source.
>
> *Nathaniel Branden*

- *I could complain to the department head that the instructor grades unfairly.*
- *I could ask my successful classmates for help.*
- *I could ask the instructor for suggestions about improving my grades.*
- *I could read about study skills and experiment with some new ways to study.*
- *I could request an opportunity to retake the test.*
- *I could take all of the online practice quizzes.*
- *I could get a tutor.*

4. **WHAT'S THE LIKELY OUTCOME OF EACH POSSIBLE CHOICE?**
Decide how you think each choice is likely to turn out. If you can't predict the outcome of one of your possible choices, stop this process and gather any additional information you need. For example, if you don't know the impact that dropping a course will have on your financial aid, find out before you take that action. Here are the possible choices from Step 3 and their likely outcomes:

- *Complain to history classmates: I'd have the immediate pleasure of criticizing the instructor and maybe getting others' sympathy.*
- *Drop the class: I'd lose three credits this semester and have to make them up later.*
- *Complain to the department head: Probably she'd ask if I've seen my instructor first, so I wouldn't get much satisfaction.*
- *Ask successful classmates for help: I might learn how to improve my study habits; I might also make new friends.*
- *Ask the instructor for suggestions: I might learn what to do next time to improve my grade; at least the instructor would learn that I want to do well in this course.*
- *Read about study skills: I would probably learn some strategies I don't know and maybe improve my test scores in all of my classes.*
- *Request an opportunity to retake the test: My request might get approved and give me an opportunity to raise my grade. At the very least, I'd demonstrate how much I want to do well.*
- *Take all of the online practice quizzes: This action wouldn't help my grade on this test, but it would probably improve my next test score.*
- *Get a tutor: A tutor would help, but it would probably take a lot of time.*

5. **WHICH CHOICE(S) WILL I COMMIT TO DOING?** Now create your plan. Decide which choice or choices will likely create your desired outcome; then commit to acting on them. If no favorable option exists, consider which choice leaves you no worse off than before. If no such option exists, then ask which choice creates the least unfavorable outcome.

I'll talk to my successful classmates, make an appointment with my instructor and have him explain what I could do to improve, and I'll request an opportunity to retake the test. I'll read the study skills sections of On Course *and implement*

A person defines and redefines who they are by the choices they make, minute to minute.

Joyce Chapman

Destiny is not a matter of chance; it is a matter of choice. It is not a thing to be waited for; it is a thing to be achieved.

William Jennings Bryant

at least three new study strategies. If these choices don't raise my next test score to at least a B, I'll get a tutor.

Each situation will dictate the best options. In the example above, if the student had previously failed four tests instead of one, the best choice might be to drop the class. Or, if everyone in the class were receiving D's and F's, and if the student had already met with the instructor, a responsible option might be to see the department head about the instructor's grading policies.

6. **WHEN AND HOW WILL I EVALUATE MY PLAN?** At some future time you will want to evaluate your results. To do so, compare your new situation to how you want it to be (as you described in Step 2). If the two situations are identical (or close enough), you can call your plan a success. If you find that you are still far from your desired outcome, you have some decisions to make. You might decide that you haven't implemented your new approach long enough, so you'll keep working your plan. Or you may decide that your plan just isn't working, in which case you'll return to Step 1 and work through Step 5 to design a plan that will work better. However, you're not starting completely over because this time you're smarter than you were when you began: Now you know what doesn't work.

After my next history test, I'll see if I have achieved my goal of getting an A. If not, I'll revise my plan.

> The principle of choice describes the reality that I am in charge of my life. I choose it all. I always have, I always will.
>
> *Will Schutz*

Here's the bottom line: Our choices reveal what we *truly* believe and value, as opposed to what we *say* we believe and value. When I submissively wait for others to improve my life, I am being a Victim. When I passively wait for luck to go my way, I am being a Victim. When I make choices that take me off course from my future success just to increase my immediate pleasure (such as partying instead of studying for an important test), I am being a Victim. When I make choices that sacrifice my goals and dreams just to reduce my immediate discomfort (such as dropping a challenging course instead of spending extra hours working with a tutor), I am being a Victim.

However, when I design a plan to craft my life as I want it, I am being a Creator. When I carry out my plan even in the face of obstacles (such as when the campus bookstore runs out of a book I need for class and I keep up with my assignments by reading a copy the instructor has placed on reserve in the library), I am being a Creator. When I take positive risks to advance my goals (such as asking a question in a large lecture class even though I am nervous), I am being a Creator. When I sacrifice immediate pleasure to stay on course toward my dreams (such as resisting the urge to buy a new cell phone so I can reduce my work hours to study more), I am being a Creator.

No matter what your final decision may be, the mere fact that you are defining and making your own choices is wonderfully empowering. By participating in the

Wise Choice Process, you affirm your belief that you *can* change your life for the better. You reject the position that you are merely a Victim of outside forces, a pawn in the chess game of life. You insist on being the Creator of your own outcomes and experiences, shaping your destiny through the power of wise choices.

JOURNAL ENTRY   6

In this activity you will apply the Wise Choice Process to improve a difficult situation in your life. Think about a current problem, one that you're comfortable sharing with your classmates and teacher. As a result of this problem, you may be angry, sad, frustrated, depressed, overwhelmed, or afraid.

Perhaps this situation has to do with a grade you received, a teacher's comment, or a classmate's action. Maybe the problem relates to a relationship, a job, or money. The Wise Choice Process can help you make an empowering choice in any part of your life.

1. Write the six questions of the Wise Choice Process and answer each one as it relates to your situation.

The Wise Choice Process

1. What's my present situation? (Describe the problem objectively and completely.)

2. How would I like my situation to be? (What is your ideal future outcome?)

3. What are my possible choices? (Create a long list of specific choices that might create your preferred outcome.)

4. What's the likely outcome of each possible choice? (If you can't predict the likely outcome of an option, stop and gather more information.)

5. Which choice(s) will I commit to doing? (Pick from your list of choices in Step 3.)

6. When and how will I evaluate my plan? (Identify specifically the date and criteria by which you will determine the success of your plan.)

2. Write what you learned or relearned by doing the Wise Choice Process. Be sure to Dive Deep. You might begin, *By doing the Wise Choice Process, I learned that I . . .*

Remember, you can enliven your journal by adding pictures cut from magazines, drawings of your own, clip art, or quotations that appeal to you.

> When I see all the choices I really have, it makes the world a whole lot brighter.
>
> *Debbie Scott, student*

Creators Wanted!

Candidates must demonstrate personal responsibilty, strong decision-making skills, and a solution-orientation to problems.

Personal Responsibility
AT WORK

I found that the more I viewed myself as totally responsible for my life, the more in control I seemed to be of the goals I wanted to achieve. *Charles J. Givens, entrepreneur and self-made multimillionaire*

A student once told me she'd had more than a dozen jobs in three years. "Why so many jobs?" I asked. "Bad luck," she replied. "I keep getting one lousy boss after another." Hmmmm, I wondered, twelve lousy bosses in a row? What are the odds of that?

Responsibility is about ownership. As long as I believe my career success belongs to someone else (like "lousy" bosses), I'm being a Victim, and my success is unlikely. Victims give little effort to choosing or preparing for a career. Instead, they allow influential others (such as parents and teachers) or circumstances to determine their choice of work. They complain about the jobs they have, make excuses for why they haven't gotten the jobs they want, and blame others or their own permanent flaws for their occupational woes. By contrast, Creators know that the foundation of success at work (as in college) is accepting this truth: *By our choices, we are each the primary creators of the outcomes and experiences of our lives.*

Accepting responsibility in the work world begins with consciously choosing your career path. You alone can decide what career is right for you. That's why Creators explore their career options thoroughly, match career requirements with their own talents and interests, consider the consequences of choosing each career (such as how much education the career requires or what the employment outlook is), and make informed choices. Choose your career wisely because few things in life are worse than spending eight hours a day, fifty weeks a year, working at a job you hate.

Taking responsibility for your work life also means planning your career path to keep your options open and your progress unobstructed. For example, you could keep your career options open in college by taking only general education courses while investigating several possible fields of work. Or you could eliminate a financial obstacle by getting enough education—such as a dental hygiene degree—to support yourself while pursuing your dream career—such as going to dental school.

In short, Creators make use of the power of wise choices. They believe that there is always an option that will lead them toward the careers they want, and they take responsibility for creating the employment they want. Instead of passively waiting for a job to come to them, they actively go out and look. One of my students lost a job when the company where she worked closed. She could have spent hours in the cafeteria complaining about her bad fortune and how she could no longer afford to stay in school. Instead she created employment for herself by going from store to store in a mall asking every manager for a part-time job until one said, "Yes." In the time she could have wasted in the cafeteria complaining about her money problems, she solved them with positive actions.

Personal Responsibility
AT WORK

When it comes to finding a full-time career position, Creators continue to be proactive. They don't wait for the perfect job opening to appear in their local paper or on an Internet job site. They don't wait for a call from an employment agency. They know that employers prefer to hire people they know and like, so Creators do all they can to get known and liked by employers in their career field. They start by researching companies that need their talents and for whom they might like to work. Then, they contact potential employers directly. They don't ask if the employer has a job opening. Instead, they seek an informational interview: "Hi, I've just gotten my degree in accounting, and I'd like to make an appointment to talk to you about your company . . . . What's that? You don't have any positions open at this time? No problem. I'm just gathering information at this point, looking for where my talents might make the most contributions. Would you have some time to meet with me this week? Or would next week be better?" Creators go to these information-gathering interviews prepared with knowledge about the company, good questions to ask, and a carefully prepared résumé. At the end of the meeting they ask if the interviewer knows of any other employers who might need their skills. They call all of the leads they get and use the referral as an opening for a job interview: "I was speaking with John Smith at the Ajax Company, and he suggested that I give you a call about a position you have open." A friend of mine got an information-gathering interview and wowed the personnel manager with her professionally prepared résumé and interviewing skills; even though the company "had no openings" when she called, two days after the interview, she was offered a position.

Accepting responsibility not only helps you *get* a great job, it makes it possible to *excel* on the job. Employers love responsible employees. Wouldn't you? Instead of complaining, blaming, making excuses, and thus creating an emotionally draining work environment, responsible employees create a positive workplace where absenteeism is low and work production is high. Instead of repeating ineffective solutions to problems, proactive employees seek solutions, take new actions, and try something new. They pursue alternative routes instead of complaining about dead ends. Creators show initiative instead of needing constant direction, and they do their best work even when the boss isn't looking. As someone once said, "There is no traffic jam on the extra mile." Creators are willing to go the extra mile, and this effort pays off handsomely.

If you run into a challenge while preparing for a career, seeking a job, or working in your career, don't complain, blame, or make excuses. Instead, ask yourself a Creator's favorite question: "What's my plan?"

▶ *Believing in Yourself*
Change Your Inner Conversation

 FOCUS QUESTION How can you raise your self-esteem by changing your self-talk?

Imagine this: Three students schedule an appointment with their instructor to discuss a project they're working on together. They go to the instructor's office at the scheduled time, but he isn't there. They wait forty-five minutes before finally giving up and leaving. As you learn what they do next, identify which student you think has the strongest self-esteem.

Student 1, feeling discouraged and depressed, spends the evening watching television while ignoring assignments in other subjects. Student 2, feeling insulted and furious, spends the evening complaining to friends about the inconsiderate, incompetent instructor who stood them up. Student 3, feeling puzzled about the mix-up, decides to email the instructor the next day to see what happened and to set up another meeting; meanwhile, this student spends the evening studying for a test in another class.

Which student has the strongest self-esteem?

> It is the mind that maketh good or ill, That maketh wretch or happy, rich or poor.
>
> *Edmund Spencer*

The Curse of Stinkin' Thinkin'

How is it that three people can have the same experience and respond to it so differently? According to psychologists like Albert Ellis, the answer lies in what each person believes caused the event. Ellis suggested that our different responses could be understood by realizing that the activating event (A) plus our beliefs (B) equal the consequences (C) (how we respond). In other words, A + B = C. For example:

Activating Event	+ Beliefs	= Consequence
Student 1: Instructor didn't show up for a scheduled conference.	My instructor thinks I'm dumb. I'll never get a college degree. I'm a failure in life.	Got depressed and watched television all evening.
Student 2: Same.	My instructor won't help me. Teachers don't care about students.	Got angry and spent the night telling friends how horrible the instructor is.
Student 3: Same.	I'm not sure what went wrong. Sometimes things just don't turn out the way you plan. There's always tomorrow.	Studied for another class. Planned to call the instructor the next day to see what happened and set up a new appointment.

> Self-esteem can be defined as the state that exists when you are not arbitrarily haranguing and abusing yourself but choose to fight back against those automatic thoughts with meaningful rational responses.
>
> *Dr. Thomas Burns*

Ellis suggests that our upsets are caused not so much by our problems as by what we *think* about our problems. When our thinking is full of irrational beliefs, what Ellis calls "stinkin' thinkin," we feel awful even when the circumstances don't warrant it. So, how we *think* about the issues in our lives is the real issue. Problems may come and go, but our "stinkin' thinkin'" stays with us. As the old saying goes, "Everywhere I go, there I am."

Stinkin' thinkin' isn't based on reality. Rather, these irrational thoughts are the automatic chatter of the Inner Critic (keeper of Negative Beliefs about the self) and the Inner Defender (keeper of Negative Beliefs about other people and the world).

So what about our three students and their self-esteem? It's not hard to see that student 1, who got depressed and wasted the evening watching television, has low self-esteem. This student is thrown far off course simply by the instructor's not showing up. A major cause of this self-defeating reaction is the Inner Critic's harsh self-judgments. Here are some common self-damning beliefs held by Inner Critics:

> The Inner Critic keeps us feeling insecure and childlike. When it is operating, we feel like children who have done something wrong and probably will never be able to do anything right.
>
> *Hal Stone & Sidra Stone*

I'm dumb.	I'm unattractive.
I'm selfish.	I'm lazy.
I'm a failure.	I'm not college material
I'm incapable.	I'm weak.
I'm not as good as other people.	I'm a lousy parent.
I'm worthless.	I'm unlovable.

A person dominated by his or her Inner Critic misinterprets events, inventing criticisms that aren't there. A friend says, "Something came up, and I can't meet you tonight." The Inner Critic responds, "What did I do wrong? I screwed up again!"

The activating event doesn't cause the consequence; rather, the judgmental chatter of the Inner Critic does. A strong Inner Critic is both a cause and an effect of low self-esteem.

What about student 2, the one who spent the evening telling friends how horrible the instructor was? Though perhaps less apparent, this student's judgmental response also demonstrates low self-esteem. The finger-pointing Inner Defender is merely the Inner Critic turned outward and is just as effective at getting the student off course. Here are some examples of destructive beliefs held by an Inner Defender:

> Everyone has a critical inner voice. But people with low self-esteem tend to have a more vicious and vocal pathological critic.
>
> *Matthew McKay & Patrick Fanning*

People don't treat me right, so they're rotten.
People don't act the way I want them to, so they're awful.
People don't live up to my expectations, so they're the enemy.
People don't do what I want, so they're against me.
Life is full of problems, so it's terrible.
Life is unfair, so I can't stand it.
Life doesn't always go my way, so I can't be happy.
Life doesn't provide me with everything I want, so it's unbearable.

A person dominated by her Inner Defender discovers personal insults and slights in neutral events. A classmate says, "Something came up, and I can't meet you tonight." The Inner Defender responds, "Who do you think you are, anyway? I can find someone a lot better to study with than you!"

The activating event doesn't cause the angry response; rather, the judgmental chatter of the judgmental Inner Defender does. A strong Inner Defender is both a cause and an effect of low self-esteem.

Only student 3 demonstrates high self-esteem. This student realizes he doesn't know why the instructor missed the meeting. He doesn't blame himself, the instructor, or a rotten world. He considers alternatives: Perhaps the instructor got sick or was involved in a traffic accident. Until he can find out what happened and decide what to do next, this student turns his attention to an action that will keep him on course to another goal. The Inner Guide is concerned with positive results, not judging self or others. A strong Inner Guide is both a cause and an effect of high self-esteem.

Disputing Irrational Beliefs

How, then, can you raise your self-esteem?

First, you can become aware of the chatter of your Inner Critic and Inner Defender. Be especially alert when events in your life go wrong, when your desired outcomes and experiences are thwarted. That's when we are most likely to complain, blame, and excuse. That's when we substitute judgments of ourselves or others for the positive actions that would get us back on course.

Once you become familiar with your inner voices, you can begin a process of separating yourself from your Inner Critic and Inner Defender. To do this, practice disputing your irrational and self-sabotaging beliefs. Here are four effective ways to dispute:

- **Offer evidence that your judgments are incorrect:** *My instructor emailed me last week to see if I needed help with my project, so there's no rational reason to believe he won't help me now.*

- **Offer a positive explanation of the problem:** *Sure my instructor didn't show up, but he may have missed the appointment because of a last-minute crisis.*

- **Question the importance of the problem:** *Even if my instructor won't help me, I can still do well on this project, and if I don't, it won't be the end of the world.*

- **If you find that your judgments are true, instead of continuing to criticize yourself or someone else, offer a plan to improve the situation:** *If I'm honest, I have to admit that I haven't done well in this class so far, but from now on I'm going to attend every class, take good notes, read my assignments two or three times, and work with a study group before every test.*

According to psychologist Ellis, a key to correcting irrational thinking is changing a "must" into a preference. When we think "must," what follows in our thoughts is typically awful, terrible, and dreadful. For example, my Inner Defender's belief

> Replacing a negative thought with a positive one changes more than just the passing thought—it changes the way you perceive and deal with the world.
>
> *Dr. Clair Douglas*

> Does it help to change what you say to yourself? It most certainly does . . . . Tell yourself often enough that you'll succeed and you dramatically improve your chances of succeeding and of feeling good.
>
> *Drs. Bernie Zilbergeld & Arnold A. Lazarus*

that an instructor "must" meet me for an appointment or he is an awful, terrible, dreadful person is irrational; I'd certainly "prefer" him to meet me for an appointment, but his not meeting me does not make him rotten—in fact, he may have a perfectly good reason for not meeting with me. As another example, my Inner Critic's belief that I "must" pass this course or I am an awful, terrible, dreadful person is irrational; I'd certainly "prefer" to pass this course, but not doing so does not make me worthless—in fact, not passing this course may lead me to something even better. Believing irrationally that I, another person, or the world "must" be a particular way, Ellis says, is a major cause of my distress and misery.

If all of the previously mentioned ideas fail, you can always distract yourself from negative, judgmental thoughts. Simply tell yourself, "STOP!" Then replace your blaming, complaining, or excusing with something positive: Watch a funny movie, tell a joke, recall your goals and dreams, think about someone you love.

Wisely choose the thoughts that occupy your mind. Avoid letting automatic, negative thoughts undermine your self-esteem. Evict them and replace them, instead, with esteem-building thoughts.

> You mainly make yourself needlessly and neurotically miserable by strongly holding absolutist irrational Beliefs, especially by rigidly believing unconditional shoulds, oughts, and musts.
>
> *Albert Ellis*

JOURNAL ENTRY 7

In this activity, you will practice disputing the judgments of your Inner Critic and your Inner Defender. As you become more skilled at seeing yourself, other people, and the world more objectively and without distracting judgments, your self-esteem will thrive.

1. **Write a sentence expressing a recent problem or event that upset you.** Think of something troubling that happened in school, at work, or in your personal life. For example, *I got a 62 on my math test.*

2. **Write a list of three or more criticisms your Inner Critic (IC) might level against you as a result of this situation. Have your Inner Guide (IG) dispute each one immediately.** Review the four methods of disputing described on page 52. You only need to use one of them for each criticism. For example,

IC: You failed that math test because you're terrible in math.

IG: It's true I failed the math test, but I'll study harder next time and do better. This was only the first test, and I now know what to expect next time.

3. **Write a list of three or more criticisms your Inner Defender (ID) might level against someone else or life as a result of this situation. Have your Inner Guide (IG) dispute each one immediately.** Again use one of the four methods for disputing. For example,

JOURNAL ENTRY **7** *continued*

ID: You failed that math test because you've got the worst math instructor on campus.

IG: I have trouble understanding my math instructor, so I'm going to make an appointment to talk with him in private. John really liked him last semester, so I bet I'll like him, too, if I give him a chance.

4. **Write what you have learned or relearned about changing your inner conversation.** Your journal entry might begin, *In reading and writing about my inner conversations, I have discovered that . . . .* Wherever possible, offer personal experiences or examples to explain what you learned.

One Student's Story

Dominic Grasseth

Lane Community College, Oregon

Enrolling in college at the age of twenty-eight was very intimidating to me. Having dropped out of high school at fifteen, I had a real problem with confidence. Even though I had a GED and was earning a decent living as a car salesman, I still doubted that I was smart enough to be successful in college. I finally took the leap and enrolled because I want a career where I don't have to work twelve hours a day, six days a week and never see my family. However, by the second week of the semester, I found myself falling back into old habits. I was sitting in the back of the classroom, asking what homework was due, and talking through most of the class. Negative thoughts constantly ran through my mind: *The teachers won't like me. I can't compete with the eighteen-year-olds right out of high school. I don't even remember what a "verb" is. I can't do this.*

Then in my College Success class, we read Chapter 2 of *On Course* about becoming a Creator and disputing "stinkin' thinkin'." I realized I had taken on the role of the Victim almost my whole life, and I was continuing to do it now. One day I was on my porch when I caught myself thinking my usual negative thoughts. It occurred to me that I was the only one holding me back, not the teachers, not the other students, not math, not English. If I wanted to be successful in college, I had to quit being scared. I had to change my thinking. So I made a deal with myself that any time I caught myself thinking negatively, I would rephrase the statement in a way that was more positive. I started to truly pay attention to the thoughts in my head and question the negative things I was telling myself. After that I began sitting up front in my classes and participating more. I've always been kind of scattered, so I started using a calendar and a dry erase board to keep track of what I had to do.

What amazes me is that I didn't really make that big of a change, yet I finished the semester with a 4.0 average! All I did was realize that what I was saying to myself was my underlying problem. I am responsible for my thoughts, and the choice about whether or not to succeed is mine. These days when I have a ridiculous thought going through my mind and I change it, I smile. It's very empowering.

Photo: Courtesy of Dominic Grasseth

Embracing Change | **Do One Thing Different This Week**

Many people resist change. It's easier to complain, blame, and make excuses. More challenging is experimenting with new beliefs and behaviors, evaluating your results, and then adopting the more helpful ones permanently. And that is exactly what Creators do. Creators crave new methods for lifting the quality of their lives up a notch. And then up another notch. And another. Creators embrace change because it's a great way—maybe the *only* way—to maximize their potential to live a rich, full life.

In this chapter, you have encountered a number of empowering beliefs and behaviors related to personal responsibility and self-esteem. Here's an opportunity to experiment with one of them. First, from the following list, choose one belief or behavior you think will make the greatest positive impact on your outcomes and experiences.

1. Think: "I accept responsibility for creating my life as I want it."
2. Write a list of Victim statements used by other people and translate the statements into Creator language.
3. Catch myself thinking or speaking Victim language, write a list of these statements, and translate them into Creator language.

4. Use the Wise Choice Process to make a decision.
5. Catch myself using stinkin' thinkin' and dispute it.
6. Demonstrate personal responsibility at my workplace.

Now, write the belief or behavior you chose under "My Commitment" in the following chart. Then, track yourself for one week, putting a check in the appropriate box each day that you keep your commitment. After seven days, assess your results. If your outcomes and experiences improve, you now have a tool you can use for the rest of your life.

My Commitment						
Day 1	Day 2	Day 3	Day 4	Day 5	Day 6	Day 7

During my seven-day experiment, what happened?

As a result of what happened, what did I learn or relearn?

Wise Choices in College | READING

The first step in the CORE Learning System is **Collecting** knowledge, and one of the most important ways you'll **Collect** knowledge in college is by reading. During your studies you can expect to read many thousands of pages. You'll read textbooks, reference books, journals, handouts, Web pages, and more. Most of the tests you'll take will be based on your reading. And so will the essays and research papers you'll write. Obviously, then, reading is one of the most important skills you can have for success in college.

Sadly, according, to American College Testing (ACT), many college-bound students lack this skill. Nearly half of the 1.2 million students who recently took the ACT college entrance test scored low in reading. This is bad news for those students. According to the ACT, the ability to read and understand complex texts is the skill that separates students who are ready for college from those who are not. And because of all of the reading that is required in college, even students with good reading skills will benefit from becoming more accomplished.

The learning strategies you'll encounter in this chapter have one thing in common: the ability to cure **mindless reading.** Mindless reading is the act of running your eyes over a page only to realize you don't recall a thing you read. The opposite of mindless reading is **active reading.** Active reading is characterized by intense mental engagement in what you are reading. This highly focused involvement leads to significant neural activity in your brain, assists deep and lasting learning, and (good news for students) leads to high grades.

Reading: The Big Picture

When reading mindfully, you are actively **Collecting** key concepts, ideas (main and secondary) and supporting details (major and minor). When placed by levels of significance, information you read looks like Figure 2.2.

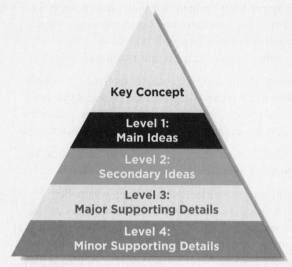

Figure 2.2 ▲

A **key concept** is the main topic you are reading about. Examples of key concepts include *inflation*, *mitosis*, *World War II*, or *symbolic interactionism*.

Ideas that expand on concepts are divided into main and secondary ideas. A **main idea** (sometimes called a "thesis") is the most important idea the author wants to convey about a key concept. Two authors may write about the same key concept but present different main ideas. For example, they may both write about *inflation* but disagree about its cause. One might say, "The primary cause of inflation is war." The other may say, "The rising cost of production is the main cause of inflation."

A **secondary idea** (sometimes called a "topic sentence") elaborates on a main idea by answering questions that readers may have about it. For example, one question about inflation might be, "What effect do taxes have on rising costs?" Another might be "How do labor unions affect the cost of production?"

Each idea—main or secondary—is typically followed by **supporting details** such as examples, evidence, explanation, and experiences.

To illustrate the relationship of levels, imagine that your instructor asks your class the following. "In Chapter 2 of *On Course*, a key concept is personal responsibility. What is the main idea about it?" (Pause for a moment and decide how you would answer, because how well you answer provides feedback about your present reading abilities.)

Imagine one of your classmates replying, "The main idea in the second chapter of *On Course* is that personal responsibility is an important inner quality for creating academic, professional, and personal success."

"Well, done," your instructor says, "and what are some of the secondary ideas?"

Another student answers, "When we are being responsible we respond to life's challenges as Creators not as Victims. Another secondary idea is that our inner conversations affect whether or not we make responsible choices. And a third idea is that using a decision-making model called the Wise Choice Process helps us make responsible choices."

"Excellent," your instructor enthuses. "You've demonstrated you understand some of the important ideas of the chapter. Now, someone please elaborate on the Wise Choice Process." In response, a third student *explains* the six steps of the Wise Choice Process and then gives an *example* of how she used it to make a recent decision. By elaborating, she offers supporting details that answer the questions a thoughtful reader would have about the Wise Choice Process, such as "What is it and how can it be used?"

So as you look at the following learning strategies, keep in mind the big picture of reading: **Your goal is to Collect key concepts, important ideas, and supporting details.**

Before Reading

1. Approach reading with a positive attitude. Attitude is the foundation of your success because it influences the choices you make. Nowhere is this truer than in reading. Do you have negative attitudes about reading in general or reading specific subjects? Or do you harbor doubts about your ability to understand what you read? Do you think of any of your reading assignments as beyond your understanding, boring, worthless, or stupid? If so, replace negative attitudes with positive ones. Realize that reading offers you access to the entire recorded knowledge of the human race. With effective reading skills, you can learn virtually any information or skill you need in order to improve your life, but only if you approach each reading assignment with a positive attitude.

2. Create a distributed reading schedule. A marathon reading session before an exam is seldom helpful. Instead, spread many shorter sessions over an entire course. For example, plan to finish your 450-page history text by reading 30 to 40 pages each week. You can easily reach that goal by reading just five or six pages a day. A distributed schedule like this keeps you current with your assignments, helps you concentrate for your entire reading session, and increases how much you recall from what you read.

3. Review past readings. As a warm-up before you read, glance at pages you have previously read. Look at chapter titles and text headings to jog your memory and prepare for what you are about to read. Review any marks or comments you made when you read earlier assignments (see Strategy 11). Look over any notes you took (see Strategy 12). Reviewing like this takes advantage of one of the three principles of deep and lasting learning: prior learning. When you connect what you are reading now to previously stored information (i.e., already-formed neural networks), you learn the new information or skill faster and more deeply.

4. Preview before reading. Like observing a valley from a high mountain, previewing a reading assignment provides the big picture of what's to come. You'll see the important ideas and their organization, which increases understanding when you read. At the beginning of a course, it's wise to preview the entire book. Most of the time, however, you'll be previewing a single chapter. Thumb through the pages, taking in chapter titles, chapter objectives, focus questions, text headings, charts, graphs, illustrations, previews, and summaries. Note any words that are specially formatted, such as with CAPITALS, **bold**, *italics*, and so on. In just a few minutes, you will have a helpful overview of what you are about to read. A chapter preview should take no longer than five minutes and include a quick look at some or all of the following features:

- **Table of Contents:** The fastest way to preview is to look at the table of contents because it provides an outline of your entire reading (for an example, see the table of contexts of this book on pages vii–xiii).

- **Chapter Objectives or Focus Questions:** Usually placed at the beginning of a chapter, these features identify what you can expect to learn from the chapter. Each section in *On Course* starts with Focus Questions.

- **Chapter Titles and Headings:** Thumb through the pages you're about to read, and note the titles and headings. They provide a helpful overview of the topics you'll be reading about. For example, here are three levels of information presented in Chapter 2 of *On Course*:

  Accepting Personal Responsibility

  Adopting the Creator Role

  Victims and Creators

  Responsibility and Choice

- **Special Formatting:** Words in CAPITALS, **bold**, *italics*, or **color** put a spotlight on key concepts and ideas. When you see special formatting, you can be confident the author is giving you a hint: *This is important information!* A common use of specially formatted text is to call attention to special vocabulary. That is why **Creator** and **Victim** were bolded earlier in this chapter.

- **Visual Elements:** Charts, graphs, illustrations, cartoons, photographs, and diagrams are included to reinforce concepts in the text and improve readers' understanding. For example, the two drawings on page 13 illustrate how learning changes neurons in the brain. Captions for visual elements usually explain their significance.

- **Chapter Summaries:** Many college texts provide a summary at the end of a chapter. This summary typically identifies the important ideas in the chapter.

While it's taken quite a few words to describe these six options for previewing a reading assignment, once you get skilled, previewing will take you only a few minutes to do.

5. Identify the purpose of what you're reading. To keep the big picture in mind, ask yourself, "What's the point of what I'm about to read?" For example, the "point" of every section of *On Course* is to present empowering beliefs and behaviors that you can add to your toolbox for success in college and in life. By keeping this purpose in mind as you read, you program yourself to **Collect** the most important ideas.

6. Create a list of questions. Create a list of questions. If the author provides focus questions, use them to start this list. Next, turn chapter titles or section headings into questions. For example, if the heading in a computer book reads "HTML Tags," turn this heading into one or more questions: *What is an HTML tag? How are HTML tags created?* If you see questions within the text, add them to your list. The process of reading for answers to questions, especially those you're really curious about, heightens your concentration, increases your active involvement, and improves your understanding.

While Reading

7. Read in chunks. Poor readers read one word at a time. Good readers don't read words; they read ideas, and ideas are found in groups of words, or chunks. For example, in the following sentence, try reading all of the words between the diamonds at once:

◆ If you read ◆ in chunks ◆ you will increase ◆ your speed ◆ and your comprehension. ◆

Like any new habit, this method will initially feel awkward. However, as you practice you'll find you can take in bigger chunks of information at increasingly faster rates of speed, like this:

◆ If you read in chunks ◆ you will increase your speed ◆ and your comprehension. ◆

Since much of your reading time occurs while you pause to take in words (called a "fixation"), the fewer times you pause, the faster you can read. In addition to taking in larger chunks of information, you can nudge yourself even faster by moving your fingers along the line of text as a speed regulator. As you get practiced at taking in more words in one fixation, you can increase the speed of your fingers and read even faster.

8. Concentrate on reading faster. In one experiment, students increased their reading speed up to 50 percent simply by concentrating on reading as fast as they could while still understanding what they were reading. You, too, can probably read faster by just *deciding* to.

9. Pause to recite. Have you ever finished reading an assignment only to realize you have no idea what you just read? Here's a remedy. Stop at the end of each section and summarize aloud what you understand to be the main ideas and supporting details. The more difficult the reading, the more often you'll want to pause to recite. Each recitation will give you instant feedback about how well you understand the author's ideas. When you can't smoothly recite the essence of what you have read, go back and read the passage again. Try reading aloud the words you have underlined or highlighted. Keep working actively with the ideas until you understand them completely.

10. Read for answers to questions on your list. If you've created a list of questions (Strategy 6), now is the time to cash in on that effort. For example, suppose you're about to read a chapter in your accounting book titled "The Double-Entry Accounting System." On your list of questions,

you've written "What is a double-entry accounting system?" As you read the chapter, look for and underline the answer. Then write the question in the margin alongside. If you finish your reading assignment and still have unanswered questions on your list, ask your instructor for answers during class or office hours.

11. Mark and annotate your text. As you read, keep asking yourself: *What's the key concept . . . what are the main ideas about the concept . . . and what support is offered?* Identifying main and supporting ideas is usually easier after you've read a whole paragraph, or even a whole section. Once you decide what's important, underline or highlight these ideas in your book. As a guideline, mark only 10 to 15 percent of your text, selecting only what is truly important. Additionally, annotate what you read. To *annotate* means to add comments. Writing your own comments in the white spaces on each page helps you minimize mindless reading and maximize your understanding. Annotations could include summaries in your own words, diagrams, or questions for which you want answers. Later, when creating study materials, your marks and annotations will help you continue **Collecting** the most important ideas to learn.

12. Take notes. Many strategies exist for **Collecting** ideas from textbooks by taking notes in a separate binder or computer file, and in future chapters you'll learn a number of nifty strategies for doing just that. However, there is one option that is particularly suited for taking notes while reading a text, so we'll look at it here. Start by writing the chapter title at the top of your note page or computer file (this is usually the key concept). Beneath the chapter title, copy the first main heading from the chapter, thus recording a level 1 main idea. Add any subheadings from your book below the main heading, indenting a few more spaces to the right, thus recording level 2 secondary ideas). Here's what this would look like for Chapter 2 of *On Course*:

Structure	Example
Key Concept	Accepting Personal Responsibility
—Level 1 Main Idea	—Adopting the Creator Role
—Level 2 Secondary Idea	—Victims and Creators
—Level 2 Secondary Idea	—Responsibility and Choice
—Level 1 Main Idea	—Mastering Creator Language
—Level 2 Secondary Idea	—Self-Talk
—Level 2 Secondary Idea	—The Language of Responsibility
—Level 1 Main Idea	—Making Wise Decisions
—Level 2 Secondary Idea	—The Wise Choice Process

13. Look up the definition of key words. Use a dictionary when you don't know the meaning of a key word. Consider starting a vocabulary list in your journal. Or create a deck of index cards with new words on one side and definitions on the other. Online dictionaries, like Merriam-Webster's (http://www.m-w.com), offer an option that lets you hear the correct pronunciation of a word. Use your new words in conversations to lock them in your memory. Developing an extensive and eloquent vocabulary is a great success strategy. In case you want to set some goals for the size of your vocabulary, linguist David Crystal estimates that the average college graduate has an active vocabulary of 60,000 words and the ability to recognize an additional 75,000.

14. Read critically. Not all ideas in print are true. Learn to read critically by being a healthy skeptic. Look for red flags that may suggest a credibility problem. Who is the author? What are the author's credentials? What assumptions does the author hold? Does the author stand to gain (e.g., money, status, revenge) by your acceptance of his or her opinion? Are the facts accurate and relevant? Is the evidence sufficient? Are the author's positions developed with logic or only strong emotions? Are sources of information identified? Are they believable? Are they current? Are various sides of an issue presented, or only one?

Given that anyone can post information on the Internet, reading critically is especially important when assessing information that you encounter online. You'll learn more about how to be a critical thinker in Chapter 7.

After Reading

15. Reflect on what you read. Upon finishing a reading assignment, lean back, close your eyes, and ask yourself questions that will help you see the big picture. For example . . .

- What are the key concepts?

- What are the main ideas about those concepts?

- What are the supporting details?

- What do I personally think and feel about the author's main ideas and supporting details?

16. Reread difficult passages. On occasion, every reader needs to revisit difficult passages to understand them fully. I recall one author whose writing made me feel like a dunce. However, somewhere around my fifth or sixth reading (and using strategies in this section), a light went on in my brain and I thought, "Oh . . . so that's what he means! That's not nearly as complicated as I thought!" Trust that by using the strategies presented here, you can comprehend any reading assignment if you stick with it long enough.

17. Recite the marked text. Read aloud the parts of the text you have underlined or highlighted. Attempt to blend the ideas into a flowing statement by adding connecting words between the words in your text. In effect, you'll be summarizing the key points of the material you just read.

18. Talk about what you read. Explain the main ideas and supporting details. Especially helpful is having this conversation with another student in your class who has read the same assignment. This study partner can give you feedback on where you may have misunderstood or left out something important.

19. Read another book on the same subject.
Sometimes another author will express the same
ideas more clearly. Ask your instructor or a librarian
to suggest other readings. Or try a book on the same
topic written for children. A book for younger learners may provide just the information or explanation
you need to make sense of your college textbook.

20. Seek assistance. Still having problems
understanding what you read? Ask your instructor to explain muddy points. Or see if your college has a reading lab or a tutoring center. For
some subjects—such as math, science, and foreign
languages—there may be dedicated personnel to
help. If all else fails, see if your college has a
diagnostician who can test you for a possible
learning disability. Such a specialist may be able
to help you improve your reading skills.

Reading Exercise

Choose your most challenging textbook and rate
your present comprehension of its content on a
scale of 1 to 10 (with 10 indicating a deep and lasting understanding of what you read). Over the next
week, apply new reading strategies when you read
this challenging text. At the end of the week, again
rate your understanding of the book on the 1-to-10
scale. Be prepared to explain why you think your
rating went up, down, or stayed the same. In particular, is there one reading strategy that was most
helpful in your quest to read this challenging text
with greater comprehension?

Discovering Self-Motivation

3

Once I accept responsibility for creating my own life, I must choose the kind of life I want to create.

I choose all of the outcomes and experiences for my life.

Successful Students . . .	Struggling Students . . .
create inner motivation, providing themselves with the passion to persist toward their goals and dreams, despite all obstacles.	**have little sense of passion and drive,** often quitting when difficulties arise.
design a compelling life plan, complete with motivating goals and dreams.	**tend to invent their lives as they live them.**
commit to their goals and dreams, visualizing the successful creation of their ideal future.	**wander aimlessly from one activity to another.**

Case Study in Critical Thinking

Popson's Dilemma

Fresh from graduate school, Assistant Professor Popson was midway through his first semester of college teaching when his depression started. Long gone was the excitement and promise of the first day of class. Now, only about two-thirds of his students were attending, and some of them were barely holding on. When Popson asked a question during class, the same few students answered every time. The rest stared off in bored silence. One student always wore a knit cap with a slender cord slithering from under it to an iPod in his shirt pocket. With ten or even fifteen minutes remaining in a class period, students would start stuffing notebooks noisily into their backpacks or book bags. Only one student had visited him during office hours, despite Popson's numerous invitations. And when he announced one day that he was canceling the next class to attend a professional conference, a group in the back of the room pumped their fists in the air and hooted with glee. It pained Popson to have aroused so little academic motivation in his students, and he began asking experienced professors what he should do.

Professor Assante said, "Research says that about 70 percent of students enroll in college because they see the degree as their ticket to a good job and fat paycheck. And they're right. College grads earn nearly a million dollars more in their lives than high school grads. Show them how your course will help them graduate and prosper in the work world. After that, most of them will be model students."

Professor Buckley said, "Everyone wants the freedom to make choices affecting their lives, so have your students design personal learning contracts. Let each one choose assignments from a list of options you provide. Let them add their own choices if they want. Even have them pick the dates they'll turn in their assignments. Give them coupons that allow them to miss any three classes without penalty. Do everything you can to give them choices and put them in charge of their own education. Once they see they're in control of their learning and you're here to help them, their motivation will soar."

Professor Chang said, "Deep down, everyone wants to make a difference. I just read a survey by the Higher Education Research Institute showing that two-thirds of first-year students believe it's essential or very important to help others. Find out what your students want to do to make a contribution. Tell them how your course will help them achieve those dreams. Even better, engage them in a service learning project. When they see how your course can help them live a life with real purpose, they'll be much more interested in what you're teaching."

Professor Donnelly said, "Let's be realistic. The best motivator for students is grades. It's the old carrot and stick. Start every class with a quiz and they'll get there on time. Take points off for absences and they'll attend regularly. Give extra points for getting assignments in on time. Reward every positive action with points and take off points when they screw up. When they realize they can get a good grade in your class by doing what's right, even the guy with the iPod will get involved."

Professor Egret said, "Most people work harder and learn better when they feel they're part of a team with a common goal, so help your students feel part of a community of learners. Give them interesting topics to talk about in pairs and small groups. Give them team assignments and group projects. Teach them how to work well in groups so everyone contributes their fair share. When your students start feeling like they belong and start caring about one another, you'll see their academic motivation go way up."

Professor Fanning said, "Your unmotivated students probably don't expect to pass your course, so they quit trying. Here's my suggestion: Assign a modest challenge at which they can all succeed if they do it. And every student *has* to do it. No exceptions. Afterward, give students specific feedback on what they did well and what they can do to improve. Then give them a slightly more challenging assignment and repeat the cycle again and again. Help them *expect* to be successful by *being* successful. At some point they're going to say, 'Hey, I can do this!' and then you'll see a whole different attitude."

Professor Gonzales said, "Learning should be active and fun. I'm not talking about a party; I'm talking engaging students in educational experiences that teach deep and important lessons about your subject. Your students should be thinking, 'I can't wait to get to class to see what we're going to do and learn today!' You can use debates, videos, field trips, group projects, case studies, learning games, simulations, role plays, guest speakers, visualizations . . . the possibilities are endless. When learning is engaging and enjoyable, motivation problems disappear."

Professor Harvey said, "I've been teaching for thirty years, and if there's one thing I've learned, it's this: You can't motivate someone else. Maybe you've heard the old saying, 'When the student is ready, the teacher will arrive.' You're just wasting your energy trying to make someone learn before they're ready. Maybe they'll be back in your class in five or ten years and they'll be motivated. But for now, just do the best you can for the students who *are* ready."

Listed below are the eight professors in this story. Based on your experience, rank the quality of their advice on the scale below. Give a different score to each professor. Be prepared to explain your choices.

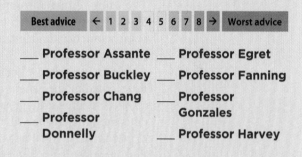

| Best advice | ← | 1 | 2 | 3 | 4 | 5 | 6 | 7 | 8 | → | Worst advice |

___ **Professor Assante** ___ **Professor Egret**

___ **Professor Buckley** ___ **Professor Fanning**

___ **Professor Chang** ___ **Professor Gonzales**

___ **Professor Donnelly**

___ **Professor Harvey**

DIVING DEEPER Is there an approach not mentioned by one of the eight professors that would be even more motivating for you?

Creating Inner Motivation

FOCUS QUESTIONS How important do educators think motivation is to your academic success? What determines how motivated you are? What can you do to keep your motivation consistently high this semester . . . and beyond?

Recently, two extensive surveys asked college and university educators to rank factors that hinder students' success and persistence. These surveys were done by American College Testing (ACT) and the Policy Center on the First Year of College. In both surveys, educators identified *lack of motivation* as the number one barrier to student success.

> There are three things to remember about education. The first is motivation. The second is motivation. The third is motivation.
>
> *Terrell Bell, former U.S. Secretary of Education*

Lack of motivation has various symptoms: students arriving late to class or being absent, assignments turned in late or not at all, work done superficially or sloppily, appointments missed, offers of support ignored, and students not participating in class discussions or activities, to name just a few. But the most glaring symptom of all is the enormous number of students who vanish from college within their first year. According to the ACT, in public four-year colleges in the United States, about one-third of students fail to return for their second year. And in public two-year colleges, it's even worse: Nearly *half* of first-year students don't make it to the second year. Despite these grim statistics, you can be among those who stay and thrive in higher education!

A Formula for Motivation

The study of human motivation—seeking to understand why we do what we do—is extensive and complex. However, one synthesis of a number of theories offers a practical understanding of academic motivation. It's represented by the formula: $V \times E = M$.

In this formula, "V" stands for "value." In terms of your education, value is determined by the benefits you believe you'll obtain from seeking and obtaining a college degree. The greater the benefits you assign to these experiences and outcomes, the greater will be your motivation. The greater your motivation, the higher the cost you'll be willing to pay in terms of time, money, effort, frustration, inconvenience, and sacrifice. Take a moment to identify the score that presently represents the personal value you place on seeking and obtaining a college education. Choose a number from 0 to 10 (where "0" represents no perceived value and "10" represents an extremely high perceived value).

The "E" in this formula stands for "expectation." In terms of your education, expectation is determined by how likely you think it is that you can earn a college degree with a reasonable effort. Here, you need to weigh your abilities (how good a student you are and how strong your previous education is) against the difficulty of achieving your goal (how challenging the courses are that you will need to take and how much you are willing to sacrifice to be successful). Take a moment to identify the score that presently represents your personal expectation of being able to complete a college degree with a reasonable effort. Choose a number from 0 to 10 (where "0" represents no expectation of success and "10" represents an extremely high expectation of success).

In a nutshell, this concept says that your level of motivation in college is determined by multiplying your value score by your expectation score. For example, if the value you place on a college degree is high (say, a 10), but your expectation of success in college is low (say, a 1), then your motivation score will be very low (10). Similarly, if your expectation for success in college is high (say, a 9), but you put little value on a degree (say, a 2), then once more, your motivation score will be very low (18). In either case, your low score suggests that you probably won't do what's required to succeed in college: to make goal-directed choices consistently, to give a high-quality effort regularly, and to

> Today's theories about motivation emphasize the importance of factors within the individual, particularly the variables of expectancy and value. Students' motivations are strongly influenced by what they think is important (value) and what they believe they can accomplish (expectancy).
>
> *K. Patricia Cross*

persist despite inevitable obstacles and challenges. Sadly, then, you'll join the multitude of students who exit college long before earning a degree.

Probably you see where all of this leads. To stay motivated in college, first, you have to find ways to raise (or keep high) the **value** you place on college, including the academic degree you'll earn, the knowledge you'll gain, and the experiences you'll have while enrolled. Second, you have to find ways to raise (or keep high) the **expectation** you have of being successful in college while making what you consider to be a reasonable effort. With our exploration of effective reading skills in Chapter 2, we've already identified some important academic skills that, if mastered, will contribute to your high expectations for success in college. Throughout *On Course,* you'll encounter literally hundreds of other skills, both academic and otherwise, that can raise your realistic expectation of success in college even higher.

For now, however, we are going to focus on value. Only you can determine how much value a college education holds for you, but let's look at some of the benefits that others have attributed to achieving a degree beyond high school.

Value of College Outcomes

One of the most widely recognized benefits of a college degree is increased earning power. According to recent U.S. Census Bureau data, high school graduates earn an average of $1.2 million dollars during their working life. However, if you complete a two-year associate's degree, that lifetime total goes up $400,000 to $1.6 million dollars. If you complete a four-year bachelor's degree, you can add another $500,000 for an average total of $2.1 million! Think what that additional money could do to help you and the people you love live a good life.

Not only does a college degree offer increased earnings, it also opens doors to employment in many desirable professions. Six out of every ten jobs now require some postsecondary education and training, according to data reported by the ERIC Clearinghouse on Higher Education. The U.S. Department of Labor predicts that by 2012 the number of jobs requiring advanced skills will grow at twice the rate of those requiring only basic skills.

A college degree confers many additional benefits. According to the Institute for Higher Education Policy and the Carnegie Foundation, college graduates enjoy higher savings levels, improved working conditions, increased personal and professional mobility, improved health and life expectancy, improved quality of life for offspring, better consumer decision making, increased personal status, more hobbies and leisure activities, and a tendency to become more open-minded, more cultured, more rational, more consistent, and less authoritarian, and these benefits are passed on to their children.

Additionally, attaining a college degree can bring personal satisfaction and accomplishment. I once had a seventy-six-year-old student who inspired us all with her determination "to finally earn the college degree that I cheated myself out of more than fifty years ago." Another valuable outcome of a college degree is the pride and esteem that many enjoy when they walk across the stage to receive their hard-earned diploma. And for some, a college degree is an essential step toward

There is evidence that the time for learning various subjects would be cut to a fraction of the time currently allotted if the material were perceived by the learner as related to his own purposes.

Carl Rogers

For learning to take place with any kind of efficiency students must be motivated. To be motivated, they must become interested. And they become interested when they are actively working on projects which they can relate to their values and goals in life.

Gus Tuberville, former president, William Penn College

fulfilling a personal vision; such was true for one of my college roommates who, for as long as he could remember, dreamed of being a doctor (and today he is one).

For some people, long-term goals are too distant to be motivating. They get fired up by the short-term goals they can nearly touch, such as outcomes they can create during this semester. Table 3.1 shows the short-term goals that one of my students chose for himself, along with his reasons why.

Table 3.1 ▼ One Student's Desired Outcomes

Desired Outcomes	Value
Earn a grade point average (GPA) of 3.8 or better and make the dean's list this semester.	A high GPA will look great on my transcript when I apply for a job. Also, it will give me a real boost of self-confidence.
In my English class, write at least one essay that contains no more than two nonstandard grammar errors.	I want to be able to write anything without worrying that someone who reads it is going to think I'm stupid or illiterate.
In my Student Success class, learn at least three strategies for managing my time more effectively.	I feel overwhelmed and stressed with all I need to do, and learning how to manage my time better will lower my stress level.
Get an A in my accounting class.	I want a career in accounting, so doing well in this course is the first step toward success in my profession.
Make three or more new friends.	My friends from high school all went to other colleges or they're working. I want to make new friends here so I'll have people to hang out with and have fun on the weekends.

Value of College Experiences

Value isn't found only in outcomes; it's also found in experiences. In fact, all human beings manage their emotions by doing their best to maximize positive experiences and minimize negative experiences. What, for example, is the value of playing an intramural sport, attending a movie, belonging to a fraternity or sorority, dancing, playing a video game, or hanging out with friends? Primarily, all are choices to manage our inner experiences. If done in excess, any one of these choices can get us off course from our desired outcomes. But done in moderation, all of these activities (and many others) can create a positive experience and contribute mightily to academic motivation. That's because if you're enjoying the journey called college, you're much more likely to persist until you reach the destination called graduation.

So, what are your desired experiences in college? If someday in the future you were to tell someone that college was one of the best experiences you ever had, what specifically would you have experienced? Many will say "fun." Fair enough. Then make fun happen. Your challenge is to experience fun while staying on course to academic success. And you can do it! Consider these options for fun: Join a club, play a sport, get to know a classmate, attend a party, learn something new that really

Setting specific goals helps learners in at least three ways: The goals focus attention on important aspects of the task; they help motivate and sustain task mastery efforts; and they serve an information function by arming learners with criteria that they can use to assess and if necessary adjust their strategies as they work.

Jere Brophy

interests you. By the way, for most college instructors, learning is high on their list of "fun," and they would love nothing more than to see you show joy in learning their subject. What if you made "joy in learning" one of your desired experiences? Would it make a difference in your overall experience of college?

So, think about it. What would you like to experience during this class or during this semester in college? Here are some additional experiences that my students desired: relaxation, mutual acceptance, respect, connection with others, self-confidence, an open mind, quiet reflection, passion for learning, total engagement, full-out participation, inspiration, excitement about this subject, synergy, courage, spirit of the group, self-acceptance, joy, pride, freedom, and a transformational "Aha." How about you?

Mohandas Gandhi said, "You must be the change you wish to see in the world." In other words, if you want to experience fun, *be* fun. If you want to experience total engagement, *be* totally engaged. If you want to experience connection with others, then *connect* with others. One of my students wanted to experience "creativity" in our student success class. To my delight, he proposed to *be* creative by asking to do an alternative to the final project. He proposed to write a rap song in which he promised to show that he had learned important success principles in our class. I told him he had my permission so long as he agreed to "rap" his project to our class on the last day of the semester. Little did I know that he was a professional rapper with a couple of CDs to his credit. As promised, he (and his whole group) showed up on the last day of the semester, handed out the words to "The College Success Rap," and treated us all to a rousing course finale. Best of all, he did a great job of demonstrating that he had learned many of the key principles of success, helping his classmates learn them even more deeply. Afterward he said, "Man, that was fun!"

Table 3.2 below lists the desired experiences that one of my students identified for herself, along with her reasons why.

> What ultimately counts most for each person is what happens in consciousness: the moments of joy, the times of despair added up through the years determine what life will be like. If we don't gain control over the contents of consciousness we can't live a fulfilling life.
>
> *Mihaly Csikszentmihaly*

Table 3.2 ▼ One Student's Desired Experiences

Desired Experiences	Value
Fun	My brother dropped out of college because he said it was all work and no play. I know I'm going to have to work hard in college, but I want to have fun, too. I think if I'm enjoying myself, that'll make all assignments more bearable.
Academic confidence	I've never done particularly well in school, although my teachers have always said I could be a good student if I applied myself more. I want to feel just as smart as any other student in my classes.
Excitement about learning	I didn't really like my classes in high school. I want to get excited about learning in at least one course, so I look forward to the homework and sometimes the class time goes so fast I can't believe when it's over.
Personal confidence	I have always been a shy person, and I want to become more outgoing so I can do well on future job interviews and be more assertive in my career so I get the promotions I deserve.

> He who puts in four hours of "want to" will almost always outperform the person who puts in eight hours of "have to."
>
> *Roger von Oech*

German philosopher Friedrich Nietzsche once said, "He who has a why to live for can endure almost any how." He affirms that few obstacles can stop us when we understand the personal value we place on the outcomes and experiences of our journey. Discover your own motivation and your chances for success soar!

> Success isn't a result of spontaneous combustion. You must set yourself on fire.
>
> *Arnold H. Glasow*

JOURNAL ENTRY 8

In this journal entry, you'll identify your desired outcomes and experiences for this course and/or this semester. Developing clarity on what you want to create this semester will help you stay motivated and on course until the end. Use the student examples earlier in this section as models, but of course record your own desired outcomes, experiences, and reasons.

1. In your journal, draw an empty table like Table 3.1. Fill in three or more of your own desired *outcomes* for this course and/or this semester. Next to each, explain why you value achieving that outcome. Remember, "outcomes" are those things you will take *away* with you at the end of the semester (such as a grade or something you learn). At this point, you don't have to know HOW you will achieve these outcomes; you only need to know WHAT you want and WHY.

2. In your journal, place an empty table like Table 3.2. Fill in three or more of your desired *experiences* for this course and/or this semester. Next to each, explain why you value having that experience. Remember, "experiences" are those things you will have *during* this semester (such as fun or a sense of community). Once again, all that matters here is WHAT you would like to experience and WHY. At this time, you don't need to worry about HOW.

3. Using the formula of V × E = M, write about your level of motivation to be successful in college. Begin as follows: *The value I place on being a success in college is _____ [0–10] and my expectation of being a success in college is _____ [0–10]. Multiplied together, this gives me an achievement motivation score of _____ [0–100].* Then continue by explaining your score and identifying specific actions you can do to raise it (or keep it high).

Remember, dive deep. When you explore your motivation at a deep level, you improve your chances of having an important insight that can change your life for the better. So dive deep and discover what really motivates you.

One Student's Story

Chee Meng Vang
Inver Hills Community College, Minnesota

When I got to college, my biggest challenge was staying motivated. I was always going out clubbing with my friends, older sisters, and cousins. I was also shooting pool and hanging out with friends until late at night. I was lazy all the time and couldn't concentrate. I missed classes, fell behind in my homework, and tried to do everything at the last minute. This caused a lot of problems for me, like getting D's on my tests and quizzes. I felt like whatever happened to me was out of my control. I was feeling down and filled with dissatisfaction.

One night I was in a club, watching people drinking and dancing, and I thought, "This is getting boring. I'm tired and this isn't taking me anywhere at all." It was a good thing that College Success was part of my full-time student schedule. Our book was called *On Course*, and it helped me big time. It taught me to see myself as the primary cause of my outcomes and experiences and to find my desires that cause me to act. I was so stupid because my desire was right in front of me. There are so many reasons why it is important that I do well in college. My parents came to the United States from Laos, and all they ever wanted was a better life for their kids. It was hard for them in a new country, and we never had very much money. I realized I was being a loser and letting them down. Also, I am the first man in my family to go to college and my lovely five little brothers look up to me. I need to show them what a good role model their big brother can be. I want a career that will allow me to help my family, and when I have children, I don't want to be a dad working in McDonald's. My dream is to be a pharmacist, but I was headed in the wrong direction.

I come from a poor family, and I don't ever want to be like that in the future, so I had to make changes right away. I stopped going out to clubs and started taking responsibility. I became more outgoing in class. I studied two hours or more every day. I started getting A's and B's on my tests and quizzes. I finished the semester by raising my D grades to B's. As you can see, I've gone from being a lazy, unmotivated guy to a responsible, outgoing, I-control-my-destiny man. Now I don't feel like a victim any more. I've actually started to feel like a hero to my parents, my little brothers, and even to the small community where we live.

Designing a Compelling Life Plan

 FOCUS QUESTIONS If your life were as good as it could possibly be, what would it look like? What would you have, do, and be?

While growing up, Joan dreamed of becoming a famous singer. Following high school, she started performing in night clubs. She married her manager, and the two of them lived in a motor home, driving from town to town in pursuit of singing jobs. After exhausting years on the road, Joan recorded a song. It didn't sell, and her dream began to unravel. Marital problems complicated her career. Career problems complicated her marriage. Joan grew tired of the financial and emotional uncertainty in her life. Finally, in frustration, she divorced her husband and gave up her dream of singing professionally.

Although disappointed, Joan started setting new goals. She needed to earn a living, so she set a short-term goal to become a hairdresser. After graduating from cosmetology school, Joan saved enough money to settle some debts, buy a car, and pay for a new long-term goal. She decided to go to a community college (where I met her) and major in dental hygiene.

Two years later, Joan graduated with honors and went to work in a dentist's office. Lacking a dream that excited her, Joan chose another long-term goal: earning her bachelor's degree. Joan worked days in the dentist's office and at night she attended classes. After a few years, she again graduated with honors.

Then, she set another long-term goal: earning her master's degree. Earlier in her life, Joan had doubted that she was "college material." With each academic success, her confidence grew. "One day I realized that once I set a goal, it's a done deal," Joan said.

This awareness inspired her to begin dreaming again. As a child, Joan had always imagined herself as a teacher, but her doubts had always steered her in other directions. Master's degree now in hand, she returned to our college to teach dental hygiene. A year later, she was appointed department chairperson. In only seven years, Joan had gone from a self-doubting first-year student to head of our college's dental hygiene department. Despite obstacles and setbacks, she continued to move in a positive direction, ever motivated by the promise of achieving personally valuable goals and dreams.

Roles and Goals

According to psychologist Brian Tracy, many people resist setting life goals because they don't know how. Let's eliminate this barrier so you, like Joan, can experience the heightened motivation that accompanies personally meaningful goals.

> Your goals are the road maps that guide you and show you what is possible for your life.
>
> *Les Brown*

> The most important thing about motivation is goal setting. You should always have a goal.
>
> *Francie Larrieu Smith*

CATHY   **by Cathy Guisewite**

© Cathy Guisewite/Universal Press Syndicate

First, think about the roles you have chosen for your life. A life role is an activity to which we regularly devote large amounts of time and energy. For example, you're presently playing the role of college student. How many of the following roles are you also playing: friend, employee, employer, athlete, brother, sister, church member, son, daughter, roommate, husband, wife, partner, parent, grandparent, tutor, musician, neighbor, volunteer? Do you play other roles as well? Most people identify four to seven major life roles. If you have more than seven, you may be spreading yourself too thin. Consider combining or eliminating one or more of your roles while in college. If you have identified fewer than four roles, assess your life again. You may have overlooked a role or two.

Once you identify your life roles, think about your long-term goals for each one. Identify what you hope to accomplish in this role in the next two to five or even ten years. For example, in your role as a student, ten years from now will you have a two-year associate of arts (A.A.) degree? A four-year bachelor of arts (B.A.) or bachelor of science (B.S.) degree? Will you have attended graduate school to earn a master of arts (M.A.) or master of science (M.S.) degree? Or gone even farther to obtain a doctor of philosophy (Ph.D.) degree, a medical doctor (M.D.) degree, or a doctor of jurisprudence (J.D.) law degree? Any of these future academic goals could be yours.

> One day Alice came to a fork in the road and saw a Cheshire cat in a tree. "Which road do I take?" she asked. "Where do you want to go?" was his response. "I don't know," Alice answered. "Then," said the cat, "it doesn't matter."
>
> *Lewis Carroll*

How to Set a Goal

To be truly motivating, a goal needs five qualities. You can remember them by applying the DAPPS rule. "DAPPS" is an acronym, a memory device in which each letter of the word stands for one of five qualities: Dated, Achievable, Personal, Positive, and Specific.

DATED. Motivating goals have specific deadlines. A short-term goal usually has a deadline within a few months (like your semester's Desired Outcomes set in Journal Entry 8). A long-term goal generally has a deadline as far in the future as one year, five years, even ten years (such as the goal you have for your most advanced academic degree). As your target deadline approaches, your motivation typically increases. This positive energy helps you finish strong. If you don't meet your deadline, you have an opportunity to examine what went wrong and create a new plan. Without a deadline, you might stretch the pursuit of a goal over your whole life, never reaching it.

> Goals are dreams with a deadline.
>
> *Napoleon Hill*

ACHIEVABLE. Motivating goals are challenging but realistic. It's unrealistic to say you'll complete a marathon next week if your idea of a monster workout has been opening and closing the refrigerator. Still, if you're going to err, err on the side of optimism. When you set goals at the outer reaches of your present ability, stretching to reach them causes you to grow. Listen to other people's advice, but trust yourself to know what is achievable for you. Apply this guideline: "Is achieving this goal at least 50 percent believable to me?" If so and you *really* value it, go for it!

PERSONAL. Motivating goals are *your* goals, not someone else's. You don't want to be lying on your deathbed some day and realize you have lived someone else's life. Trust that you know better than anyone else what *you* desire.

POSITIVE. Motivating goals focus your energy on what you *do* want rather than on what you *don't* want. So translate negative goals into positive goals. For example, a negative goal to not fail a class becomes a positive goal to earn a grade of B or better. I recall a race car driver explaining how he miraculously kept his spinning car from smashing into the concrete racetrack wall: "I kept my eye on the track, not the wall." Likewise, focus your thoughts and actions on where you *do* want to go rather than where you *don't* want to go, and you, too, will stay on course.

> I always wanted to be somebody, but now I realize I should have been more specific.
>
> *Lily Tomlin*

SPECIFIC. Motivating goals state outcomes in specific, measurable terms. It's not enough to say, "My goal is to do better this semester" or "My goal is to work harder at my job." How will you know if you've achieved these goals? What specific, measurable evidence will you have? Revised, these goals become, "I will complete every college assignment this semester to the best of my ability" and "I will volunteer for all offerings of overtime at work." Being specific keeps you from fooling yourself into believing you've achieved a goal when, in fact, you haven't. It also helps you make choices that create positive results.

Through the years, I've had the joy of working with students who have had wonderful and motivating long-term goals: becoming an operating room nurse, writing and publishing a novel, traveling around the world, operating a refuge for homeless children, marrying and raising a beautiful family, playing professional baseball, starting a private school, composing songs for Aretha Franklin, becoming a college professor, swimming in the Olympics, managing an international mutual fund, having a one-woman art show, becoming a fashion model, getting elected state senator, owning a clothing boutique, and more. How about you? What do you *really* want?

Discover Your Dreams

Perhaps even more than goals do, dreams fuel our inner fire. They give our lives purpose and guide our choices. They provide motivating energy when we run headlong into an obstacle. Martin Luther King, Jr., had a dream that all people, regardless of differences, would live in a world of respect and harmony. When Candy Lightner's daughter was killed by a drunk driver, she transformed this tragedy into her dream to stop drunk driving, and her dream became the international organization Mother's Against Drunk Driving (MADD). I found my dream only after twenty years of college teaching: My passion is empowering students with the beliefs and behaviors essential for living a rich and personally fulfilling life. While it's difficult to define a dream, they're grand in size and fueled by strong emotions. Unlike goals, which usually fit into one of our life roles, dreams often take over our lives, inspire other people, and take on a life of their own. I sometimes wonder if people have dreams or if dreams have people.

> The future belongs to those who believe in the beauty of their dreams.
>
> *Eleanor Roosevelt*

If you presently have a big dream, you know how motivating it is. If you don't have a big dream, you're certainly in the majority. Most people have not found a guiding dream, yet they can still have a great life. College, though, offers a wonderful opportunity to discover or expand your dreams. You'll be exposed to hundreds, even thousands, of new people, ideas, and experiences. With each encounter, be aware of your energy. If you feel your voltage rise, pay attention. Something within you is getting inspired. If you're fortunate enough to find such a dream, consider the pithy advice of philosopher Joseph Campbell: "Follow your bliss."

Your Life Plan

Wise travelers use maps to locate their destination and identify the best route to get there. Similarly, Creators identify their goals and dreams and the most direct path there. In creating such a life plan, it helps to start with your destination in mind and work backwards. If you have a dream, accomplishing it becomes your ultimate destination. Or maybe your destination is the accomplishment of one or more long-term goals for your life roles. Since you can't complete a long journey in one step, your short-term goals become steppingstones, and each one completed brings you closer to the achievement of a long-term goal or dream.

Take a look at a page of a life plan that one student, Pilar, designed for herself. Although Pilar recorded her dream, not everyone will be able to do that. Her full life plan includes a page for each life role that she identified for herself, all of them with the same dream. Obviously, some life roles are going to make a more significant contribution to her dream than others. Notice that each long- and short-term goal adheres to the DAPPS rule.

MY DREAM: *I help families adopt older children (ten years old or older) and create home environments in which the children feel loved and supported to grow into healthy, productive adults.*

MY LIFE ROLE: *College student*

MY LONG-TERM GOALS IN THIS ROLE:

1. *I earn an associate of arts (A.A.) degree by June 2013.*
2. *I earn a bachelor of arts (B.A.) degree by June 2015.*
3. *I earn a master of social work (M.S.W.) degree by June 2017.*

MY SHORT-TERM GOALS IN THIS ROLE: *(this semester)*

1. *I achieve an A in English 101 by December 18.*
2. *I write a research paper on the challenges of adopting older children by November 20.*

> What is significant about a life plan is that it can help us live our own lives (not someone else's) as well as possible.
>
> *Harriet Goldhor Lerner*

We . . . believe that one reason so many high-school and college students have so much trouble focusing on their studies is because they don't have a goal, don't know what all this studying is leading to.

Muriel James & Dorothy Jongeward

3. *I achieve an A in Psychology 101 by December 18.*

4. *I learn and apply five or more psychological strategies that will help my family be happier and more loving by November 30.*

5. *I achieve an A in College Success by December 18.*

6. *I dive deep in every* On Course *journal entry, writing a minimum of 500 words for each one.*

7. *I learn five or more new success strategies and teach them to my younger brothers by November 30.*

8. *I take at least one page of notes in every class I attend this semester.*

9. *I turn in every assignment on time this semester.*

10. *I learn to use a computer well enough to prepare all of my written assignments by October 15.*

This is the first page of Pilar's six-page life plan. She wrote a similar page for each of her other five life roles: sister, daughter, friend, athlete, and employee at a group home for children.

Consciously designing your life plan, as Pilar did, has many advantages. A life plan defines your desired destinations in life and charts your best route for getting there. It gives your Inner Guide something positive to focus on when the chatter of your Inner Critic or Inner Defender attempts to distract you. And, like all maps, a life plan helps you get back on course if you get lost.

Perhaps most of all, a life plan is your personal definition of a life worth living. With it in mind, you'll be less dependent on someone else to motivate you. Your most compelling motivation will be found within.

JOURNAL ENTRY   9

In this activity, you will design one or more parts of your life plan. To focus your thoughts, glance back at Pilar's life plan and use it as a model.

Many people fail in life, not for lack of ability or brains or even courage but simply because they have never organized their energies around a goal.

Elbert Hubbard

1. Title a new page in your journal: **MY LIFE PLAN. Below the title, complete the part of your life plan for your role as a student.**

My Dream: [If you have a compelling dream, describe it here. If you're not sure what your dream is, you can simply write, "I'm searching."]

My Life Role: Student

My Long-Term Goals in This Role: [These are the outcomes you plan to achieve as a student in the next two to ten years, or even longer if necessary.]

My Short-Term Goals in This Role: [These are the outcomes you plan to achieve as a student this semester; each one accomplished

➡

JOURNAL ENTRY   9   *continued*

brings you closer to your long-term goals as a student. To begin your list of short-term goals, you can write the same Desired Outcomes that you chose in Journal Entry 8; then add other short-terms goals as appropriate.]

Remember to apply the DAPPS rule, making sure that each long- and short-term goal is **d**ated, **a**chievable, **p**ersonal, **p**ositive, and **s**pecific. With this in mind, you may need to revise the Desired Outcomes that you transfer here from Journal Entry 8.

If you wish, repeat this process for one or more of your other life roles: employee, parent, athlete, and so on. The more roles you plan, the more complete your vision of life will be. Taken together, these pages map your route to a rich, personally fulfilling life.

At this time you don't have to know how to achieve your goals and dreams, so don't even think about the method. All you need to know is what you want. In the following chapters, you'll learn dozens of powerful strategies for turning your life plan into reality. For now, keep your eye on your destination!

2. **Write about what you have learned or relearned by designing your life plan.** In particular, identify any impact this effort has had on your level of motivation to do well in college this semester, or do well in any other parts of your life.

> I started getting successful in school when I saw how college could help me achieve my dreams.
>
> *Bobby Marinelli, student*

Committing to Your Goals and Dreams

 FOCUS QUESTIONS Do you start new projects (such as college) with great enthusiasm, only to lose motivation along the way? How can you keep your motivation strong?

Many people doubt they can achieve what they truly want. When a big, exciting goal or dream creeps into their thoughts, they shake their heads. "Oh, sure," they mumble to themselves, "how am *I* going to accomplish that?"

In truth, you don't need to know how to achieve a goal or dream when you first think of it. What you do need is an unwavering commitment, fueled by a strong desire. Once you promise yourself that you will do whatever it takes to accomplish your goals and dream, you often discover the method for achieving them in the most unexpected ways.

> Always bear in mind that your own resolution to succeed is more important than any one thing.
>
> *Abraham Lincoln*

Commitment Creates Method

A commitment is an unbending intention, a single-mindedness of purpose that promises to overcome all obstacles regardless of how you may feel at any particular moment. During the summer between my sophomore and junior years in college, I learned the power of commitment.

That summer, I used all of my savings to visit Hawaii. While there, I met a beautiful young woman, and we spent twelve blissful days together.

One of my desires was to have a wonderful love relationship, so I promised to return to Hawaii during Christmas break. However, back in college 6,000 miles away, my commitment was sorely tested. I had no idea how, in just three months, I could raise enough money to return to Hawaii. Committed to my dream, though, I spent weeks inventing and rejecting one scheme after another. (Though I didn't realize it at the time, I was actually using the Wise Choice Process to find my best option.)

Then one day, I happened upon a possible solution. I was glancing through *Sports Illustrated* magazine when I noticed an article written by a student-athlete from Yale University. Until that moment, all I'd had was a commitment. When I saw that article, I had a plan. A long shot, yes, but a plan, nonetheless: Maybe the editors of *Sports Illustrated* would buy an article about the sport I played, lightweight football. Driven by my commitment, I worked on an article every evening for weeks. Finally, I dropped it in the mail and crossed my fingers.

A few weeks later, my manuscript came back, rejected. On the printed rejection form, however, a kind editor had handwritten, "Want to try a rewrite? Here's how you might improve your article . . . ."

I spent another week revising the article, mailed it directly to my encouraging editor, and waited anxiously. Christmas break was creeping closer. I had just about given up hope of returning to Hawaii in December.

Then one day my phone rang, and the caller identified himself as a photographer from *Sports Illustrated*. "I'll be taking photos at your football game this weekend. Where can I meet you?"

And that's how I learned that my article had been accepted. Better yet, *Sports Illustrated* paid me enough money to return to Hawaii. I spent Christmas on the beach at Waikiki, with my girlfriend on the blanket beside me.

Suppose I hadn't made a commitment to return to Hawaii? Would reading *Sports Illustrated* have sparked such an outrageous plan? Would I, at twenty years of age, have ever thought to earn money by writing a feature article for a national magazine? Doubtful!

What intrigues me as I recall my experience is that the solution for my problem was there all the time; I just couldn't see it until I made a commitment.

By committing to our dreams, we program our brains to look for solutions to our problems and to keep us going when the path gets rough. Whenever you're tempted to look for motivation outside yourself, remember this: Motivation surges up from a *commitment* to a passionately held purpose.

> When you have a clear intention, methods for producing the desired results will present themselves.
>
> *Student Handbook, University of Santa Monica*

> Once a commitment is made without the option of backing out, the mind releases tremendous energy toward its achievement.
>
> *Ben Dominitz*

Visualize Your Ideal Future

Human beings seek to experience pleasure and avoid pain. Put this psychological truth to work for you by visualizing the pleasure you'll derive when you achieve your goals or dreams.

Cathy Turner explained how she visualized her way to winning two Olympic gold medals in speed skating: "As a little girl, I used to stand on a chair in front of the mirror and pretend I had won a gold medal. I'd imagine getting the medal, I'd see them superimposing the flag across my face just like they did on TV, and I would start to cry. When I really did stand on the podium, and they raised the American flag, it was incredible. I was there representing the United States, all of the United States. The flag was going up and the national anthem was being played, and there wasn't a mirror in front of me and it wasn't a chair I was standing on. I had dreamt that for so long. All my life. And my dream was coming true right then and there."

To make or strengthen your commitment to achieve success in college, do what Cathy Turner did. Visualize yourself accomplishing your fondest goal and imagine the delight you'll experience when it actually happens. Let this desired outcome and the associated positive experiences draw you like a magnet toward a future of your own design.

Some years ago, I happened to glance at a three-ring notebook carried by one of my students. Taped to the cover was a photo showing her in a graduation cap and gown.

"Have you already graduated?" I asked.

"Not yet. But that's what I'll look like when I do."

"How did you get the photo?"

"My sister graduated from college a few years ago," she explained. "After the ceremony, I put on her cap and gown and had my mother take this picture. Whenever I get discouraged about school, I look at this photo and imagine myself walking across the stage to receive my diploma. I hear my family cheering for me, just like we did for my sister. Then I stop feeling sorry for myself and get back to work. This picture reminds me what all my efforts are for."

A few years later at her graduation, I remember thinking, "She looks just as happy today as she did in the photo. Maybe happier."

Life will test our commitments. To keep them strong in times of challenge, we need a clear picture of our desired results. We need a motivating mental image that, like a magnet, draws us steadily toward our ideal future.

The power of visualizing makes sense when you remember that getting anywhere is difficult if you don't know where you're going. A vivid mental image of your chosen destination keeps you on course even when life's adversities conspire against you.

> From my own experience, there is no question that the speed with which you are able to achieve your goals is directly related to how clearly and how often you are able to visualize your goals.
>
> *Charles J. Givens*

> I see a Chicago in which the neighborhoods are once again the center of our city, in which businesses boom and provide neighborhood jobs, in which neighbors join together to help govern their neighborhood and their city.
>
> *Harold Washington, Chicago's first black mayor*

How to Visualize

Here are four keys to an effective visualization.

Visualization takes advantage of what almost might be called a "weakness" of the body; it cannot distinguish between a vivid mental experience and an actual physical experience.

Dr. Bernie Siegel

1. **RELAX.** Visualizing seems to have the most positive impact when experienced during deep relaxation. One way to accomplish deep relaxation is to breathe deeply while you tighten muscle groups one by one from the tips of your toes to the top of your head.

2. **USE PRESENT TENSE.** Imagine yourself experiencing success *now*. Therefore, use the present tense for all verbs: *I am walking across the stage to receive my diploma.* OR *I walk across the stage.* (Not past tense: *I was walking across the stage;* and not future tense: *I will be walking across the stage.*)

3. **USE ALL FIVE SENSES.** Imagine the scene concretely and specifically. Use all of your senses. What do you see, hear, smell, taste, touch?

4. **FEEL THE FEELINGS.** Events gain power to motivate us when accompanied by strong emotions. Imagine your accomplishment to be just as grand and magnificent as you wish it to be. Then feel the excitement of your success.

Psychologist Charles Garfield notes that athletes have used visualizations to win sports events; psychologist Brian Tracy writes about salespeople using visualizations to succeed in the business world; and Dr. Bernie Siegel, a cancer specialist, has even chronicled patients improving their health with visualizations.

Finally, consider this: the act of *keeping* your commitment may be as important, if not even *more* important, than achieving a particular goal or dream. In this way, you raise your expectations for the success of future commitments, knowing that when you make a promise to yourself, you keep it.

So, create lofty goals and dreams. And, from deep within you, commit to their achievement.

JOURNAL ENTRY   10

In this activity, you will visualize the accomplishment of one of your most important goals or dreams. Once you vividly picture this ideal outcome, you will have strengthened your commitment to achieve it, and you will know how to do the same thing with all of your goals and dreams.

1. Write a visualization of the exact moment in the future when you are experiencing the accomplishment of your biggest goal or dream in your role as a *student.* Describe the scene of your success as if it is happening to you *now.* For example, if your desire is to graduate from a four-year university with a 4.0 average, you might write, *I am dressed in a long, blue robe, the tassel from my graduation cap tickling my face. I look out over the thousands of people in the audience, and I see my mother, a smile spreading across her face. I hear the announcer call my name. I feel a rush of adrenaline, and chills tingle on my back as I take my first step onto the stage. I see the college president smiling, reaching her hand out to me in congratulations. I hear the announcer repeat my name, adding that I am graduating with highest honors, having obtained a 4.0 average. I see my classmates standing to applaud me. Their cheers flow over me, filling me with pride and happiness. I walk . . .*

For visual appeal, consider also drawing a picture of your goal or dream in your journal. Or cut pictures from magazines and use them to illustrate your writing. If you are writing your journal on a computer, consider adding clip art that depicts your visualization. Allow your creativity to support your dream.

Remember the four keys to an effective visualization:

1. **Relax** to free your imagination.
2. Use **present-tense verbs** . . . the experience is happening now!
3. Use **all five senses.** What do you see, hear, smell, taste, and feel (touch)?
4. Include **emotion.** Imagine yourself feeling great in this moment of grand accomplishment. You deserve to feel fantastic!

Read your visualizations often. Ideal times are right before you go to sleep and when you first awake in the morning. You may even wish to record your visualizations and listen to them often.

> Until one is committed there is hesitancy, the chance to draw back, always ineffectiveness. Concerning all acts of initiative (and creation), there is one elementary truth, the ignorance of which kills countless ideas and splendid plans: that the moment one definitely commits oneself, then Providence moves too. All sorts of things occur to help one that would never otherwise have occurred. A whole stream of events issues from the decision, raising in one's favour all manner of unforeseen incidents and meetings and material assistance, which no man could have dreamt would have come his way.
>
> *William Hutchison Murray, Scottish mountaineer*

One Student's Story

Amanda Schmeling
Buena Vista University, Iowa

Coming to college hundreds of miles from home meant leaving behind my family and friends, but most important my identical twin sister. My eyes filled with tears as I hugged my sister goodbye. All our lives, we had done everything together, we relied on each other, and everyone knew us as a pair. In the first weeks of school without my sister, I felt homesick and lost. I was pulled in two directions, one half toward my familiar past and the other toward my unknown future. At college, all my energies went into acting like everything was okay, hiding my feelings from everyone. Despite this show on the outside, I was miserable on the inside. After weeks of struggling, I began to lose sight of why I had even come to college in the first place.

Just when I began thinking of quitting, we wrote a journal entry in my First-Year Seminar class. The directions asked us to visualize ourselves achieving an important goal or dream. In class we discussed the importance of seeing ourselves being successful and feeling the confidence we would gain. My professor asked us to draw a picture of the moment in our future when we were accomplishing our biggest dream after college. Some people drew sky scrapers and dollar signs; another drew a large family on a beautiful farm. After staring at the blank paper for a while, I began to draw the day when I achieve my dream of opening my own business. I sketched the unique colors of green, pink, blues, and purples that decorate the walls of my tea shop. I am preparing fragrant tea and baking delicious scones and cookies for my new customers. In the center of each table are gerbera daisies, tulips, and greens, each arrangement different from the next. My sister and mother are there to help me finish setting up for the day. Everything around me is exactly how I want it, exactly how I dreamed it, and for now that is all that matters. Finally the day I have dreamed about since childhood has finally arrived.

Later that night as I was doing homework, my mind wandered back to my visualization. I could feel myself in that moment, I could see the doors opening, and I could hear the excitement. I thought to myself, *Maybe my future isn't so unclear; I know what I want, all I need to do is take hold of it.* My dreams had been there all along. I had just lost sight of them. My little "escape" to my future left me rejuvenated, and most important, I reconnected with my purpose for attending college—to earn my degree in business management. Since that day, my road continues to climb, twisting and turning, a new direction each day. I wake up not knowing how I will fare on my journey, but I know that no matter how hard the day may be, I still have my dream to look forward to. It's like a compass guiding me to my destination, my dream.

Self-Motivation AT WORK

Figure out what kind of job would make you happiest because the kind that would make you happiest is also the one where you will do your best and most effective work. *Richard Bolles, career expert, author of What Color Is Your Parachute?*

Creators Wanted!

Candidates must demonstrate self motivation, a strong sense of purpose, and effective goal-setting abilities.

One of the most important choices you will ever make is whether to seek a job or a career. When you have a job, you work for a paycheck. When you have a career, you work for the enjoyment and satisfaction you earn from your daily efforts . . . and you also get paid, possibly very well. I've had both, and I assure you, a career makes life a whole lot sweeter. If you want to feel motivated to get up and go to work fifty weeks a year, you'll definitely want to choose a career.

College is a great place to prepare for a career. But, to stay self-motivated, you'll want to match your career choice and college major with your unique interests, talents, and personality. I once had a student who was majoring in accounting because he'd heard that accountants make a lot of money. He saw no problem with the fact that he hated math. He thought he was preparing for a career when in fact he was preparing for a job.

Some of the most motivated students in higher education are those who see college as the next logical step on the path to their career goals. Sometimes these are younger students who are pursuing a lifelong dream of working in a particular profession. More often they are older students who've grown weary of working at uninspiring jobs and have come to college to prepare for rewarding careers. These self-motivated students are the ones who not only make the most of their education but who also enjoy the journey.

If you have a dream of a particular career, stay open to the possibility of finding something even more suited for you. If you're not yet sure what you want to do, keep exploring. The answer will probably reveal itself to you, and when it does, your life will change. One student I knew went from barely getting C's and D's to earning straight A's when she discovered her passion to be a kindergarten teacher.

Use your life-planning skills to design a motivating career path for yourself, identifying the long- and short-term goals that will act as steppingstones to your success. Using the DAPPS rule that you learned in this chapter, you might create a career path like this:

Two years: I've received my A.A. degree in accounting with high honors and, by thoroughly researching accounting firms nationally, I've decided on five firms that look promising to work for after earning my B.A. degree.

Five years: I've earned my B.A. in accounting with high honors, and I'm employed in an entry-level accounting position in a firm of my choice earning $50,000 or more per year.

Ten years: I own my own accounting firm, and I'm earning $150,000 or more per year, contributing to the financial prosperity and security of my clients.

Keep in mind that there is more to choosing an employer than how much money you're offered. Choosing an employer whose purpose and values are compatible with your own will assist you greatly to stay motivated. By reading a company's mission statement, you can find out what it claims are its purpose and values. For example, suppose you wanted to work in retail sales or marketing for one of the giant office products companies. Here is the mission statement for Staples:

Slashing the cost and hassle of running your office! Our vision is supported by our core values: C.A.R.E.

- *Customers*—Value every customer
- *Associates*—Support them as valuable resources
- *Real Communications*—Share information with people when they need it
- *Execution*—Achieve our business goals

Now, here is the mission statement for a major competitor, Office Depot:

Office Depot's mission is to be the most successful office products company in the world. Our success is driven by an uncompromising commitment to:

- *Superior Customer Satisfaction:* A company-wide attitude that recognizes that customer satisfaction is everything.
- *An Associate-Oriented Environment:* An acknowledgment that our associates are our most valuable resource. We are committed to fostering an environment where recognition, innovation, communication, and the entrepreneurial spirit are encouraged and rewarded.
- *Industry Leading Value, Selection, and Services:* A pledge to offer only the highest-quality merchandise available at everyday low prices, providing customers with an outstanding balance of value, selection, and services.
- *Ethical Business Conduct:* A responsibility to conduct our business with uncompromising honesty and integrity.
- *Shareholder Value:* A duty to provide our shareholders with superior Return-On-Investment.

Based on their mission statements, which company do you think has a purpose and value system that would create a more motivating work environment for you?

Once you actually begin your search for a position in your chosen career, your goal-setting abilities and visualizing skills will help you stay motivated. You can expect to make dozens of contacts with potential employers for each one that responds with interest to your inquiry. One way to keep yourself motivated during your search is to set a goal of making a specific number of contacts each week. *Goal: I will send a letter of inquiry and my résumé to ten or more potential employers each week.* In this way, you focus your energy on what you have control over—your own actions.

Self-Motivation
AT WORK

Additionally, take a few minutes each day to visualize yourself already in the career of your choice; see your office, your coworkers, and imagine yourself doing the daily activities of your career. This mental movie will reduce anxieties and remind you of the purpose for your hard work. Visualizing yourself in your ideal career will help keep you motivated when you encounter delays and disappointments on the path to your goal.

When you actually begin your career, self-motivation strategies will become extremely important to your success. You can't read many employment ads without noticing how many businesses are seeking employees who are "self-motivated." The ad might say "Must work well on own" or "Seeking a self-starter," but you know what such buzz words really mean. These employers want a worker who is able to take on a task and stick with it until completion despite obstacles or setbacks. Who wouldn't want a self-motivated worker? If you were an employer, wouldn't you?

Finally, your ability to set goals in your career is critical to your success. Goals and quotas are inevitable for those in sales positions, but many employers require all of their workers to set goals and create work plans. Your ability to set effective goals will not only help you excel at achieving goals for yourself, but also for your team, office, and company. As you move up in responsibility, your ability to coach others to set goals will be a great asset to the entire organization.

You will likely be working thirty, forty, or even more years. Your ability to discover inner motivation will have a great deal to do with the quality of the outcomes and experiences you create during all of these years.

▶ *Believing in Yourself*
Write a Personal Affirmation

? **FOCUS QUESTIONS** What personal qualities will you need to achieve your dreams? How can you strengthen these qualities?

Certain personal qualities will be necessary to achieve your goals and dreams. For example, if you desire a happy family life, you'll need to be loving, supportive, and communicative. To discover the cure for cancer, you'll need to be creative, persistent, and strong-willed.

Think of the short- and long-term goals you have for your education. What are the personal qualities you'll need to accomplish them? Will you need to be intelligent, optimistic, articulate, responsible, confident, goal-oriented, mature, focused, motivated, organized, hard-working, curious, honest, enthusiastic, self-nurturing?

We are what we imagine ourselves to be.

Kurt Vonnegut, Jr.

The potential for developing all of these personal qualities, and more, exists in every healthy human being. Whether a particular person fulfills that potential is another matter.

During childhood, a person's judgment of his or her personal qualities seems to be based mostly on what others say. If your friends, family, or teachers told you as a child that you're smart, you probably internalized this quality and labeled yourself "smart." But if no one said you we're smart, perhaps you never realized your own natural intelligence. Worse, someone important may have told you that you are dumb, thus starting the negative mind chatter of your Inner Critic.

How we become the labels that others give us is illustrated by a mistake made at a school in England. A group of students at the school were labeled "slow" by their scores on an achievement test. Because of a computer error, however, their teachers were told these children were "bright." As a result, their teachers treated them as having high potential. By the time the error had been discovered, the academic scores of these "slow" students had risen significantly. Having been treated as if they were bright, the kids started to act bright. Perhaps, like these children, you have positive qualities waiting to blossom.

As adults, we can consciously choose what we believe. As one of my psychology professors used to say, "In your world, your word is law." In other words, my thoughts create my reality, and then I act according to that reality (regardless of its accuracy). For example, suppose I'm taking a large lecture class and I keep getting confused. Students sitting around me ask questions when they're confused, but I don't because, well, I've just never been comfortable asking questions in a large lecture hall—that's just the way I am. I'm shy. My Inner Defender is fine with this explanation because it protects me from doing something uncomfortable. The trouble is, the questions I don't ask keep popping up on tests, and I'm about to fail the course if I don't do something different.

Another part of me, my Inner Guide, knows I'd benefit from being bolder. In fact, if I want to pass this course, I *have* to be bolder! So I try an experiment. I start telling myself, *I am bold . . . I am bold . . . I am bold.* Of course, life keeps giving me chances to test my claim. A few class sessions later, I have another question, but I don't ask it. This time, though, I'm keenly aware of what I did: I took the wimpy way out. Undaunted, I continue my experiment, thinking, *I am bold . . . I am bold . . . I am bold.* The next time I have a question, I wait until after class and ask a fellow student. A little better, but still not *bold.* Then one day in class, I'm totally confused. *I am bold.* I shoot my hand in the air. Gulp. The professor calls on me, I ask my question, she answers, and, amazingly enough, I live to tell about it. Better yet, I get the answer correct on the next test. And best of all, my action finally corresponds with my claim. I came to a fork in the road (one I know so well), I consciously chose the bold path, I got the answer I needed, and I realize: My new thought generated new behaviors that, in turn, changed my outcomes and experiences for the better. And, if I did it once, I can do it again. Any time I need to. Any time I *choose* to!

We continue to be influenced by our earliest interactions with our parents. We hear their voices as our own internal self-talk. Those voices function like posthypnotic suggestions. They often govern our lives.

John Bradshaw

I was saying "I'm the greatest" long before I believed it.

Muhammad Ali

Claiming Your Desired Personal Qualities

An effective way to strengthen desired qualities is to create a personal affirmation, a statement in which we claim desired qualities as if we already have them in abundance. Here are some examples:

- I am a bold, joyful, loveable man.
- I am a confident, creative, selective woman.
- I am a spiritual, wise, and curious man, finding happiness in all that I do.
- I am a supportive, organized, and secure woman, and I am creating harmony in my family.

Affirmations help us breathe life into personal qualities that we choose to strengthen. One of my colleagues recalls that whenever she made a mistake as a child, her father would say, "I guess that proves you're NTB." "NTB" was his shorthand for "not too bright." Imagine her challenge of feeling intelligent when she kept getting that message from her father! Today, she doesn't even need her father around; her Inner Critic is happy to remind her that she's NTB. She could benefit from an affirmation that says, "I am VB (very bright)."

What limiting messages did you receive as a child? Perhaps others said you were "homely," "stupid," "clumsy," or "always screwing up." If so, today you can create an affirmation that empowers your desired qualities. For example, you could say, "I am a beautiful, intelligent, graceful woman, turning any mistake into a powerful lesson." Some people report that their positive affirmations seem like lies. The negative messages from their childhood (chanted today by their Inner Critics) feel more like the truth. If so, try thinking of your affirmation as prematurely telling the truth. You may not feel beautiful, intelligent, or graceful when you first begin claiming these qualities, but, just as the "slow" children at the English school responded to being treated as bright, with each passing day you can behave your way into believing the truth of your chosen qualities. Using affirmations is like becoming your own parent: You acknowledge the positive qualities that no one has thought to tell you about . . . until now. And then, most important, you act on them, changing your outcomes and experiences in the process.

> To adopt new beliefs, we can now systematically choose affirming statements, then consciously live in them.
>
> *Joyce Chapman*

> My "Born to Lose" tattoo was written on my mind long before it was written on my arm. Now I'm telling myself I'm "Born to Win."
>
> *Steve R., student*

Living Your Affirmation

Of course, simply creating an affirmation is insufficient to offset years of negative programming. Affirmations need reinforcement to gain

"Mother, am I poisonous?"

© The New Yorker Collection, 1960. Frank Modell from cartoonbank.com. All Rights Reserved.

influence in your life. Here are three ways to empower your affirmation: Repeat . . . Dispute . . . Align.

Assume a virtue, if you have it not.

William Shakespeare

1. **REPEAT YOUR AFFIRMATION.** In this way you'll remember the qualities you have chosen to strengthen. One student repeated her affirmation during workouts on a rowing machine. The steady pace of the exercise provided the rhythm to which she repeated her affirmation. What would be a good occasion for you to repeat your affirmation?

2. **DISPUTE YOUR INNER CRITIC.** Realize that you already possess the qualities you desire. You already *are* creative, persistent, loving, intelligent . . . whatever. These are your natural human qualities waiting to be re-empowered. To confirm this reality (and quiet your Inner Critic), simply recall a specific event in your past when you displayed a quality that is in your affirmation.

Affirmations have to be supported by the behavior that makes them happen.

Charles Garfield

3. **ALIGN YOUR WORDS AND DEEDS.** At each choice point, be what you affirm. If you say that you're "bold," make a bold choice. If you claim that you're "organized," do what an organized person does. If you assert that you're "persistent," keep going even when you don't feel like it. At some point, you'll have the evidence to assert, "Hey, I really am bold, organized, and persistent!" Your choices will prove the truth of your affirmation and your new outcomes and experiences will be the reward.

So, decide which personal qualities will help you stay on course to your goals and dreams and prepare to write a personal affirmation that will help you bring them forth!

In this activity, you will create a personal affirmation. If you repeat your affirmation often, it will help you make choices that will strengthen the personal qualities needed to achieve your goals and dreams.

1. **Write a one-sentence statement of one of your most motivating goals or dreams in your role as a student.** You can simply copy one that you wrote in Journal Entry 9 (or create a new one if you prefer).

2. **Write a list of personal qualities that would help you achieve this educational goal or dream.** Use adjectives such as *persistent, intelligent, hard-working, loving, articulate, organized, friendly, confident, relaxed,* and so on. Write as many qualities as possible.

> An affirmation is self-talk in its highest form.
>
> *Susan Jeffers*

3. **Circle the three qualities on your list that seem the most essential for you to achieve your goal or dream as a student (from Step 1).**

4. **Write three versions of your personal affirmation.** Do this by filling in the blanks in sentence formats A, B, and C below. Fill the blanks with the three personal qualities you circled in Step 3 above. NOTE: Use the same three personal qualities in each of the three formats.

Format A: I am a _____, _____, _____ man/woman.

Example: I am a strong, intelligent, persistent woman.

Format B: I am a _____, _____, _____ man/woman, _____ing _____.

Example: I am a strong, intelligent, persistent woman, creating my dreams.

Format C: I am a _____, _____, _____ man/woman, and I _____.

Example: I am a strong, intelligent, persistent woman, and I love life.

Don't copy the examples; create your own unique affirmation.

5. **Choose the one sentence from Step 4 that you like best and write that sentence five or more times.** This repetition helps you to begin taking ownership of your affirmation and desired qualities.

6. **Write three paragraphs—one for each of the three qualities in your affirmation.** In each of these paragraphs, write about a specific experience when you displayed your desired quality. For example, if one of your desired qualities is persistence, tell a story about a time in your life when you were persistent (even a little bit!). Write the story like a scene from a book, with enough specific details that readers will feel as though they are seeing what you experienced. Your paragraph might begin, *The first quality from my affirmation is . . . A specific experience in my life when I demonstrated that quality was . . .*

> The practice of doing affirmations allows us to begin replacing some of our stale, worn out, or negative mind chatter with more positive ideas and concepts. It is a powerful technique, one which can in a short time completely transform our attitudes and expectations about life, and thereby totally change what we create for ourselves.
>
> *Shakti Gawain*

You can add creativity to your journal by writing your affirmation with colors, maybe adding pictures or key words cut from magazines, drawings of your own, clip art, or quotations that appeal to you.

One Student's Story

Donna Ludwick
Carteret Community College, North Carolina

Twenty-three years after dropping out of high school, I finally enrolled in college. In between, I got married, worked as a waitress, had three children, and adopted a fourth. My first baby got cancer and had three serious operations between the ages of two and five. What she and the other kids in the hospital went through touched my heart, and I knew I wanted to help kids who were dealing with serious illnesses. I had always thought that school was useless and that I didn't have the smarts to finish, but I started to see that the only way I was going to make something of myself was to go to college. When I was in my thirties, I got my GED and became a certified nursing assistant. A few years later, I took the big step and came to college.

It was scary sitting in classes with people my daughter's age. They had such young minds and it all came so natural to them. One day while trying to do my math homework, I found myself saying, "I can't do this. I'm too stupid." Then I remembered my affirmation. We were reading *On Course* in my developmental English class, and the affirmation I wrote was, "I am a persistent, confident, hardworking woman, and I love to learn new things; I will be successful." At that moment, I felt like a boulder had been lifted off my shoulders. It took me four hours to finish that assignment, but I wouldn't quit. I passed the next math test, and that made me feel more confident and work even harder. I applied my affirmation qualities in English, too.

I knew what I wanted to say, but I couldn't put it on paper. I'd write, revise, tear it up, and start all over. But I wouldn't quit! I swear I worked more than one hundred hours on some of those essays, and pretty soon I started to turn my thoughts into what I really meant.

Sometimes it's a real struggle to work thirty-five hours a week, raise my kids, and go to school, too. Then I think, "This is going to get me what I want in life." I want to become a Licensed Practical Nurse, then go on for my RN degree and work in a hospital with those kids. I keep my affirmation on my refrigerator so I see it every day. With my affirmation staring me in the face, it reminds me I've come this far, and I'm not going to give up now. I really am a persistent, confident, hardworking woman, and I do love to learn new things. I *will* be successful!

Embracing Change   Do One Thing Different This Week

You can wait until someone else (such as your instructor) motivates you . . . or you can be a Creator and do it for yourself. From the following list, pick ONE new belief or behavior that you will experiment with for one week. Check off each day that you do the action. See if this new choice increases the **value** you place on your academic efforts, increases your **expectations** that you will be successful in your academic efforts, or both. After seven days, assess your results. If your outcomes and experiences improve, you now have a **tool** you can use for the rest of your life.

From the following list, choose one belief or behavior you think will make the greatest positive impact on your self-motivation or self-esteem.

1. Think: "I choose all of the outcomes and experiences for my life."
2. Review and, if appropriate, revise my desired outcomes and desired experiences for this semester (recorded in Journal Entry 8).
3. Set a goal using the DAPPS rule.
4. Review my life plan (recorded in Journal Entry 9).
5. Focusing on an additional role in my life, write another page of my life plan.
6. Reread my visualization of achieving my goal or dream as a student (recorded in Journal Entry 10).
7. Write a visualization in which I am achieving a goal or dream in another life role.
8. Demonstrate self-motivation at my workplace.
9. Say my affirmation _____ times every day (recorded in Journal Entry 11).

Now, write the one you chose under "My Commitment" in the following chart. Then, track yourself for one week, putting a check in the appropriate box when you keep your commitment. After seven days, assess your results. If your outcomes and experiences improve, you now have a tool you can use to heighten your self-motivation for the rest of your life.

My Commitment						
Day 1	Day 2	Day 3	Day 4	Day 5	Day 6	Day 7

During my seven-day experiment, what happened?

As a result of what happened, what did I learn or relearn?

Wise Choices in College TAKING NOTES

In Chapter 2, we discussed the many hours you will spend in college **Collecting** information and skills from your reading assignments. In this chapter, we will examine the second most time-consuming way you will **Collect** information while in college: attending classes. In the pursuit of a four-year degree, students spend nearly 400 hours in a formal classroom. Students pursuing a two-year degree spend about half that time in class.

Your instructors, of course, expect you to learn what they cover in these class sessions. Unless you're motivated to take effective notes, however, most of what you hear in class will zip through your short-term memory and be quickly forgotten. More than one hundred years ago, Hermann Ebbinghaus conducted the first studies of memory and discovered that we lose about 75 percent of what we learn within twenty-four hours. That's why effective note-taking is an essential skill for achieving academic success in college.

Taking notes while attending a class is similar to taking notes while reading a textbook. However, taking notes during a class offers additional challenges. For one thing, as you mark or annotate a textbook, you stop reading. Thus, while reading you are in total control of how fast you receive new information. By contrast, when you take notes during a class, the speaker keeps talking. You have little or no control over the speed of information delivery. This situation places greater demands on your ability to identify key concepts, main ideas, and supporting details and write them down accurately and completely.

And that's not all. You're likely to encounter instructors who will provide their own unique obstacles to note-taking: They may speed talk until your head spins. Or . . . drone . . . on . . . so . . . sloooowly . . . you . . . have . . . trouble . . . staying . . . awake. They may be poorly organized. Or have

accents that you have difficulty understanding. Some instructors may wander maddeningly from the topic or distract you with irritating mannerisms. Or all of the above.

A summary of research on note-taking compiled by Kenneth Kiewra reports sobering news. Lecture notes taken by first-year students contain, on average, only 11 percent of the critical ideas presented during a class. No matter how well you study, you can't pass tests if you are studying only 11 percent of the important ideas in a course.

You can choose to complain, blame, and make excuses for why it's impossible to take good notes in a class. Or, you can take full responsibility for your learning outcomes and experiences. Regardless of how many obstacles the instructor or the subject presents, it's your job to take effective notes. In this chapter you'll learn how.

Taking Notes: The Big Picture

To take effective class notes, you need to answer two key questions: *What* should I write in my notes and *how* should I write that information?

First, consider what to write in your notes. Despite a popular misconception, the answer is not "everything the instructor says." Even if you could write that fast, having a word-for-word transcript of a class is not the goal of note-taking. As with reading, the goal of note-taking is **Collecting** key concepts, main ideas, and supporting details. Thus, much of what you learned earlier about taking notes while reading also applies to taking notes in class. But you'll need some new strategies to compensate for the challenges of writing notes while someone is speaking.

As for how to write your notes, a number of note-taking systems have been invented, but essentially they all fit into one of two categories: linear or graphic. Examples of these methods will be explained in this chapter.

Many students worry about taking perfect class notes because they use their notes to study for tests. In the CORE Learning System, however, you do not study from either your class notes or your textbooks. Instead, as you'll learn in the next chapter, after **Collecting** key concepts, main ideas, and supporting details from all sources, you'll **Organize** this information into effective study materials. It is these materials that will help you create deep and lasting learning. For now, simply examine the note-taking strategies that follow and choose the ones that you think will best help you **Collect** important knowledge during each class. No single method of note-taking works best for everyone, so experiment and personalize a note-taking system that works best for you.

As you examine the following strategies, keep in mind that the big picture of note-taking is essentially the same as for reading: **You are Collecting key concepts, important ideas, and supporting details.**

Before Taking Notes

1. Create a positive affirmation about taking notes. Some students hold negative beliefs about their ability to take good notes or the value of doing so. Create an affirming statement about taking notes. For example, *I take notes that record all of the main ideas and supporting details, making learning easy and fun.* Along with your personal affirmation, repeat this note-taking affirmation to motivate new learning attitudes and behaviors.

2. Assemble appropriate supplies. Experiment and decide on the best note-taking supplies for you. Find a pen you like writing with. Keep your notes in ring binders, composition books, spiral binders, or a laptop computer. Ring binders are handy because you can add and remove pages easily. This option is helpful when an instructor provides handouts or you revise your notes. If you use one binder for all of your classes, use tabs to separate the notes for each class. If you take class notes on a laptop computer, be sure to back up your files often to avoid the disaster of losing notes because of a hard-drive crash.

3. Complete homework assignments before class. Remember, neural networks created by prior learning make new learning easier. That's why completing assignments before class increases your ability to understand lectures and discussions. Also, you'll know what belongs in your notes. For example, you'll know if the instructor is repeating what was in the reading or adding new information. And, suppose the instructor's presentation style presents a challenge (such as speed talking). Because the information is already familiar, you'll more easily spot key concepts, main ideas, and supporting details. If your homework includes solving problems, complete them before class as well.

4. Prepare a list of questions. After completing homework assignments, write questions you have about the information. If you write them on binder paper, leave a space after each question for the answer. If you write questions on 3″ × 5″ cards, you can put answers on the other side. If you place questions in a computer file, it's easy to type in the answers. Bring these questions to class, study group meetings, tutoring sessions, or a conference with your instructor.

5. Attend every class. As obvious as this suggestion may seem, some students don't create good notes simply because they aren't in class. Sure, you can borrow notes from another student. But is it smart to bet your academic success on another student's note-taking skill? Remember, research reveals that first-year students' notes contain only 11 percent of the important ideas presented during a class. Your notes, after applying the strategies in this chapter, will be far more effective than that!

6. Be organized. At the end of each term, you'll have note pages galore for each course. To keep them organized, write some or all of the following information at the top of each note page:

- Course name
- Date of the class
- Topic of the class (usually listed in the course syllabus)
- Any associated reading assignments (also usually listed in the course syllabus)
- Page number (in case your notes get mixed up later)

While Taking Notes

First, let's consider WHAT to write in your notes.

7. Listen actively for key concepts, main ideas, and supporting details. Collecting this information *accurately* and *completely* takes active listening. When you listen actively, you're able to reflect back what a speaker says. In a conversation with a friend, you might reflect: *Sounds like you had an exciting time white water rafting last weekend.* Or in a music class, you might reflect, *So, you're saying a divertimento is a short musical piece that was popular during the Classical period.* When taking notes, you'd simply write an abbreviated version of this reflection: *Divertimento—a short musical piece popular during the Classical period.* Be aware that inner chatter competes with active listening, so quiet your Inner Critic and Inner Defender during class. Don't judge yourself: *I have no clue what she's talking about; I am such a dunce.* And don't judge others: *This jerk is the worst teacher on the planet.* Replace judgments with an active effort to hear all of the speaker's key concepts, main ideas, and supporting details. After all, if you don't **Collect** the course information completely and accurately, then your entire learning effort is sabotaged from the start. See pages 152–153 for more suggestions to improve active listening.

8. Ask and answer questions. When you bring questions to class, raise your hand and ask. When your instructor asks a question, raise your hand

and answer. When you don't understand an idea, raise your hand and ask: *Excuse me, Professor, what holds atoms together in a molecule?* Or, if you're too confused to formulate a question, simply request more information: *Would you please say more about Kant's idea that metaphysics can be reformed through epistemology?* If asking a question isn't an option, leave a space in your notes and write a question in the margin. Many options exist for later filling in the answer: Listen for the instructor to answer your question during the class. Visit the instructor during his or her office hours. Look for the missing information in your textbook. Ask a classmate or study group member for help. Seek assistance at your college's tutoring center.

9. Listen for verbal cues. Instructors will often provide verbal cues to introduce a main idea or supporting detail, thus helping you decide *what* to write in your notes. When you hear any of the following, get ready to record an important idea: *The point is . . . The following is very important . . . Be sure to write this next idea in your notes . . . On page 135 underline the following . . . Let me repeat that. . . The key here is . . . That's a great answer to my question . . . A third component is . . . The main symptom of this problem is . . . The next step for solving this problem is . . . If you remember only one thing from today's class, remember that . . . The key point here is . . .* (and the granddaddy of them all) *This will be on the test.* Also, instructors often give verbal cues before presenting supporting details. When you hear any of the following, get ready to record one or more supporting details: *To illustrate this point . . . Evidence for this includes . . . A good example is . . . To explain that idea further . . . This was proven in a study that showed . . .* Listen for additional kinds of supporting details such as personal experiences, experiments, dates, anecdotes, definitions, lists, names, facts, and data.

Now, we'll consider HOW to write your notes.

10. Take notes with an outline. Now that we've looked at ways to determine *what* to put in your notes, let's consider the second critical choice: *how* to write your notes. As mentioned earlier, the two general methods of note-taking are linear and graphic. First, we'll consider linear notes, which are the more common of the two. When you take notes in a linear fashion, you record ideas as much as possible in the order they are presented ("linear" means in a line). Outlines are good for this. They record ideas and supporting details on separate lines, using indentations to indicate levels of importance. You can view an example of an informal outline in Figure 3.1. Note the use of short phrases instead of full sentences to greatly condense what the speaker says. Here's how to take notes with an outline:

- Write a *key concept* at the top of a page. This information is usually expressed in a word or phrase. This might be the title of a chapter or a key word in the instructor's course outline. For example, the key concept in a history class might be "Causes of World War II," in a biology class it might be "Cell Communication," and in a psychology class it could be "Abraham Maslow."

- Record *main ideas (level 1)* beginning at the left margin. For a formal outline, start each level 1 line with a Roman numeral (e.g., I, II, III, IV).

- Under each main idea, indent a few spaces and record related *secondary ideas (level 2)*. For a formal outline, start each level 2 line with a capital letter (e.g., A, B, C, D).

- Under each secondary idea, indent a few more spaces and record any related *major supporting details (level 3)*. For a formal outline, begin each level 3 line with an Arabic numeral (e.g., 1, 2, 3, 4).

- If you need to add *minor supporting details (level 4),* indent those lines a few more spaces and, for a formal outline, begin those lines with small letters (e.g., a, b, c, d).

Outlines are most helpful when instructors present well-organized lectures. If your instructor provides printed lecture notes or uses PowerPoint slides, you've probably got an organized instructor. If, however, your instructor jumps from topic to topic and back again, all is not lost. That's when a concept map can ride to the rescue.

11. Take notes with a concept map. In this graphic note-taking method, *where* you place information (key concepts, main ideas, and supporting details) on the page shows both their level of importance and their relationship to one another. In general, ideas placed closer to the middle are more important than ideas placed farther away from the middle. Figure 3.2 shows an example of a concept map with content. Here's how to take notes with a concept map:

- Write the *key concept* in the middle of a page; then underline or draw a circle around it. This information is usually just a word or phrase. For example, if the topic of a class session is "Photosynthesis" or "Logical Fallacies" or "Abraham Maslow," that is what you would write in the middle of the page.

- Write *main ideas (level 1)* near the key concept, underline or circle them, and draw lines connecting them to the key concept.

- Write *secondary ideas (level 2)* near their related main idea, underline or circle them, and draw lines connecting them to the related main ideas.

- Write *major supporting details (level 3)* near their related secondary idea, underline or circle them, and draw lines connecting them to the related secondary idea.

- Write *minor supporting details (level 4)* near their related major supporting idea, underline or circle them, and draw lines connecting them to the related major supporting idea.

Concept maps are helpful when lecturers leap from idea to idea. They are also good for taking notes on class discussions that move back and forth between topics. As a speaker returns to an earlier idea, go to

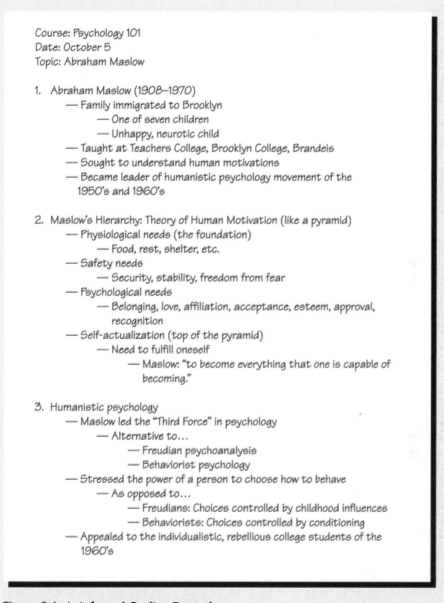

Course: Psychology 101
Date: October 5
Topic: Abraham Maslow

1. Abraham Maslow (1908–1970)
   — Family immigrated to Brooklyn
     — One of seven children
     — Unhappy, neurotic child
   — Taught at Teachers College, Brooklyn College, Brandeis
   — Sought to understand human motivations
   — Became leader of humanistic psychology movement of the 1950's and 1960's

2. Maslow's Hierarchy: Theory of Human Motivation (like a pyramid)
   — Physiological needs (the foundation)
     — Food, rest, shelter, etc.
   — Safety needs
     — Security, stability, freedom from fear
   — Psychological needs
     — Belonging, love, affiliation, acceptance, esteem, approval, recognition
   — Self-actualization (top of the pyramid)
     — Need to fulfill oneself
       — Maslow: "to become everything that one is capable of becoming."

3. Humanistic psychology
   — Maslow led the "Third Force" in psychology
     — Alternative to...
       — Freudian psychoanalysis
       — Behaviorist psychology
   — Stressed the power of a person to choose how to behave
     — As opposed to...
       — Freudians: Choices controlled by childhood influences
       — Behaviorists: Choices controlled by conditioning
   — Appealed to the individualistic, rebellious college students of the 1960's

Figure 3.1 ▲ **Informal Outline Example**
Source: From Carol Kanar, *The Confident Student*, Third Edition, p.353. Copyright © 1998 by Houghton Mifflin Company. Used by permission.

that part of the concept map, add the new information, circle or underline it, and draw a line connecting it to related information. The visual nature of a concept map makes it especially appealing to students who like a picture of what they are learning.

12. Use three-column notes for mathematics.
Since math instructors spend much class time demonstrating how to solve problems, a three-column approach is extremely helpful for **Collecting** their methods. First, divide your note page into three

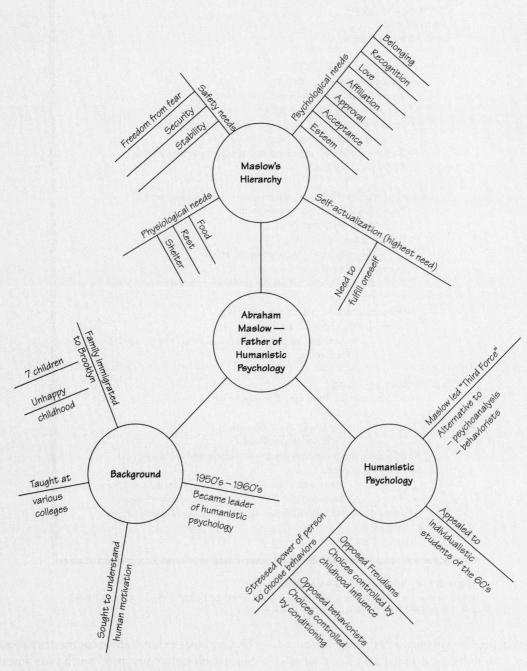

Figure 3.2 ▲ Concept Map Example

columns. Title the left-hand column "Problem," the middle column "Solution," and the right-hand column "Explanation." When the instructor presents a problem, write it in the left column. As the instructor demonstrates how to solve the problem, write all steps in the middle column, making sure you understand each one. In the right-hand column, add any explanation that will help you understand how to solve similar problems. For example, you might add an explanation of each step or convert unfamiliar symbols into words.

Structure of Three-Column Math Notes

Problem	Solution	Explanation
The math problem as presented by the instructor	Step 1 Step 2 Step 3 Step 4 Step 5 Etc.	Elaboration to explain steps of the solution

You'll find an example of three-column math notes on page 134.

13. Speed up note-taking. Most speakers talk much faster than you can write (or even type, if using a computer), so here are three strategies for speeding up your note-taking:

- *Condense*: Instead of attempting to write everything, listen for a couple of minutes, identify the key concept, a main idea, and one or two secondary ideas, and then paraphrase them in your own words.

- *Leave a blank space:* When you miss something, skip down a few lines, and pick up writing what is being said now. As with unanswered questions, you can return later to fill in the blank space in a number of ways: ask the instructor (in class, if appropriate, or during office hours), ask a classmate, ask a tutor, or review your reading assignment for the missing information.

- *Use abbreviations:* Create your own personal shorthand. The following are some possible abbreviations:

Ex	example	&	and
con't	continued	dept	department
imp	important	→	leads to
#	number	=	equals
1st	first	vs	versus
w/	with	w/o	without
nec	necessary	etc	and other things

14. Record the class. If you try the previous suggestions and still aren't happy with the quality of your notes, ask your instructor for permission to record the class. You can listen to the recording as many times as needed to fill in gaps in your notes or review difficult concepts. *Caution*: Don't procrastinate until you have forty-five hours of recorded class sessions to listen to and only twenty-four hours before the final exam. Instead, listen often to short segments. Each time, practice different note-taking strategies until you perfect your own personalized system.

After Taking Notes

15. Polish your notes within twenty-four hours. As soon as possible after each class, make sure your notes are *accurate*, *complete*, and *understandable*. Do some or all of the following:

- Finish partial sentences.

- Expand on key words.

- Fill in spaces with missing information.

- Correct misspellings.

- Clarify unreadable words and confusing sentences.

- Delete unnecessary information.

- Revise drawings or charts.

- Correct steps in problem solving.

Afterward, if you still have gaps or confusion in your notes, meet with classmates, a tutor, or your instructor to address the problems. Not only does this action provide you with polished notes, it continues the active process of creating deep and lasting learning.

16. Compare notes. Compare your notes with those of your study group members or other motivated classmates. See if others have **Collected** important information that you missed. See where their notes may have different information and decide whose version is more accurate. This effort will help you all **Collect** additional information and further polish your notes.

Note-Taking Exercise

In an upcoming class, take notes in a new way. Compare your experimental notes with those of a classmate, seeing which of you has recorded more complete and accurate information for later studying.

A bit of heresy: In many study skills books, another method of note-taking is usually presented. Named for the university where it originated, the Cornell Method calls for note paper to be divided into three sections (see page 135 for the structure). Section A is used for recording notes from a reading assignment or class session. However, the Cornell Method offers no unique suggestions about *how* to record notes in that section. Sections B and C are employed later for adding key words, questions, and summaries, so they also offer no guidance about *how* to take notes. Thus, although the Cornell Method is usually presented as a note-taking system, it actually offers no strategies for *how* to take notes while reading or attending class (only *where* to record them). So, in the CORE Learning System, the Cornell Method is not considered a note-taking method. It is, however, a very powerful method for **Rehearsing** and **Evaluating** learning, so we will examine the use of this valuable learning strategy in Chapter 4.

Mastering Self-Management

4

Once I accept responsibility for choosing and creating the life I want, the next step is taking purposeful actions that will turn my desires into reality.

I am taking all of the actions necessary to achieve my goals and dreams.

Successful Students . . .	Struggling Students . . .
act on purpose, choosing deeds that move them on course to their goals and dreams.	**wait passively or wander from one unpurposeful activity to another.**
employ self-management tools, regularly planning and carrying out purposeful actions.	**live disorganized, unplanned lives,** constantly responding to whims of the moment.
develop self-discipline, showing commitment, focus, and persistence in pursuing their goals and dreams.	**quit or change course when their actions don't lead to immediate success.**

Case Study in Critical Thinking

The Procrastinators

Two students from Professor Hallengren's English composition class sat in the cafeteria discussing the approaching deadline for their fourth essay.

"There's no way I can get this essay done on time," **Tracy** said. "I've turned in every essay late, and I still owe him a rewrite on the second one. Professor Hallengren is going to be furious!"

"You think you're in trouble!" **Ricardo** said. "I haven't even turned in the last essay. Now I'm going to be two essays behind."

"How come?" Tracy asked. "I would have thought a young guy right out of high school would have all the time in the world."

"Don't ask me where my time goes," Ricardo answered, shrugging. "Deadlines keep sneaking up on me, and before I know it, I'm weeks behind. I live on campus, and I don't even have to commute. But something always comes up. Last weekend I was going to write that other essay and study for my sociology test, but I had to go to a wedding out of state on Saturday. I was having such a good time, I didn't drive back until Monday morning. Now I'm even further behind."

"So that's why you missed English class on Monday," Tracy said. "Professor Hallengren lectured us because so many students were absent."

"I know I miss too many classes. One time I stayed home because I didn't have my essay ready. And sometimes I stay up late talking to my girlfriend on the phone or playing video games. Then I can't get up in the morning."

"My situation is different," Tracy said. "I'm in my thirties and I'm a single mother. I have three kids: five, seven, and eight. I work twenty hours a week, and I'm taking four courses. I just can't keep up with it all! Every time I think I'm about to catch up, something goes wrong. Last week one of my kids got sick. Then my refrigerator broke, and I had to work overtime for money to get it fixed. Two weeks ago they changed my schedule at work, and I had to find new day care. Every professor acts like his class is all I have to do. I wish! The only way I could do everything is give up sleeping, and I'm only getting about five hours a night as it is."

"What are you going to do?" Ricardo asked.

"I don't think I can make it this semester. I'm considering dropping all of my classes."

"Maybe I should drop out, too."

1. **Who do you think has the more challenging self-management problem, Ricardo or Tracy? Be prepared to explain your choice.**

2. **If this person asked for your advice on how to do better in college, what specific self-management strategies would you recommend that he or she adopt?**

DIVING DEEPER Which person's situation, Ricardo's or Tracy's, is more like yours? Explain the similarities and identify what you do to keep up with all of the things you need to do.

Acting on Purpose

 FOCUS QUESTIONS Have you ever noticed how much highly successful people accomplish? How do they make such effective use of their time?

Creators do more than dream. They have developed the skill of translating their desired outcomes into purposeful actions. They make a plan and then take one step after another . . . even when they don't *feel* like it . . . until they achieve their objective. Goals and dreams set your destination, but only persistent, purposeful actions will get you there.

Thomas Edison did more than dream of inventing the light bulb; he performed more than ten thousand experiments before achieving his goal. Martin Luther King, Jr., did more than dream of justice and equality for people of all races; he spoke and organized and marched and wrote. College graduates did more than dream of their diplomas; they attended classes, read books, wrote essays, conferred with instructors, rewrote essays, formed study groups, did library research, asked questions, went to support labs, sought out tutors, and more!

When we consider the accomplishments of successful people, we may forget that they weren't born successful. Most achieved their success through the persistent repetition of purposeful actions. Creators apply a powerful strategy for turning dreams into reality: **Do important actions first, *before* they become urgent**.

> Do not confuse a creator with a dreamer. Dreamers only dream, but creators bring their dreams into reality.
>
> *Robert Fritz*

Harness the Power of Quadrant II

The significance of **importance** and **urgency** in choosing our actions is illustrated in the chart of the Quadrant II Time Management System® on the next page (from Stephen Covey's book *The 7 Habits of Highly Effective People*). This chart shows that our actions fall into one of four quadrants, depending on their importance and urgency.

Only you can determine the importance of your actions. Sure, others (such as friends and relatives) will have their opinions, but they don't really know what you value. If an action will help you achieve what you value, then it's *important* and you'd be crazy not to do it. Sadly, though, many people fill their time with unimportant actions, thus sabotaging their goals and dreams.

Likewise, only you can determine the urgency of your actions. Sure, others (such as instructors and counselors) will set deadlines for you, but these external finish lines won't be motivating unless you make them personally important. If meeting an approaching deadline will help you achieve something you value, it's *urgent* and you'd be crazy not to meet that deadline. Sadly, though, many people miss urgent deadlines, thus sabotaging their goals and dreams.

I've heard all sorts of excuses for why students "couldn't" get an assignment in on time. However, when I asked if they could have met the deadline if it was worth one million dollars, their answer was almost always, "Sure, but it wasn't." So now we know the real problem. It wasn't that they "couldn't" meet the deadline. They just

> I am personally persuaded that the essence of the best thinking in the area of time management can be captured in a single phrase: organize and execute around priorities.
>
> *Stephen Covey*

didn't make the deadline valuable enough to do what needed to be done. Creators choose their own goals and meet deadlines (even those set by others) because it's what *they* want, because it's important to creating the life *they* desire.

As you read on about the four quadrants, ask yourself, "In which quadrant am I choosing to spend most of my time?" No quadrant is "better" than others, but the choice you make will dramatically affect the outcomes and experiences you create.

Not all of your daily activities are of equal importance, and your mission is to organize and prioritize all activities into a working plan.

Charles J. Givens

- **QUADRANT I ACTIONS (Important and Urgent)** are important activities done under the pressure of nearing deadlines. One of my college roommates began his junior paper (the equivalent of two courses) just three days before it was due. He claimed that success in college was *important* to him, and the impending deadline certainly made this assignment *urgent*. He worked on the paper for seventy-two hours straight, finally turning it in without time even to proofread. Although he squeaked by this time, he fell deeper and deeper into this pattern of procrastination, until in our senior year he failed out of college. Procrastination is the choice to do unimportant tasks while neglecting important tasks. It's a violation of priorities, acting on low priorities while neglecting high priorities. At the last minute, procrastinators dive desperately into Quadrant I to handle an action that has always been important but is now urgent. People who spend their lives in Quadrant I are constantly dashing about putting out brush fires in their lives. They frantically create modest achievements in the present while sacrificing extraordinary success in the future. Worse, Quadrant I is the one in which people experience stress, develop ulcers, and flirt with nervous breakdowns.

It is not enough to be busy . . . the question is: What are we busy about?

Henry David Thoreau

- **QUADRANT II ACTIONS (Important and Not Urgent)** are important activities done *without* the pressure of looming deadlines. When you engage in an important activity with time enough to do it well, you can create your greatest dreams. Lacking urgency, Quadrant II actions are easily postponed. Almost all of the suggestions in this book belong in Quadrant II. For example, you could postpone forever keeping a journal, using the Wise Choice Process, adopting the language of Creators, discovering and visualizing your dreams, designing a life plan, and creating personal affirmations. However, when you do take purposeful actions such as these, you create a rich, full life. Quadrant II is where you will find Creators.

	Urgent	**Not Urgent**
Important	**Quadrant I** *Example:* Staying up all night cramming for an 8:00 A.M. test.	**Quadrant II** *Example:* Creating a study group in the first week of the semester.
Not Important	**Quadrant III** *Example:* Attending a hastily called meeting that has nothing to do with your goals.	**Quadrant IV** *Example:* Mindlessly watching television until 4:00 A.M.

- **QUADRANT III ACTIONS (Not Important and Urgent)** are unimportant activities done with a sense of urgency. How often have you responded to the demand of your ringing phone only to be trapped in long, unwanted conversations? Or you agree to something because you can't bring yourself to say "no"? When we allow someone else's urgency to talk us into an activity unimportant to our own goals and dreams, we have chosen to be in Quadrant III.

- **QUADRANT IV ACTIONS (Not Important and Not Urgent)** are simply time wasters. Everyone wastes some time, so it's not something to judge yourself for, though your Inner Critic may try. Instead, listen to your Inner Guide. Become more conscious of your choices, and minimize wasting the irreplaceable hours of each day. A college professor I know surveyed his classes and found that many of his students watch more than forty hours of television per week. That's the equivalent of a full-time job without pay or benefits!

What to Do in Quadrant II

Creators spend as much time as possible in Quadrant II. In college, Creators attend class regularly. They do all assignments to the best of their ability. They schedule conferences with their instructors. They organize study groups. They rewrite their notes on graphic organizers and study them for short periods nearly every day. They predict questions on upcoming tests and carry the answers on 3″ × 5″ study cards. No external urgency motivates them to take these purposeful actions. They create their own urgency by a strong commitment to their valued goals and dreams.

By contrast, Victims spend much of their time in Quadrants III and IV, where they repeat unproductive actions such as complaining, excusing, blaming, and wasting time. Not surprisingly, they move farther and farther off course.

If you want to know which quadrant you are in at any moment, ask yourself this question: "Will what I'm doing now positively affect my life one year from today?" If the answer is "yes," you are in Quadrant I or II. If the answer is "no," you are probably in Quadrant III or IV.

Creators say "no" to Quadrant III and Quadrant IV activities. Sometimes the choice requires saying "no" to other people: *No, I'm not going to be on your committee this semester. Thank you for asking.* Sometimes this choice requires saying "no" to themselves: *No, I'm not going to sleep late Saturday morning. I'm going to get up early and study for the math test. Then I can go to the movies with my friends without getting off course.*

When we say "no" to Quadrants III and IV, we free up time to say "yes" to Quadrants I and II. Imagine if you spent just thirty additional minutes each day taking purposeful actions. Think how dramatically that one small choice could change the outcome of your life!

While it is true that without a vision the people perish, it is doubly true that without action the people and their vision perish as well.

Johnetta B. Cole, president, Spelman College

A vision without a task is but a dream, a task without a vision is drudgery, a vision and a task is the hope of the world.

From a church in Sussex, England, ca. 1730

JOURNAL ENTRY | **12**

In this activity, you will assess the degree to which you are acting on purpose. *Your* purpose! As you spend more time in Quadrants I and II, you will notice a dramatic improvement in the results you are creating.

1. Write a list of fifteen or more specific actions you have taken in the past two days. (The actions will be considered *specific* if someone could have recorded you doing them with a video camera.)

2. Using an entire journal page, draw a four-quadrant chart like the example on page 104. Remember to reread the visualization of your dream (Journal Entry 10) often to help you stay motivated. Also, remember to say your affirmation (Journal Entry 11) each day to enhance the personal qualities that will keep you on course to your dreams! These are both great Quadrant II actions.

3. Write each action from your list in Step 1 in the appropriate quadrant on your chart. After each action, put the approximate amount of time you spent in the activity. For example, Quadrant IV might be filled with actions such as these:

1. Watched TV (2 hours)
2. Phone call to Terry (1 hour)
3. Watched TV (3 hours)
4. Went to the mall and wandered around (2 hours)
5. Hung out in the cafeteria (2 hours)
6. Played video game (2 hours)

4. Write about what you have learned or relearned concerning your use of time. Effective writing anticipates questions that a reader may have and answers these questions clearly. To dive deep in this journal entry, answer questions such as the following:

- What exactly did you discover after analyzing your time?
- In which quadrant do you spend the most time?
- What specific evidence did you use to draw this conclusion?
- If you continue using your time in this way, are you likely to reach your goals and dreams? Why or why not?
- What most often keeps you from taking purposeful actions?
- How do you feel about your discoveries?
- What different choices, if any, do you intend to make about how you use time?

One Student's Story

Jason Pozsgay
Oakland University, Michigan

When I started college as a freshman engineering student, I knew I would have a little trouble with the transition from high school to college. What I didn't know was that my main challenge would come from distractions. There's a mall only five minutes from campus, and when my friends wanted to hang out there, I wouldn't say no. Other times we'd play video games, or go out to dinner, or watch television. There was always something to distract me and no one to tell me to get to work. I was an A/B student in high school, and I was used to things coming easy to me. In college there's a lot more work and it's definitely not work you can do in five minutes and be done like in high school. I always found some excuse not to do my work, and then I'd try to do it the day it was due. I remember waiting until about 30 minutes before my first chemistry test to start studying. When my grades started dropping, I realized I needed to change but I wasn't sure how.

That's when we read about self-management in the *On Course* book. In class we did an activity where we divided a paper into four quadrants. Then we put what we had done the last two days onto those quadrants. I only had a few things in Quadrants I and II (Important). But Quadrant IV (Unimportant) was full. I realized I was studying only about three hours a week, but I was going to the mall about five hours, watching movies and television about six to ten hours, playing video games about twenty hours, and surfing the Internet about thirty hours. I had never had a high-speed connection before, and things like YouTube and Facebook were consuming a good part of my life.

Now that I had figured out my problem, I needed a solution. I started by hanging up the quadrants in my room with my wasted time on them. I then put up another blank quadrant chart next to it. I decided to try new ways to manage my time over the next week and keep track of how I spent my time every day. I set a goal to reduce my time in Quadrants III and IV to no more than twenty hours per week and increase my time in Quadrants I and II up to thirty or forty hours. At first I tried to completely cut out everything that was a waste of time, but I found myself stressed out. I was studying so much I thought my brain would explode and I couldn't remember what I was studying. Then I tried getting all of my work done before I did anything that could be seen as a waste of time. But, again I was unable to focus on

my work. Then I found the strategy that has helped. I put my schedule on a dry erase board and I adjust it to what I have going on that week. I make sure that I put both work and leisure time on the schedule. Also, if I have something important going on, like a test, I write it on my schedule in bold letters so I don't forget. Essentially I have made a reusable planner.

This strategy has helped me out a lot since I put it into effect. When I filled in the quadrants at the end of the first week, I was about halfway to my goals. Toward the end of the semester, I tracked my time again, and I reached my goals. My new system makes me more aware of what I'm choosing to do. I spend less time on the Internet, and I learned to say no. I remember when a bunch of my friends wanted to go to the movies the night before I had a math test. They asked me to go at least ten times, but I stayed home and studied. I actually did really well on the test. Probably the best choice I made was taking my video games home. Since I started writing my important work on the white board, I've missed almost no assignments and my grades have improved in every class. I have found a strategy that arranges my time so that I can get my important work done and still have time for fun things. My reusable planner has helped me a lot in my freshman year, and I plan to keep using it throughout college.

Photo: Courtesy of Jason Pozsgay

Creating a Self-Management System

 FOCUS QUESTION How can you devote more time to creating the outcomes and experiences that matter most to you?

At the beginning of a class, I asked my students to pass in their assignments. A look of panic came over one man's face. "What assignment?" he moaned. "You mean we had an *assignment* due today?" On another day, I overheard a student ask a friend: "Did you study for the math test today?" "No," the friend replied, "I didn't have time." Not long ago, a student told me, "I'm doing fine in my classes, but that's because I'm letting the rest of my life go down the drain."

Do these situations sound familiar? Do important actions leak through your hands like water? Do you sometimes give a half-hearted effort on important tasks . . . or finish them late . . . or not even do them at all? Do you neglect one important role in your life to do well in another? It's no easy matter getting everything done, especially if you're adding college to an already demanding life. But there are proven tools that can help you work more effectively and efficiently.

Typically these are called *time management* tools, but the term is misleading because no one can actually manage time. No matter what we mortals do, time just keeps on ticking. What we *can* manage, however, is ourselves. More specifically, we can manage the choices we make daily. **The secret to effective self-management is making choices that maximize the time you spend in Quadrants I and II.** These are the quadrants, you'll recall, where all of your actions are important to achieving your goals and dreams.

Understand that there's no "right" self-management tool that you *have* to use. Rather, there are many tools with which to experiment. You'll know you've found your best self-management system when you start achieving more of your desired outcomes and experiences with less stress. As a bonus, when you find the self-management approach that feels right for you, your expectations of success in college (and elsewhere) will go up because now you'll be confident you can get the required work done. Here are three of the best tools for making sure that you spend most of your time creating a great future.

Monthly Calendars

The first self-management tool, a **monthly calendar** (page 113), provides an overview of your upcoming Quadrant I and II commitments, appointments, and assignments. Use it to record classes, labs, work hours, doctor's appointments, family responsibilities, parties, job interviews, and conferences with instructors. Also put on your calendar the due dates of tests, research papers, final exams, projects, lab reports, and quizzes. A monthly planner is an easy and effective self-management tool to use all by itself. In a glance, you can see what you're scheduled to do in the days, weeks, even months to come.

Time is the coin of your life. It is the only coin you have, and only you can determine how it will be spent.

Carl Sandburg

I think that learning about and using time is a very complicated kind of learning. Many adults still have difficulty with it.

Virginia Satir

Scheduling purposeful actions is one thing; actually doing them is quite another. Once you have chosen your priorities, let nothing keep you from completing them except a rare emergency or special opportunity. Make a habit of saying "no" to unscheduled, low-priority alternatives found in Quadrants III and IV.

In addition to paper calendars, many people today keep their appointment schedule on a personal digital assistant (PDA). PDAs, which cost between $60 and $750, are tiny, handheld computers that can do a lot more than merely store your calendar. Depending on the model, a PDA can also record your important contact information (address and phone book), play music, take digital pictures, surf the Internet, and allow you to download and respond to email. A free electronic alternative is an online calendar hosted by a number of Internet sites (simply do an Internet search for "online calendar"). A unique advantage of these services is that most allow you to create calendars that can be accessed and updated by members of a group. So, if you have a project group, a study team, or a large family, an online calendar service might be just the right tool for managing your collective schedules.

Next Actions Lists

A **next actions list** (page 114) records everything you need to do "next" (as opposed to a calendar, where you schedule actions on a particular day or at a particular time). Whenever you have some free time that you might otherwise waste, your next actions list provides Quadrant I or II actions to complete. Here's how to use one:

1. Write your life roles and corresponding goals, which you defined in Chapter 3, in the shaded boxes. This first step makes your next actions list more effective than a mere to-do list by ensuring that your actions are directed at the accomplishment of all of your important goals.

2. List Quadrant I (Important and Urgent) actions for each of your goals. For example, if your short-term goal for Math 107 is to earn an A, your list might contain actions like these:

   Role: Math 107 student

   Goal: Grade A

   - *Attend classes on time (MWF).*
   - *Read pages 29–41 and do problems 1–10 on page 40.*
   - *Study 2 hours or more for Friday's test on Ch's 1–3.*

Each of these three actions is **important,** and each is relatively **urgent.** Notice that each action is written to heed the DAPPS rule, just as your goals are. Each action is dated, achievable, personal, positive, and specific. Especially be specific. Vague items such as *Do homework* provide little help when the time comes to take action. Much more helpful are specifics such as *Read pages 29–41 and do problems 1–10 on page 40.*

In college I learned how to manage more tasks than anyone could possibly finish. Literally. We learned how to keep a lot of balls in the air at the same time. You couldn't study for every class every day, so you had to decide what could be put off till later. The experience taught us to set priorities.

Dennis Hayes, Hayes Microcomputer Products

Asking "What's the next action?" undermines the victim mentality. It presupposes that there is a possibility of change, and that there is something you can do to make it happen.

David Allen

3. List Quadrant II (Important and Not Urgent) actions under each of your goals. For example, your list for Math 107 might continue with actions like these:

- *Make appointment with Prof. Finucci and ask her advice on preparing for Friday's test.*
- *Reschedule appointment with math lab tutor.*
- *Meet with study group and compare answers on practice problems.*

These Quadrant II behaviors are the sorts of activities that struggling students seldom do. You could go through the entire semester without doing any of these purposeful actions because none of them is urgent. But when you consistently choose Quadrant II actions, this decision makes a big difference in the results you create.

Whenever you have free time during the day, instead of slipping unconsciously into Quadrants III or IV, check your next actions list for purposeful actions. As you complete an action, cross it off your list. As you think of new important actions, add them to your list under the appropriate role. A bonus of keeping a next actions list is that it eliminates the burden of remembering numerous small tasks, freeing your brain to do more creative and critical thinking.

Tracking Forms

The third self-management tool, a **tracking form** (on page 115), is a variation of an old friend. You've already used a version of a tracking form in the "Embracing Change" experiment within previous chapters. As demonstrated there, a tracking form is ideal for scheduling actions that you decide are important to reach a personal goal. A tracking form helps you coordinate many actions all directed at a common goal. Elite athletes typically use some form of this tool to plan and monitor their training.

In college, a tracking form is ideal for helping you plan and take actions that will help you succeed in a challenging course. Suppose, for example, you decide to use a tracking form to help you gain a deep understanding of sociology and earn an A in the course. One helpful outer (physical) action might be "Read the textbook one or more hours." A possible inner (mental) action is "Say my affirmation five or more times." So, you write these two actions in the appropriate left-hand column, and put the dates of the next fourteen days at the top of the check-box columns.

Each day that you take these actions, you check the appropriate box, and at the end of fourteen days, you'll see exactly what you have (or have not) done to achieve your goal. One of my students commented, "Before I used the tracking form, I thought I was studying a lot. Now I realize I'm not studying enough." She started studying more, and her grades improved dramatically. A tracking form keeps your Inner Defender from fooling you into thinking you're doing what's necessary to stay on course when, in fact, you're not.

You've got to put down on paper the ten things that you absolutely have to do. That's what you concentrate on. Everything else—forget it.

Lee Iacocca

All the best work is done the way ants do things—by tiny untiring and regular additions.

Lefcadio Hearn

The Rewards of Effective Self-Management

Some people resist using a written self-management system. "These forms and charts are for the anally retentive," one student objected. "Everything I need to do, I keep right here in my head." I know this argument well, because I used to make it myself. Then one day, one of my mentors replied, "If you can remember everything you need to do, I guess you're not doing very much." Ouch.

I decided it wouldn't kill me to experiment with written self-management tools. Over time, I came up with my own combination of the tools we've been examining. In the process I became aware of how I had been wasting precious time. With my old self-management system (mostly depending on my memory, with an occasional "note to self"), the best I did was remember to do what was important and urgent. The worst I did was forget something vital, then waste time cleaning up the mess I had made. With my new system, I not only complete my Quadrant I actions now, I also spend large chunks of time in Quadrant II, where I take important actions before they become urgent. I'm better at keeping commitments to myself and others. I'm less tempted to go off course. Relieved of remembering every important task I need to do, my mind is free to think more creatively and boldly. And, most of all, my written self-management system helps me carry out the persistent, purposeful actions necessary to achieve my goals and dreams.

If you're already achieving all of your greatest goals and dreams, then keep using your present self-management system because it's working! However, if your Inner Guide knows you could be more successful than you are now, then maybe it's time to implement a new approach to managing your choices. You'll rarely meet a successful person who doesn't use some sort of written self-management system, whether in the world of work or in college. In fact, researchers at the University of Georgia found that students' self-management skills and attitudes are even better predictors of their grades in college than their Scholastic Aptitude Test (SAT) scores.

Consistently using a written self-management system is a habit that takes time to establish. You may begin with great energy, only to find later that a week has gone by without using it. Avoiding self-judgment, simply examine where you went astray and begin your plan a new. Experiment until you find the system that works best for your personality and creates the outcomes and experiences you desire. In time, your skills in using your personally designed written self-management system will excel. And then watch how much more you accomplish!

> When the seniors in the College Board study were asked what contributed to a successful and satisfying career in college, 73 percent said the "ability to organize tasks and time effectively."
>
> *Tim Walter & Al Siebert*

> When people with whom you interact notice that without fail you receive, process, and organize in an airtight manner the exchanges and agreements they have with you, they begin to trust you in a unique way.
>
> *David Allen*

I used to wonder how other students got so much done. Now that I'm using a planner, I wonder how I settled for doing so little.

John Simmons, student

JOURNAL ENTRY | **13**

In this activity, you'll explore how you could improve your present self-management system. By becoming more effective and efficient in the use of time, you'll complete a greater number of important actions and maximize your chances of attaining your goals and dreams.

1. **Write about the system (or lack of system) that you presently use to decide what you will do each day.** There is no "wrong" answer, so don't let your Inner Critic or Inner Defender get involved. Consider questions such as how you know what homework to do, when to prepare for tests, what classes to attend, and what instructor conferences to go to. How do you track what you need to do in other roles, such as your social or work life? Why do you currently use this approach? How well is your system working (giving examples wherever possible)? How do you *feel* while using this approach to self-management (e.g., stressed, calm, energized, frantic, etc.)?

2. **Write about how you *could* use or adapt the three self-management tools in this chapter to create a leak-proof self-management system and improve your outcomes and experiences. Or, if you do not want to use or adapt any of these tools, explain why.** Consider the monthly calendar, the next actions list, and the tracking form. How might you use them separately or in combination? How could you use computers or other technology in your self-management approach? How might you use written self-management tools not mentioned here that you may know about? In short, invent your own system for managing your choices that you think will maximize the quality of your outcomes and experiences. Should you need them, copies of a monthly calendar, a next actions list, and tracking form can be found on the Internet at www.cengage.com/success/Downing/OnCourse6e.

Monthly Calendar

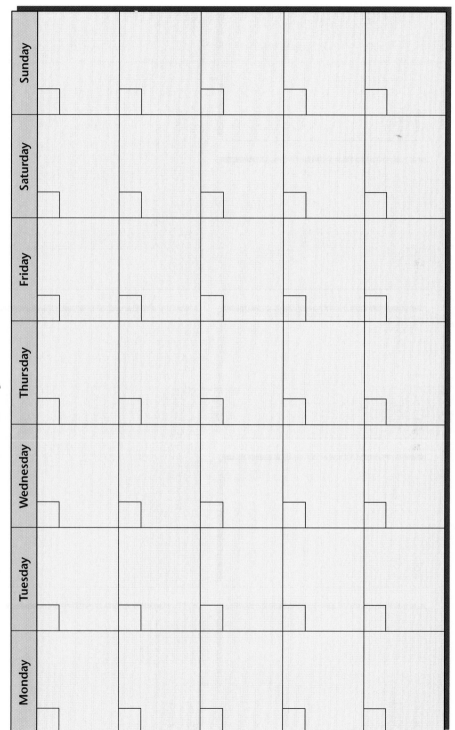

Monday	Tuesday	Wednesday	Thursday	Friday	Saturday	Sunday

Month _____

Next Actions List

Role:
Goal:

Role:
Goal:

Role:
Goal:

Role:
Goal:

Role:
Goal:

Telephone calls

Miscellaneous actions

Role:
Goal:

Tracking Form

Role:

Dream:

Long-term goal:

Short-term goals (to be accomplished this semester):

      1.

      2.

      3.

      4.

OUTER (Physical) Action Steps

    Dates:

INNER (Mental) Action Steps

    Dates:

One Student's Story

Allysa LePage

Sacramento City College, California

When the fall semester began, I wasn't sure how I was going to fit everything into my schedule. In addition to taking three college courses, I was waitressing twenty-four hours a week, taking dance classes, teaching dance classes to kids, spending time with my boyfriend, doing housework and errands, hanging out with friends from three different groups (high school, college, and church), and rehearsing two evenings a week for an annual December musical at Memorial Auditorium, an event that draws thousands of people. I'd stay up late to get my homework done, then wake up exhausted. I was struggling in math, and in my heart I knew I could be doing better in my other classes. I'd forget to turn in homework, I was skimping on preparation for my dance classes, I wasn't calling friends back, and I'd forget to bring costumes and makeup to rehearsals for the musical. I was sick all the time with colds and headaches. I was seriously stressed and not doing full justice to anything.

Before I lost all hope, my Human Career Development class went over self-management tools. I developed my own system and started writing down everything I needed to do. I keep a big calendar by my bed so I see it in the morning, and I carry a smaller calendar in my purse. My favorite tool is a list of everything I have to do put into categories. I make a new list every day and put important things at the top so it's okay if I don't get to the ones on the bottom. My system helps me see what my priorities are and get them done first so I don't feel so scattered.

By doing important things first, I began having more focus, not rushing as much, and getting more done. Of course I had to let a few lower-priority things go for a while, like doing housework and spending as much time with some of my friends. I started getting more sleep, completing my homework, and getting A's on all of my tests while doing everything else that I needed to do. After a while, I began to accomplish so much more and I realized that I *do* have enough time to fit all of the important things into my schedule. In fact, every once in a while now I actually find myself with a luxury I haven't had in a long while—free time.

Developing Self-Discipline

 FOCUS QUESTIONS Do you find yourself procrastinating, even on projects that mean a great deal to you? How can you keep taking purposeful actions even when you don't feel like it?

Every semester perfectly capable students abandon their goals and dreams. Somewhere along the path, they get distracted and stop or they wander off in another direction.

"Hey," their instructors want to shout, "the goals and dreams you say you want are over here! Keep coming this way. You can do it!"

Maybe these students believe college is a sprint, over in a flash. Not so. Like most grand victories, college is a marathon with many hurdles along the way. It may take only thirty seconds to stride proudly across the stage to receive your college diploma, but it will have taken you thousands of persistent small steps taken over years to get there.

Self-discipline is self-caring.

Dr. M. Scott Peck

In a word, success takes self-discipline—the willingness to do whatever has to be done, whether you feel like it or not, until you reach your goals and dreams. Every January, athletic clubs are wall-to-wall with people who made New Year's resolutions to get in shape. You know what happens. A month later, the crowds are gone, reminding us that getting and staying in shape takes commitment, focus, and persistence.

So it goes with every important goal we set. Our actions reveal whether we have the self-discipline to stay on course in the face of tempting alternatives. Most students want to be successful, but *wanting* and *doing* are worlds apart. Partying with friends is easier than going to class . . . day after day. Talking on the phone is easier than reading a challenging textbook . . . hour after hour. Watching television is easier than doing research at the library . . . night after night.

Many people choose instant gratification. Few choose the far-off rewards of persistent and purposeful actions. Many begin the journey to their dreams; few finish. Yet all we need to do is put one foot in front of the other . . . again and again and again. A journey of a thousand miles may begin with a single step, but many more better follow.

Self-discipline has three essential ingredients: **commitment, focus,** and **persistence.** In Journal Entry 10, you explored how to strengthen your commitment. Now we'll take a look at focus and persistence.

Staying Focused

Distractions constantly tug at our minds, and, like an unruly child, the unfocused mind dashes from one distraction to another. Everyone has experienced losing focus for a minute, an hour, even a day. But struggling students lose focus for weeks and months at a time. They start arriving late, skipping classes, doing sloppy work, ignoring assignments. They take their eyes off of the prize and forget why they are in college.

For many students, the time to beware of losing focus is at midterm. The excitement of the new semester has been replaced by the never-ending list of assignments. That's when Inner Defenders start offering great excuses to quit: *I've got boring teachers; my schedule stinks; I'm still getting over the flu; next semester I could start all over.* And Inner Critics chime in with practiced self-judgments: *I never could do math; I'm not as smart as my classmates; I'm too old; I'm too young; I'm not really college material.*

Your Inner Guide, however, knows that winners stay focused and finish strong. They complete the semester with a bang, not a snivel. Their efforts go up as the semester winds down. Your Inner Guide can help you regain focus by addressing one question: *What are my goals and dreams?* If you need a reminder, revisit your life plan in Journal Entry 9 and the visualization of your biggest academic goals or dream in Journal Entry 10. If your goals and dreams don't motivate you

> To be disciplined or nondisciplined is a choice you make every minute and every hour of your life. Discipline is nothing more than the process of focusing on any chosen activity without interruption until that activity is complete.
>
> *Charles J. Givens*

> You always have to focus in life on what you want to achieve.
>
> *Michael Jordan*

Calvin and Hobbes   by Bill Watterson

© CALVIN AND HOBBES ©1992, Watterson. Reprinted with permission of Universal Press Syndicate. All rights reserved.

to keep taking purposeful actions right to the finish line, then perhaps you need to rethink where you want to go in life.

Being Persistent

If focus is self-discipline in thought, then persistence is self-discipline in action. Here's the question your Inner Guide can ask when you slow down or quit: "Do I love myself enough to keep going?" After all, you are the one who'll benefit most from the accomplishment of your goals and dreams . . . and you're the one who will pay the price of disappointment if you fail.

Here's the thing, though. While failure is certain if you quit, success isn't guaranteed simply because you persist. Sometimes wisdom requires more than simply repeating the same thing over and over expecting a better result. If Plan A isn't working, don't quit. But also don't keep doing what isn't working! Change your approach. Move on to Plan B. Or C or D if necessary.

One of my students learned just how powerful persistence and a willingness to try something different can be. When Luanne enrolled in my English 101 class, she had taken and failed the course three times before. She had actually developed some good writing skills, but she definitely needed to master Standard English to pass the course. "I know," she said, "that's what all my other teachers told me." She paused, took a deep breath and added, "At least I'm not a quitter."

I asked Luanne why she was going to college. As she told me about her dream to work in television, her eyes sparkled. I asked if mastering standard grammar would help her achieve her dream. She hesitated, perhaps nervous about where her answer might lead.

Finally she said, "Yes."

> Perhaps the most valuable result of all education is the ability to make yourself do the thing you have to do, when it ought to be done, whether you like it or not; it is the first lesson that ought to be learned; and however early a man's training begins, it is probably the last lesson that he learns thoroughly.
>
> *Thomas Henry Huxley*

"Great! So, what's one action that, if repeated every day for a month or more, would improve your grammar?" She needed to discover a Quadrant II activity and make it a new habit.

"Probably studying my grammar book."

I handed her a **32-Day Commitment Form** (see page 121). "Okay, then, I'm inviting you to make a commitment to study your grammar book for thirty-two days in a row. You can put a check on this form each day that you keep your promise to yourself. Will you do it?"

"I'll try."

"C'mon, Luanne. You've been *trying* for three semesters. My question is, 'Will you commit to studying grammar for thirty minutes every day for the next thirty-two days?'"

She paused again. Her choice at this moment would surely affect her success in college, and probably the outcome of her life.

"Okay," she said, "I'll do it."

And she did. Each time I passed the writing lab, I saw Luanne working on grammar. The tutors joked that they were going to start charging her rent.

But that's not all Luanne did. She attended every English class. She completed every writing assignment. She met with me to discuss her essays. She created flash cards, writing problem sentences on one side and corrections on the other. In short, Luanne was taking the persistent actions of a self-disciplined student.

As mentioned earlier, to receive a passing grade in English 101, students had to pass one of two exit exam essays graded by other instructors. The first exam that semester brought Luanne some good news: She had gotten her highest score ever. But there was the usual bad news as well: Both exam graders said her grammar errors kept them from passing her.

Luanne was at another important choice point. Did she have the self-discipline to persist in the face of discouraging news? Would she quit or finish strong?

"Okay," she said finally, "show me how to correct my errors." We reviewed her essay, sentence by sentence. The next day she went to the writing lab earlier; she left later. She rewrote the exam essay for practice, and we went over it again. Applying self-discipline, Luanne's mastery of standard grammar continued to improve.

That semester, the second exam was given on the Friday before Christmas. In order to finalize grades, all of the English 101 instructors met that evening to grade the essays. I promised to call Luanne with her results.

The room was quiet except for rustling papers as two dozen English instructors read one essay after another. At about ten o'clock that night, I received my students' graded essays. I looked quickly through the pile and found Luanne's. She had passed! As I dialed the phone to call her, Luanne's previous instructors told others about her success.

"Merry Christmas, Luanne," I said into the phone, "you passed!"

I heard her delight, and at that moment, two dozen instructors in the room began to applaud.

The major difference I've found between the highly successful and the least successful is that the highly successful stick to it. They have staying power. Everybody fails. Everybody takes his knocks, but the highly successful keep coming back.

Sherry Lansing, chairman,
Paramount Pictures

A dream doesn't become reality through magic; it takes sweat, determination, and hard work.

Colin Powell

In this activity, you will apply self-discipline by planning and carrying out a thirty-two-day commitment that will help you achieve a goal in college. Making and keeping a thirty-two-day commitment has a number of benefits. First, it guarantees that you spend significant time on task, which is essential to college success. Second, a thirty-two-day commitment automatically provides distributed practice, one of the keys to deep and lasting learning. And third, it helps you make visible progress toward your goal, thus raising your expectations of success and your motivation to persist.

> My Daddy used to ask us whether the teacher had given us any homework. If we said no, he'd say, "Well, assign yourself." Don't wait around to be told what to do. Hard work, initiative, and persistence are still the nonmagic carpets to success.
>
> *Marian Wright Edelman*

1. From your life plan in Journal Entry 9, copy one of your most important and challenging short-term goals from your role as a *student*.

2. Write and complete the following sentence stem five or more times: I WOULD MOVE STEADILY TOWARD THIS GOAL IF EVERY DAY I . . .

Write five or more different physical actions that *others can see you do* and that you can do every day of the week, including weekends. So you wouldn't write, "be motivated" or "attend class." Others cannot see your motivation, and you can't attend class every day for thirty-two days straight. Instead, if your short-term goal is to earn an A in English, you might complete the sentence with specific actions such as these:

1. **I WOULD MOVE STEADILY TOWARD THIS GOAL IF EVERY DAY I** *spend at least fifteen minutes doing exercises in my grammar book.*
2. **I WOULD MOVE STEADILY TOWARD THIS GOAL IF EVERY DAY I** *write at least two hundred words in my journal.*
3. **I WOULD MOVE STEADILY TOWARD THIS GOAL IF EVERY DAY I** *revise one of my previous essays, correcting the grammar errors that my teacher marked.*

Chances are, all of these actions will fall in Quadrant II.

> Becoming a world-class figure skater meant long hours of practice while sometimes tolerating painful injuries. It meant being totally exhausted sometimes, and not being able to do all the things I wanted to do when I wanted to do them.
>
> *Debi Thomas*

3. On a separate page in your journal, create a 32-Day Commitment Form or attach a photocopy of the one on page 121. Complete the sentence at the top of the form ("Because I know . . . .") with ONE action from your list in Step 2. For the next thirty-two days, put a check beside each day that you keep your commitment.

4. Write your thoughts and feelings as you begin your thirty-two-day commitment. Develop your journal paragraphs by asking and answering readers' questions, such as, How self-disciplined have you been in the past? What is your goal? What were some possible actions you considered? What action did you choose for your thirty-two-day commitment? How will this action, when performed consistently, help you reach your goal? What challenges might you experience in keeping your commitment? How will you overcome these challenges? How do you feel about undertaking this commitment? What is your prediction about whether or not you will succeed in keeping your thirty-two-day commitment?

IMPORTANT: If you miss a day on your 32-Day Commitment form, don't judge yourself or offer excuses. Simply ask your Inner Guide what got you off course, renew your commitment to yourself, and start over at Day 1.

32-Day Commitment

Because I know that this commitment will keep me on course to my goals, I promise myself that every day for the next 32 days I will take the following action:

_____

_____

_____

Day 1			Day 17	
Day 2			Day 18	
Day 3			Day 19	
Day 4			Day 20	
Day 5			Day 21	
Day 6			Day 22	
Day 7			Day 23	
Day 8			Day 24	
Day 9			Day 25	
Day 10			Day 26	
Day 11			Day 27	
Day 12			Day 28	
Day 13			Day 29	
Day 14			Day 30	
Day 15			Day 31	
Day 16			Day 32	

One Student's Story

Holt Boggs

Belmont Technical College, Ohio

I was a first-year student and enjoying college, but I was having a hard time in my electronics class. The teacher lectured about things like current, watts, volts, and resistance, and even though I read the book, took notes in class, and asked questions, I still wasn't understanding what I needed to. When I got back my first test, I didn't fail but I did pretty badly. I was scared because, if this is what the first test was like, how hard would the rest of them be? This was a new experience for me because I never had to study much to do well in school. I knew that I had to try something different if I was going to pass electronics.

In my Student Learning and Success class, I read about the thirty-two-day commitment, and I decided to give it a try. I decided to read one section from my electronics book twice every day for thirty-two days. I figured that if I read the section twice, maybe I would understand it better the second time around. However, as the semester went on, I still wasn't doing so hot. At times I felt like quitting my commitment because, even though I was reading every section twice, I still wasn't getting it. By midterm, I was ahead of the class in the book, and when the instructor taught the section, it was all review for me. Then one day he was putting examples on the board, and I realized, "Hey, I know this stuff." Since I already understood most of

the material, I had time to focus on the things that I didn't understand. Everything that was still blurry to me he made clear. On the next chapter test, I got a 93, and in the end I passed the class with a B.

It's amazing what doing one little thing for thirty-two days can do for you. I never would have thought committing thirty-two days to reading a section from my book twice would help so much. Before, I'd say, "Yeah, I read it," but I was only skimming. When I read it a second time, I picked up things that I missed the first time through and I really understood what I was reading. In the end the thirty-two-day commitment was able to help me pass my electronics class, but even more important, this experience gave me a lot more confidence. Now I know that I can pass all of the challenging classes on the way to my degree.

Creators Wanted!

Candidates must demonstrate effective self-management, self-discipline, and the ability to manage complex actions to achieve goals.

Self-Management AT WORK

Success in business requires training and discipline and hard work. But if you're not frightened by these things, the opportunities are just as great today as they ever were. *David Rockefeller, former chairman, The Chase Manhattan Bank*

As it is in college, success in the workplace means converting your goals into a step-by-step plan and having the self-discipline to spend the majority of your time doing what is important, preferably before it becomes urgent. Here in the realm of action, doers separate themselves from dreamers. Folks in business often refer to this aspect of success as "doing diligence."

In college, "doing diligence" is wise because the effort usually nets you good grades, and a high GPA impresses potential employers with both your intelligence and your work ethic. But getting good grades isn't all you can do in college to stand out in a job interview. Here are some other Quadrant II actions that will look great on your résumé: gain experience in your career field through part-time jobs, volunteer work, internships, or cooperative-education experiences; demonstrate leadership qualities through your involvement with the student

Self-Management
AT WORK

government; create a portfolio of your best college work; join clubs or activities that relate to your future career. Wise choices like these offer employers something that distinguishes you from all the other applicants for the job.

When it comes time to search for a position in your field, your effective self-management skills will once more serve you well. Consider using the **tracking form** to direct your outer and inner action steps toward your employment goal. The **next actions list** is a great tool for keeping track of essential one-time actions like returning calls or sending thank-you notes after an interview. **Monthly calendars** help you avoid the embarrassment of arriving late or having to cancel a job interview because of a scheduling conflict. All of these tools will allow you to monitor your use of time, assuring that you spend the bulk of your time productively in Quadrants I and II.

As you begin your career search, consider doing the following outer action steps. Develop a list of careers that interest you. Make a list of potential employers in each career. Attend a résumé-writing workshop. Write a résumé and cover letter to showcase the talents and experiences you offer an employer. Personalize each cover letter to fit the job you're applying for. Develop your telephone skills. Participate in mock interviews where others ask you likely questions. Your college's career center or a career development course can help you take these job-search actions effectively.

Searching for employment can get discouraging, and you would be wise to take some inner actions to maintain a positive attitude. You could create an affirmation as a mental pick-me-up. For example, "I am enthusiastically taking all of the actions necessary to find the ideal position to start my career." Or "I optimistically send out ten job inquiries each week." If you find an important action difficult to do (such as calling employers to see if they have unadvertised openings), you could visualize yourself doing it and having the experience go extraordinarily well.

Once you move into your career, your self-management skills will become essential for accomplishing all you have to do. Notice how many people at your workplace carry planners, either paper or electronic. If you don't already have a planner that works for you, experiment to see if one will help you to manage the avalanche of tasks that will come your way in a new position. There's no one-size-fits-all self-management system for everyone, but there is one self-management system that will fit you. And it's your responsibility to find or invent it.

At the beginning of your career, tasks will likely take you twice as long to do as they will after a few years of practice. So not only do you need to manage your next actions list, you'll also need to make some sacrifices to get them all done. People with a "job" mentality sometimes stop short of getting all of their work done because work inevitably leaks into their personal time. They work only until their "shift" is over. On the other hand, people with a "career" mentality know that sometimes they'll need to stay late or take work home. They have the discipline to work until the task is done. Of course, these folks have to find a balance that allows them to have a personal life as well. The important thing to know is that the workload is always heavy at the beginning of a career, and this is the time when you establish your reputation as someone who can be counted on to get the job done.

▶ *Believing in Yourself*
Develop Self-Confidence

 FOCUS QUESTIONS In which life roles do you feel most confident? In which do you experience self-doubt? What can you do to increase your overall self-confidence?

On the first day of one semester, a woman intercepted me at the classroom door.

"Can I ask you something?" she said. "How do I know if I'm cut out for college?"

"What's your opinion?" I asked.

"I think I'll do okay."

"Great," I said.

She stood there, still looking doubtful. "But . . . my high school counselor said . . . ." She paused.

"Let me guess. Your counselor said you wouldn't do well in college? Is that it?"

She nodded. "I think he was wrong. But how do I know for sure?"

Indeed! How *do* we know? There will always be others who don't believe in us. What matters, however, is that we have confidence in ourselves. Self-confidence is the core belief that *I CAN,* the unwavering trust that I can successfully do whatever is necessary to achieve my goals and dreams.

Ultimately, it matters little whether someone else thinks you can do something. It matters greatly whether *you* believe you can. Luck aside, you'll probably accomplish just about what you believe you can. In this section we'll explore three effective ways to develop greater self-confidence.

Create a Success Identity

Are you confident that you can tie your shoes? Of course. And yet there was a time when you weren't. So how did you move from doubt to confidence? Wasn't it by practicing over and over? You built your self-confidence by stacking one small victory upon another. As a result, today you have confidence that you can tie your shoes every time you try. By the same method, you can build a success identity in virtually any endeavor.

The life of Nathan McCall illustrates the creation of a success identity under difficult circumstances. McCall grew up in a Portsmouth, Virginia, ghetto where his involvement with crimes and violence led to imprisonment. After his release, McCall attended college and studied journalism. As you might imagine, one of his greatest challenges was self-doubt. But he persevered, taking each challenge as it came—one more test passed, one more course completed. After graduation, he got a job with a newspaper, and over the years he steadily rose to the position of bureau chief. Recalling his accumulated successes, McCall wrote in his journal, "These experiences solidify my belief that I can do anything I set my mind to

> If people don't feel good about themselves and believe that they'll win a championship, they never will.
>
> *Tara VanDerveer, head coach of the 1990 NCAA Championship Stanford women's basketball team*

> Success brings its own self-confidence.
>
> *Lillian Vernon Katz*

do. The possibilities are boundless." Boundless indeed! McCall went from street-gang member and prison inmate to successful and respected reporter for the *Washington Post,* and his book, *Makes Me Wanna Holler,* climbed to the *New York Times* bestseller's list.

Genuine self-confidence results from a history of success, and a history of success results from persistently taking purposeful actions. That's why a thirty-two-day commitment (Journal Entry 14) is not only an effective self-management tool but also a great way to start building a success identity. After we experience success in one area of our life, self-confidence begins to seep into every corner of our being, and we begin to believe *I CAN.*

Celebrate Your Successes and Talents

A friend showed me a school assignment that his eight-year-old daughter had brought home. At the top of the page was written: *Nice job, Lauren. Your spelling is very good. I am proud of you.* What made the comments remarkable is this: The teacher had merely put a check on the page; Lauren had added the compliments herself.

At the age of eight, Lauren has much to teach us about building self-confidence. It's great when someone else tells us how wonderful our successes and talents are. But it's even more important that we tell ourselves.

One way to acknowledge your success is to create a deck of victory cards: Every day, write at least one success (big or small) on a $3'' \times 5''$ card. Add it to your growing deck of victory cards and read through the deck every day. Or post the cards on a wall where you'll be reminded often of your accomplishments: *Got an 86 on history test . . . Attended every class on time this week . . . Exercised for two hours at gym.* In addition to acknowledging your successes, you can celebrate them by rewarding yourself with something special—a favorite dinner, a movie, a night out with friends.

> **Research studies show that people who have high self-esteem regularly reward themselves in tangible and intangible ways . . . . By documenting and celebrating their successes, they insure that these successes will reoccur.**
>
> *Marsha Sinetar*

Visualize Purposeful Actions

We can also strengthen our self-confidence by visualizing purposeful actions done well, especially actions outside our comfort zone. Psychologist Charles Garfield once performed an experiment to determine the impact of visualizations on a group of people who were afraid of public speaking. These nervous speakers were divided into three subgroups:

> **Peak performers develop powerful mental images of the behavior that will lead to the desired results. They see in their mind's eye the result they want, and the actions leading to it.**
>
> *Charles Garfield*

Group 1 read and studied how to give public speeches, but they delivered no actual speeches.

Group 2 read about speechmaking and also gave two talks each week to small audiences of classmates and friends.

Group 3 read about effective speaking and gave one talk each week to small groups. This group also watched videotapes of effective speakers and, twice a day, *mentally rehearsed* giving effective speeches of their own.

Experts on public speaking, unaware of the experiment, evaluated the effectiveness of these speakers both before and after their preparation. Group 1 did not improve at all. Group 2 improved significantly. Group 3, the group that had visualized themselves giving excellent speeches, improved the most.

Mentally rehearsing purposeful actions will not only help you improve your ability to do the action but will also reduce associated fears. Suppose you're feeling anxious about an upcoming test. Your Inner Critic is probably visualizing a disaster: *As soon as I walk into the exam room, my pulse starts racing, I start sweating, I start feeling weak, and my mind goes totally blank. I fail!*

What if you visualized a more positive experience? You could imagine yourself taking the test confidently, creating an ideal outcome. Your revised mental movie might look like this: *I walk into the exam fully prepared. I've attended all of my classes on time, done my very best work on all my assignments, and studied effectively. Feeling confident, I find a comfortable seat and take a few moments to breathe deeply, relax, and focus myself. I concentrate on the subject matter of this test. I release all my other cares and worries, feeling excited about the opportunity to show how much I have learned. The instructor walks into the room and begins handing out the exams. I know that any question the instructor asks will be easy for me to answer. I glance at the test and see questions that my study group and I have prepared for all semester. Alert and aware, I begin to write. Every answer I write flows easily from the storehouse of knowledge I have in my mind. I work steadily and efficiently, and, after finishing, I check my answers thoroughly. I hand in the exam with a comfortable amount of time remaining, and as I leave the room, I feel a pleasant weariness. I am confident that I have done my very best.*

Since you choose the movies that play in your mind, why not choose to star in a movie in which you successfully complete purposeful actions?

Creators know there are many choices that will strengthen self-confidence. When we consciously choose options such as creating a success identity, celebrating our successes and talents, and visualizing the successful completion of purposeful actions, we will soon be able to say with supreme confidence: *I CAN.*

> If we picture ourselves functioning in specific situations, it is nearly the same as the actual performance. Mental practice helps one to perform better in real life.
>
> *Dr. Maxwell Maltz*

JOURNAL ENTRY   15

In this activity, you will practice ways to increase your self-confidence. Self-confident people *expect* success, which in turn strengthens their motivation and fuels their energy. If what they are doing isn't working, they don't quit. Instead, they switch to Plan B (or C or D) and persist. Then they finish strong, consistently giving their best to achieve their goals and dreams! In this way, the very success they expect often becomes a reality.

I wanted to be the best dentist that ever lived. People said, "But she's a woman; she's colored," and I said, "Ha! Just you wait and see."

Bessie Delany, dentist and author

1. **List the successes you have created in your life.** The more successes you list, the more you will strengthen your self-confidence. Include small victories as well as big ones.

2. **List your personal skills and talents.** Again, the longer your list, the more you will strengthen your self-confidence. What are you good at doing? Don't overlook talents that you use daily. No talent is too insignificant to acknowledge.

3. **List positive risks that you have taken in your life.** When did you stretch your comfort zone and do something despite your fear?

4. **List important actions that you presently have some resistance about doing.** What purposeful actions cause anxious rumblings in the pit of your stomach? For example, maybe you fear asking a question in your biology lecture or you're nervous about going to a scheduled job interview.

5. **Write a visualization of yourself successfully doing one of the actions you listed in Step 4.** Remember to use the four keys to effective visualizing discussed in Journal Entry 10:

1. Relax.
2. Use present-tense verbs.
3. Be specific and use many senses.
4. Feel the feelings.

As a model for your writing, reread the positive visualization on page 126.

If you have no confidence in self, you are twice defeated in the race of life. With confidence, you have won even before you have started.

Marcus Garvey

Embracing Change   Do One Thing Different This Week

Creators take important actions daily, both urgent (Quadrant I) and not urgent (Quadrant II). From the following list, pick ONE new belief or behavior you think will improve your self-management. Then experiment with it for a week to see if this new choice helps you create more positive outcomes and experiences.

1. Think: "I am taking all of the actions necessary to achieve my goals and dreams."
2. Pause, look at what I am doing, and decide what quadrant I am in at that moment.
3. Use a monthly calendar.
4. Use a next actions list.
5. Use a tracking form.
6. Make and keep a 32-Day Commitment.
7. Demonstrate effective self-management skills at my workplace.
8. Celebrate a success, big or small.
9. Visualize myself taking a purposeful action.

Now, write the one you chose under "My Commitment" in the following chart. Then, track yourself for one week, putting a check in the appropriate box when you keep your commitment. After seven days, assess your results. If your outcomes and experiences improve, you now have a tool you can use to improve your self-management for the rest of your life. As author and philosopher Henry David Thoreau noted, "Things do not change, we change."

My Commitment						
Day 1	**Day 2**	**Day 3**	**Day 4**	**Day 5**	**Day 6**	**Day 7**

During my seven-day experiment, what happened?

As a result of what happened, what did I learn or relearn?

Wise Choices in College   ORGANIZING STUDY MATERIALS

To pass the many quizzes, tests, and exams they will take in college, students obviously need to know how to study. But, many do not.

In fact, the study methods of many students—even those who were "good" students in high school—are only marginally effective in college. Even when they pass tests, many students understand and remember only a fraction of what they studied. Imagine the problems this missing knowledge causes when it's needed later in the course. Or later in a more advanced course. Or even later in a career. Relying on ineffective study skills leads to shallow and short-lived learning. Such ineffective learning is a sure-fire way to undermine academic, professional, and even personal success.

You're about to explore a number of strategies that will help you *learn in a deep and lasting way.* Mastering these strategies will provide you with the ability to improve your learning outcomes and experiences for the rest of your life. And, yes, your grades in college will almost surely go up as well.

Organizing Study Materials: The Big Picture

Recall from Chapter 1 that effective learners take advantage of three principles that contribute to deep and lasting learning. First is **prior learning**—relating new information to what you already know. Second is the **quality of processing**—creating many different kinds of deep-processing strategies. And third is the **quantity of processing**—using frequent practice sessions of sufficient length distributed over time.

In this chapter we will examine study strategies that address the *quality of processing*. Quality processing leads to a deep understanding of what we are learning. To develop deep understanding, we begin by **Organizing** the knowledge we have **Collected**

from all course materials. Our goal is the creation of many different kinds of effective study materials. Later in Chapter 5, we will look at strategies for **Rehearsing** these study materials in order to take advantage of the third learning principle: *quantity of processing.* Using this combined approach will create learning that is both deep and lasting.

So, experiment with the many study strategies that follow and continue personalizing your own CORE Learning System. As you do, keep in mind the big picture of this step in studying: **You are Organizing the information and skills you have Collected from all course resources, and your goal is the creation of many different kinds of effective *study materials.* Engaging actively in this process greatly enhances your understanding of what you are learning.**

Before Organizing Study Materials

1. Adopt a growth mind-set. Having positive beliefs about the value of studying improves your learning outcomes. According to psychologist Carol Dweck, one important belief is that *the ability to learn can be improved.* Dweck calls this belief a "**growth mind-set.**" The opposite mind-set is that you're stuck with whatever learning ability you were born with (which is stinkin' thinkin'). To begin developing a growth mind-set about learning, create an affirming statement about the value of using high-quality study strategies. For example, *My CORE Learning System makes learning more effective and fun.* Along with your personal affirmation, repeat this learning affirmation in order to make new choices about studying.

2. Create an ideal study space. Having one comfortable place where you usually study has many advantages. Your learning resources are always close at hand. You aren't distracted by unfamiliar sights or sounds. And your mind becomes accustomed to shifting into learning gear whenever you enter your study area. Design your study area so you enjoy being there. Minimum requirements include a comfortable chair, plenty of light, room to spread out your course materials, and space to store your books and supplies. Personalize your study area to make it even more inviting. For example, display pictures of loved ones or add plants. Do whatever it takes to create a space you look forward to entering.

3. Arrange to be undisturbed. Do whatever is necessary to minimize interruptions while you study. Schedule regular study times and ask friends and relatives not to contact you during those times. Put a Do-Not-Disturb sign on your door. Let voice mail take telephone calls. Resist checking emails or text messages. If necessary, study where no one can easily disturb you, such as at your campus library. Protect the sanctity of your study time.

4. Create a distributed study schedule. As you know, active learners engage in numerous study sessions spread over time. So refer to your calendar where you have recorded all of the announced tests for your classes (you *have* done this, right?). Then choose a date before each test when you will begin serious studying. As a guideline, start seven days before a regular test and up to fourteen days before a major exam. Plan to use one quarter to one third of the days for creating study materials (as you will learn to do in this chapter). Use the remaining days to **Rehearse** these materials using the strategies you'll learn in Chapter 5. A tracking form is ideal for creating a distributed study schedule.

5. Gather all course materials. Start with your textbooks (marked and annotated) and your class notes. Add to them all other course documents, such as handouts, study guides, graded tests and essays, and study group notes.

While Organizing Study Materials

6. Condense course materials. Since you have already marked and annotated all of your reading assignments and taken detailed notes in class, you will have a large **Collection** of information and skills. As a result, you may think you have all you

need for studying. Not true. Learning from these raw materials is seldom effective. Instead, good learners condense all of these materials into the key concepts, main ideas, and supporting details of the course. Then they **Organize** this condensed knowledge into effective *study materials.* But one thing at a time. Here's an effective way to condense:

- Read through the markings, annotations, and notes you added to your course materials. As you do, place a star beside key concepts, important ideas, and supporting details.

- Now, reread only the information you marked with a star, find the most important ideas within those, and put a second star beside them.

- Finally, reread just the ideas you have marked with two stars, identify the most important of these, and put a third star beside them.

- Read through all starred information one more time and circle the key concepts.

By doing this process, you should have condensed your course materials by at least half (preferably more) and identified various levels of information:

- Key concepts (circled)
- Level 1: main ideas (three stars)
- Level 2: secondary ideas (two stars)
- Levels 3 and 4: supporting details—major and minor (one star)

Now your goal is to **Organize** this condensed information in ways that will help you understand it thoroughly. The **Organizing** options described next fall into one of two broad categories: *linear* or *graphic* (just as with note taking). Experiment to find which options work best for you. Keep in mind that while a particular **Organizational** approach may work well for one subject (e.g., sociology), a different approach may be better for another (e.g., mathematics).

7. Create outlines (linear organizer). Using the key concepts, ideas, and supporting details you have just identified with circles and stars, you can now create an outline using the process described on pages 95–96. However, an even easier way to craft an outline for study purposes is to copy your textbook's table of contents to a blank page. Sometimes you can find the book's table of contents on the publisher's or author's website. Then you can simply copy and paste it into your own study document. Once you have the table of contents converted into an outline, add to it starred information from *all* of your course materials. It's likely that you will have some starred information (e.g., lecture notes) that does not fit into the outline created from the textbook. In that case, simply create a new section in the outline and add the new information. Outlines make particularly valuable study materials when preparing for essay tests or writing a paper (composition) to demonstrate your learning.

8. Create test questions (linear organizer). Put yourself in the mind of the instructor preparing a test. What information or skill does she expect you to learn? Write questions that will reveal your understanding of that target knowledge. Although any questions about the key concepts and main ideas of the course make helpful study materials, they are most effective when you know the kinds of questions that will be on the test. The best way to find out is to ask. "*Professor, what kinds of questions will be on the midterm exam? True/false? Multiple choice? Matching? Short answer? Essay? Word problems? Translations?*" Some instructors will tell you exactly what to expect. Others won't answer your question directly but may offer hints, provide sample questions, or even give you copies of past tests. Here are additional ways to generate test questions:

- Turn headings from your textbook into questions.

- Turn chapter learning objectives and/or summaries into questions.

- Find questions in your class notes that the instructor asked during class.

- Find concepts (circled) and main ideas (starred) in your textbook or class notes and turn them into questions.

- Make a list of key terms and turn them into questions.

- See if your textbook has practice problems either in the book or on a related website.

- Exchange possible test questions with study group members.

It's a great feeling to begin a test and find that you have practiced answering nearly every question on it.

9. Create flash cards (linear organizer). On one side of an index card, write a question that your instructor might ask on a test. On the back of the card, write the answer. Examples include a . . .

- question and its answer

- date and what happened on that date

- word and its definition

- graph and its meaning

- person's name and what he or she is noted for

- math problem and its solution

- quotation and who said it

Show your flash cards to your instructor or a tutor. Ask them to verify the appropriateness of the questions and the accuracy of the answers. Carry flash cards with you everywhere. Pull them out for a quick review whenever you have a few extra minutes. If you study them only twenty minutes per day, that's over two extra hours of studying each week. A number of free Internet sites allow you to create flash cards and even play games with the content. To find such a site, simply type "flash cards" into an Internet search engine. (Be cautious about using flash cards created by other students, as their answers may be incorrect.) Flash cards make valuable study materials in courses where you expect objective tests such as true/false, definitions, matching, multiple choice, fill in the blank, and some kinds of math problems. See examples of flash cards shown on the next page.

10. Create concept maps (graphic organizer). In Chapter 3, you learned how to take class notes using

Front

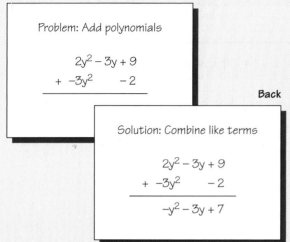

Back

Sample Problem-Solution Flash Cards

Front

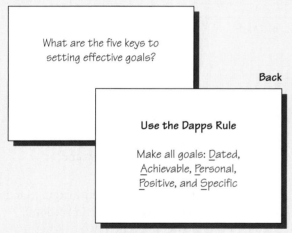

Back

Sample Question-and-Answer Flash Card
Source: From Carol Kanar, *The Confident Student,* Third Edition, p.353. Copyright © 1998 by Houghton Mifflin Company. Used by permission.

a concept map. Whether or not you choose to take class notes with concept maps, strongly consider them for creating study materials. You'll see an example of a concept map on page 98 and the steps for creating one on pages 96–97. Concept maps have a number of benefits when used as study materials. First, they clearly show the relationship among levels

of information (i.e., key concepts, main ideas, and supporting details). They aid learning by combining the left brain's verbal and analytical skills with the right brain's spatial and creative abilities. Concept maps are simple to expand, so you can easily add new information from various sources. And they are especially useful when preparing for an essay test or term paper.

11. Create three-column study charts for math (graphic organizer): If you took math notes using three-column charts (see page 134), you are well on your way toward **Organizing** helpful study materials for that course. If not, simply begin now by dividing blank pages into three columns and titling them: Problem, Solution, and Explanation. Now add one problem at the top of the left-hand column of each page; include problems representing different levels of difficulty:

- **Easy problems:** These could be problems your instructor solved in class that you immediately "got." These might be problems you correctly solved on a test or homework assignment. Or they could even be problems you initially did wrong but have since learned how to solve.

- **Challenging problems:** These might be problems that you got wrong on a test or homework assignment and still don't understand how to solve. Or they might be problems your instructor solved in class but continue to baffle you. Or, they could be sample problems you haven't tried to solve, but just looking at them, you doubt whether you can. These challenging practice problems could come from sources such as class notes, homework, tests, the tutoring center, or the website for your textbook.

Now do your best to solve each problem in the middle column, while writing explanations (e.g., directions, key terms, and rules) in the right-hand column. Because you are creating study materials, it is essential that you understand each step in the solution as well as its explanation. If you get stuck on a problem, set it

Problem	Solution	Explanation
Find an equation of the line with slope 4 that contains the point (2, −1).	Step 1: $y = 4x + b$	Substitute 4 for the "m" in $y = mx + b$; "m" is the slope.
	Step 2: $-1 = 4(2) + b$	Replace x with 2 and y with −1 in the equation.
	Step 3: $-1 = 8 + b$	In ordered pairs, the first value is for x, the second is for y.
	Step 4: $-9 = b$	Multiply to simplify.
	Step 5: Equation: $y = 4x - 9$	Solve for b by subtracting 8 from both sides.
	Step 6: $-1 = 4(2) - 9$ Is this true?	Replace the "b" with −9 in the equation $y = 4x + b$.
	Step 7: $-1 = 8 - 9$ YES	Check the answer by substituting the x and y values in the answer.

Figure 4.1 ▲ **Three-Column Study Chart for Math**

aside and save it. You'll learn how to deal with these challenging problems in Chapter 5. For now, include as many solved problems as you can. Figure 4.1 shows an example of a three-column study chart for math.

12. Create Cornell study sheets. Walter Pauk, an educator at Cornell University, devised a simple and helpful way to organize study materials. Cornell study sheets are very useful later on when you **Rehearse** and **Evaluate** the target knowledge, as you'll learn to do in Chapter 5. Here's how to construct one:

• Create a blank Cornell study sheet by drawing lines on notebook paper to create the three sections depicted in Figure 4.2. If working on a computer, use the table feature in your word processing program. Simply create a table with two rows and two columns. Drag the middle vertical line to the left to widen Section A and narrow Section B. Drag the middle horizontal line toward the bottom to lengthen Section A.

Then merge the bottom two columns to create Section C.

• In Section A, copy study materials you have already created, especially outlines and concept maps.

• Compose questions about the information found in Section A. Write each question in Section B alongside its answer in Section A.

• Circle or underline key concepts in Section A. Write each key concept in Section B alongside its definition or explanation in Section A.

• In Section C, write a summary of the key concepts, main ideas, and supporting details that appear in Section A.

See Figure 4.3 for an example of a completed Cornell study sheet. Note that Section A (the largest section) contains an informal outline that was created (as described in Strategy 7), polished, and then copied onto the study sheet.

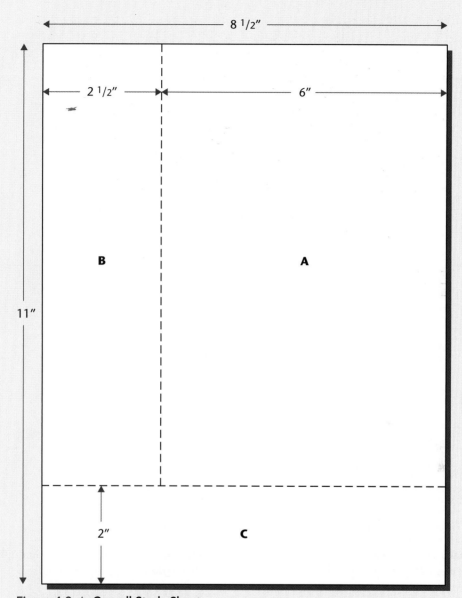

Figure 4.2 ▲ Cornell Study Sheet
Source: From Walter Pauk, *How to Study in College*, Sixth Edition, p. 205. Copyright © 1997 by Houghton Mifflin Company. Used by permission.

After Organizing Study Materials

13. Read more on the same subject. Are you having difficulty understanding the information in your notes? Consider **Collecting** more. Ask your instructor, tutor, or a librarian to suggest additional reading materials. Sometimes another author will express the same idea in a way that will flip a switch in your head and get your neurons firing. This extra information may clarify muddy areas or fill in gaps in your study materials. If you have difficulty understanding your textbook, look for a book on the same subject written for younger students. It may present the same information in a way that is easier to comprehend. After reading this simpler version, you can return to your study materials with an improved understanding.

	Course: Psychology 101
	Topic: Abraham Maslow
	Abraham Maslow (1908–1970)
	– Family immigrated to Brooklyn from Russia
	– One of seven children
	– Unhappy, neurotic child
What was the psychological	– Taught at Teachers College, Brooklyn College, Brandeis
movement that Maslow led?	– Sought to understand human motivations
When did he become leader	– Became leader of humanistic psychology movement of
of this movement?	the 1950s and 1960s.
What are the five levels of	Maslow's hierarch: theory of Human Motivation (like a pyramid)
motivation, according to	– Physical (the foundation)
Maslow's Hierarchy?	– Food, water, air, rest, health, exercise, etc.
What are examples of	– Safety needs
each level?	– Security, stability, shelter, freedom from fear
	– Social needs
	Love, belonging, connection, affiliation
	– Psychological needs
	– self-esteem, power, approval, recognition, confidence
Self-actualization	– Self-actualization (top of the pyramid)
	– Need to fulfill oneself, creation
	– Maslow: "To become everything that one is capable
	of becoming."
	Humanistic psychology
	– Maslow led the "Third Force" in psychology
	– Third Force—alternative to other approaches of psychology
How does humanistic	– Freudian psychoanalysis
psychology differ from	– Behaviorist psychology
Freudian and behavioral	– Stressed the power of a person to choose how to behave
psychology regarding	– Other approaches minimized the importance of conscious choice
"choice" in human behavior?	– Freudians: Choices controlled by childhood influences
	– Behaviorists: Choices controlled by conditioning
	– Appealed to the individualistic, rebellious college students
	of the 1960s
Abraham Maslow became the leader of the humanistic psychology movement in the 1950's and 60's. Unlike Freudian and behavioral psychologists, humanists believe people have the power to choose their own behaviors. Maslow is most noted for his efforts to identify forces that motivate human beings. His "hierarchy" proposes that some needs must be addressed before others. The most primary needs are physical (air, water, food). Next comes safety (freedom from fear, shelter from cold). Then social needs such as love and belonging. Next, psychological needs such as self-esteem, power, approval, recognition and confidence. Self-Actualization sits atop the pyramid of motivation.	

Figure 4.3 ▲ Cornell Study Sheet Completed Example

14. Get feedback on your study materials. Show them to classmates and study group members. Show them to a tutor. Show them to your instructor. Ask for their suggestions to improve the accuracy, completeness, and organization of your study materials.

15. Seek help. If you don't understand something you're studying or need more one-on-one explanations, make an appointment with your instructor. You can also go to the tutoring center on your campus to get assistance. If the first tutor you see isn't much help, ask for a different tutor the next time. Keep seeking help until you understand the information or skill well enough to create well-**Organized** study materials.

Studying Exercise

Interview successful students and ask for their favorite ways to create effective study materials. See if you can discover additional strategies not on the list presented here. However, be ready to hear that many students don't create study materials. Rather, they skip this step of learning and study directly from their unorganized class notes or textbook markings. Now you need never make this mistake again.

A note about Cornell study sheets: As mentioned in Chapter 3, many study skills books suggest writing all of your notes from reading assignments and class sessions directly on Cornell-formatted pages. This approach is usually called the "Cornell note-taking system." By contrast, I recommend that you take your reading and class notes on regular paper or a computer. Next, do three things to deep process the information you have **Collected**:

1. Polish your notes, making sure they are complete and accurate.

2. Condense your notes, identifying key concepts, ideas, and supporting details.

3. **Organize** the condensed notes, creating effective study materials (e.g., outlines, concept maps) that include information from *all* course materials.

Now, if you wish, copy your polished, condensed, and organized study materials onto a Cornell study sheet.

Here's why I urge you to wait to create Cornell study sheets until you have thoroughly processed your original notes. If you write your original notes on Cornell study sheets, you will be tempted to study from them without polishing, condensing, or **Organizing** the information. This means you will be skipping essential steps necessary for creating deep and lasting learning. But suppose you resist the temptation and you do polish, condense, and **Organize** the notes you took on Cornell-formatted pages. Now you'll need to write them on other pages anyway, so there was no real purpose for taking them on Cornell-formatted pages to begin with. Here's the bottom line: The best use for Cornell-formatted pages is for **Rehearsing** and **Evaluating** (not **Collecting**) what you are learning, and you will learn how to do this in Chapter 5.

Employing Interdependence

5

Once I accept responsibility for taking purposeful actions to achieve my goals and dreams, I then develop mutually supportive relationships that make the journey easier and more enjoyable.

I am giving and receiving help.

Successful Students . . .	Struggling Students . . .
develop mutually supportive relationships, recognizing that life is richer when giving to and receiving from others.	**remain dependent,** codependent, or independent in relation to others.
create a support network, using an interactive, team approach to success.	**work alone,** seldom cooperating with others for the common good of all.
strengthen relationships with active listening, showing their concern for the other person's thoughts and feelings.	**listen poorly,** demonstrating little desire to understand another person's perspective.

Case Study in Critical Thinking

Professor Rogers' Trial

Professor Rogers thought her Speech 101 students would enjoy role-playing a real court trial as their last speech for the semester. She also hoped the experience would teach them to work well in teams, a skill much sought after by employers. So, she divided her students into groups of six—a team of three defense attorneys and a team of three prosecuting attorneys—providing each group with court transcripts of a real murder case. Using evidence from the trial, each team would present closing arguments for the case, after which a jury of classmates would render a verdict. Each team was allowed a maximum of twenty-four minutes to present its case, and all three team members would receive the same grade.

After class, **Anthony** told his teammates, **Sylvia** and **Donald**, "We'll meet tomorrow at 4:00 in the library and plan a defense for this guy." Sylvia felt angry about Anthony's bossy tone, but she just nodded. Donald said, "Whatever," put headphones on, and strolled away singing louder than he probably realized.

"Look," Anthony said to Sylvia at 4:15 the next day, "we're not waiting for Donald any more. Here's what we'll do. You go first and take about ten minutes to prove that our defendant had no motive. I'll take the rest of the time to show how it could have been the victim's brother who shot him. I want an A out of this."

Sylvia was furious. "You can't just decide to leave Donald out. Plus, what about the defendant's fingerprints on the murder weapon! We have to dispute that evidence or we'll never win. I'll do that. And I'll go last so I can wrap up all the loose ends. I want to win this trial."

The defense team met twice more before the trial. Donald came to only one of the meetings and spent the entire time reading the case. He said he wasn't sure what he was going to say, but he'd have it figured out by the day of the trial. Anthony and Sylvia argued about which evidence was most important and who would speak last. At one point, the college librarian shushed them when Sylvia lost her temper and started shouting at Anthony that no one had elected him the leader.

The day before the trial, Anthony went to Professor Rogers. "It's not fair that my grade depends on my teammates. Donald couldn't care less what happens, and Sylvia is always looking for a fight. I'll present alone, but not with them."

"If you were an actual lawyer," Professor Rogers replied, "do you think you could go to the judge and complain that you aren't getting along with your partners? You'll have to figure out how to work as a team. The trial goes on as scheduled, and all three of you will get the same grade."

On the day of the trial, the three student prosecutors presented one seamless and persuasive closing argument. Then Anthony leapt up, saying, "I'll go first for my team." He spoke for twenty-one minutes, talking as fast as he could to present the entire case, including an explanation of how the defendant's fingerprints had gotten on the murder weapon. Sylvia, greatly flustered, followed with a seven-minute presentation in which she also explained how the defendant's fingerprints had gotten on the murder weapon. At that point, Professor Rogers announced that the defense was already four minutes over their time limit. Donald promised to be brief. He assured the jury that the defendant was innocent and then read three unconnected passages from the transcript as "proof." His presentation took seventy-five seconds. The jury deliberated for five minutes and unanimously found the defendant guilty. Professor Rogers gave all members of the defense team a D for their speeches.

Listed below are the characters in this story. Rank them in the order of their responsibility for the group's grade of D. Give a different score to each character. Be prepared to explain your answer.

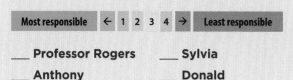

Most responsible   ← 1 2 3 4 →   **Least responsible**

___ **Professor Rogers**   ___ **Sylvia**
___ **Anthony**   ___ **Donald**

DIVING DEEPER Imagine that you have been assigned to a group project in one of your college courses and that the student whom you scored above as most responsible for the group's grade of D (Anthony, Sylvia, or Donald) is in your group. What positive actions could you take to help your group be a success despite this person?

Developing Mutually Supportive Relationships

 FOCUS QUESTION How could you make accomplishing your success a little easier and a lot more fun?

One semester, in the eleventh week, Martha made an announcement. "This is the last time I'll be in class. I'm withdrawing from college. I just wanted to say how much I'll miss you all."

A concerned silence followed Martha's announcement. Her quiet, solid presence had made her a favorite with classmates.

"My babysitter just moved," Martha explained, "and I've been trying to find someone I trust to look after my one-year-old . . . with no luck. My husband took his vacation this week to take care of her, but he has to go back to work. I have to drop out of school to be with my baby. Don't worry," she added weakly, "I'll be back next semester. Really, I will."

"But there are only a few more weeks in the semester. You can't drop out now!" someone said. Martha merely shrugged her shoulders, clearly defeated.

Then one of the other women in the class said, "My kids are grown and out of the house, and this is the only class I'm taking this semester. I'd be willing to watch your child for the next few weeks if that would help you get through the semester. The only thing is, you'll need to bring your baby to my house because I don't have a car."

"I don't have a car either," Martha said. "Thanks anyway."

"Wait a minute," a young man in the class said. "Not so fast. Aren't we learning that we're all in this together? I have a car. I'll drive you and your child back and forth until the semester's over."

Martha sat for a moment, stunned. "Really? You'd do that for me?" In three minutes Martha's fate had changed from dropping out of school to finishing her courses with the help of two classmates.

No man is an island, entire of itself; every man is a piece of the continent, a part of the main.

John Donne

Nobody but nobody can make it out here alone.

Maya Angelou

All of us decide whether we'll go for our dreams alone or if we'll seek and accept assistance from others along the way. In Western culture we often glorify the solitary hero, the strong individual who stands alone against all odds. This script makes good cinema, but does it help us stay on course to our dreams?

After all, who of us actually goes unaided by others? We eat food grown *by others*. We wear clothes sewn *by others*. We live in houses built *by others*. We work at businesses owned *by others*. And so it goes.

We are all interdependent. Do things for others—tribe, family, community—rather than just for yourself.

Chief Wilma Mankiller

Ways to Relate

When it comes to relating to others, we generally choose one of four paths, depending on the beliefs we hold about ourselves and other people:

- When I believe, *I can't achieve my goals by myself*, I choose **dependence.**
- When I believe, *I have to help other people get their goals before I can pursue my own goals*, I choose **codependence.**
- When I believe, *By working hard, I can get some of what I want all by myself*, I choose **independence.**
- When I believe, *I know I can get some of what I want by working alone, but I'll accomplish more and have more fun if I give and receive help*, I choose **interdependence.**

Which belief do you hold? More important, which belief will best help you stay on course to your goals and dreams?

A Sign of Maturity

Moving from dependence or codependence to independence is a major step toward maturity. However, Creators know that life can be easier and more enjoyable when people cooperate. They know that moving from independence to *inter*dependence demonstrates the greatest maturity of all.

Interdependent students maximize their results in college by seeking assistance from instructors, study partners, librarians, academic advisors, counselors, community services, and family members. Interdependent students know that it's a lot easier getting to graduation with a supportive team than it is by themselves.

Don't be fooled into thinking you are alone on your journey. You're not. Your struggle is everyone's struggle. Your pain is everyone's pain. Your power is everyone's power. It is simply that we take different paths along our collective journey toward the same destination.

Benjamin Shield

Interdependence will help you stay on course in college and support your success in ways you can't even imagine now. A friend of mine who buys old houses, remodels them, and resells them for a tidy profit ran into difficult times. His renovated houses weren't selling, he was short of money to begin new projects, and bankers were unwilling to lend him additional money. Creditors began to harass him, and for a few weeks he considered declaring bankruptcy. Then he created an ingenious plan to raise capital: He asked friends to contribute money to his "investment fund," agreeing to pay them higher interest rates than banks were paying at the time. Within two weeks, he had accumulated enough money not only to sustain himself until his properties sold, but also to buy two new houses to remodel. With the help of friends, he was back in business.

Among the most destructive relationships are those based on codependence. Codependent people are motivated not by their own successes, but by someone else's approval or dependence upon them. *I am worthwhile*, the codependent believes, *only if someone else can't get along without me.* Codependent people abandon their own dreams and even endure abuse to keep the approval of others.

John was a bright fellow who had been in college for seven years without graduating. During a class discussion, he related an experience that he said was typical of him: He had been studying for a midterm test in history when a friend called and asked for help with a test in biology, a course John had already passed. John set aside his own studies and spent the evening tutoring his friend. The next day John failed his history exam. In his journal, he wrote, "I've learned that in order to be successful, I need to make my dreams more important than other people's approval. I have to learn to say 'no.'" Codependent people like John often spend time in Quadrant III, engaged in activities that are urgent to someone else but unimportant to their own goals and dreams.

With codependence, dependence, and independence, giving and receiving are out of balance. The codependent person *gives* too much. The dependent person *takes* too much. The independent person seldom gives or receives. By contrast, the interdependent person finds a healthy balance of giving and receiving, and everyone benefits. That's why building mutually supportive relationships is one of the most important Quadrant II behaviors you'll ever undertake.

> Taking on responsibilities that properly belong to someone else means behaving irresponsibly toward oneself.
>
> *Nathaniel Branden*

Giving and Receiving

A story is told of a man who prayed to know the difference between heaven and hell. An angel came to take the man to see for himself. In hell, the man saw a huge banquet table overflowing with beautifully prepared meats, vegetables, drinks, and desserts. Despite this bounty, the prisoners of hell had withered, sunken looks. Then the man saw why. The poor souls in hell could pick up all the food they wanted, but their elbows would not bend, so they could not place the food into their mouths. Living amidst all that abundance, the citizens of hell were starving.

Then the angel whisked the man to heaven, where he saw another endless banquet table heaped with a similar bounty of splendid food. Amazingly, just as in hell, the citizens of heaven could not bend their elbows to feed themselves.

"I don't understand," the man said. "Is heaven the same as hell?"

The angel only pointed. The residents of heaven were healthy, laughing, and obviously happy as they sat together at the banquet tables. Then the man saw the difference.

The citizens of heaven were feeding each other.

> Surround yourself with only people who are going to lift you higher.
>
> *Oprah Winfrey*

> No matter what accomplishments
> you make, somebody helps you.
>
> *Althea Gibson Darben*

JOURNAL ENTRY 16

In this activity, you will explore your beliefs and behaviors regarding giving and receiving.

1. Write and complete the following ten sentence stems:

1. A specific situation when someone assisted me was . . .
2. A specific situation when I assisted someone else was . . .
3. A specific situation when I made assisting someone else more important than my own success and happiness was . . .
4. When someone asks me for assistance I usually feel . . .
5. When I think of asking someone else for assistance I usually feel . . .
6. What usually gets in the way of my asking for help is . . .
7. If I often asked other people for assistance . . .
8. If I joyfully gave assistance to others . . .
9. If I gratefully accepted assistance from others . . .
10. One goal that I could use assistance with today is . . .

2. Write about what you discovered by completing the sentence stems in Step 1: Is your typical relationship to others (1) dependent, (2) codependent, (3) independent, or (4) interdependent? Describe how you have most often related to others in the past and how you intend to relate to others in the future.

Remember, to squeeze the most learning from your effort, dive deep!

One Student's Story

Jason Matthew Loden
Avila University, Missouri

During my first semester in college, I struggled in my Calculus class. I didn't understand anything my instructor taught, and his mathematical terms bounced off me like a foreign language. I dreaded going to class and frequently zoned out when I did. After class, I attempted to teach myself the material, but I couldn't understand the confusing terms. I started turning in my homework late and incomplete, and my first two test grades were in the low sixties. I knew I needed help, but I was too independent to admit it.

One day, in my freshman seminar class, my instructor began discussing independent individuals. He informed us that it takes a strong person to be independent, but what he went on to say hit me like a brick: "It takes a stronger individual to be *inter*dependent." I stared at him for a while, pondering his last few words. That night, I cracked open the *On Course* textbook and began to read through Chapter 5. It stressed that people who are interdependent (rely on others as well as themselves) are happier and have greater success in life than those who are independent (rely only on themselves). Persuaded by the readings, I met with my Calculus instructor and arranged twice-a-week tutoring sessions. I also formed a calculus study group with my friends Joey and Amy, and we began meeting every Friday.

At the beginning of each tutoring session, my instructor gave me a quiz. Then we would focus on one specific element of calculus, such as derivatives as they relate to velocity. In my study group, we dove into our homework, sharing our answers along with the processes we used to solve them. At first, I was very frustrated, but after a month of hard work and interdependent studying, I started to grasp the whole idea of calculus. By the end of the semester, I had become a Quadrant II student in calculus. I no longer worried about my homework or stressed over class because I prepared a little each day with the help of my instructor and friends. My grade steadily improved throughout the semester, leading to a fabulous 94 on my final, which allowed me to achieve an A for the course. Before this experience, I knew that I had a good chance of success in life as an independent individual. Now that I know the power of a support group, there's no stopping me!

Creating a Support Network

FOCUS QUESTION How could you create and sustain an effective support network to help achieve your greatest dreams in college and in life?

For solving most problems, ten brains are better than one and twenty hands are better than two. Although Victims typically struggle alone, Creators know the incredible power of a network of mutually supportive people.

This ingredient of success has been called **OPB: Other People's Brains** or **Other People's Brawn.** The Internet has provided an explosion of networking that makes possible the opportunity to benefit from the wisdom of people you will likely never meet. Companies such as InnoCentive create opportu-

> I not only use all the brains that I have, but all that I can borrow.
>
> *Woodrow Wilson*

nities for Seekers (businesses and organizations with problems) to find Solvers (people with possible solutions). For example, a chemist in Bloomington, Illinois, solved a problem for the Oil Spill Recovery Institute located thousands of miles away in Alaska. The problem was how to keep oil in Alaskan storage tanks from freezing, and the solution was the same as how to keep concrete from setting up before being used: Keep them both vibrating.

Like the Internet, college provides a great place to develop the skill of using OPB to achieve maximum success. Let's consider some choices you could make to create a support network, one that will help you not only achieve your goals in college but enjoy the experience as well.

Seek Help from Your Instructors

Building positive relationships with your college instructors is a powerful Quadrant II action that can pay off handsomely. Your instructors have years of specialized training. You've already paid for their help with your tuition, and all you have to do is ask.

Find out your professors' office hours and make appointments. Arrive prepared with questions or requests, and you'll likely get very good help. As a bonus, by getting to know your instructors, you may find a mentor who will help you in college and beyond.

> My driving belief is this: great teamwork is the only way to reach our ultimate moments, to create the breakthroughs that define our careers, to fulfill our lives with a sense of lasting significance.
>
> *Pat Riley, professional basketball coach*

Get Help from College Resources

Nearly every college spends a chunk of tuition money to provide support services for students, but these services go to waste unless you use them. Do you know what support services your college offers, where they are, and how to use them?

CONFUSED ABOUT FUTURE COURSES TO TAKE? Get help from your advisor or someone in the counseling center. They can help you decide on a major and create an academic plan that includes all of your required courses and their prerequisites.

ACADEMIC PROBLEMS? Get help at one of your college's tutoring labs. Many colleges have a writing lab, a reading lab, and a math lab. Other sources of academic assistance might include a science learning center or a computer lab. Your college may also have a diagnostician who tests students for learning disabilities and suggests ways of overcoming them.

MONEY PROBLEMS? Get help from your college's financial aid office. Money is available in grants and scholarships (which you don't pay back), loans (which you do pay back, usually at low interest rates), and student work programs (which offer jobs on campus). Your college may also have a service that can locate an off-campus job, perhaps one in the very career field you want to enter after graduation. In Chapter 8, you'll find detailed information about addressing your money problems (see pages 271–278).

PERSONAL PROBLEMS? Get help from your college's counseling office. Trained counselors are available at many colleges to help students through times of emotional upset. It's not unusual for students to experience some sort of personal difficulty during college; Creators seek assistance.

HEALTH PROBLEMS? Get aid from your college's health service. Many colleges have doctors who see students at little or no cost. Health-related products may be available inexpensively or even for free. Your college may even offer special health insurance for students.

> Alone we can do so little; together we can do so much.
> *Helen Keller*

PROBLEMS DECIDING ON A CAREER? Get help from your college's career office. There you can take aptitude tests, discover job opportunities, learn to write or improve your résumé, and practice effective interviewing skills.

PROBLEMS GETTING INVOLVED SOCIALLY AT YOUR COLLEGE? Request assistance from your college's student activities office. Here you'll discover athletic teams, trips, choirs, dances, service projects, student professional organizations, the college newspaper and literary magazine, clubs, and more, just waiting for you to get involved.

Create a Project Team

If you're tackling a big project, why not create a team to help? A project team accomplishes one particular task. In business, when a project needs attention, an ad hoc committee is formed. *Ad hoc* in Latin means "toward this." In other words, an ad hoc committee comes together for the sole purpose of solving one problem. Once the task is complete, the committee disbands.

One of my students created a project team to help her move. More than a dozen classmates volunteered, including a fellow who provided a truck. In one Saturday morning, the team packed and delivered her possessions to a new apartment.

What big project do you have that would benefit from the assistance of a group? The only barrier standing between you and a project team is your willingness to ask for help.

> To reach your goals you need to become a team player.
> *Zig Ziglar*

Start a Study Group

In the late 1970s and early 1980s, mathematics graduate student Uri Treisman at the University of California, Berkeley, showed the value of academic study groups. He had noticed that students who succeeded in calculus met outside of class and, among other things, talked about solving math problems. Struggling students didn't. As a result of this observation, Treisman created a program for struggling calculus students. His approach encouraged these students to gather for the purpose of talking about mathematics and solving challenging problems. The program was so successful that it has since been offered at many other colleges and universities. You can create a variation of Triesman's program in any course you want. Simply start a study group with some of your classmates. A study group differs from a project team in two ways. First, a study group is created to help everyone on the team excel in a particular course. Second, a study group meets many times throughout a semester. In fact, some study groups are so helpful that their members stay together throughout college.

Study groups offer a number of benefits. Participation increases your active involvement with the course content, which in turn leads to deeper learning and higher grades. The resulting academic success raises your expectations for success and increases your level of motivation. Study group participation helps you develop the skill of working with a group, a skill much sought after by employers. And some study group members may become your lifelong friends. Here are three suggestions for maximizing the value of your study group:

> Love thy neighbor as thyself, but choose your neighborhood.
>
> *Louise Beal*

1. **Choose only Creators.** As the semester begins, make a list of potential study group members: classmates who attend regularly, come prepared, and participate actively. Also watch for that quiet student who doesn't say much but whose occasional comments reveal a special understanding of the subject. After the first test or essay, find out how the students on your list performed and invite three or four of the most successful to study with you.

2. **Choose group goals.** Regardless of potential, a study group is only as effective as you make it. Everyone should agree upon common goals. You might say to prospective study group members, "My goal in our math class is to master the subject and earn an A. Is that what you want, too?" Team up with students whose goals match or exceed your own.

3. **Choose group rules.** The last step is establishing team rules. Pat Riley, one of the most successful professional basketball coaches ever, had his players create a "team covenant." Before the season, they agreed on the rules they would follow to stay on course to their goal of a championship. Your team should do the same. Decide where, how often, and what time you'll meet. Most important, agree on what will happen during the meetings. Many study groups fail because they turn into social gatherings. Yours will succeed if you adopt rules like these:

> If people around you aren't going anywhere, if their dreams are no bigger than hanging out on the corner, or if they're dragging you down, get rid of them. Negative people can sap your energy so fast, and they can take your dreams away from you, too.
>
> *Earvin (Magic) Johnson*

   Rule 1: *We meet in the library every Thursday afternoon from one o'clock to three o'clock.*

   Rule 2: *All members bring their favorite study materials, including twenty new questions with answers and sources (e.g., textbook page or class notes).*

   Rule 3: *All study materials are discussed and all written questions are asked, answered, and understood before any socializing.*

One student I know took this advice and started a study group in his anatomy and physiology class, a course with a notoriously high failure rate. At the end of the semester, he proudly showed me a thank-you card signed by the other four members of his group. "We couldn't have done it without you," they wrote. "Thanks for *making* us get together!" Defying the odds, everyone in the group had passed the course.

Whom you spend time with will dramatically affect your outcomes and experiences in college. If you hang out with people who place little value on learning or a college degree, it's challenging to resist their negative influence. However, if you associate with highly committed, hard-working students, their encouragement can motivate you to stay on course to graduation even when the road gets rough. One of my students actually moved to a new apartment when he realized that "friends" from his old neighborhood spent most of their time putting down his efforts to get a college degree. When it comes to selecting your "group" in college, be sure to choose people who want out of life what you do.

Many people collaborate only with others who are like them. One of the greatest benefits of your college experience is meeting people of diverse backgrounds, with different ideas, skills, experiences, abilities, and resources. Be sure to network with those who are older or younger than you, who are from different states or countries, who are of different races or cultures, and who have different religions or political preferences. Exposure to such differences will expand your horizons and enhance your life.

© Estate of Ed Arno

Start a contact list of the people you meet in college. You might even want to write a few notes about them: their major or career field, names of family members, hobbies, interests, and especially their strengths. Keep in touch with these people during and after college.

Creators develop mutually supportive relationships in college that continue to support them for years—even for a lifetime. Don't get so bogged down with the daily demands of college that you fail to create an empowering support network.

Until recently, the "old girls" did not know how the "old boys" network operated .... Women now know that, besides hard work and lots of skill, the move to the top requires a supportive network.

June E. Gabler

JOURNAL ENTRY | 17

In this activity, you will explore the creation of a support network. Afterward, you may decide to start networking more, using OPB to help you achieve your greatest goals and dreams.

> Individually, we are one drop. Together, we are an ocean.
>
> *Ryunosuke Satoro*

1. Write and complete the following sentence stems:

1. An outer obstacle that stands between me and my success in college is . . . (Examples might be a lack of time to study or a teacher you don't understand.)

2. Someone besides me who could help me overcome this outer obstacle is . . .

3. How this person could help me is by . . .

4. An inner obstacle that stands between me and my success in college is . . . (Examples might be shyness or a tendency to procrastinate.)

5. Someone besides me who could help me overcome this inner obstacle is . . .

6. How this person could help me is by . . .

7. The most challenging course I'm taking in college this semester is . . .

8. This course is challenging for me because . . .

9. Someone besides me who could help me overcome this challenge is . . .

10. How this person could help me is by . . .

2. Write about two (or more) choices you could make to create a stronger support network for yourself in college. Consider the choices you could make to overcome the challenges and obstacles to your success that you identified in Step 1. Consider also any resistance you may have about taking steps to create a support network. Dive deep as you explore each choice fully.

One Student's Story

Neal Benjamin

Barton County Community College, Kansas

In the first semester in my freshman year, one of the most challenging things for me was my sociology class. It was a lecture class, and all the teacher did was talk for the whole hour while we took notes. I wasn't used to that way of learning, and from the first day most of it went right over my head. In high school, teachers usually gave us some leeway on assignments and tests, but my sociology instructor expected everything explained in depth. After I did horribly on the first test, I went to see the teacher during his office hours to get some help.

He gave me some ideas about how to study for his class, and then he suggested that I meet with some other students in the class who were getting it. I hadn't been in a study group before, but it made sense to study with people in my class who understood sociology better than I did. There were three of us, a girl who knew about as much as I did and a guy who really understood the class. When we ran into each other in the library, we'd meet to get ready for the next test. The guy in our group would ask questions about what the teacher went over to see how much we already knew. Then he would explain what we didn't know. I felt that I was getting a better understanding of the class and my test scores started to improve little by little.

I wound up getting a C in sociology, but without my study group I probably would have gotten a D or an F. Next semester, I'm going to join a study group for my hardest subjects, but this time I'm going to use more of what I learned from my experience with the sociology study group and also from the *On Course* book in my student success seminar. I'll start the study group earlier in the semester before I fall behind. I think a study group should be made up of people you know and get along with so there aren't problems that get you away from studying. I'll also make sure that my next group is a little more organized, with scheduled times to meet. And finally, we'll have a plan of what we're going to do so we won't meet for a long time without accomplishing anything. It's good to talk to a teacher, but sometimes you need another student to explain ideas in layman's terms so you can really understand them.

Strengthening Relationships with Active Listening

 FOCUS QUESTIONS Do you know how to strengthen a relationship with active listening? What are the essential skills of being a good listener?

Once we have begun a mutually supportive relationship, we naturally want the relationship to grow. Books on relationships abound, suggesting untold ways to strengthen a relationship. At the heart of all of these suggestions is a theme: We must show that we value the other person professionally, personally, or both.

Many ways exist to demonstrate another's value to us. Some of the most powerful methods include keeping promises, giving honest appreciation and approval, resolving conflicts so that both people win, staying in touch, and speaking well

> When people talk, listen completely. Most people never listen.
>
> *Ernest Hemingway*

of someone when talking to others. However, for demonstrating the high esteem with which you value another person, there may be no better way than active listening.

Few people are truly good listeners. Too often, we're thinking what we want to say next. Or our thoughts dash off to our own problems, and we ignore what the other person is saying. Or we hear what we *thought* the person was going to say rather than what he actually said.

Good listeners, by contrast, clear their minds and listen for the entire message, including words, tone of voice, gestures, and facial expressions. No matter how well one person communicates, unless someone else listens actively, both the communication and the relationship are likely to go astray. Imagine the potential problems created if good listening skills are absent when an instructor says to a class, "I need to change the date of the final exam from Monday to the previous Friday. I just found out that I need to turn in my final grades on Monday." Suppose a student assumes that the instructor said the exam will be moved to the *following* Friday (instead of the *previous* Friday). When that student shows up on the "following" Friday, not only will the exam be long over, but the instructor will have turned in the final course grades as well. Talk about an unpleasant surprise!

Listening actively means accepting 100 percent responsibility for receiving the same message that the speaker sent, uncontaminated by your own thoughts or feelings. That's why active listening begins with empathy, the ability to understand the other person as if, for that moment, you *are* the other person. To empathize doesn't mean that you necessarily agree. Empathy means understanding what the other person is thinking and feeling. And you actively reveal this understanding.

With active listening, you send this message: *I value you so much that I am doing my very best to see the world through your eyes.*

How to Listen Actively

Active listening is a learned skill. You will become an excellent listener if you master the following four steps:

STEP 1: LISTEN TO UNDERSTAND. Listening isn't effective when you're simply waiting for the first opportunity to insert your own opinion. Instead, focus fully on the speaker, activate your empathy, and listen with the intention of fully understanding what the other person thinks and feels.

STEP 2: CLEAR YOUR MIND AND REMAIN SILENT. Don't be distracted by judgmental chatter from your Inner Critic and Inner Defender. Clear your mind, stay focused, and be quiet. Let your mind listen for thoughts. Let your heart listen for the undercurrent of emotions. Let your intuition listen for a deeper message hidden beneath the words. Let your companion know that you are actively listening. Sit forward. Nod your head when appropriate. Offer verbal feedback that shows you are actively listening: "Mmmmm . . . I see . . . Uh huh . . . "

> For the lack of listening, billions of losses accumulate: retyped letters, rescheduled appointments, rerouted shipments, breakdowns in labor management relations, misunderstood sales presentations, and job interviews that never really get off the ground.
>
> *Michael Ray & Rochelle Myers*

> Active listening, sometimes called reflective listening, involves giving verbal feedback of the content of what was said or done along with a guess at the feeling underneath the spoken words or acts.
>
> *Muriel James & Dorothy Jongeward*

STEP 3: ASK THE PERSON TO EXPAND OR CLARIFY. Don't make assumptions or fill in the blanks with your own experience. Invite the speaker to share additional information and feelings.

- *Tell me more about that.*
- *Could you give me an example?*
- *Can you explain that in a different way?*
- *How did you feel when that happened?*
- *What happened next?*

STEP 4: REFLECT THE OTHER PERSON'S THOUGHTS AND FEELINGS. Don't assume you understand. In your own words, restate what you heard, both the ideas and the emotions. Then verify the accuracy of your understanding.

- To a classmate: *Sounds like you're really angry about the instructor's feedback on your research paper. To you, his comments seem more sarcastic than helpful. Is that it?*
- To a professor: *I want to be clear about the new date for the final exam. You're postponing the exam from Monday to the following Friday. Have I got it right?*

Notice that reflecting adds nothing new to the conversation. Don't offer advice or tell your own experience. Your goal is merely to understand.

Use Active Listening in Your College Classes

Active listening not only strengthens relationships with people, it strengthens our understanding of new concepts and helps us learn. In class, successful students clear their minds and prepare to hear something of value. They reflect the instructor's ideas, confirming the accuracy of what they heard. When confused, they ask the instructor to expand or clarify, either in class or during the instructor's conference hours. As Creators, these students actively listen to understand. And, ultimately, they record their understanding in their notes. Obviously, the more accurate the information is in your class notes, the more you will learn when studying.

So, choose today to master active listening. You'll be amazed at how much this choice will improve your relationships, your learning, and your life.

> If I were to summarize in one sentence the single most important principle I have learned in the field of interpersonal relations, it would be this: Seek first to understand, then to be understood.
>
> *Stephen Covey*

> What few people realize is that failure to be a good listener prevents us from hearing and retaining vital information, becoming a roadblock to personal and professional success.
>
> *Jean Marie Stine*

If there is any one secret of success, it lies in the ability to get the other person's point of view and see things from his angle as well as your own.

Henry Ford

JOURNAL ENTRY | **18**

In this activity, you will practice the skill of active listening by writing out a conversation with your Inner Guide. As discussed earlier, thoughts are dashing through our minds much of the time. Writing a conversation with your Inner Guide applies this knowledge in a new and powerful way. First, it helps us become more aware of the thoughts that are guiding our choices. Second, writing this conversation encourages us to sort through confusion and find a positive solution. Third, it reminds us that we are not our thoughts and we can change them when doing so would benefit us. And, finally, writing this conversation with our Inner Guide gives us practice with an important mental skill used by highly intelligent and adaptive people: *metacognition*. Metacognition is the skill of thinking about our thinking. Developing metacognition helps us see where our thinking is flawed. It allows us to change our thinking to achieve better outcomes and experiences. If you've ever talked out loud to yourself while working on a problem, you were probably using metacognition. You may find writing this dialogue to be a new (and perhaps unusual) experience. However, the more you practice, the more you'll see what a valuable success skill it is to have a conversation with yourself as an active listener. And, of course, becoming an active listener with others will strengthen those relationships immeasurably.

Dr. Eliot's listening was not mere silence, but a form of activity. Sitting very erect on the end of his spine with hands joined in his lap, making no movement except that he revolved his thumbs around each other faster or slower, he faced his interlocutor and seemed to be hearing with his eyes as well as his ears. He listened with his mind and attentively considered what you had to say while you said it . . . . At the end of an interview the person who had talked to him felt that he had his say.

*Henry James about
Charles W. Eliot, former
president of Harvard University*

1. Write a conversation between you (ME) and your Inner Guide (IG) about a problem you are facing in college. Label each of your IG's responses with the listening skill it uses: silence, expansion, clarification, reflection (be sure to reflect feelings as well as thoughts). Let your IG demonstrate the skills of active listening without giving advice.

Here's an example of such a conversation:

ME: I've been realizing what a difficult time I have asking for assistance.

IG: Would you like to say more about that? **(Expansion)**

ME: Well, I've been having trouble in math. I know I should be asking more questions in class, but . . . I don't know, I guess I feel dumb because I can't do the problems myself.

IG: You seem frustrated that you can't solve the math problems without help. **(Reflection)**

ME: That's right. I've always resisted that sort of thing.

IG: What do you mean by "that sort of thing"? **(Clarification)**

ME: I mean that ever since I can remember, I've had to do everything on my own. When I was a kid, I used to play alone all the time.

IG: Uh-huh . . . **(Silence)**

ME: As a kid, I never had anyone to help me. And I don't have anyone to help me now.

➡

JOURNAL ENTRY | **18** | *continued*

IG: So, no one is available to help you? Is that how it seems? **(Reflection)**

ME: Well, I guess I could ask Robert for help. He seems really good in math, but I'm kind of scared to ask him.

IG: What scares you about asking him? **(Expansion)** . . . etc.

Imagine that the conversation you create here is taking place over the phone. Don't hang up until you've addressed all aspects of the problem and know what your next action step will be. Let your Inner Guide demonstrate how much it values you by being a great listener.

2. **Write what you learned or relearned about active listening during this conversation with your Inner Guide.** Remember to dive deep to discover a powerful insight. When you think you have written all you can, see if you can write at least one more paragraph.

Interdependence AT WORK

Over 90 percent of us who work for a living do so in organizations, and the ability to function effectively as a member of a team is usually an imperative of success. *Nathaniel Branden, psychologist*

You may have noticed that many employment ads say, "Looking for a team player" or "Must relate well to others." Few abilities have more impact on your success at work than your ability to interact well with supervisors, peers, subordinates, suppliers, and customers. And enhancing this ability starts now.

Creators Wanted!

Candidates must demonstrate interdependence, a team-orientation, and a strong ability to work cooperatively with others.

Someday you'll probably ask a former professor or employer to write you a letter of recommendation. What they write on that future day will depend on the relationships you're building with them now. Are you someone who works well with others? Someone who completes assignments and does them with excellence? Attends classes regularly and on time? Is respectful of others? Self-aware? Responsible? A former student called me with a request that I write her a recommendation. After much thought, I said no. Based on her performance in my class, I could not honestly write anything that would help her chances of getting hired. Sadly, when she was "blowing off" my course, she hadn't anticipated the day when she would need me to speak well of her to a potential employer.

In the work world, most people must interact well with others to keep their jobs or to advance. In college, one way to continue developing effective interdependence is by participating actively in study groups. Learning to work collaboratively now will contribute to your success tomorrow (not to mention that your grades will likely be higher).

PERSONAL SKILLS for CAREER SUCCESS TURN RIGHT

Interdependence
AT WORK

As you begin a search for your ideal job, one of the best sources of information about what a career is *really* like is someone who is doing it now. By conducting information-gathering interviews with enough people who are working in your chosen profession, you'll learn about qualifications, employment outlook, work conditions, and salaries. If you don't know anyone in the career of your choice, be a Creator and ask people you know for referrals. If that fails, try the Yellow Pages. Call a company you find there, ask for the Public Information Office, and explain the information you're seeking. Besides the information you may uncover, who knows who might be impressed with your professional approach to job hunting!

The same information-gathering strategy is helpful when it comes to learning important information about a particular employer you may be considering. Talk to people who work at the company and find out from the inside what it's really like. For example, if you find the company's mission statement appealing, ask employees if the company backs up those words with actions. Of course, it's important to talk to a number of people to avoid being swayed by one or two biased opinions.

Many people limit their job search to employment agencies and advertised positions, jobs listed in the "visible" marketplace. However, some career specialists estimate that as many as 85 to 90 percent of the available jobs are unlisted and found only by uncovering them in the "invisible" marketplace. Creators discover these unpublished openings by networking. Do that by seeking informational interviews with possible employers, and ask them if they know of others who might have a job for which you'd qualify. Additionally, you can ask friends and acquaintances if they know of positions that are available where they work. Ask professors if they've heard of job openings. Ask at church and club meetings. Ask all of these folks to spread the word that you're looking for a position. You never know who might help you discover an opening that would be ideal for you. A great job might become visible only because you asked a friend who asked a coworker who asked his sister who asked her boss who said, "Sure, we've got a job like that. Have the person call me."

Another great strategy during a job search is to develop a support group, especially one made up of other job seekers. Support groups not only provide emotional support when disappointments (and your Inner Critic) strike, they can also give you helpful suggestions and practice at essential skills. For example, support groups can critique your résumé and cover letters. They can help you practice your interviewing skills. Someone in your support group may share an experience that can teach you a valuable lesson. For instance, if someone reports going blank when an interviewer asked, "Do you have any questions for me?" you'll learn to prepare questions to ask at your own interviews.

Okay, let's say you've gotten your dream position in the company you wanted. Teamwork continues to have a big impact on

EMPLOY TEAMWORK

your work life. The *Harvard Business Review* reported a study that discovered why some scientists at Bell Labs in New Jersey were considered "stars" by their colleagues. Interestingly, the stars had done no better academically than their less successful colleagues. In fact, the study found that the stars and their coworkers were very similar when measured on IQ and personality tests. What distinguished the stars was their strong networks of important colleagues. When problems struck, the stars always had someone to call on for advice, and their requests for help were responded to quickly. Interdependence transformed good scientists into stars.

I once asked a very successful investment banker (he retired at the age of thirty-five) how important networking was in his profession. "Well, there's networking up here," he said, holding his hand as high in the air as he could reach, "and then there's everything else down here." He dropped his hand to within inches of the floor. "In this business, you either build relationships or you fail."

One last suggestion about interdependence could apply anywhere on your career path, but is particularly important once you are in your job: Find a mentor. A mentor is someone further along in his or her career development and willing to guide and help newer employees like you. Keep your eyes open for someone successful whose qualities you admire. You can create an informal mentoring relationship by making choices that put you into frequent contact with this person, or you can create a formal relationship by actually asking the person to be your mentor. With the wisdom of experience, a mentor can help keep you on course to career success.

▸ *Believing in Yourself*
Be Assertive

 FOCUS QUESTION How can you communicate in a style that strengthens relationships, creates better results, and builds strong self-esteem?

On rare occasions, we may encounter someone who doesn't want us to achieve our goals and dreams. Much more often, though, we run across folks who are too busy, too preoccupied, or couldn't care less about helping us. Meeting such people is especially likely in a bureaucracy such as a college or university. How we communicate our desires to them has a profound impact not only on the quality of the relationships and results we create, but on our self-esteem as well.

According to family therapist Virginia Satir, the two most common patterns of ineffective communication are **placating** and **blaming.** Both perpetuate low self-esteem.

- **Placating.** Victims who placate are dominated by their Inner Critic. They place themselves below others, protecting themselves from the sting of criticism and rejection by saying whatever they think will gain approval.

> Once a human being has arrived on this earth, communication is the largest single factor determining what kinds of relationships she or he makes with others and what happens to each in the world.
>
> *Virginia Satir*

Picture placators on their knees, looking up with a pained smile, nodding and agreeing on the outside, while fearfully hiding their true thoughts and feelings within. "*Please, please approve of me,*" they beg as their own Inner Critic judges them unworthy. To gain this approval, placators often spend time in Quadrant III doing what is urgent to others but unimportant to their own goals and dreams. Satir estimated that about 50 percent of people use placating as their major communication style.

Learning to perceive the truth within ourselves and speak it clearly to others is a delicate skill, certainly as complex as multiplication or long division, but very little time is spent on it in school.

Gay & Kathlyn Hendricks

- **Blaming.** Victims who blame are dominated by their Inner Defender. They place themselves above others, protecting themselves from disappointment and failure by making others fully responsible for their problems. Picture them sneering down, a finger jabbing judgmentally at those below. Their Inner Defender snarls, "*You never . . . . Why do you always . . . ? Why don't you ever . . . ? It's your fault that . . . .*" Satir estimated that about 30 percent of people use blaming as their major communication style.

Either passively placating or aggressively blaming keeps Victims from developing mutually supportive relationships, making the accomplishment of their dreams more difficult. The inner result is damaged self-esteem.

Leveling

What, then, is the communication style of Creators? Some have called this style *assertiveness*: boldly putting forth opinions and requests. Satir calls this communication style *leveling*. Leveling is characterized by a simple, yet profound, communication strategy: asserting the truth as you see it.

Creators boldly express their personal truth without false apology or excuse, without harsh criticism or blame. Leveling requires a strong Inner Guide and a commitment to honesty. Here are three strategies that promote leveling:

We should replace our alienating, criticizing words with "I" language. Instead of, "You are a liar and no one can trust you," say, "I don't like it when I can't rely on your words—it is difficult for us to do things together."

Ken Keyes

1. **COMMUNICATE PURPOSEFULLY.** Creators express a clear purpose even in times of emotional upset. If a Creator goes to a professor to discuss a disappointing grade, she will be clear whether her purpose is to (1) increase her understanding of the subject, (2) seek a higher grade, (3) criticize the instructor's grading ability, or accomplish some other option. By knowing her purpose, she has a way to evaluate the success of her communication. The Creator states purposefully, *When I saw my grade on this lab report, I was very disappointed. I'd like to go over it with you and learn how to improve my next one.*

2. **COMMUNICATE HONESTLY.** Creators candidly express unpopular thoughts and upset feelings in the service of building mutually supportive relationships. The Creator says honestly, *I'm angry that you didn't meet me in the library to study for the sociology test as you agreed.*

3. **COMMUNICATE RESPONSIBLY.** Because responsibility lies within, Creators express their personal responsibility with I-messages. An I-message allows

Creators to take full responsibility for their reaction to anything another person may have said or done. An effective I-message has four elements:

A statement of the situation:	*When you . . .*
A statement of your reaction:	*I felt/thought/decided . . .*
A request:	*I'd like to ask that you . . .*
An invitation to respond:	*Will you agree to that?*

Let's compare Victim and Creator responses to the same situation. Imagine that you feel sick one day and decide not to go to your history class. You phone a classmate, and she agrees to call you after class with what you missed. But she never calls. At the next history class, the instructor gives a test that was announced the day you were absent, and you fail it. Afterward, your classmate apologizes: "Sorry I didn't call. I was swamped with work." What response do you choose?

Placating: *Oh, don't worry about it. I know you had a lot on your mind. I probably would have failed the test anyway.*

Blaming: *You're the lousiest friend I've ever had! After making me fail that test, you have some nerve even talking to me!*

Leveling: *I'm angry that you didn't call. I realize that I could have called you, but I thought I could count on you to keep your word. If we're going to be friends, I need to know if you're going to keep your promises to me in the future. Will you?*

> I speak straight and do not wish to deceive or be deceived.
>
> *Cochise*

Notice that the leveling response is the only one of the three that positively addresses the issue, nurtures a relationship of equals, and demonstrates high self-esteem.

Making Requests

Making effective requests is another demonstration of both assertiveness and high self-esteem. Creators know they can't reach their greatest goals and dreams alone, so they ask for help. The key to making effective requests is applying the DAPPS rule. Whenever possible, make your requests **dated**, **achievable**, **personal**, **positive**, and (above all) **specific**. Here are some translations of vague Victim requests to specific, clear Creator requests:

Victim Requests	**Creator Requests**
1. I'm going to be absent next Friday. It sure would be nice if someone would let me know if I miss anything.	1. John, I'm going to be absent next Friday. Would you be willing to call me Friday night and tell me what I missed?
2. I don't suppose you'd consider giving me a few more days to complete this research paper?	2. I'd like to request an extension on my research paper. I promise to hand it in by noon on Thursday. Would that be acceptable?

When you make specific requests, the other person can respond with a clear "yes" or "no." If the person says "no," all is not lost. Try negotiating:

1. *If you can't call me Friday night, could I call you Saturday morning to find out what I missed?*

2. *If Thursday noon isn't acceptable to you, could I turn my paper in on Wednesday by 5:00?*

A Creator seeks definite yes or no answers. Victims often accept "maybe" or "I'll try" for fear of getting a "no," but it's better to hear a specific "no" and be free to move on to someone who will say "yes."

One of my mentors offered a valuable piece of advice: "If you go through a whole day without getting at least a couple of 'no's,' you aren't asking for enough help in your life."

Saying "No"

Saying "no" is another tool of the assertive Creator. When I think of the power of saying "no," I think of Monique. One day after class she took a deep breath, sighed, and told me she was exhausted. She complained that everyone at her job kept bringing her tasks to do. As a result, she had virtually no social life, and she was falling behind in college. She wanted advice on how to manage her time better.

"Sounds like you're working 60 hours a week and doing the work of two people," I observed. She nodded modestly. "Here's an outrageous thought: The next time someone at work brings you more to do, say 'no.'"

"That sounds so rude."

"Okay then, say, 'I'm sorry, but my schedule is full, and I won't be able to do that.'"

"What if my boss asks? I can't say 'no' to her."

"You can say, 'I'll be glad to take that on. But since I have so many projects already, I'll need you to give one of them to someone else. That way I'll have time to do a good job on this new project.'"

Monique agreed to experiment with saying "no." The next time I saw her, she was excited. "I sent my boss a memo telling her I had too much work and I couldn't take on the latest project she had assigned me. Before I'd even talked to her about the memo, one of my coworkers came by. He said our boss had sent him to take over some of my projects. Not only did I not get the new project, I got rid of two others. I just might be able to finish this semester after all."

Monique's voice had a power that hadn't been there before. With one "no" she had transformed herself from exhausted to exhilarated. That's the power of a Creator being assertive.

If you go to somebody and say, "I need help," they'll say, "Sure, honey, I wish I could," but if you say, "I need you to call so-and-so on Tuesday, will you do that?" they either will say yes or they'll say no. If they say no, you thank them and say, "Do you know someone who will?" If they say yes, you call on Wednesday to see if they did it. You wouldn't believe how good I've gotten at this, and I never knew how to ask anybody for anything before.

Barbara Sher

When two people are relating maturely, each will be able to ask the other for what he or she wants or needs, fully trusting that the other will say "no" if he or she does not want to give it.

Edward Deci

JOURNAL ENTRY 19

In this activity, you will explore assertiveness. This powerful way of being creates great results, strengthens relationships, and builds self-esteem.

1. **Write three different responses to the instructor described in the following situation.** Respond to the instructor by (1) placating, (2) blaming, and (3) leveling. For an example of this exercise, refer to the dialogues on page 159.

Situation: You register for a course required in your major. It is the last course you need to graduate. When you go to the first class meeting, the instructor tells you that your name is NOT on the roster. The course is full, and no other sections of the course are being offered. You've been shut out of the class. The instructor tells you that you'll have to postpone graduation and return next semester to complete this required course.

Remember, in each of your three responses, you are writing what you would actually say to the instructor—first as a placator, second as a blamer, and third as a leveler.

2. **Now, think about one of your most challenging academic goals. Decide who could help you with this goal. Write a letter to this person and request assistance.** You can decide later if you actually want to send the letter.

Here are some possibilities to include in your letter:

- Tell the person your most challenging academic goal for this semester.
- Explain how this goal is a steppingstone to your dream.
- Describe your dream and explain its importance to you.
- Identify your obstacle, explaining it fully.
- Discuss how you believe this person can help you overcome your obstacle.
- Admit any reluctance or fear you have about asking for assistance.
- Request *exactly* what you would like this person to do for you and persuade him or her to give you helpful assistance.

Remember, for effective requests, use the DAPPS rule.

3. **Write what you have learned or relearned about being assertive.** How assertive have you been in the pursuit of your goals and dreams? How has this choice affected your self-esteem? What changes do you intend to make in communicating (placating, blaming, leveling), making requests, and saying "no"? Be sure to dive deep!

> When things really get difficult, all I can say is, ask for help.
>
> *Dr. Bernie Siegel*

One Student's Story

Amy Acton
Southern State Community College, Ohio

I returned fall quarter feeling broken. I had hoped some time off would help my marriage and my mental state. But I felt exhausted and overwhelmed. I barely slept or ate. I was grinding my teeth and having nightmares. In class, I daydreamed because I didn't really want to be there. I already have a bachelor's degree from Wilmington College, but I'm back in school because I want to be a nurse. In the past, my GPA has always been high. But because of challenges in my marriage, studying was no longer on my A list. Maybe not even on my B or C list. I had to read an assignment several times to get it, and I was definitely not doing my best work. When I got a C on the first test in Anatomy and Physiology, I panicked. The worst part was pretending everything was okay. I couldn't ask for help or admit the level of suffering. Not me. Instead, I smiled my best Pollyanna grin and went through the motions to keep up the appearance of a healthy life.

I was taking PYSC 108: College Success because the previous term someone had come into my English class and raved about it. *That sounds like a course I could use,* I thought. In the first week, I took the self-assessment. Ouch. Kick a girl while she's down. I scored remarkably low in interdependence. I was shocked that creating a support system was so important. I'd always valued my independent nature. But I knew I had to do something different. I had to start somewhere.

So I started by asking for help. At first, it made me feel like vomiting. But it got easier. I trusted *On Course* and decided there must be benefits to interdependence. With practice, it got more comfortable. Now, it's wonderful. I began by asking students who were doing well in Anatomy and Physiology to start a study group. We would meet and go over what we covered in class. They told me about strategies they use to memorize all the bones we had to know. We made study cards and I carry them everywhere. I even started asking for help from coworkers at the hospital where I work. I usually did all of the patient charting, but I started asking others to share the task.

Next, I practiced the art of saying "no." I was raised to say "yes," followed by "please." Saying "no" took some work. I literally broke out in hives at first. I took allergy medicine and kept trying. I've gotten so good at it that now I say it every day, usually followed by "thank you." My mom is famous for calling me and asking me to pick up something at the store. I finally told her I had to choose activities that were important to my goals, like studying my nursing courses. I even said "no" to cleaning my house all the time. I prefer a clean house, but saying no to cleaning means I can say yes to more important things. The results have been life changing.

I also made a conscious effort to tell people how I truly feel. Living as my authentic, quirky self feels right. Many relationships where I was doing all the work have disappeared. For example, I asked my husband to help more around the house. He got angry at first, but I told him how important it is to me to get help so I can succeed in school and become a nurse. Now he helps more than he used to. I've finally made living the life that I want a priority, and the people who really care about me are glad.

I am so happy and grateful that I signed up for this course. Also, that I took it seriously and dove deep. I was off course in September, but the New Year is looking brighter. When I got my grades at the end of the quarter, I had all A's. My marriage is way better and my husband tells me I've changed. He doesn't say how, but I can tell that he likes me better now. This process didn't happen overnight. The journal entries were a valuable tool to inspire healing. While writing the journals, I felt very reserved at first. But soon I realized that I had something to say. I was hearing my voice again . . . *my* voice! Hearing my voice was like running into an old friend. There was a moment when I giggled. I thought, "I remember you." I like you. Where have you been my old friend?

Photo: Courtesy of Amy Acton

Embracing Change   Do One Thing Different This Week

Creators build mutually supportive relationships, giving and receiving help. Experiment with being more interdependent by picking ONE new belief or behavior from the following list and trying it for one week.

1. Think: "I am giving and receiving help."
2. Ask an instructor for help.
3. Seek help from a college resource.
4. Find and work with a study partner.
5. Create and meet with a study group.
6. Have a meaningful conversation with someone very different from myself.

7. Use an "I" statement in assertively expressing something that upsets me.
8. Make a request for help with a problem.
9. Offer help to someone with a problem.
10. Say "no" to a request of me.

Now, write the one you chose under "My Commitment" in the following chart. Then, track yourself for one week, putting a check in the appropriate box when you keep your commitment. After seven days, assess your results. If your outcomes and experiences improve, you now have a tool you can use for the rest of your life. As Russian author Leo Tolstoy said, "Everyone thinks of changing the world, but no one thinks of changing himself."

My Commitment						
Day 1	**Day 2**	**Day 3**	**Day 4**	**Day 5**	**Day 6**	**Day 7**

During my seven-day experiment, what happened?

As a result of what happened, what did I learn or relearn?

| *Wise Choices in College* | # REHEARSING AND MEMORIZING STUDY MATERIALS |

No matter how good your study materials are, if you can't remember what you're learning, you're going to fail. This outcome is likely whether the test is given by an instructor, an employer, or by life itself. That's why the ability to understand *and* remember what you learn is essential to success.

In Chapter 4, we explored strategies for developing a deep and lasting *understanding* of what we want to learn. To do so, we gathered all of the knowledge we had **Collected** from reading assignments and class sessions. Then we **Organized** that knowledge to create a variety of helpful study materials. In this way we continued to build the neural networks that store our knowledge for future use.

In this chapter, we'll take these efforts another step toward creating deep and lasting learning. We'll look at strategies to *remember* what we are learning. To do so, we'll explore effective ways to **Rehearse** study materials. Here is the learning principle that guides our efforts: *To strengthen neural networks, use many different kinds of* **Rehearsal** *strategies and distribute these efforts over time.*

As may be obvious, *understanding* and *remembering* reinforce one another. Thus, efforts to remember also help you understand, just as efforts to understand help you remember. That's why it is so important to include in your CORE Learning System both **Organizing** for understanding and **Rehearsing** for remembering. In fact, I hope you are experiencing confidence that you can rightfully have in your ability to learn virtually any information or skill. The key is choosing effective study strategies and spending sufficient time on task. You are not only fully responsible for your learning; you are also completely up to the challenge!

Rehearsing and Memorizing Study Materials: The Big Picture

Rehearsal is a term that learning researchers use for mental efforts to remember something. **Rehearsal** strategies generally fall into one of two kinds—elaborative and rote. In this chapter, we will look at both. In most cases, however, **elaborative rehearsal** will better serve your learning goals in college. These strategies use deep processing that strengthens both understanding *and* remembering. They do so by focusing on meaning, by showing relationships between ideas, and by connecting new knowledge with old. As such, elaborative rehearsal enhances deep and *lasting* learning.

By contrast, **rote rehearsal** is more about remembering than understanding. As such, it employs surface processing such as memorizing by sheer repetition. There is both good news and bad about rote rehearsal. The good news is that memorized facts and details can be valuable. For example, rote rehearsal is probably how you learned both the alphabet and multiplication tables, and they have certainly come in handy over the years. But there's bad news as well. Mindlessly memorizing information can fool you into thinking you understand something when you don't. Then you stroll into a test feeling prepared . . . only to discover how wrong you were. And even if you do pass the test, the knowledge you memorized without understanding will probably be gone when you need it later on.

So, experiment with the many **Rehearsal** strategies in this chapter. As you do, continue personalizing a CORE Learning System that helps you create deep and, in particular, *lasting* learning. As a bonus, most **Rehearsal** strategies perform double duty. As you **Rehearse**, you also generate feedback that allows you to **Evaluate** your learning. For example, when you **Rehearse** by quizzing yourself and get a wrong answer, that's valuable feedback. It prompts you to **C**ollect more information, **O**rganize it differently, and/or keep **R**ehearsing.

While examining the following strategies, keep in mind the big picture of **R**ehearsing your study materials. **First, use *elaborative* Rehearsal strategies to learn and remember complex ideas; use *rote* Rehearsal strategies to memorize facts and details. Second, schedule frequent Rehearsal sessions of sufficient length distributed over time. Third, use all feedback to Evaluate and, if needed, revise your approach to learning.**

Before Rehearsing and Memorizing Study Materials

1. Form a study team. Many of the following learning strategies are enhanced by doing them with others. That's why teaming up with fellow Creators can increase the effectiveness of your study time. Follow the suggestions on page 148 to ensure that your study team functions at top form.

2. Create a distributed study schedule. Remember: *Learning is enhanced by frequent practice sessions of sufficient length distributed over time.* Here's an example. Suppose two classmates each study a total of twenty hours for a final exam. One classmate crams twenty hours of studying into the twenty-four hours before the test. The other distributes her effort by studying two hours each day for ten days before the test. The second student will almost always experience deeper and longer lasting learning. If you began the distributed study schedule suggested in Chapter 4, you devoted the first 25 to 33 percent of your total study time to **O**rganizing a variety of effective study materials. Now, use the remaining time to deep-process those study materials using the **R**ehearsal strategies that follow. Your payoff will be improved learning, not to mention better grades.

3. Assemble all study materials. In Chapter 4, you learned to create a great variety of study materials.

Have them all handy as you begin the second stage of your study efforts. You will understand and remember more of what you study if you **R**ehearse different kinds of study materials. For example, you might **R**ehearse with an outline one day, a concept map the next, and flash cards the next.

While Rehearsing and Memorizing Study Materials

4. Review your study materials. *Reviewing* means reading over your study materials silently and with great concentration on the meaning. To avoid mindless reviewing, do the following three steps:

- Review a section of your study materials.

- Look away and ask yourself, *What are the key concepts, main ideas, and supporting details of what I just read?* Think through complete answers to those questions.

- Look back at your study materials to confirm the accuracy of your thinking.

Keep repeating these three steps with additional sections of your study materials. Reviewing in this way causes you to make sense of and remember what you have just read. This process also provides immediate feedback on how well you understand the content of your study materials.

5. Recite your study materials. *Reciting* is similar to reviewing but is done *aloud*. You've probably used reciting when you met a person for the first time. Perhaps you said the person's name aloud to help you remember it. "It's nice to meet you, *Clarissa*. I've never met anyone named *Clarissa* before. Is *Clarissa* a family name?" As you read aloud from your study materials, add any related information that comes to mind. Now look away from your study materials and do your best to say the same information again. Pretend you are explaining the information to someone who isn't in the course but is interested in the information. Look back at your study materials and compare the information there with what you have been saying. Repeat the process with each section of your study materials. Continue doing this look-away technique until what you recite captures the essence of what is in your notes. By reciting aloud, you engage multiple senses (sight and sound), thus creating stronger neural networks.

6. Use Cornell study sheets. (See page 136 for an example.) Remember that Section A of a Cornell study sheet contains information you have **Organized** in your preferred way (e.g., outlines or concept maps). Section B contains key words and questions about the information in Section A. And Section C contains a summary of the key concepts and main ideas in Section A. To **Rehearse** information on Cornell study sheets, do the following:

- Study the content of Section A using either reviewing or reciting. Keep rehearsing the content in Section A until you feel confident that you understand it fully.

- Now cover Section A with a blank sheet of paper and look at Section B. There you will see the key words and questions you have written. Explain the key words and answer the questions as thoroughly as you can. Afterward, uncover the information in Section A and check the accuracy of your responses.

- Finally, cover the whole page and write a summary of the information in Section A. Then, uncover Section C on your Cornell study sheet and compare summaries. As your learning deepens, you may find that your latest summary is even better than the one you wrote earlier.

Note how this process offers both an excellent study technique and an instant **Evaluation** of your learning. If you can't explain the key concepts or answer the questions in Section B, you know you have more studying to do. The same is true if you can't create a summary as good as—or better than—the one you originally wrote in Section C.

7. Test yourself. Get out the list of possible test questions you prepared earlier (see page 132 for

how to prepare questions). Taking a practice test is a great way to both **Rehearse** and **Evaluate** your knowledge. Think of a self-test as a dress **Rehearsal** for the real thing. To that end, do your best to duplicate the actual test situation. For example, practice answering the kinds of questions that will be on the real test (e.g., multiple choice, short answer, true/false, essay, problems). If the test will be timed, time your own practice test. If possible, test yourself in the room where the real test will be given. If you expect distractions during the test, reproduce them as well. As a bonus, when you excel in a practice test, confidence will replace self-doubts. After taking the practice test, get feedback on your answers. The best person to provide this feedback is your instructor. Others to ask include tutors in the learning center, friends who already took the class and did well, and classmates.

8. Hold a study team quiz. Here's a variation on a self-test. Ask study team member to bring questions to a meeting and quiz each other. Don't move on until everyone agrees on an answer. If needed, find the correct answer in your course materials (e.g., textbook or class notes). Or set it aside to ask your instructor. To add fun to your efforts, search the Internet for sites that allow you to create learning games such as *Jeopardy* (the television quiz show). For those motivated by friendly competition, make a game out of the quiz by awarding points for correct answers. Perhaps the person with the highest score gets treated to lunch by the others. This competition is one in which everyone wins by enhancing their learning.

9. Study three-column math charts. (See page 134 for an example.) The key to studying mathematics is solving problems, solving problems, and solving more problems. Here's where the three-column math charts you created are so helpful. Take a blank sheet of paper and place it over Column 2 (Solution) and Column 3 (Explanation). Now all you can see is the problem in Column 1. Solve the problem on the blank sheet of paper (which is covering the Solution and Explanation columns). If you have difficulty solving the problem, give yourself hints by uncovering part of the solution or explanation. After solving the problem, uncover Columns 2 and 3. Then check both your solution and your understanding of the process. If a problem continues to stump you, seek help from your instructor, a tutor, or classmates who excel in math. Trust that with enough practice and enough help, you'll be able to solve even the most difficult problems. Remember, you don't learn to solve math problems by only watching your instructor solve them. You don't even learn to solve math problems by only reading how. You learn to solve math problems by *solving* math problems.

10. Study with flash cards. (See page 132 for suggestions on creating flash cards.) Carry a deck of rubber-banded flash cards with you at all times. Pull them out for a quick review whenever you have a few extra minutes. If you study your flash cards just fifteen minutes per day (say in three sessions of five minutes each), that's nearly two extra hours of studying each week! The process is simple. Look at the front side of a flash card and recite the answer you believe is on the back. Turn it over and look. If you got the answer correct, put a dot in the upper right hand corner of the answer side. Now place the card on the bottom of your deck and keep repeating the process, perhaps shuffling the deck now and then. When you place the third dot on a card (meaning you got it correct three times), transfer that card to a second deck. Keep studying Deck 1 until all cards are moved to Deck 2. Review Deck 2 occasionally to keep your learning fresh. Flash cards are great study tools when preparing for short-answer tests, such as multiple choice and fill in the blank.

11. Memorize by chunks. Occasionally you may find it desirable—or even required—to memorize something for a course (e.g., a poem, a formula, or a summary from your Cornell study sheets). An important thing to know about memorizing is that *reading* information and *recalling* information

strengthen different neural connections. Since you need to *recall* the information on a test, you want to strengthen the neural networks that manage recall (not reading). That's why simply reading something over and over is an ineffective way to memorize it. Here is one way to create strong neural networks for recalling information. If you memorize the words with a full understanding of their meaning, you'll be engaged in *elaborative* **Rehearsal**. However, if all you do is memorize the words like a parrot, you're using *rote* **Rehearsal**.

- Recite the entire text you want to memorize (e.g., poem, formula, summary, etc.)

- Recite the first chunk of information (e.g., line, string of symbols, sentence, etc.) from the text.

- Recite the first chunk without looking at the text.

- Recite the first *and* second chunks of information while looking at the text.

- Recite this longer chunk aloud without looking at the text.

- Keep adding chunks until you can correctly recite the entire text aloud five times without looking at it.

- Take a ten-minute break and again recite the entire text aloud from memory until you do it correctly five times in a row.

- Thereafter, recite daily the entire text from memory; give extra practice to sections that are a challenge for you to recall.

If you wish, you can substitute writing for reciting in any of the steps. In fact, you'll probably find it helpful to alternate back and forth between reciting and writing.

12. Memorize with acronyms. An acronym is a word made from the first letters of other words that you want to remember. For example, in Chapter 4 of *On Course*, you encountered the DAPPS Rule, an acronym that helps you remember the qualities of an effective goal: **D**ated, **A**chievable, **P**ersonal, **P**ositive,

Specific. If you want to remember the names of the Great Lakes, you can use the acronym HOMES: **H**uron, **O**ntario, **M**ichigan, **E**rie, **S**uperior. In this way, remembering one word (the acronym) cues you to recall all of the other words represented by the individual letters. Acronyms can be real words (HOMES) or made-up words (DAPPS).

13. Memorize with acrostics. Acrostics are sometimes called sentence acronyms. Like acronyms, acrostics are made from the first letters of other words you want to memorize. However, instead of creating a new word from the initial letters, you create a sentence. For example, biology students may be required to know the taxonomic classifications: kingdom, phylum, class, order, family, genus, species. Taking the first letter of each word in this list, you can create the sentence "**K**ing **P**eter **c**ame **o**ver **f**or **g**rape **s**oda." Music students can recall the notes on the lines of a musical staff (E-G-B-D-F) by the sentence "**E**very **g**ood **b**oy **d**oes **f**ine." To remember the order of operations for math (parentheses, exponents, multiply, divide, add, and subtract), remember the acrostic of "**P**lease **e**xcuse **m**y **d**ear **A**unt **S**ally." Notice that an acrostic is an especially helpful tool when you need to remember items in a particular order.

14. Memorize with associations. When you associate something new with something you already know, the new information is easier to recall. Suppose you want to remember the name of your new mathematics teacher, Professor Getty; you could associate his name with the Battle of Gettysburg that you studied in American history. You might even visualize him wearing a uniform and carrying a musket. Now you'll remember his name. Have you ever thought of something important in the middle of the night but you can't recall it in the morning? Try tossing a pillow (or some other item) into the middle of your room and consciously associating that item to the important thought. When you see the pillow in the morning, you'll usually remember.

15. Memorize with the loci technique. The loci (pronounced *low'-sigh*) technique is a variation of association. *Loci* is Latin for "places," so with this strategy, you associate items you want to memorize with familiar places. Suppose you're studying parts of the brain and you want to remember the *amygdala*, which plays an important role in processing and remembering emotional reactions. Think of a familiar place, such as your living room. Picture your television turned to your favorite talk show and the host introducing an angry woman wearing a bright red dress. The host is saying, "Please welcome Amy G. Dala." Review this mental image several times a day for two or three days. When you need to recall the *amygdala*, mentally visit your living room, turn on the television, and there's angry ol' Amy G. Dala waiting to be introduced. You can now associate other parts of the brain with additional places in your living room. Say, isn't that a neo-cortex sitting on your couch?

After Rehearsing and Memorizing Study Materials

16. Review, Review, Review. Repetition strengthens memory. Shortly after a study period, spend a few minutes reviewing your outlines, graphic organizers, flash cards, Cornell study sheets, or whatever study materials you prefer. Two hours later review again. For the next three days, review your study materials daily. Next, review them weekly. I've found that reviewing before going to sleep helps me to remember. But the ideal time to review is any time you can. Repeated review takes little effort but creates much learning.

17. Teach what you learn. If you ask your instructors when they achieved a deep and lasting understanding of their subject, most will say it was when they started teaching it. Explaining a complex idea requires a thorough understanding. And stumbling over an explanation is clear evidence of incomplete learning. So find people to teach. Say, "Let me tell you something fascinating that I learned in one of my classes." Teaching is also a great activity to do in a study group. Suppose each time your group met, each member gave a five-minute lecture on something important they had learned in the course that week. Other teaching possibilities are only limited by your imagination. One student I knew put her children to bed each night in a most ingenious way. She donned hand puppets and delivered animated lectures to her children about what she had learned in college that day. Every night her kids couldn't wait for Professor Hand to tuck them in. Now that is a Creator!

Memorizing Exercise

Suppose you were asked to memorize all of the memory strategies you just read about. How would you go about it? Fully describe your methods.

Gaining Self-Awareness

6

Despite all of my efforts to create success in college and in life, I may still find myself off course. Now is the perfect time to identify and revise the inner obstacles to my success.

I am choosing core beliefs and habit patterns that support my success.

Successful Students . . .	Struggling Students . . .
recognize when they are off course.	**wander through life unaware of being off course.**
identify their self-defeating patterns of thought, emotion, and behavior.	**remain unaware of their self-defeating patterns of thought, emotion, and behavior.**
rewrite their outdated scripts, revising limited core beliefs and self-defeating patterns.	**unconsciously persist in making choices based on outdated scripts,** finding themselves farther and farther off course with each passing year.

Case Study in Critical Thinking

Strange Choices

"Do your students make really strange choices?" Professor Assante asked.

The other professors looked up from their lunches. "What do you mean?" one asked.

"At the beginning of each class, I give short quizzes that count as 50 percent of the final grade," **Professor Assante** replied. "One of my students comes late to every class, even though I keep telling her there's no way she can pass the course if she keeps missing the quizzes. But she still keeps coming late! What is she thinking?"

"That's nothing," **Professor Buckley** said. "I've got a really bright student who attends every class and offers great comments during discussions. But the semester is almost over, and he still hasn't turned in any assignments. At this point, he's too far behind to pass. Now that's what I call a strange choice."

"You think that's strange," **Professor Chen** said, "I'm teaching composition in the computer lab. Last week I sat down next to a woman who was working on her essay, and I suggested a way she could improve her introduction. I couldn't believe what she did. She swore at me, stormed out of the room, and slammed the door."

Professor Donnelly chimed in. "Well, I can top all of you. In my philosophy class, participation counts for one-third of the final grade. I've got a student this semester who hasn't said a word in twelve weeks. Even when I call on him, he just shakes his head and says something under his breath that I can't hear. One day after class, I asked him if he realized that if he didn't participate in class discussions, the best grade he could earn is a D. He just mumbled, 'I know.' Now there's a choice I don't get!"

"How about this!" **Professor Egret** said. "I had a student last semester with a B average going into the final two weeks. Then he disappeared. This semester, I ran into him on campus, and I asked what happened. 'Oh,' he said, 'I got burned out and stopped going to my classes.' 'But you only had two more weeks to go. You threw away thirteen weeks of work,' I said. You know what he did? He shrugged his shoulders and walked away. I wanted to shake him and say, 'What is wrong with you?'"

Professor Fanning said, "Talk about strange choices. Last week I had four business owners visit my marketing class to talk about how they promote their businesses. Near the end of the period, a student asked if the business owners had ever had problems with procrastination. While the panelists were deciding who was going to answer, I joked, 'Maybe they'd rather answer later.' Okay, it was weak humor, but most of the students chuckled, and then one panelist answered the question. The next day I got a call from the dean. The student who'd asked about procrastination told him I'd mocked her in front of the whole class, and now she's going to drop out of college. I had videotaped the class, so I asked her if she'd be willing to watch the tape. Later she admitted I hadn't said what she thought I had, but she still dropped out of school. What is it with students today and their bizarre choices?"

Listed below are all of the professors' students. Choose the one you think made the strangest choice and speculate why this student made the choice. Dive deeper than obvious answers such as "He's probably just shy." Why do you suppose he is shy? What past experiences might have made him this way? What might the inner conversation of his Inner Critic and Inner Defender sound like? What emotions might he often feel? What beliefs might he have about himself, other people, or the world? In what other circumstances (e.g., work, relationship, health) might a similar choice sabotage his success?

____ **Professor Assante's** student

____ **Professor Buckley's** student

____ **Professor Chen's** student

____ **Professor Donnelly's** student

____ **Professor Egret's** student

____ **Professor Fanning's** student

DIVING DEEPER Recall a course you once took in which you made a choice that your instructor might describe as "strange." Explain why you made that choice. Dive deep, exploring what *really* caused your choice.

Recognizing When You Are Off Course

FOCUS QUESTIONS In which of your life roles are you off course? Do you know how you got there? More important, do you know how to get back on course to your desired outcomes and experiences?

Take a deep breath, relax, and consider your journey so far.

You began by accepting personal responsibility for creating your life as you want it. Then you chose personally motivating goals and dreams that give purpose and direction to your life.

Next, you created a self-management plan and began taking effective actions. Most recently, you developed mutually supportive relationships to help you on your journey. Throughout, you have examined how to believe in yourself.

Despite all these efforts, you may still be off course—in college, in a relationship, in your job, or somewhere else in your life. You just aren't achieving your desired outcomes and experiences. Once again, you have an important choice to make. You can listen to the blaming, complaining, and excusing of your Inner Critic and Inner Defender. Or you can ask your Inner Guide to find answers to important questions such as . . .

- *What habits do I have that sabotage my success?*
- *What beliefs do I have that get me off course?*
- *How can I consistently make wise choices that will create a rich, personally fulfilling life?*

The Mystery of Self-Sabotage

Self-sabotage has probably happened to everyone who's set off on a journey to a better life. Consider Jerome. Fresh from high school, Jerome said his dream was to start his own accounting firm by his thirtieth birthday. He set long-term goals of getting his college degree and passing the C.P.A. (certified public accountant) exam. He set short-term goals of earning A's in every class he took during his first semester. He developed a written self-management system and demonstrated interdependence by starting a study group. But at semester's end, the unthinkable happened: Jerome failed Accounting 101!

Wait a minute, though. Jerome's Inner Guide has more information. You see, Jerome made some strange choices during his first semester. He skipped his accounting class three times to work at a part-time job. On another day, he didn't attend class because he was angry with his girlfriend. Then he missed two Monday classes when he was hungover from weekend parties. He was late five times because parking was difficult to find. Jerome regularly put off doing

> Consider this: If at first you don't succeed, something is blocking your way.
>
> *Michael Ray & Rochelle Myers*

> Progressively we discover that there are levels of experience beneath the surface, beneath our consciousness, and we realize that these may hold the key both to the problems and the potentialities of our life.
>
> *Ira Progoff*

homework until the last minute because he was so busy. He didn't hand in an important assignment because he found it confusing. And he stopped going to his study group after the first meeting because . . . well, he wasn't quite sure why. As the semester progressed, Jerome's anxiety about the final exam grew. The night before, he stayed up late cramming, then went to the exam exhausted. During the test, his mind went blank.

Haven't you, too, made choices that worked against your goals and dreams? Haven't we all! We take our eyes off the path for just a moment, and some invisible force comes along and pulls us off course. By the time we realize what's happened—if, in fact, we ever do—we can be miles off course and feeling miserable.

What's going on around here, anyway?

Unconscious Forces

One of the most important discoveries in psychology is the existence and power of unconscious forces in our lives. We now know that experiences from our past linger in our unconscious minds long after our conscious minds have forgotten them. As a result, we're influenced in our daily choices by old experiences we don't even recall.

Dr. Wilder Penfield of the Montreal Neurological Institute found evidence that our brains may retain nearly every experience we have ever had. Dr. Penfield performed brain surgery on patients who had local anesthesia but were otherwise fully awake. During the operation, he stimulated brain cells using a weak electric current. At that moment his patients reported re-experiencing long-forgotten events in vivid detail.

Further research by neuroscientist Joseph LeDoux suggests that a part of our brain called the amygdala stores emotionally charged but now unconscious memories. The amygdala, like a nervous watchman, examines every present experience and compares it to past experiences. When a key feature of a present event is similar to a distressing event from the past, it declares a match. Then, *without our conscious knowledge*, the amygdala hijacks our rational thought processes. It causes us to respond to the present event as we learned to respond to the past event. The problem is, the outdated response is often totally inappropriate in our present situation. By the time the amygdala loosens its grip on our decision-making power, we may have made some very bad choices.

If many of the forces that get us off course are unconscious, how can we spot their sabotaging influence? By analogy, the answer appears in a fascinating discovery in astronomy. Years ago, astronomers developed a mathematical formula to predict the orbit of any planet around the sun. However, one planet, Uranus, failed to follow its predicted orbit. Astronomers were baffled as to why Uranus was "off course." Then the French astronomer Leverrier proposed an ingenious explanation: The gravitational pull of an invisible planet was getting Uranus off course. Sure enough, when stronger telescopes were created, the planet Neptune was discovered, and Leverrier was proven correct.

We know from surgical experiences that electrical stimulation delivered to the temporal area of the brain elicits images of events that occurred in the patient's past. This is confirmation that such memories are "stored," but in most instances they cannot be voluntarily recollected. Thus, all of us "know" more than we are aware that we know.

Richard Restak, M.D.

In the entire history of science, it is hard to find a discovery of comparable consequence to the discovery of the power of unconscious belief as a gateway—or an obstacle—to the hidden mind, and its untapped potentialities.

Willis Harman

Here's the point: Like planets, we all have invisible Neptunes tugging at us every day. For us, these invisible forces are not in outer space. They exist in inner space, in our unconscious minds. As with Uranus, the first clue to spotting the existence of these unconscious forces is recognizing that we are off course. So, be candid. Where are you off course in your life today? What desired outcomes and experiences are you moving away from instead of toward? What goals and dreams seem to be slipping away? Self-awareness allows you to identify that you are off course. Then you can start making wiser choices that will get you back on course to the life you want to create.

> I learned that I could not look to my exterior self to do anything for me. If I was going to accomplish anything in life I had to start from within.
>
> *Oprah Winfrey*

JOURNAL ENTRY 20

In this activity, you will recall times in your life when you were off course and took effective actions to get back on course. Everyone gets off course at times, but only those who are self-aware can consistently make positive changes to improve their lives.

1. **Write about a time when you made a positive change in your life.** Examples include ending an unhealthy relationship, entering college years after high school, changing careers, stopping an addiction, choosing to be more assertive, or changing a negative belief you held about yourself, other people, or the world. Dive deep in your journal entry by asking and answering questions such as the following:

- In what area of my life was I off course?
- What choices had I made to get off course?
- What changes did I make to get back on course?
- What challenges did I face while making this change?
- What personal strengths helped me make this change?
- What benefits did I experience as a result of my change?
- If I hadn't made this change, what would my life be like today?

2. **Write about an area of your life in which you are off course today.** If you need help in identifying an area, review your desired outcomes and experiences from Journal Entry 8 and your goals and dreams from Journal Entry 9. Explain which area of your life is furthest from the way you would like it to be. What choices have you made that got you off course? What will be the effect on your life if you continue to stay off course?

> The truth is that our finest moments are most likely to occur when we are feeling deeply uncomfortable, unhappy, or unfulfilled. For it is only in such moments, propelled by our discomfort, that we are likely to step out of our ruts and start searching for different ways or truer answers.
>
> *M. Scott Peck, M.D.*

The fact that you've made positive changes in the past is a good reminder that you have the personal strengths to make similar changes whenever you wish. All you need is the awareness that you're off course and the motivation to make new choices.

One Student's Story

Sarah Richmond

Missouri University of Science and Technology, Missouri

I was in the emergency room when it hit me how far off course I was. My friend Matt had driven me to the ER because the Student Health Center couldn't supply the antibiotics I needed for a bad sore throat. As we sat in the waiting room talking, I told Matt that I was failing math, and I broke down and cried. I told him I was doing things in college that I had never done at home. When I was in high school, my parents were very strict. They didn't let me go out late during the week, and they'd wake me up in the morning to make sure I went to school. But in college, no one cares if you stay out all night or even if you get up and go to class. I had adopted "Why not?" as my motto, and I started doing things I knew I shouldn't be doing. My weekends had become a blur of boys and parties, and I had even started partying during the week. The parties I went to in high school were mostly small girls' nights, nothing like the drunken fraternity parties I was going to on campus. In high school I was one of the smart kids, and even though I hardly

ever studied, I was an honor student. But college was different. I was doing terrible in math and not much better in biology. It was a shock to not do as well as I had in high school.

I started getting a bleak outlook on life, and I didn't really want to be at the university. I had no idea what I wanted to major in. I thought of myself as lazy and irresponsible. I remember telling one of my friends that I should just get married, have kids, and then I'd probably be divorced by forty. After that I'd spend the rest of my life in a lousy job, struggling to survive. I felt like I couldn't do anything right. I don't know why I let everything bother me so much, but I felt awful.

Talking with Matt in the emergency room, I started realizing how lonely I felt in college. I missed my family, especially my sister. I wasn't getting along with my roommate, and we competed about everything: going out, boys, drinking, staying up late, playing video games, you name it. A lot of the students at my university are really into playing Halo.

I tried to fit in, but I'm no good at video games. At my school, if you're not in engineering, they tease you non-stop. One time a guy picked up my *On Course* book and starting teasing me about the class. "So what do you do in that class," he asked, "sit around and talk about your *feelings*? Maybe you need to go on Oprah." I didn't bother saying that the course helped me think things out, things I wouldn't have thought about, like all of the mistakes I was making.

That day in the emergency room was my wake up call. Sitting there talking with Matt, I not only realized that I was way off course, I also realized that deep down I didn't believe in myself, and therefore I couldn't take actions today to improve my tomorrow. After that, I realized I had to make some dramatic changes. I got a new roommate, stopped partying, buckled down, and passed my math class. That was two years ago. Today I'm a junior and my life is very different. I've found a major that I love, I just finished an internship that was great, and my GPA is 3.4. Making positive changes isn't always easy. But my life started to get better that day in the emergency room when I took a good look at myself and realized just how far off course I was.

Photo: Courtesy of Sarah Richmond

Identifying Your Scripts

 FOCUS QUESTIONS What habit patterns in your life get you off course? How did these habit patterns develop?

Once you realize you're off course, you need to figure out how to get back on course. Unfortunately, the forces pulling us off course are often just as invisible to us as the planet Neptune was to Leverrier and his fellow observers of outer space.

As observers of inner space, psychologists seek to identify what they can't actually see: the internal forces that divert human potential into disappointment. In various psychological theories, these unconscious inner forces have been called names such as ego defenses, conditioned responses, programs, mental tapes, blind spots, schemas, and life-traps.

The term I like best to describe our internal forces was coined by psychologist Eric Berne: **scripts**. In the world of theater, a script tells an actor what words, actions, and emotions to perform onstage. When the actor gets a cue from others in the play, he doesn't make a choice about his response. He responds automatically as his script directs. Performance after performance, he reacts the same way to the same cues.

Responding automatically from a dramatic script is one sure way to succeed as an actor. However, responding automatically from a *life* script is one sure way to struggle as a human being.

© 1990 by S. Gross

Anatomy of a Script

Everyone has scripts. I do, your instructor does, your classmates do, you do. Some scripts have helped us achieve our present success. Other scripts may be getting us off course from our goals and dreams. Becoming aware of our unique personal scripts helps us make wise choices at each fork in the road, choices that help us create the life we want.

Scripts are composed of two parts. Closest to the surface of our consciousness reside the directions for how we are to think, feel, and behave. **Thought patterns** include habitual self-talk such as *I'm too busy, I'm good at math, I always screw up, I can't write.* **Emotional patterns** include habitual feelings such as anger, excitement, anxiety, sadness, or joy. **Behavior patterns** include habitual actions such as smoking cigarettes, always arriving on time, never asking for help, and exercising regularly. When people know us well, they can often predict what we will say, feel, or do in a given situation. This ability reveals their recognition of our patterns.

> A psychological script is a person's ongoing program for his life drama which dictates where he is going with his life and how he is to get there. It is a drama he compulsively acts out, though his awareness of it may be vague.
>
> *Muriel James & Dorothy Jongeward*

Deeper in our unconscious mind lies the second, and more elusive, part of our scripts, our **core beliefs**. Early in life, we form core beliefs about the world (e.g., *The world is safe* or *The world is dangerous*), about other people (e.g., *People can be trusted* or *People can't be trusted*), and about ourselves (e.g., *I'm worthy* or *I'm unworthy*). Though we're seldom aware of our core beliefs, these unconscious judgments dictate what we consistently think, feel, and do. These beliefs become the lenses through which we see the world. Whether accurate or distorted, our beliefs dictate the choices we make at each fork in the road. What do you believe that causes you to make choices that other people think are strange? More important, what do you believe that keeps you from creating the outcomes and experiences you want?

> The grooves of mindlessness run deep. We know our scripts by heart.
>
> *Ellen J. Langer*

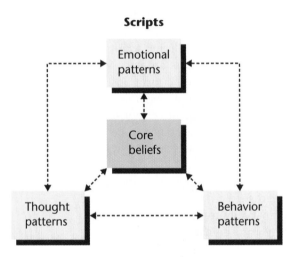

How We Wrote Our Scripts

> The hearts of small children are delicate organs. A cruel beginning in this world can twist them into curious shapes. The heart of a hurt child can shrink so that forever afterward it is hard and pitted as the seed of a peach.
>
> *Carson McCullers*

How We Wrote Our Scripts

Though no one knows exactly how we wrote our life scripts as children, reasonable explanations exist. One factor seems to be **how others responded to us**. Imagine this scene: You're two years old. You're feeling lonely and hungry, and you begin to cry. Your mother hurries in to pick you up. "There, there," she croons. "It's all right." She hugs you, feeds you, sings to you. You fall asleep full and content. If this happens often enough, what do you suppose you'd decide about the world, about other people, about yourself? Probably you'd believe *The world is kind; People will help me; I am lovable*. In turn, these beliefs would dictate your thoughts, emotions, and behaviors. With positive beliefs such as these at the core of your scripts, very likely you'd develop optimistic thought patterns (e.g., *If I ask, I'll get help*), positive emotional patterns (e.g., joy and harmony), and empowering behavior patterns (e.g., asking for what you want).

Now imagine the same childhood scene with a different response. You cry but no one comes. You scream louder, but still no one comes. Finally you abandon hope that anyone will respond. You cry yourself to sleep, alone and hungry. Imagine also that being ignored happens often. You'd probably develop core beliefs such as *The world doesn't care about me; People won't help me; I'm not important.* You could very well develop pessimistic thought patterns (e.g., *I'm alone*), negative emotional patterns (e.g., anxiety and anger), and passive behavior patterns (e.g., not asking for what you want).

Now, imagine this scene one more time. As you're crying for attention and food, an adult storms into your room, screams "Shut up!" and slaps your face. After a few wounding experiences like this, you may decide *The world is a dangerous and painful place; People will hurt me; I'm unlovable!* These beliefs may lead to defensive thought patterns (e.g., *People are out to get me*), defensive emotional patterns (e.g., fear and rage), and defensive behavior patterns (e.g., immediately fighting or fleeing at the first sign of danger). Imagine how easily these patterns could get you off course later in life.

> Parents, deliberately or unaware, teach their children from birth how to behave, think, feel, and perceive. Liberation from these influences is no easy matter.
>
> *Eric Berne*

A second factor that seems to shape our scripts is **what significant adults said to us.** What did they say about the world: Is it safe or dangerous? What did they say about other people: Can they be trusted or not? And, perhaps most important, what did important adults say about us? Psychologists have a term for qualities that tell us how we "are" or "should be": **attributions.** Common attributions tell us to be *good, quiet, rebellious, devoted, helpful, athletic, sexy, tough, independent, dependent, invisible, macho, dominant, competitive, smart, shy,* or *confident.*

Psychologists also have a term for the qualities that tell us what we "are not" or "should not be": **injunctions.** Common injunctions include *don't be yourself, don't talk back, don't feel, don't think, don't be intimate, don't say no, don't say yes, don't get angry, don't trust, don't love yourself, don't be happy, don't be weak, don't believe in yourself, don't exist.*

A third way we seem to write our scripts is by **observing the behavior of significant adults.** Children notice, *What did important adults do? If it's right for them, it's right for me.* When children play, we see them trying on adult behaviors, conversations, and emotions. It doesn't take a detective to figure out where they learned them. From significant adults we learn not only our unique personal scripts but also our cultural scripts. For example, some cultures encourage individuality while others place family and community above all other concerns. Each belief is deeply imbedded in the culture and becomes the lens through which its members see the world, influencing their choices whether they are aware of the beliefs or not.

> We first make our habits, and then our habits make us.
>
> *John Dryden*

In these ways we develop our unique scripts comprised of core beliefs and their resulting patterns of thoughts, feelings, and behaviors. At critical choice points, especially when we are under stress, we unconsciously refer to our scripts for guidance: *What similar experience have I had in the past? What thoughts, emotions, or actions did I choose back then? Did that choice increase or decrease my pain or pleasure? Oh, look, here's a response that seemed to work back then. I'll use it again now.*

The good news about our unconscious scripts is that their intention is always positive—always to minimize our pain, always to maximize our pleasure. Many of us made it through the mental, emotional, and physical challenges of growing up with the help of our childhood scripts. Some of us would not have survived without them.

But, as you might guess, there is bad news as well: When we make unconscious, script-guided choices as adults, we often get off course. That's because the scripts we developed in childhood seldom apply to the situations of our present lives. Imagine an actor in a Broadway show who can't stop playing a role from his grade school play! Many of us do the equivalent of this in our daily lives.

To others, a choice I make may seem strange. To me, it makes perfect sense. The important issue, though, is: Do my habitual choices help or hinder me in the pursuit of the life I want to create?

> The more you are keenly aware of your misery-creating thoughts, feelings, and behaviors, the greater your chances are of ridding yourself of them.
>
> *Albert Ellis*

Self-Defeating Habits

Though our unconscious scripts are as invisible to us as the planet Neptune was to early astronomers, we can often see their influence in our lives. Put a check next to any of the following patterns of thought, emotion, and behavior that are often true of you. These habits may reveal the presence of outdated scripts that get you off course. In particular, see if you can identify any habits that may have gotten you off course in the area you wrote about in Journal Entry 20.

> What lies behind us and what lies before us are tiny matters compared to what lies within us.
>
> *Oliver Wendell Holmes*

- ☐ **1.** I waste a lot of time doing unimportant things (e.g., television, video games).
- ☐ **2.** I wonder if I'm "college material."
- ☐ **3.** I easily get upset (e.g., angry, sad, anxious, depressed, guilty, frustrated).
- ☐ **4.** I hang out with people who don't support my academic goals.
- ☐ **5.** I believe that most people don't like me.
- ☐ **6.** I often turn in college assignments late.
- ☐ **7.** I get nervous around my instructors.
- ☐ **8.** I worry excessively about doing things perfectly.
- ☐ **9.** I think most of my classmates are smarter than I am.
- ☐ **10.** I quit on things that are important to me.
- ☐ **11.** I allow a person in my life to treat me badly.

- ☐ **12.** I don't believe I deserve success as much as other people do.
- ☐ **13.** I miss more college classes than I should.
- ☐ **14.** I'm very critical of myself.
- ☐ **15.** I wait until the last minute to do important college assignments.
- ☐ **16.** I don't ask questions in class or participate in class discussions.
- ☐ **17.** I often break promises I have made to myself or others.
- ☐ **18.** I am addicted to something (e.g., caffeine, alcohol, cigarettes, soft drinks, video games, social networking Internet sites, drugs).
- ☐ **19.** I experience severe test anxiety.
- ☐ **20.** I feel uncomfortable about asking for help.
- ☐ **21.** I don't get along with one or more people with whom I live.
- ☐ **22.** I often side-talk or daydream in my college classes.
- ☐ **23.** I seldom do my best work on college assignments.
- ☐ **24.** I am very critical of other people.
- ☐ **25.** I get extremely nervous when I speak to a group.
- ☐ **26.** I keep promising to study more in college, but I don't.
- ☐ **27.** I get my feelings hurt easily.
- ☐ **28.** I am a loner.
- ☐ **29.** I . . . _____
- ☐ **30.** I . . . _____

Are you aware of any other of your patterns—mental, emotional, or behavioral? If so, add them to the list.

> It is not true that life is one damn thing after another—it's one damn thing over and over.
>
> *Edna St. Vincent Millay,*
> *American poet*

JOURNAL ENTRY   21

In this activity, you will explore self-defeating patterns in your life that may reveal unconscious scripts. You're about to embark on an exciting journey into your inner world! There you can discover—and later revise—the invisible forces that have gotten you off course from your goals and dreams.

1. **Write about one of your self-defeating *behavior* patterns.** Choose a behavior pattern that you checked on the list or identify a self-defeating behavior that isn't on the list but that you do often. Remember to develop your journal paragraphs by anticipating questions that someone reading it might have about this behavior pattern. (Even you might have questions when you read your journal ten years from now.) For example,

- What exactly is your self-defeating behavior pattern?
- What are some specific examples of when you did this behavior?
- What may have caused this habit?
- What undesirable effects has it had on your life?
- How would your life be improved if you changed it?

One student began by writing, *One of my self-defeating behavior patterns is that I seldom do my best work on college assignments. For example, in my biology lab . . .*

2. **Repeat Step 1 for one of your self-defeating *thought* patterns or for one of your self-defeating *emotional* patterns.** Once again, choose a pattern that you checked on the list or identify a habit that isn't on the list but that you often think or feel. You might begin, *One of my self-defeating thought patterns is that I often wonder if I am smart enough to be successful in college. I especially think this during exams. For example, last Thursday I . . . Or . . . One of my self-defeating emotional patterns is that I often feel frustrated. For example . . .*

All serious daring starts from within.

Eudora Welty

One Student's Story

James Floriolli

Foothill College, California

At different points in my life I've given up when I ran into a challenge. As a child, I loved baseball, but when I got hit in the face with a ball, I stopped playing. In school, I started having problems with my writing skills, and I was diagnosed with a learning disability. I got all kinds of accommodations, even more than I deserved, and I started goofing off. I convinced myself that success was getting the best grades possible with the least amount of work. After high school, college didn't seem like a viable option, so I joined the Marine Corps Reserve. Boot camp was even harder than I thought it would be. Once again, I used the minimum amount of effort necessary to complete each task, and I failed to achieve the level of success in the Marines that I could have. When I left the Marines to get a civilian job, I defined success as getting maximum compensation for minimum effort.

I got a job at the phone company and at first it seemed perfect. I'm very well paid for very little effort. However, this situation isn't as rewarding as I thought it would be. After a few years I began to want a greater challenge. I knew I needed an education to advance in the workplace, so I started taking college courses part-time. For the first year I avoided classes that involved a lot of writing, as I was still intimidated by past failures in this area. But when poor writing began to affect my grades in other courses, I decided to take a composition class. In that class we read *On Course*, and in the chapter about self-awareness, I began to see how negative scripts could cause problems. I started wondering if there was a script contributing to the frustration I was feeling in my life. An idea kept coming up that at first I was unwilling to accept. I had always thought of myself as a hard worker, but looking back on my life I could not deny there were challenges I had run away from. When baseball had required extra work to get past my fear of the ball, I quit. When school stopped coming easily to me, I quit. When I realized how hard I'd have to work to be a success in the Marines, I quit. Seeing this pat-

tern was powerful for me. Finally, I felt like I understood how I ended up in the situation I am in. I realized that I'll do anything to avoid feeling bad. If I feel down in any way, I'm willing to throw everything out the window to feel better. In the past, I have doubted myself and been afraid to take risks. I overvalued security and undervalued me. I need to believe I am capable of accomplishing anything I want to.

Soon I have to pick my college major. One option is to get a computer science degree and continue working at the phone company. This would probably lead to the greatest profit and security. Or, I could choose a major that would prepare me for my dream job working in the front office of a professional baseball team. Obviously, going for my dream would be very difficult and call for a large initial pay cut. Knowing I have an issue with not following through on my most challenging commitments, I need to set my goals very carefully. No matter what I choose, I hope that when everything is said and done I will be proud of what I have accomplished. This will mean I have successfully revised my negative script of running from important challenges in my life.

Rewriting Your Outdated Scripts

 FOCUS QUESTION How can you revise the self-defeating patterns that keep you from achieving your full potential?

Once in a writing class, I was explaining how to organize an essay when a student named Diana told me she didn't understand. She asked if I'd write an explanation on the board.

Earlier in the class, we'd been talking about the differences between left-brain and right-brain thinking. We'd discussed how the left side of the brain deals with logical, organized information, while the right side deals with more creative, intuitive concepts. "No problem," I said to Diana, "I hear your left brain crying out for some order. Let's see if I can help."

As I turned to write on the blackboard, she screamed, "You have no right to talk to me that way!"

I was stunned. Talk about a strange response! I took a deep breath to compose myself. "Maybe we could talk about this after class," I said.

> We don't see things as they are, we see them as we are.
>
> *Anais Nin*

The Impact of Outdated Beliefs

Diana and I did talk, and I learned that she was in her late thirties, a single mother of an eight-year-old daughter. Our conversation wandered for a while; then Diana mentioned that she had always disliked school. In elementary school, she had consistently gotten low grades, while her sister consistently earned A's. One day, when Diana was about twelve, she overheard her father and mother talking. "I don't know what we're going to do with Diana," her father said. "She's the *half-brain* of the family."

Diana accepted as a fact other people's belief that she couldn't think or learn. She developed patterns of thoughts, emotions, and behaviors that supported this belief. She decided that school was a waste of time (thought), she exploded when anyone questioned her about schoolwork (emotion), and she was often absent (behavior). Diana barely graduated from high school, then got a menial job that bored her.

> We are what we think.
> All that we are arises
> With our thoughts.
> With our thoughts,
> We make the world.
>
> *The Buddha*

For nearly twenty years, Diana heard her Inner Critic (sounding much like her father) telling her that something was wrong with her brain. Finally, another inner voice began to whisper, *Maybe—just maybe* . . . . Then one day she took a big risk and enrolled in college.

"So what happens?" she said, getting angry again. "I get a teacher who calls me a *half-brain*! I knew this would happen. I ought to just quit."

I used my best active listening skills: I listened to understand, not to respond. I reflected both her thoughts and her anger. I asked her to clarify and expand. I allowed long periods of silence.

Finally, her emotional storm subsided. She took a deep breath and sat back.

I waited a few moments. "Diana, I know you think I called you a 'half-brain.' But what I actually said was *left* brain. Remember we had been talking in class about the difference between left-brain and right-brain thinking? Two different approaches to planning your essay? I was talking about that."

"But I *heard* you!"

"I know that's what you *heard*. But that isn't what I *said*. I've read two of your essays, and I know your brain works just fine. What really matters, though, is what *you* think! You need to believe in your own intelligence. Otherwise, you'll always be ready to hear people call you a 'half-brain' no matter what they really said."

Diana had come within an inch of dropping out of college, of abandoning her dreams of a college degree. And all because of her childhood script.

Doing the Rewrite

Until we revise our limiting scripts, we're less likely to achieve some of our most cherished goals and dreams. That's why realizing we're off course can be a blessing in disguise. By identifying the self-defeating patterns of thought, emotion, and behavior that got us off course, we may be able to discover and revise the underlying core beliefs that are sabotaging our success.

Diana stuck it out and passed English 101. She persevered and graduated with an Associate of Arts degree in early childhood education. When I spoke to her last, she was working at a nursery school and talking about returning to college to finish her bachelor's degree. Like most of us, she'll probably be in a tug of war with her scripts for the rest of her life. But now, at least, she knows that she, and not her scripts, can be in charge of making her choices.

One of the great discoveries about the human condition is this: We are not stuck with our scripts. We can re-create ourselves. By revising our outdated scripts, we can get back on course and dramatically change the outcomes of our lives for the better.

JOURNAL ENTRY   22

In this activity, you'll practice revising your scripts, thus taking greater control of your life. As in Journal Entry 18, you'll once again be writing a conversation with your Inner Guide, a critical thinking skill that empowers you to become your own best coach, counselor, mentor, and guide through challenging times. This practical application of critical thinking greatly enhances your self-awareness, helping you make the wise choices necessary to create your desired outcomes and experiences.

1. Write a dialogue with your Inner Guide that will help you revise your self-sabotaging scripts.

Have your Inner Guide ask you the following ten questions. After answering each question, let your Inner Guide use the active listening skills that will help you dive deep:

1. **Silence**
2. **Reflection** (of your thoughts and feelings)

In developing our own self-awareness many of us discover ineffective scripts, deeply embedded habits that are totally unworthy of us, totally incongruent with the things we really value in life.

Stephen Covey

JOURNAL ENTRY   22 *continued*

3. **Expansion** (by asking for examples, evidence, and experiences)
4. **Clarification** (by asking for an explanation)

Ten questions from your Inner Guide:

1. In what area of your life are you off course?
2. What self-defeating **thought patterns** of yours may have contributed to this situation?
3. What different thoughts could you choose to get back on course?
4. What self-defeating **emotional patterns** of yours may have contributed to this situation?
5. What different emotions could you choose to get back on course?
6. What self-defeating **behavior patterns** of yours may have contributed to this situation?
7. What different behaviors could you choose to get back on course?
8. What limiting **core beliefs** of yours (about the world, other people, or yourself) may have led you to adopt the self-defeating patterns that we've been discussing?
9. What different beliefs could you choose to get back on course?
10. As a result of what you've learned here, what new behaviors, thoughts, emotions, or core beliefs will you adopt?

A sample dialogue follows.

Sample Dialogue with your Inner Guide

IG: In what area of your life are you off course? (Question 1)

ME: My grades are terrible this semester.

IG: Would you say more about that? **(Expansion)**

ME: In high school I got mostly A's and B's even though I played three sports. My goal this semester is to have at least a 3.5 grade point average, but the way things are going, I'll be lucky if I even get a 2.0.

IG: What self-defeating **thought patterns** of yours may have contributed to this situation? (Question 2)

ME: I guess I tell myself I shouldn't have to work hard to get good grades in college.

IG: Why do you think that? Is there a deeper meaning? **(Clarification)**

ME: If I have to study hard, then I must not be very smart.

IG: That's a good awareness! What different thoughts could you choose to get back on course to your goal of getting at least a 3.5 average? (Question 3)

ME: I could remind myself that going to college is like moving from the minor leagues to the major leagues. The challenge is a lot greater,

> It is a marvelous faculty of the human mind that we are also able to stop old programming from holding us back, anytime we choose to. That gift is called conscious choice.
>
> *Shad Helmstetter*

➡

JOURNAL ENTRY   **22**   *continued*

and I better start studying like a major league student or I'm not going to succeed.

IG: What self-defeating **emotional patterns** of yours may have contributed to this situation? (Question 4)

ME: I get really frustrated when I don't understand something right away.

IG: So you want to understand it immediately. **(Reflection)**

ME: Absolutely. When I don't get it right away, I switch to something else.

IG: That's understandable since everything came so easy to you in high school. What different emotion could you choose to get you back on course to your goal of a 3.5 GPA? (Question 5)

ME: I could do the same thing I do in basketball when the coach asks me to shut down the other team's top scorer. I can psych myself up and push myself to study harder. My college degree is worth a lot more to me than winning a basketball game.

IG: What self-defeating **behavior patterns** of yours may have contributed to this situation? (Question 6)

ME: Like I said before, I get frustrated when I don't understand something right away, and then I put it aside. I always plan to come back to it later, but usually I don't.

IG: Are there any other self-defeating behaviors you can think of? **(Expansion)**

ME: I don't ask my teachers for help or go to the tutoring center either. I guess I hate asking for help. It's like admitting that I'm not very smart.

IG: There's that concern again about not being smart enough. **(Reflection)**

ME: I hadn't realized my Inner Critic is so loud!

IG: Now you can prove your Inner Critic wrong. What different behaviors could you choose to get back on course to your goal? (Question 7)

ME: I could ask my teachers for more help and go to the tutoring center. Also, when I set homework aside, I could write on my calendar when I'm going to work on it again. I'm really good about doing things that I write down.

IG: I like it! What limiting **core beliefs** of yours (about the world, other people, or yourself) may have led you to adopt the self-defeating patterns that we've been discussing? (Question 8)

ME: This conversation has made me realize I have some doubts about whether I'm as smart as I think I am. Maybe I don't believe I can really succeed in college unless studying comes easy for me. Maybe I got a little spoiled and lazy in high school.

IG: What different core belief could you choose to get back on course to your goal? (Question 9)

Whatever we believe about ourselves and our ability comes true for us.

Susan L. Taylor, editor-in-chief,
Essence Magazine

➡

JOURNAL ENTRY   **22**   *continued*

ME: I can succeed in college if I'm willing to do the work . . . and give it my best.

IG: That's great! Do the work and do your best! As a result of what you've learned here, what new behaviors, thoughts, emotions, or core beliefs will you commit to? (Question 10)

ME: When I feel like putting an assignment aside, I'll work on it at least fifteen more minutes. Then, if I stop before I'm finished, I'll write on my calendar when I'm going to work on it again and I'll go back and finish later. If I'm still having trouble with the assignment, I'll ask my professor for help. And I'll keep reminding myself, "Do the work and do my best." If that doesn't help, I'll be back to talk to you some more. I *will* get a 3.5 average! Thanks for listening.

CALVIN and HOBBES © 1990, Watterson. Reprinted with permission of Universal Press Syndicate. All rights reserved.

One Student's Story

Annette Valle
The Victoria College, Texas

Mrs. Turner, my seventh-grade math teacher, lives in my head. I haven't seen her in more than 30 years, but I can still picture her on the day I went up to her desk at the front of the room. She had fair skin, long brown hair, and hazel eyes. I can see her elbows on her big wooden desk, her eyes staring off into the distance, clicking the nail of a finger against the nail on her thumb. When I asked her to help explain the math, she turned and waved my paper at me and told me I was too stupid to learn math. All these years later, I can still hear her words. *I have no idea why you even come to this class, Annette. You're never going to pass math. You're just stupid.* Then she dismissed me with a wave of her hand.

I grew up in Houston, Texas, in the 1970s. College was something that rich, smart people did. It wasn't an option for poor Hispanic children living in the barrio. In our neighborhood, no one talked about going to college. Conversations were about drug dealers, drive-bys, and the latest girl who'd been beaten up by her husband. Our biggest goal in life was to survive. Like many of my friends, I dropped out of school. I got married at 15 and had two children by the time I was 17. After my brother got his GED in the military in 1980, he talked me into getting a GED, too. That diploma qualified me for higher-paying jobs, like working

security in a chemical plant or loading ATM machines. But they were all boring jobs that required physical labor, and I wasn't very happy.

Now fast forward to 2005. That's when I was diagnosed with rheumatoid arthritis. The doctor said I couldn't work at physical jobs any more, and I became eligible for a rehabilitation program that offered an opportunity for me to attend college. When I started my first semester at the age of 46, I was overwhelmed and scared. The campus seemed huge. I was intimidated by all of the young students and the academic requirements that I didn't understand. The teachers said, "Here's your syllabus," but I had no idea what a "syllabus" was. My English teacher told us to do our research paper in MLA format, but I had no idea what that meant either. I didn't want to ask because I figured everyone else knew. So I pretended I knew, too. I walked around campus with my head down and watched the cement. If I had a problem and someone didn't say, *Can I help you?* I would just try to figure it out on my own.

One of my courses was called Strategic Learning, where we read *On Course*. In this class I learned to overcome my fears and accept every challenge placed before me. It helped me become armed with the belief that the choices I make and the strategies I use are what will deter-

mine what happens to me. I learned to combat the scripts in my head that were saying *You're not smart enough; You can't do this; You'll never be a good college student.* I replaced those negative thoughts with *I can do this; I will do whatever it takes to get the work done; Only I can change my path.* It's a good thing I had this class, because I was also taking math. Mrs. Turner was still in my head telling me I was stupid and would never pass math. Instead of giving in like I had when I was in her class, I tried my newly learned strategies with determination. One thing I did was take inspirational quotations from *On Course* and write them on my workspace wall at home. When I feel like giving up, I read them out loud. Then I remind myself that I am just as smart as my younger classmates and I can accomplish my dreams just as well as they can. I'm willing to do whatever it takes, even if that means spending forty hours a week in tutoring. Maybe I'll never be a great math student, but I did pass the course.

I'm now in my fourth semester in college, and I walk across campus with my head up. When I see another student who's confused, I offer to help. I've even used some of the *On Course* techniques to encourage other students who have the same obstacles I had. The course made me a stronger person and helped me change my life. Still, I get sad when I realize that I believed Mrs. Turner for so long. I wasted a lot of years listening to her criticisms in my mind, and for a long time let her steal my thunder of achievement.

Photo: Courtesy of Annette Valle

Creators Wanted!

Candidates must demonstrate self-awareness, self-confidence, and positive work and life habits.

Self-Awareness AT WORK

Looking inward is the first place we need to look to find our own direction, not the last. *Clarke G. Carney & Cinda Field Wells in* Career Planning

Many people spend more time choosing a movie than choosing their career. As a result, the unlucky ones later dread going to work, perhaps for the rest of their lives! Creators, by contrast, devote time and effort to one of life's most important Quadrant II activities: conscious career planning. As a result, many of them actually enjoy going to work.

Conscious career planning requires self-awareness. How else can you find a match between you and the thousands of career possibilities open to you? A place to start your planning is taking an inventory of your **hard skills.** Hard skills are the special-knowledge skills that you've learned to do throughout your life. They include such abilities as swimming, writing, programming computers, playing racquetball, solving mathematics problems, building a house, creating a budget, giving a speech, drawing blood, writing a business plan, designing a garden, cooking lasagna, backpacking, playing chess, and reading. You probably learned many of your hard skills from a teacher, coach, mentor, or book. These skills can typically be filmed on a camcorder, and they tend to be applicable only in limited and specific situations; for example, writing a business plan isn't a skill of much value when you're programming computers. To begin your inventory of hard skills, ask yourself, "What talents have gotten me compliments, recognition, or awards? In which school courses have I received good grades? When did I feel fully alive, extremely capable, or very smart, and what skills was I using at the time?" Finding a match between your hard skills and the requirements of a career is essential for success.

Continue your self-assessment with an inventory of your **soft skills** (sometimes referred to as "necessary skills"). Soft skills are the ones you have developed to cope with life. They include the ones you're exploring in this book: making choices as a Creator, motivating yourself, being industrious, developing relationships, demonstrating self-awareness, finding lessons in every experience, managing your emotions, and believing in yourself. Many of these soft skills you learned unconsciously as you faced life's challenges. Usually, they are attitudes and beliefs, so they can't be filmed for playback. They are as invisible as oxygen but just as important to the quality of your life. Unlike hard skills, soft skills tend to be helpful in any career; for example, feeling confident is valuable whether you are an accountant, computer programmer, or nurse. To create an inventory of your soft skills, ask yourself, "What personal qualities have earned me compliments? What accomplishments am I proud of, and what inner qualities helped me achieve them?" Finding a match between your soft skills and the demands of a career further increases your chances of rising to the top of your profession.

To create a third component of your self-assessment, identify your **personal preferences.** To do so, go to your college's career center and ask to take one of the well-known interest inventories: the *Strong Interest Inventories* (SII), the *Self-Directed Search* (SDS), or the *Myers-Briggs Type Indicator®* (MBTI®) instrument.

Self-Awareness
AT WORK

These tools help you discover personal preferences and suggest possible college majors and career choices that will match your interests. An additional tool, the *Holland Code,* places you in one of six personality types and suggests possible careers for each. Which of the following personality types sounds most like you?

1. **Realistic** personalities prefer activities involving objects, tools, and machines. Possible careers: mechanic, electrician, computer repair, civil engineer, forester, industrial arts teacher, dental technician, farmer, carpenter.

2. **Investigative** personalities prefer activities involving abstract problem solving and the exploration of physical, biological, and cultural phenomena for the purpose of understanding and controlling them. Possible careers: chemist, economist, detective, computer analyst, doctor, astronomer, mathematician.

3. **Artistic** personalities prefer activities involving self-expression, using words, ideas, or materials to create art forms or new concepts. Possible careers: writer, advertising manager, public relations specialist, artist, musician, graphic designer, interior decorator, inventor.

4. **Social** personalities prefer activities involving interaction with other people to inform, train, develop, help, or enlighten them. Possible careers: nurse, massage therapist, teacher, counselor, social worker, day-care provider, physical therapist.

5. **Enterprising** personalities prefer activities involving the persuasion and management of others to attain organizational goals or economic gain. Possible careers: salesperson, television newscaster, bank manager, lawyer, travel agent, personnel manager, entrepreneur.

6. **Conventional** personalities prefer activities involving the application of data to bring order out of confusion and develop a prescribed plan. Possible careers: accountant, computer operator, secretary, credit manager, financial planner.

The research of Dr. John Holland, creator of the Holland Code, shows that people tend to be satisfied in careers that are compatible with their personality type, and people are less satisfied when the match isn't there. Becoming aware of your interest preferences and personality type improves your chances of finding a satisfying career match.

Another important area of self-knowledge is your scripts, those that support your success and especially those that don't. For example, what beliefs do you hold that might keep you from pursuing or succeeding in your chosen career? If one of your scripts is to distrust other people, then it will be difficult for you to develop the support systems that will enhance your success. This awareness allows you to make a conscious choice about revising the script. Remember, since you wrote your script originally, you can rewrite it in the service of a successful career.

Self-awareness in the workplace will also help you notice when your self-sabotaging habits get you off course. For example, you'll stop arriving at meetings late; instead, you'll arrive a few minutes early. You'll stop interrupting when others are talking;

Self-Awareness
AT WORK

instead, you'll listen actively. You'll stop acting as if you know all the answers; instead, you'll ask others for their opinions. In short, you'll become conscious of converting your destructive behavior into constructive behavior. If you've ever had bosses or coworkers who demonstrate any of these negative behaviors, you'll know how you wished they would become aware of what they were doing and change.

To summarize, cultivating the soft skill of self-awareness will help you choose a career that you will enjoy and bring out the behaviors, beliefs, and attitudes that will help you to excel in that profession.

▶ *Believing in Yourself*
Write Your Own Rules

> **(?) FOCUS QUESTIONS** What personal rules do you have that dictate the choices you make daily? Which of these rules help you create high self-esteem?

Few things affect self-esteem more than our sense of personal power. When we feel like mere passengers, with no apparent choice in where we're going in life, self-esteem shrivels. When we feel like the pilots of our lives, with the power to choose wisely and reach our destinations, self-esteem grows.

Outdated scripts can steal our sense of personal power and drag down our self-esteem. When these unconscious programs take over, we essentially turn over the controls of our lives to the scared and confused child of our past. Then we make those strange choices that push us far off course and leave us wondering, "How the heck did I get way over here?" If we want to reclaim our personal power and increase self-esteem, we need to choose wise rules to live by.

> I think you're going to be very surprised to discover that you may be living by rules of which you're not even aware.
>
> *Virginia Satir*

As an example, former first lady Eleanor Roosevelt chose these life rules: *Do whatever comes your way as well as you can. Think as little as possible about yourself; think as much as possible about other people. Since you get more joy out of giving joy to others, you should put a good deal of thought in the happiness that you are able to give.*

According to psychologist Virginia Satir, we are all living by rules; the important question is *Are we aware of our rules?* You'll want to identify and preserve any empowering rules that are keeping you on course. You'll want to become conscious of and revise any self-defeating rules that are holding you back. Finally, you'll want to write new rules that will support you in achieving even greater victories.

> The most important thing is to have a code of life, to know how to live.
>
> *Hans Selye, M.D.*

Three Success Rules

I have polled thousands of college instructors, and they consistently identify three behaviors that their most successful students demonstrate. As you'll see, these rules apply just as well to creating great outcomes in other life roles such as your career and relationships. Consider, then, these three rules as the foundation of your personal code of conduct.

RULE 1: I SHOW UP. Commit to attending every class from beginning to end. Someone once said that 90 percent of success is simply showing up. Makes sense, doesn't it? How can you be successful at something if you're not there? Studies show a direct correlation between attendance and grades (as one measure of success). At Baltimore City Community College, a study found that, on average, the more classes students missed, the lower their grades were, especially in introductory courses. A study by a business professor at Arizona State University showed that, on average, his students' grades went down one full grade for every two classes they missed. If you can't get motivated to show up, maybe you need new goals and dreams.

RULE 2: I DO MY BEST WORK. Commit to doing your best work on all assignments, including turning them in on time. You'd be amazed at how many sloppy assignments instructors see. But it isn't just students who are guilty. A friend in business has shown me hundreds of job applications so sloppily prepared that they begged to be tossed in the trash. Doing your best work on assignments is a rule that will propel you to success in all you do.

RULE 3: I PARTICIPATE ACTIVELY. Commit to getting involved. College, like life, isn't a spectator sport. Come to class prepared. Listen attentively. Take notes. Think deeply about what's being said. Ask yourself how you can apply your course work to achieve your goals and dreams. Read ahead. Start a study group. Ask questions. Answer questions. If you participate at this high level of involvement, you couldn't keep yourself from learning even if you wanted to.

Some students resist adopting these three basic rules of success. They say, "But what if I get sick? What if my car breaks down on the way to class? What if . . . ?" I trust that by now you recognize the voice of the Inner Defender, the internal excuse maker.

Of course something may happen to keep you from following your rules. Each rule is simply your *intention*. Each rule identifies an action you believe will help you achieve your desired outcomes and experiences. So you *intend* to be at every class from beginning to end. You *intend* to do your very best work and turn assignments in on time. You *intend* to participate actively. Your promise is never to break your own rules for a frivolous reason. However, you'll always break your own rules if something of a higher value (like your health) demands it. At each fork in the road, the key to your success is being aware of which choice leads to the future you want. When you are a Creator, you make each choice uncontaminated by the past (your scripts), informed by your own rules of conduct, and ultimately determined by which option, in that moment, will best support the achievement of your goals and dreams.

Changing Your Habits

Exceptional students follow not only these three basic rules of success; they also add their own for college and life. By choosing personal rules, they commit to replacing their scripts with consciously chosen habits. Here are a few of my own life rules:

- I keep promises to myself and others.
- I seek feedback and make course corrections when appropriate.

> People who lead a satisfying life, who are in tune with their past and with their future—in short, people whom we would call "happy"—are generally individuals who have lived their lives according to rules they themselves created.
>
> *Mihaly Csikszentmihalyi*

> I'll give you the Four Rules of Success:
> 1. Decide what you want.
> 2. Decide what you want to give up in order to get what you want.
> 3. Associate with successful people.
> 4. Plan your work and work your plan.
>
> *Blair Underwood, actor*

- I arrive on time.
- I do my very best work on all projects important to me.
- I play and create joy.
- I care for my body with exercise, healthy food, and good medical care.

What is hateful to you do not to your fellowman. That is the entire Law; all the rest is commentary.

The Talmud

Do I follow these rules every day of my life? Unfortunately, no. And when I don't, I soon see myself getting off course. Then I can reelect to follow my self-chosen rules and avoid sabotaging the life I want to create.

Once we follow our own rules long enough, they're no longer simply rules. They become habits. And once our positive actions, thoughts, and feelings become habits, few obstacles can block the path to our success.

JOURNAL ENTRY   23

In this activity, you will write your own rules for success in college and in life. By following your own code of conduct, you will more likely stay on course toward your greatest dreams.

To focus your mind, ask yourself, "What do successful people do consistently? What are their thoughts, attitudes, behaviors, and beliefs?"

Sow a thought, reap an act; Sow an act, reap a habit; Sow a habit, reap a character; Sow a character, reap a destiny.

Anonymous

1. Title a clean journal page "MY PERSONAL RULES FOR SUCCESS IN COLLEGE AND IN LIFE." Below that, write a list of your own rules for achieving your goals in college. List only those actions to which you're willing to commit to do consistently. You might want to print your rules on certificate paper and post them where you can see them daily (perhaps right next to your affirmation). Consider adopting the following as your first three rules:

1. I show up.
2. I do my very best work.
3. I participate actively.

2. Write your thoughts and feelings about your personal rules. As you write your response, consider answering questions such as the following:

- Which of my rules is the most important? Why?
- What experiences have I had that suggest the value of these rules?
- With which rule(s) will I most easily cooperate? Why?
- Which rule(s) will challenge me the most to keep? Why?

What if one of your rules was: I dive deep! How much would that rule improve your results in college and in life?

One Student's Story

Brandeé Huigens

Northeast Iowa Community College, Iowa

I was never a drinker in high school, but when I turned twenty-one, I started going out to bars with my friends. I found that "liquor courage" made me feel better about myself. When I was drinking, I was funny, had a great time, and I was happy. Then I started having blackouts. One time I woke up in my truck, surrounded by policemen, and I had no idea how I had gotten there or where I had been. Another time, I woke up in my bed and there were traffic citations all over the place. I found out later that I had spent the night in jail and the police had sent me home in a cab, but what made it worse was that I didn't remember a second of it. I had always gotten good grades before, but now I started missing my college classes. I wasn't doing as well as I wanted, especially in my nursing classes, like microbiology. I felt crappy and started putting even more pressure on myself. Then I would drink and it made me feel better, almost like a good friend. Trouble was, I'd wake up the next day and my life was falling apart. People were telling me that I could get a medical withdrawal, and I started thinking about dropping out of college.

Looking back on it now, I realize that I had completely lost control of my inner core. I've never been a quitter, though, and I started using my journal entries for this course to figure out my challenges and how to fix them. My entries would run on for five or six pages as I poured myself emotionally into my writing. I was excited because it was a way to express myself positively. About half way through the semester, I made a new rule for myself and told my class about it: *I will abstain from drinking alcohol.* From day one, it was a rule that took over my life, and I decided to track it with a thirty-two-day commitment. To support my change, I started going to AA meetings and I got a counselor at the Substance Abuse Services Center. I reread my journals for inspiration, and every day in this class we'd share how we were doing on our commitments.

Of course there were times I was tempted to drink, but I successfully completed my thirty-two days, and then I just kept going. In the last six months, I have abstained from drinking every day but one.

Today, I think about how powerful it was to write that little sentence and make a new rule for myself. It set so many other things in motion. Some are obvious, like I got sober and stopped having blackouts. My final grades were awesome, and I even got a B in micro, the hardest course I ever took. I also got a new perspective on grades. I always wanted to be perfect so I could get approval from my family, but now I see a B as a success instead of a failure. Perhaps most of all, I learned that in trying to please everyone else but me, I had lost focus on what is important to me and all I want to accomplish. Now I've created an assertiveness rule. I've starting speaking up for myself and saying "no," and I can feel my confidence and self-esteem getting stronger. From this class and from the people I shared it with, I have learned how to stand up for myself. My inner core is not fully complete, but the seed has been planted and it is definitely starting to grow.

Embracing Change   Do One Thing Different This Week

Creators do all they can to become aware of the habits of thought, emotion, and behavior that sabotage their success. With this awareness, they take steps to revise any self-sabotaging habit patterns or beliefs, empowering them to create greater success. Experiment with being more self-aware by picking ONE of the following new beliefs or behaviors and trying it for one week:

1. Think: "I am choosing habit patterns and core beliefs that support my success."

2. Identify a "strange choice" that someone else makes and consider what belief about themselves, other people, or life would generate such a choice.

3. Identify a choice I make that someone else might think is "strange" and consider what belief about myself, other people, or life would cause me to make such a choice.

4. Identify an area of my life in which I am off course (even a little).

5. Identify a **behavior** that gets me off course and replace it with one that is more self-supporting.

6. Identify a **thought** that gets me off course and replace it with one that is more self-supporting.

7. Identify an **emotion** that gets me off course and replace it with one that is more self-supporting.

8. Identify a **belief** that gets me off course and replace it with one that is more self-supporting.

9. Identify the experience that I most enjoyed this week and identify careers that would provide similar experiences on a regular basis.

10. Review my personal rules (Journal Entry 23) and identify which ones I kept that day.

Now, write the one you chose under "My Commitment" in the following chart. Then, track yourself for one week, putting a check in the appropriate box when you keep your commitment. After seven days, assess your results. If your outcomes and experiences improve, you now have a tool you can use to improve your self-awareness for the rest of your life.

My Commitment						
Day 1	Day 2	Day 3	Day 4	Day 5	Day 6	Day 7

During my seven-day experiment, what happened?

As a result of what happened, what did I learn or relearn?

Wise Choices in College Taking Tests

A test is a game . . . an important game, but a game nonetheless.

First, let's review why tests in college are important (as if you didn't know). Tests contribute to your course grade, and that grade becomes a part of your permanent record. If your grades are consistently low, you will be put on probation or even expelled. Low grades may cause you to lose financial aid. If you're an athlete, low grades can cost you eligibility for intercollegiate sports. However, if your grades are consistently high enough, you'll eventually earn a degree. Then your grades will be of interest to future employers, graduate schools, and car insurance companies, to name a few. One of my students told me that even the parents of his fiancé asked to see a copy of his transcript. Perhaps they thought his grades would reveal what kind of husband he would make for their daughter.

So tests are important. But they *are* just a game, and you win the test game by scoring the maximum number of points possible. Three factors determine how well you score on tests:.

• **Factor one: How well have you prepared?** If you have diligently completed each step of the CORE Learning System, you are extremely well prepared! Look around the room at the other students taking the test. Remind yourself that you are as well prepared as all of them and more prepared than most of them. You have worked hard, used a powerful learning system, and the result is deep and lasting learning. You have every reason to be confident!

• **Factor two: How well do you take tests?** Most people assume that tests reveal how much you know and maybe even how intelligent you are. In an ideal world, perhaps this would be true. Here on planet Earth, however, another critical factor influences your grades: Your skill at taking tests. Without this skill, your grades may only vaguely represent how much you know or how intelligent you are. Every

game requires special skills for scoring points. In this chapter, you'll learn some of the very best skills for maximizing the number of points you earn on every test. Get ready to learn how to be "test smart."

• **Factor three: How much have you learned from previous tests?** Every test provides feedback. As you know, self-aware Creators pay attention to feedback and use it to their advantage. If a test score reveals that you're on course, you can confidently keep doing whatever you've been doing. However, if a test score reveals that you are off course, it's time to change tactics.

Taking Tests: The Big Picture

In previous chapters you discovered how to be a good learner. In this chapter you'll learn how to be a good "test taker." The good news is there are only so many ways an instructor can ask you to demonstrate your knowledge and skills. Your challenge is to determine the most likely ways and prepare accordingly. So, experiment with the many following strategies and, as you do, keep in mind the big picture of test taking: **Your goal for each test is to score the maximum number of points possible. Just as there is an art to learning, so is there an art to taking tests. It's called being *test smart*.**

Before Taking Tests

1. Actively use the CORE Learning System. This means when you walk into the test room, you have already . . .

A. **Collected** complete and accurate information from all reading assignments and class sessions,

B. **Organized** many different kinds of effective study materials,

C. **Rehearsed** these study materials with a distributed study schedule, and

D. **Evaluated** to confirm your understanding of all study materials.

2. Visualize success. Create a mental movie of yourself taking the exam with great success. In your mind, picture yourself understanding every question, answering each one quickly and correctly, finishing on time, and, later, getting your test back with the grade you want (or even higher). Playing this positive movie in your mind often will build your confidence and prepare you to think, feel and act positively during the real test. (Review Journal Entry 10 for a refresher on how to create a visualization.)

3. Prepare yourself physically and emotionally. Be sure to get a good night's sleep and eat well before a test. You don't want to be distracted by tiredness or hunger. As your instructor hands out the test, breathe deeply and relax. Your studying is done. Now it's game time and your goal is simple: Earn the most points possible. You're ready. Repeat your affirmation. Visualize your success. Take another deep breath and get ready to score! You can do this!

While Taking Tests

4. Preview the test. Just as previewing a reading assignment is valuable, so is previewing a test. Note the kinds of questions. Note the point value of various questions. Read the directions carefully so you understand the rules of the game. For example, on a multiple-choice test, if the directions ask you to mark *two or more* answers and you mark only one, you'll lose points. Also, be alert for directions that change the rules. In one part of the test a wrong answer may be penalized whereas in another part of the test it may not be. This knowledge will determine whether or not you guess at an answer. Be sure you understand exactly what you are being asked to do. If unsure, ask the instructor to clarify.

5. Make a test-smart plan. Remember, your goal is to earn as many points as possible. The first rule of a test-smart plan is *Answer easy questions first.* Skim the test and answer any questions you can answer quickly and correctly. Answering easy questions first has three advantages: It makes sure you pocket these points. It builds confidence that

calms test anxiety. And, while answering the easy questions, you may come across answers to other questions on the test.

The second rule of a test-smart plan is *Spend time in proportion to points available.* Having answered the easy questions, now answer the remaining questions that are worth the most points. Suppose you're taking a fifty-minute test with fifty true/false questions worth two points each. Your plan is obvious. Assign one minute to answer each question. If you spend five minutes answering one question and five minutes answering another, now you have only forty minutes to answer the remaining forty-eight questions. Or consider a different situation: You're taking a fifty-minute test with ten true/false questions worth two points each and two short-answer essay questions worth forty points each. You want to make sure you get as many of those eighty essay points as possible. Since each essay is worth 40 percent of the total points available, you assign 40 percent of the time available (twenty minutes) to each . . . which leaves ten minutes to answer the true/false questions. Without this plan, you might spend twenty minutes answering the true/false questions, leaving yourself less time to gobble up all those essay points.

6. Answer true/false questions. Obviously, the best situation is when you know whether the statement is true or false. However, all is not lost if you are unsure. Even by guessing, you'll likely get half of them correct, and here are six test-smart strategies for improving those odds:

A. If any part of a statement is false, the answer is false.

B. If the question contains an **unconditional** word (100% with no exception), such as *all, every, only, never,* or *always,* the answer is probably false.

C. If the question contains a **conditional** word (less than 100% with some exceptions), such as *generally, some, a few, occasionally, seldom, usually, sometimes,* or *often,* the answer is probably true.

D. If the statement has two negatives, cross them both out and see if the statement is true or false.

E. If the sentence contains words you've never heard of, guess false. (This suggestion assumes you've studied thoroughly and will recognize key terms in the course.)

F. If you are reduced to taking a pure guess, choose "True." It is easier for instructors to write a true statement; plus, most would prefer that you think about the correct answer.

7. Answer multiple-choice questions. Multiple-choice questions offer a statement or question, and then present alternative ways to complete the statement or answer the question. A multiple-choice question is actually a group of true/false questions. Your task, then, is to read each statement and choose the correct (true) answer. When you are stumped, here are ways to be test smart. The following options won't always get you the correct answer, but when you are reduced to making pure guesses, they can improve your odds of choosing the correct answer.

A. Note in the directions whether you can choose only one answer or more than one answer for each question.

B. Be sure to read all answers before making a choice. Answer A may be partly accurate and tempting, but Answer D may be more accurate and therefore is the answer you should choose.

C. Cross out all obviously incorrect answers, such as those that are intended to be humorous.

D. Cross out answers with unconditional (100%) words like *all, always, never, must,* or *every.*

E. Look for grammatical clues to cross out an answer (e.g., the subject in the question doesn't agree with the verb in a possible answer).

F. When the answers are numbers, cross out the highest and lowest.

G. If two answers are similar (e.g., such as *independent* and *interdependent*), choose one of them as the correct answer.

H. If you know two or more answers are correct, choose "All of the above" as the correct answer.

I. If one answer has a more thorough answer than the others, choose that answer as correct.

J. If the question is based on a reading passage, read the question and possible answers *before* reading the passage. Then read the passage with the specific purpose of finding the answer.

8. Answer fill-in-the-blank questions. Fill-in-the-blank questions present a sentence with one or more words (or phrases) left out. Your task is to insert the correct word or phrase. Despite the increased level of challenge, being test smart can improve your chances of earning points on fill-in-the-blank questions.

A. Unless the directions say you will be penalized for a wrong answer, always write something in the blank.

B. Make sure your answer fits grammatically into the sentence (e.g., don't insert a noun if the space in the sentence requires a verb).

C. Use the length of the blank to indicate whether the correct answer is one or more words.

D. If you see two or more blanks, realize you need to have a different word or phrase in each blank.

E. Since fill-in-the-blank questions usually ask about key concepts, these concepts are often mentioned elsewhere in the test. Keep alert for them as you do other parts of the test.

F. After inserting the answer, read the sentence to make sure it makes sense.

9. Answer short-answer questions. Short-answer questions are mini-essays, usually one paragraph in length. The best approach, then, is to state a main idea. Then offer specific supporting details to demonstrate your thorough understanding of the idea. It's difficult to fake knowledge on a short-answer question, but there are some test-smart strategies that can maximize the number of points you earn.

A. Always write something. Your instructor can't give you points for a blank space.

B. Circle the *guide word* in the writing prompt. (e.g., Describe the advantages of using a tracking form.) Guide words reveal the way in which the instructor expects you to develop the topic. See Figure 6-1 for a description of twelve common guide words.

C. Underline the topic in the writing prompt. (e.g., Describe the advantages of using a tracking form.) Referring to the underlined words helps you stay focused on the topic.

D. On a blank sheet of paper or the back of a test page, jot down any related ideas and supporting details you can think of. If you have time, write a rough draft of your answer and copy it onto the test.

E. Begin writing your answer by turning the question or writing prompt into your main idea. Again, imagine that the prompt is "Describe the advantages of using a tracking form." Begin your answer, "Using a tracking form has a number of advantages." This beginning helps you stay focused on the topic as you write your paragraph.

F. Flesh out your paragraph with supporting details such as examples, evidence, explanations, and experiences. If you're at a loss for supporting details, see if you can find some in other questions on the test.

G. The space provided usually indicates how much writing your instructor expects, so plan your answer to fit in that space (unless there's a note

such as "Continue your answer on the back of this page").

H. End your paragraph with a wrap-up sentence (e.g., "There are other advantages to using a tracking form, but these are three of the most valuable").

I. Proofread your paragraph. Even if instructors don't consciously take off points for errors, such distractions can undermine an otherwise positive impression of your answer.

10. Answer essay questions. Essay questions require an in-depth discussion of a topic. In Chapter 7, you will learn many writing skills that will help you excel in answering essay questions. Here we will address two writing challenges that are unique to taking an essay test. First, you usually need to write your essay from information stored in your memory (not in your notes). Second, you have a time limit in which to write (unless it is a take-home exam). Thus, essay questions not only test your knowledge of the course content, they also test your writing ability. Here are some test-smart strategies for answering essay questions:

A. Read the directions carefully. As with short-answer questions, circle guide words in the essay prompt. Words such as *define, compare, contrast, describe, evaluate, summarize,* and *explain the cause* require different sorts of responses. Be sure you understand what you are being asked to write. (See Figure 6.1: One Dozen Common Guide Words.)

B. Underline all key terms in the writing prompt. Suppose the topic says "Describe the following economic theories: Classical, Marxist, and Keynesian." If you do a great job on Classical and Keynesian theories but don't mention Marxist theory, you'll lose many possible points.

C. If the question gives you a choice of topics to write about, be sure to write the correct number of essays. If you write more than asked for, you're wasting precious time on questions you didn't need to answer (and probably won't get points for). And if you answer fewer, you'll certainly lose points.

Guide Words	What to Do	Example Questions
1. **Analyze**	Identify the parts of something and explain how those parts contribute to the whole.	*Analyze* the skills of a test-smart student. *Analyze* the symbolism of the white whale in Herman Melville's *Moby Dick*.
2. **Compare**	Show similarities of two or more things. (Note: some instructors also want you to show differences as well.)	*Compare* linear and graphic organizers. *Compare* democracy and socialism.
3. **Contrast**	Show differences between two or more things.	*Contrast* Creators and Victims. *Contrast* Flemish and Italian painters during the Renaissance.
4. **Define**	State the meaning of something.	*Define* a self-sabotaging script. *Define* standard deviation.
5. **Describe**	Tell about in some detail.	*Describe* an effective self-management system. *Describe* the efforts of England's King Henry VII to consolidate royal power.
6. **Discuss (or Explain) Why**	Provide a detailed account showing cause.	*Discuss* why it is important to be an active learner. *Explain* why Chebyshev's theorem is important.
7. **Discuss (or Explain) Effect**	Give the results of something.	*Discuss* the long-term effects of stress on physical health. *Explain* the effect of global warming.
8. **Discuss (or Explain) How**	Provide the details of a process.	*Discuss* how students can maintain or increase their academic motivation. *Explain* how hydrogen and oxygen combine to make water.
9. **Evaluate**	Assess strengths and weaknesses, providing reasons.	*Evaluate* the quality of writing in your first *On Course* journal entry. *Evaluate* a vegetarian diet.
10. **Explain**	Make clear or comprehensible.	*Explain* the three components of a logical argument. *Explain* how nicotine affects human cells.
11. **Illustrate**	Offer an example.	*Illustrate* the use of the Wise Choice Process. *Illustrate* the benefits of using cascading style sheets in the creation of a website.
12. **Summarize**	Provide a condensed version, highlighting main points only.	*Summarize* the reasons that interdependence is important in the workplace. *Summarize* the plot of *Huckleberry Finn* by Mark Twain.

Figure 6.1 ▲ **One Dozen Common Guide Words**

For Better or For Worse®   by Lynn Johnston

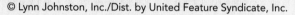

© Lynn Johnston, Inc./Dist. by United Feature Syndicate, Inc.

D. Don't start writing immediately. Instead, brainstorm by jotting down ideas related to the topic. If you need more ideas, glance over the rest of the test to see if other questions or answers suggest additional ideas or supporting details to add to your brainstorm.

E. Revise the question or topic and use it as the first sentence of your essay. (See Strategy 9E for how to do this.)

F. Organize your ideas with your preferred method (e.g., outline or concept map). Creating a clear organization helps you maximize points earned. If you have more main ideas in your plan than you have time to write about, cross out the ones for which you have the fewest supporting details. You're likely to earn more points for four to six well developed paragraphs than you will for seven to ten poorly developed paragraphs.

G. Develop each main idea in a separate paragraph, offering specific support such as examples, evidence, explanations, and experiences. Don't leave information out of your essay because you think the instructor already knows it. Remember, this is not a test to see if your *instructor* can answer the question; the

test is to determine if *you* can. You'll be wise to write to a general audience: a group of intelligent, interested readers who know very little about your topic. This approach will assure that you include all relevant information that could earn you points. (Strategy 15 in Chapter 7 offers more information on how to develop a paragraph effectively.)

H. Write a satisfying conclusion, perhaps summarizing the main points you have made. (Strategy 17 in Chapter 7 provides suggestions for concluding your essay.)

I. Save time for revising. As you read over what you have written, identify and answer questions your reader may have about your ideas. For example, readers often want to know "Why?" and "How do you know?" Add additional supporting details (examples, evidence, explanations, experiences) to undeveloped paragraphs.

J. Proofread carefully for grammar, spelling, and punctuation errors.

K. If your handwriting is difficult to read, recopy for legibility. For further neatness, consider printing, writing on every other line, and writing on one side of the paper only.

Here are some final tips for maximizing essay points:

- Always write something. Your instructor can't give you points for a blank page.

- Leave three or four blank lines after each answer in case you think of something later that you can add at the end.

- If you can't finish, provide an outline or concept map for what you would have written with more time. You may get partial points for your plan.

- If you can type, consider asking if you can bring a laptop to the test. You'll be able to write faster and make corrections more easily. Of course, you'll need some way to print your test before handing it in.

11. Solve math problems. Mathematics tests usually ask you to solve problems of the type you have been studying. If you have been solving practice problems successfully throughout the course, you are well prepared. Here are some test-smart strategies to apply during a math test:

A. As soon as you get the test, write notes and formulas on the test. If you freeze up later, you'll have access to this essential information.

B. Do a first pass through the test and solve all of the problems you can do easily. You never want to lose points by leaving a problem undone that you could have solved, but ran out of time.

C. Make a second pass through the test to work on the more challenging problems. Begin to solve each problem by estimating the answer.

D. As you do a problem, write out every step of your solution. Even if you get the answer wrong, the instructor may give you some points.

E. When finished with each problem, compare your answer with your estimate. If the two answers are very different, recheck your computations.

F. As time allows, revisit each problem and double-check all calculations.

12. If you get stuck, move on. Don't sit there wasting time on a question you can't answer. Not only will you lose time that you need for earning points, you'll also undermine your confidence by focusing on what you *don't* know instead of what you *do* know. If you doubt an answer that you've given or you've given no answer at all, put a light check mark next to the question. If time allows, return later and review your answer with fresh eyes.

13. Review your answers. Start with the sections that offer the most points. Then, check answers in other parts of the test in descending order of points available. For math problems, look for possible errors in each line of your solution.

14. Provide an answer for every question. When you have reviewed all of your answered questions, revisit unanswered questions. Run your finger along the words and read the question aloud (whisper). Highlight key words. Close your eyes and see if you can picture the answer in your study materials. Glance through the test to see if the answer may be included in another question. As a final resort, guess. You might just get some points if your guess is close.

After Taking Tests

15. Reward yourself. No matter how you think you did on the test, give yourself at treat for your efforts before and during the test—go out to dinner, call an old friend, take a bubble bath, rent a movie.

16. Study the instructor's feedback. When you get the test back, don't just look at the grade. Read the instructor's comments. For recognition questions (e.g., true/false, multiple-choice, or matching), all you may see are X's to indicate errors. For recall questions (e.g., essay or math problems), your instructor may provide commentary to explain why you earned or lost points. Whatever feedback the instructor provides, its purpose is to get you on course. Gobble it up. If there's an error or comment you don't understand, make an appointment with your instructor to discuss your confusion.

17. Analyze your errors. By analyzing your errors, you can determine how to score more points on the next test. There are seven problems that typically cost students points on a test. For example, you might have lost points because you studied the wrong material or because you didn't have a test-smart plan. Use the Test Debrief (Figure 6.2 on page 206) to identify where you lost points, and make a plan for earning more points on your next test.

18. Get help. Before the next test, seek help from your instructor, tutors, or classmates. Go to the learning center on your campus. If you haven't already created a study group, start one. If offered, attend workshops on test preparation and test anxiety. By seeking help, you can learn the information

you got wrong on the previous test and improve your preparation for the next one.

Test-Taking Exercise

Create a twenty-five-question test for a course you are now taking; write out your answers to each question. Include five questions each of the following kinds: (1) true/false, (2) matching, (3) fill in the blank, (4) multiple choice, and (5) short answer or essay. Or, for a mathematics or science course, prepare problems similar to the ones you have been studying. Design your questions so that a student who answers correctly will be demonstrating the essential knowledge/ skills covered in this course. Have a meeting with your instructor and ask for feedback on the quality of your questions and answers. Revise them based on what you discover in the conversation with your instructor. BONUS: Exchange tests with a partner and each of you create a test-smart plan for taking the other's test.

TEST DEBRIEF

Directions: *Consider the seven test-taking problems below, and estimate the number of points you lost on the test for each problem. Circle the problem(s) that cost you the most points, and implement the solution(s) as you prepare for the next test.*

Problem 1: I didn't study some of the information or skills covered on the test.
Points lost: _____
Solution: Be more assertive about discovering what content will be covered on the test. Check the course syllabus; ask classmates, tutors, and especially the instructor. Add this material to your CORE Learning System.

Problem 2: I did study the information or skills covered on the test, but I got questions wrong anyway.
Points lost: _____
Solution: Experiment with **Organizing** new kinds of study materials. Try different ways of **Rehearsing** your study materials. Distribute your studying over longer periods of time and increase your time on task. Implement more **Evaluations** to assess your understanding (e.g., have study team members and/or tutors test your knowledge).

Problem 3: I wasn't good at answering the kind of questions the instructor asked.
Points lost: _____
Solution: Do all you can to determine what kind of questions will be on the test. Construct and take practice tests that use those kinds of questions. Have study team members also construct questions of this kind. Show the questions you create and your answers to a tutor or your instructor for feedback. Keep creating and answering these kinds of questions until you become skilled at answering them.

Problem 4: I didn't follow the directions.
Points lost: _____
Solution: Take time to read all of the directions carefully, circle guide words, and underline key terms. When you proofread, confirm that you have done what was asked.

Problem 5: I lost points for questions I could have answered but didn't get to.
Points lost: _____
Solution: Make a test-smart plan that focuses on accumulating the greatest number of points possible. Determine where the easy, point-rich questions are and make a plan to answer those questions first. Set time limits for each section so you don't get stuck and lose points by not answering questions in other parts of the test.

Problem 6: I knew the answers but made careless mistakes.
Points lost: _____
Solution: Move steadily through the test, but don't rush. Think carefully about what each question is asking and about the best way to answer it. Allow time at the end to check all answers and proofread carefully before handing in the test.

Problem 7: I panicked and was too stressed to answer questions, even those for which I knew the answer.
Points lost: _____
Solution: Overlearn the content and take numerous practice tests under "game" conditions to build test-taking skills and confidence. Visualize your success and create a positive affirmation about your test-taking ability. Make and follow a test-smart plan. If you get stuck during the test, don't waste time on a tough question; move on. If you feel anxious, refocus. Keep reminding yourself that taking tests is a game and that your job is simply to earn the most points possible. If test anxiety continues to plague you, consider seeing a counselor for further suggestions and help.

Points lost for the Seven Problems should total the number of points you lost on the test.

Figure 6.2 ▲ Test Debrief

Adopting Lifelong Learning

7

As a Creator, I take personal responsibility for learning all of the information, skills, and life lessons necessary to achieve my goals and dreams.

I learn valuable lessons from every experience I have.

Successful Students . . .	Struggling Students . . .
discover their preferred learning style, utilizing strategies that allow them to maximize their learning of valuable new information and skills.	**often experience frustration, boredom, or resistance when their instructors don't teach the way they prefer to learn.**
develop critical thinking, using probing questions and higher-order reasoning skills to evaluate complex situations, make wise choices, and solve important problems.	**use poor thinking skills that result in confusion, unsound judgment, enduring problems, and even exploitation by others.**
learn to make course corrections, giving them the flexibility to change their approach, improve their results, and learn powerful life lessons.	**keep doing what they are doing in college and in life even when it isn't working.**

Case Study in Critical Thinking

A Fish Story

One September morning, on their first day of college, two dozen first-year students made their way into the biology laboratory. They sat down six at a lab table and glanced about for the professor. Because this was their first college class, most of the students were a bit nervous. A few introduced themselves. Others kept checking their watches.

At exactly nine o'clock, the professor, wearing a crisply pressed white lab coat, entered the room. "Good morning," he said. He set a white plate in the middle of each table. On each plate lay a small fish.

"Please observe the fish," the professor said. "Then write down your observations." He turned and left the room.

The students looked at each other, puzzled. This was *bizarre!* Oh, well. They took out scrap paper and wrote notes such as, *I see a small fish.* One student added, *It's on a white plate.*

Satisfied, they set their pens down and waited. And waited. For the entire class period, they waited. A couple of students whispered that it was a trick. They said the professor was probably testing them to see if they'd do something wrong. Time crawled by. Still they waited, trying to do nothing that would get them in trouble. Finally, one student mumbled that she was going to be late for her next class. She picked up her books and stood. She paused. Others rose as well and began filing out of the room. Some looked cautiously over their shoulders as they left.

When the students entered the biology lab for their second class, they found the same white plates with the same small fish already waiting on their laboratory tables. At exactly nine o'clock, the professor entered the room. "Good morning. Please take out your observations of the fish," he said.

Students dug into their notebooks or book bags. Many could not find their notes. Those few who could held them up for the professor to see as he walked from table to table.

After visiting each student, the professor said, "Please observe the fish. Write down all of your observations."

"Will there be a test on this?" one student asked. But the professor had already left the room, closing the door behind him. Frustrated, the student blurted, "Why doesn't he just tell us what he wants us to know?"

The students looked at one another, more puzzled. They peered at the fish. Those few who had found their notes glanced from the fish to their notes and back again. Was the professor crazy? What else were they supposed to notice? It was only a stupid fish.

About then, one student spied a book on the professor's desk. It was a book for identifying fish, and she snatched it up. Using the book, she quickly discovered what kind of fish was lying on her plate. She read eagerly, recording in her notes all of the facts she found about her fish. Others saw her and asked to use the book, too. She passed the book to other tables, and her classmates soon found descriptions of their fish. After about fifteen minutes the students sat back, very pleased with themselves. Chatter died down. They waited. But the professor didn't return. As the period ended, all of the students carefully put their notes away.

The same fish on the same white plate greeted each student in the third class. The professor entered at nine o'clock. "Good morning," he said. "Please hold up your observations." All of the students held up their notes immediately. They looked at each other, smiling, as the professor walked from table to table, looking at their work. Once again, he walked toward the door. "Please . . . *observe* the fish. Write down *all* of your observations," he said. And then he left.

The students couldn't believe it. They grumbled and complained. *This guy is nuts. When is he going to teach us something? What are we paying tuition for, anyway?* Students at one table, however, began observing their fish more closely. Other tables followed their example.

The first thing all of the students noticed was the biting odor of aging fish. A few students recorded details about the fish's color that they had failed to observe in the previous two classes. They wondered if the colors had been there originally or if the colors had appeared as the fish aged. Each group measured its fish. They poked it and described its texture. One student looked in its mouth and found that he could see light through its gills. Another student found a small balance beam, and each group weighed its fish. They passed around someone's pocket knife. With it, they sliced open the fish and examined its insides. In the stomach of one fish they found a smaller fish. They wrote quickly, and their notes soon overflowed onto three and four sheets of paper. Finally someone shouted, "Hey, class was over ten minutes ago." They carefully placed their notes in three-ring binders. They said good-bye to their fish, wondering if their finny friends would be there on Monday.

They were, and a vile smell filled the laboratory. The professor strode into the room at exactly nine o'clock. The students immediately thrust their notes in the air. "Good morning," the professor said cheerfully, making his way from student to student. He took longer than ever to examine their notes. The students shifted anxiously in their chairs as the professor edged ever closer to the door. How could they endure the smell for another class period? At the door, the professor turned to the students.

"All right," he said. "Now we can begin."

—Inspired by Samuel J. Scudder,
"Take This Fish and Look at It" (1874)

Based on what you observed in this biology class, rate the professor on the scale below:

| Terrible | ← | 1 | 2 | 3 | 4 | 5 | 6 | 7 | 8 | 9 | 10 | → | Excellent |

Be prepared to explain your rating.

DIVING DEEPER If you had been in this biology lab class, what lessons about college and life would you have learned from the experience? When you think you have discovered one life lesson, dive deeper and find another even more powerful lesson. And then another and another.

Discovering Your Preferred Learning Style

 FOCUS QUESTIONS What is your preferred way of learning? What can you do when your instructor doesn't teach the way you prefer to learn?

Today, well into the information age, staying on course to our goals and dreams requires learning vast amounts of information, facts, theories, and skills. Once you master the CORE Learning System introduced in Chapter 1, all that learning shouldn't be a problem, right? Not quite. Further understanding of how the human brain learns reveals a complication. In addition to approaches to learning

> Education is our passport to the future, for tomorrow belongs to the people who prepare for it today.... Give your brain as much attention as you do your hair and you'll be a thousand times better off.
>
> *Malcolm X*

> It is very natural to teach in the same way we learn. It may be difficult for us to believe that others could learn in a way that is foreign and difficult for us.
>
> *Carolyn Mamchur*

that are common to us all, each of us has our own preferred way of learning as well. Each of us has our own preferred way of taking in and deeply processing our learning experiences. Each of us has our own preferred way of creating meaning from the rush and jumble of information we encounter in college, at work, at home, and everywhere else in life. Knowing how *you* prefer to learn gives you a great advantage everywhere in life, but especially in college when you encounter an instructor who doesn't teach the way you prefer to learn.

Self-Assessment: How I Prefer to Learn

Before reading on, take the following self-assessment inventory. It will give you insights about how your brain, with its unique set of past learning experiences, prefers to gather and process information.

Preferred Learning Style Inventory

In each group below, rank all four answers (A, B, C, D) from the least true of you to the most true of you. Give each possible answer a different score. There are no right or wrong answers; your opinion is all that matters. Remember, items that are MOST TRUE OF YOU get a 4. You can also take this self-assessment on the Internet at www.cengage.com/success/Downing/OnCourse6e.

Least true of you   1   2   3   4   Most true of you

1. I would prefer to take a college course
   _____ A. in science.
   _____ B. in business management.
   _____ C. in group dynamics.
   _____ D. as an independent study that I design.

2. I solve problems by
   _____ A. standing back, thinking, and analyzing what is wrong.
   _____ B. doing something practical and seeing how it works.
   _____ C. leaping in and doing what feels right at the time.
   _____ D. trusting my intuition.

3. Career groups that appeal to me are
   _____ A. engineer, researcher, financial planner.
   _____ B. administrator, city manager, military officer.
   _____ C. teacher, social worker, physical therapist.
   _____ D. entrepreneur, artist, inventor.

4. Before I make a decision, I need to be sure that
   _____ A. I understand all of the relevant ideas and facts.
   _____ B. I'm confident my solution will work.
   _____ C. I know how my decision will affect others.
   _____ D. I haven't overlooked a more creative solution.

5. I believe that
   _____ A. life today needs more logical thinking and less emotion.
   _____ B. life rewards the practical, hard-working, down-to-earth person.
   _____ C. life must be lived with enthusiasm and passion.
   _____ D. life, like music, is best composed by creative inspiration, not by rules.

6. I would enjoy reading a book titled
   _____ A. *Great Theories and Ideas of the Twentieth Century.*
   _____ B. *How to Organize Your Life and Accomplish More.*
   _____ C. *The Keys to Developing Better Relationships.*
   _____ D. *Tapping into Your Creative Genius.*

7. I believe the most valuable information for making decisions comes from
   _____ A. logical analysis of facts.
   _____ B. what has worked in the past.
   _____ C. gut feelings.
   _____ D. my imagination.

8. I am persuaded by an argument that
   _____ A. offers statistical or factual proof.
   _____ B. presents the findings of recognized experts.
   _____ C. is passionately presented by someone I admire.
   _____ D. explores innovative possibilities for future change.

9. I prefer a teacher who
   _____ A. lectures knowledgeably about the important facts and theories of the subject.
   _____ B. provides practical, step-by-step, hands-on activities with clear learning objectives.
   _____ C. stimulates exciting class discussions and group projects.
   _____ D. challenges me to think for myself and explore the subject in my own way.

10. People who know me would describe me as
    _____ A. logical.
    _____ B. practical.
    _____ C. emotional.
    _____ D. creative.

Total your ten scores for each letter and record them below:

_____ A. THINKING   _____ C. FEELING
_____ B. DOING   _____ D. INNOVATING

Your scores suggest the following:

30–40   You have a strong preference to learn this way.

20–29   You are capable of learning this way when necessary.

10–19   You avoid this way of learning.

Discoveries about learning styles can help us maximize what we learn. These discoveries suggest that each of us develops a preferred way of learning. This preferred way of learning requires less effort from our brain and produces more learning than a less preferred style. For a quick understanding of learning preferences, sign your name twice, once with each hand. Notice that your preferred hand allows you to write quickly, easily, effectively, much as your preferred learning style(s) allows you to learn. Your nonpreferred hand usually writes more slowly, painstakingly, less effectively, much the way you learn with your less preferred style(s) of learning. You are able to sign your name with either hand, but you *prefer* one over the other.

Although there is no preferred way for everyone to learn, there is a preferred way for *you* to learn, and the self-assessment you just took begins your understanding of what that way is. Your scores indicate your order of preference for four different learning approaches: THINKING, DOING, FEELING, and INNOVATING. More specifically, your scores suggest what types of questions motivate you, how you prefer to gather relevant information, and how you prefer to process information to discover meaningful answers.

Traditional college teaching—characterized by lectures and textbook assignments—typically favors the learning preference of Thinkers, and, to a somewhat lesser degree, Doers. As more instructors discover the importance of individual learning styles, however, many are adapting their teaching methods to help all learners maximize their academic potential.

However, if you encounter an instructor who doesn't teach the way you prefer to learn (and most won't), take responsibility for your learning and experiment with some of the suggestions that follow. Perhaps most important of all, develop flexibility in how you learn. The more choices you have, the richer your learning experience and the greater your success.

In the table on pp. 213–214, you'll discover how Thinkers, Doers, Feelers, and Innovators prefer to learn. You may want to start by reading the section about your own learning preference(s), based on your self-assessment score. There you'll find options to use when your instructors don't teach as you prefer to learn. By looking at the other learning styles as well, you'll see additional ways to expand your menu of effective learning strategies. Your goal here is to find deep-processing strategies that are compatible with and supportive of your preferred way of learning.

Highly effective learners realize that not all instructors will teach to their preferred way of learning. They take responsibility for not only *what* they learn in every class but also *how* they learn it. They discover deep-processing methods that maximize their learning, regardless of the subject or the way the instructor teaches.

> **Knowledge of our brain dominance empowers us as individuals and groups to achieve more of our full potential.**
>
> *Ned Herrmann*

	Thinking Learners	Doing Learners	Feeling Learners	Innovating Learners
Motivating questions that energize	**"What?" questions** *What theory supports that claim?* *What does a statistical analysis show?* *What is the logic here?* *What facts do you have?* *What experts have written about this?*	**"How?" questions** *How does this work?* *How can I use this?* *How will this help me or others?* *How did this work in the past?* *How can I do this more efficiently?* *How do experts do this?*	**"Why?" or "Who?" questions** *Why do I want or need to know this subject?* *Who is going to teach me?* *Who is going to learn this with me?* *Why do they want to know this information?* *Who here cares about me?* *Who here do I care about?*	**"What if?" or "What else?" questions** *What if I tried doing this another way?* *What else could I do with this?* *What if the situation were different?* *What is this similar to?*
Preferred ways of gathering information	• enjoy pondering facts and theories • learn well from instructors who present information with lectures, visual aids, PowerPoint slides, instructor-modeled problem solving, textbook readings, independent library research, and activities that call upon logical skills, such as debates • benefit from time to reflect on what they are learning	• enjoy taking action • learn well from instructors who present factual information and practical skills in a step-by-step, logical manner; who present models or examples from experts in the field; and who allow students to do hands-on work in guided labs or practice applications • benefit from the opportunity to dive right in and do the work	• enjoy personal connections and an emotionally supportive environment • learn well from instructors who are warm and caring; who value feelings as well as thoughts; and who create a safe, accepting classroom atmosphere with activities such as group work, role playing, and sharing of individual experiences • benefit from an opportunity to relate personally with both their instructors and classmates	• enjoy imagining new possibilities and making unexpected connections • learn well from instructors who encourage students to discover new and innovative applications; who allow students to use their intuition to create something new; and who use approaches such as independent projects, flexible rules and deadlines, a menu of optional assignments, metaphors, art projects, and visual aids • benefit from the freedom to work independently and let their imaginations run free
Preferred ways of processing information	• respect logical argument supported by documented facts and data • are uncomfortable with answers that depend on tradition, emotion, personal considerations, or intuition • excel at analyzing, dissecting, figuring out, and using logic to arrive at reasoned answers • like well-organized and well-documented information • benefit from deep-processing strategies that bring order to complex information, such as creating outlines or comparison charts	• honor objective testing of an idea or theory, whether their own or an expert's • are uncomfortable with answers based on abstract theories, emotion, personal considerations, or intuition • excel at being unbiased, taking action and observing outcomes, following procedures, and using confirmed facts to arrive at reasoned answers • appreciate well-organized and well-documented information • benefit from deep-processing strategies that bring order to complex information, such as creating flow charts or a model of the concepts to be learned	• honor their emotions and seek answers that are personally meaningful • are uncomfortable with answers based on abstract theories or dispassionate facts and data • excel at responding to emotional currents in groups, empathizing with others, considering others' feelings in making decisions, and using empathy and gut feelings to arrive at personally relevant answers	• honor personal imagination and intuition • are uncomfortable with answers based on abstract theories, cold facts, hard data, emotion, or personal considerations • excel at trusting their inner vision, their intuitive sense of novel and exciting possibilities, and their imaginations

(continued)

	Thinking Learners	Doing Learners	Feeling Learners	Innovating Learners
When your instructor doesn't teach to your preferred style *What you can do:*	• Construct important "What?" questions and search for their answers in class sessions and homework assignments. • Construct and answer other types of questions your instructor might ask: How? Who? Why? What if? • Read all of your textbook assignments carefully, creating well-organized notes that identify the key points. • Resist getting upset if your instructor asks you to work in groups or has students do some of the teaching. • Organize your lecture and reading notes in a logical fashion, using outlines and comparison charts wherever appropriate. • Study with classmates who have different preferred ways of learning from your own, as they may provide insights about how to learn best from your instructor's teaching style.	• Construct important "How?" questions and search for their answers. • Construct and answer other types of questions your instructor might ask: What? Who? Why? What if? • Practice using the course information or skills outside of class. • Find someone who uses the course information or skills in their work and shadow them for a day or more. • Resist getting upset if your instructor seems more interested in theories than in application. • Organize your lecture and reading notes in a step-by-step fashion, using outlines and comparison charts wherever appropriate. • Study with classmates who have preferred ways of learning different from your own, as they may provide insights into how to learn best from your instructor's teaching style.	• Construct important "Who?" and "Why?" questions and search for their answers. • Construct and answer other types of questions your instructor might ask: What? How? What if? • Discover the value of this subject for you personally. • Organize your notes and study materials using concept maps. • Resist feeling upset if your instructor seems distant or aloof. • Practice using the course information or skill with people in your life. • Make friends with classmates and discuss the subject with them outside of class. • Record class sessions (with permission) and listen to recordings during free time. • Study with classmates who have different preferred ways of learning from your own, as they may provide insights into how to learn best from your instructor's teaching style. • Teach what you are learning to someone else.	• Construct important "What if?" and "What else?" questions and search for their answers. • Construct and answer other types of questions your instructor might ask: What? How? Who? Why? • Resist feeling upset when your instructor or classmates don't immediately see something as you do. • Organize your notes and study materials using concept maps and personally meaningful symbols or pictures. • Think about the content creatively (how could I adapt this?) and metaphorically (what is this like?) • Study with classmates who have different preferred ways of learning from your own, as they may provide insights into how to learn best from your instructor's teaching style.
Ask your instructor to do the following:	• Answer your important "What?" questions in class or in a conference. • List important points on the board or on handouts. • Provide handouts of PowerPoint presentations. • Allow students time to answer discussion questions in writing before answering them aloud. • Suggest additional readings, especially those written by recognized authorities in the subject. • Provide examples of past test questions. • Demonstrate the step-by-step solution of a math or science problem. • Provide data or other objective evidence that supports theories presented.	• Answer your important "How?" questions in class or in a conference. • Explain practical applications for theories taught in the course. • Provide a visual model of the concept (such as the Scripts Model in Chapter 6). • List important steps on the board or on handouts. • Demonstrate the information or skill in a step-by-step manner. • Invite guest speakers who can explain real-world application of the course information or skill in their daily work. • Observe and give corrective feedback as you demonstrate your hands-on understanding of the subject.	• Answer your important "Who?" and "Why?" questions in class or in a conference. • Explain how you might make a personal application of the course information. • Meet with you outside of class, perhaps for tutoring, so you can get to know one another better and feel more comfortable in the class. • Provide occasional opportunities for small-group activities within the classroom. • Tell stories about how he or she (or someone else) has personally used the information or skills taught in the course. • Let you do some of the course assignments with a partner or in a group. • Allow students time to talk in pairs about discussion questions before answering them in front of the whole class.	• Answer your important "What if?" and "What else?" questions in class or in a conference. • Allow you to design some of your own assignments for the course. • Use visual aids to explain concepts in class. • Recommend a book for you to read by the most innovative or rebellious thinker in the field. • Evaluate your learning with essays and independent projects rather than with objective tests.

JOURNAL ENTRY   24

In this activity, you'll apply what you have learned about your preferred ways of learning to improve your results in a challenging course.

1. **Write about the most challenging course you are taking this semester.** Using what you just learned about how you prefer to learn, explain why the course may be difficult for you: Consider the subject matter, the teaching methods of the instructor, the textbook, and any other factors that may contribute to making this course difficult for someone with your preferred way(s) of learning. (If you are not taking a challenging course this semester, write about the most challenging course you have taken any time in your education.)

2. **Using what you now know about the way you prefer to learn, write about choices you can make that will help you learn this challenging subject more easily.** Refer to pages 213–214 for possible choices.

By choosing different ways of learning in a challenging course, you can avoid the excusing, blaming, and complaining of a Victim and apply the solution-oriented approach of a Creator.

> Young cat, if you keep your eyes open enough, oh, the stuff you would learn! The most wonderful stuff!
>
> *Dr. Seuss*

One Student's Story

Melissa Thompson

Madison Area Technical College, Wisconsin

The challenge for me was chemistry. In lecture, the words were coming at me but the material wasn't sticking. The teacher was dry, stand-offish, and intimidating, and he never joked around. I could read the book, reread it, and still wonder what I had just read. I was so frustrated because I needed to pass chemistry to get into my major. Realizing this, I was spending ten to twelve hours a week studying, and I even started a study group and got a tutor. With all this help, I was doing fine on the assignments, but the tests were killing me. I would take one look at them and my mind would go blank. I was stressed and so tempted to drop the course.

About that time I took the self-assessment in *On Course* about how I prefer to learn. I scored highest as a *feeling* learner, with *doing* learner second. I learned it's important for me to relate well personally with my instructors and classmates. Also, I want to see and touch what I'm learning, and I'm not comfortable with abstract theories and dispassionate facts. BINGO! The light went on. My favorite subjects in high school were classes like art and English where I could be creative and hands on. My favorite teacher was my art teacher, a kind, caring person who told lots of stories that related art to lessons in life. Now I'm in chemistry, which is exactly the type of subject I'm uncomfortable with, and I have a professor who is distant and intimidating. I knew what I had to do, and I probably wouldn't have done it before taking my College Success class.

I asked my chemistry instructor if I could stay after class to talk with him. I explained what I had discovered about my learning preference and why I was so challenged by chemistry. He agreed to meet with me after every class. During lecture, I'd write questions in the margins of my notes or leave a space wherever I got lost. I'd also highlight things in my book that I didn't understand. Going over my questions with him after class was helpful because everything was fresh in my mind. He would take my questions and answer them in different ways than he had in class. Then I would tell him what I thought he was saying and he would coach me until I had it right. Once I got to know him, I realized he was actually very friendly and helpful. He's a quiet person, but I could tell how much he loves chemistry. Before, when I walked into class, I felt intimidated, but before long I felt more comfortable.

Soon after these meetings started, my grades began to come up. I was retaining the information and it showed. I worked hard, and in the end I did pass chemistry. If I hadn't found out about my learning preference and done something different, I don't think I would have passed. My professor is definitely a "thinker," and he handles things so differently than I do. Once I understood the situation, though, I knew I had to step up and be in control of my life, and I did.

Employing Critical Thinking

 FOCUS QUESTIONS How can you determine the truth in this complex and confusing world? How can you present your truths in a way that is logical and persuasive to others?

Imagine this: While deciding what classes to take next semester, you decide to register for Psychology 101. After checking the various times it will be offered, you're delighted to discover that a section of the course taught by Professor Skinner fits perfectly into your schedule. Since two of your friends are taking the course with Professor Skinner this semester, you wisely ask for their opinions.

One friend says, "Dr. Skinner is terrible. Don't even think about taking his course!" But your second friend says, "Dr. Skinner is the best instructor I've ever had! You should definitely take his class." Darn. Now what do you do?

Before deciding, you'd be smart to apply some critical thinking. The term "critical" derives from the Greek word *kritikos,* which means having the ability to understand or decide by using sound judgment. Critical thinking helps us better understand our complex world, make wise choices, and create more of our desired outcomes and experiences. Knowing the importance of critical thinking in many realms of life, most college educators place it high on the list of skills they want their students to master.

Here's good news. You've already been using one of the most powerful critical thinking skills—the Wise Choice Process. As you've seen, thoughtfully answering the six questions of the Wise Choice Process guides you through the critical thinking process of identifying options, looking at likely outcomes, and choosing the best option available at the time.

In addition to helping you make wise choices, critical thinking helps in another important realm: constructing and analyzing persuasive arguments. Think of the countless times others have tried to persuade you to think or do something: *Mathematics is a fascinating subject* (think this), *Let me copy your chemistry notes* (do that), *Global warming is a huge threat* (think this), *Major in accounting* (do that), *My roommate is so inconsiderate* (think this), *Go to graduate school* (do that). And, of course, you're doing the same to them. Think this . . . do that.

Thus, much of life is a mental tug-of-war. Efforts to influence others' thoughts and actions lie at the heart of most human interaction, from conversations to wars. Think this . . . do that. It's no wonder the quality of your life is so greatly affected by your ability to construct and analyze persuasive arguments. You can even use these skills to decide whether or not to register for Professor Skinner's Psychology 101 class.

> Higher-order thinking, critical thinking abilities, are increasingly crucial to success in every domain of personal and professional life.
>
> *Richard Paul*

> Intelligence is something we are born with. Thinking is a skill that must be learned.
>
> *Edward de Bono*

Constructing Logical Arguments

At many colleges, entire courses, even majors, are devoted to the study of argumentation. Here, we'll focus on two skills that are essential to the construction and analysis of persuasive arguments. The first skill is the ability to **construct a *logical* argument.** Three components of a logical argument are (1) reasons, (2) evidence, and (3) conclusions. As the building blocks of a logical argument, these ingredients may be offered in any order. Suppose, for example, someone wants to convince you to participate in your college's Sophomore Year Abroad Program. Here's how she might present her argument: *You should apply for our college's Sophomore Year Abroad Program. It'll change your life. I read an article in our college newspaper about the Sophomore Year Abroad Program. The author surveyed students who have completed the program, and 80% rated their experience as "life changing."*

Here's what this argument looks like when broken into its components:

The problem with many youngsters today is not that they don't have opinions but that they don't have the facts on which to base their opinions.

Albert Shanker

1. **REASONS** (also called *premises, claims,* or *assumptions*) answer the question "Why?" Reasons explain why the audience should think or do something. Reasons are presented as true, but they may not be.	WHY? *The Sophomore Year Abroad Program will change your life.*
2. **EVIDENCE** (also called *support*) answers the question "How do you know?" Evidence provides support to explain how the persuader knows the reason(s) to be true. Evidence should be verifiable as true. Three common kinds of evidence are facts, data, and stories.	HOW DO I KNOW? *I read an article in our college newspaper about the Sophomore Year Abroad Program. The author surveyed students who have completed the program, and 80% rated their experience as "life changing."*
3. **CONCLUSIONS** (also called *opinions, beliefs,* or *positions*) answer the question "What?" Conclusions state what the persuader wants the audience to think or do.	WHAT SHOULD YOU THINK OR DO? *You should apply for our college's Sophomore Year Abroad Program.*

Asking Probing Questions

Essential to analyzing a logical argument is a second critical thinking skill: **asking probing questions.** A probing question exposes conclusions built on unsound reasons, flawed evidence, and faulty logic. Probing questions are the kind that a good lawyer, doctor, educator, parent, detective, lover, shopper, or friend asks to expose a hidden truth. The following chart lists some of the questions that critical thinkers might ask of any persuasive argument. Asking and answering these questions (and others) can help you both construct powerful arguments of your own and analyze the arguments of others.

Always the beautiful answer. Who asks a more beautiful question.

e.e. cummings

Questions about Reasons	Sample Probing Questions
• What reasons have been offered to support the conclusion?	• *When your brother studied for a year in Australia, was the experience life changing for him?*
• Based on your experience and knowledge, do the reasons make sense?	• *What did the students mentioned in the newspaper article mean by "life changing"?*
• Did the reasons derive from careful reflection and logical thinking, or are they misguided beliefs or prejudices?	• *Does it seem likely that such a program would change my life?*
• Are there important exceptions to the reason?	• *Do I even want to change my life?*
• Are the definitions of all key terms clear?	
• Are strong emotions being substituted for reasons?	

(continued)

Questions about Evidence	Sample Probing Questions
• Is the source of the evidence reliable? • Is the evidence true? • Is the evidence objective and unbiased? • Is the evidence relevant? • Is the evidence current? • Is there enough evidence? • Does contradictory evidence exist? • Has important evidence been omitted? • What do authorities say?	• *Could the group of students polled have been specially selected to support the author's point of view about the Sophomore Year Abroad Program?* • *Does the person persuading me stand to gain if I choose to participate in the program?* • *Were enough students polled to make their results significant?* • *What percent of students from all previous Sophomore Year Abroad groups rated the experience as "life changing"?*
Questions about Conclusions	**Sample Probing Questions**
• Why? • Is the conclusion logical, or are there errors in the reasoning? • Could a different conclusion be drawn from the same reasons and/or evidence?	• *Could there be another cause for the students' life-changing experiences besides the Sophomore Year Abroad Program?* • *Did the students who rated their experience as "life changing" have anything else in common that might have been the cause of their life-changing outcome instead of the program?* • *Is the program today the same program that changed the lives of students in the survey?*

> The real value of learning lies in answering questions and questioning answers.
>
> *Marty Grothe*

Applying Critical Thinking

Let's observe these critical thinking skills in action. Listen in as two students debate their conclusions about the biology professor described in "A Fish Story" (the case study that opens this chapter). Note how they explain the reasons and evidence that lead them to their conclusions. And watch as each uses probing questions to challenge the argument of the other.

> **Emiko:** I rated the biology professor as "terrible." I'd hate to have him as my instructor. **[Conclusion]**
>
> **Frank:** Why? **[Probing question]**
>
> **Emiko:** Are you kidding? College instructors are called "professors" for a reason. They're paid to "profess," and to profess means to *tell*. Professors are supposed to be the experts, so their job is to *tell* students what they need to know. **[Reason]**
>
> **Frank:** Of course college instructors need to be experts in their subject. But is it really their job to tell students what they need to know? **[Probing question]** I think an instructor's job is to help students learn to think for themselves, not just memorize facts. **[Reason]** I'd love to have an instructor like that. I rated him as "excellent." **[Conclusion]**

> The abilities you develop as a critical thinker are designed to help you think your way through all of life's situations.
>
> *John Chaffee*

I had learned at twenty-one that you couldn't just say a thing is so because it might not be so, and somebody brighter, smarter, and more thoughtful would come out and tell you it wasn't so. Then if you still thought it was, you had to prove it. Well, that was a new thing for me. I cannot, I really cannot describe what that did to my insides and to my head. I thought: I'm being educated finally.

Barbara Jordan

Emiko: In the whole first week of the class, all he did was give his students a fish and then leave the room. **[Evidence]** Don't you think an instructor has a responsibility to at least be in the room? **[Probing question]**

Frank: The issue isn't whether the instructor was in the room. The issue is whether he was helping students learn. **[Reason]** The biology instructor did a lot more than give his students a fish and leave the room. He asked students to observe the fish and write down everything they observed. That got them actively engaged in thinking like biologists on the first day of the course. **[Evidence]** In my opinion, that makes him an excellent instructor. **[Conclusion]**

Emiko: If a professor wants to get students actively engaged in their education, that's fine. But an instructor shouldn't frustrate and make students anxious on their very first day in college. Good instructors make their students feel comfortable. **[Reason]** Look at how anxious they were while waiting for the professor to return. They had no clue what was going on. **[Evidence]** That's why I think this instructor is terrible. **[Conclusion]**

Frank: Maybe the students were a bit anxious, but isn't that a good thing? **[Probing question]** Sometimes we need to be a little uncomfortable to learn something. **[Reason]** The best teacher I ever had in high school made everyone in the class uncomfortable by firing questions at us as fast as she could, especially at people who weren't paying attention or hadn't done the homework. I learned more in that class than in all my other high school classes combined. **[Evidence]** I would rather get a C from a professor who makes me think than get an A from a professor who simply feeds me answers to put on a test. **[Reason]**

Emiko: You wouldn't think that way if you wanted to be a doctor like I do. If I get a couple of C's, I can pretty much forget about getting into a good medical school. **[Reason]** That's why I would avoid this professor like the plague. He's terrible! **[Conclusion]**

While their arguments aren't air tight, these students deserve credit for using critical thinking skills. They are clearly making an effort to provide reasons and evidence to support their conclusions. Additionally, they're asking probing questions about each other's reasons, evidence, and conclusions. Like all critical thinkers, they are respectful skeptics.

To some, it may appear that the purpose of critical thinking is to win arguments. While critical thinking can certainly do that, it actually has a loftier goal. Critical thinking helps us find the truth. That's why, to be an effective critical thinker, you must be willing to abandon your position whenever you find another view that is a better explanation of reality. The ultimate goal of a critical thinker is not victory, then, but learning.

Education's purpose is to replace an empty mind with an open one.

Malcolm S. Forbes

JOURNAL ENTRY | **25**

1. Return to the beginning of this section where you were asked to imagine getting contradictory opinions about Dr. Skinner, the Psychology 101 instructor. Make a list of at least ten probing questions you could ask your two friends to help you find the "truth" and make a wise choice about whether or not to take Dr. Skinner's class. Your questions should probe their reasons, their evidence, and their conclusions. Among others, consider asking questions that use your knowledge of learning preferences.

2. Write a logical argument that explains which character you think is most responsible for the group's grade of D in the case study "Professor Roger's Trial" (found at the beginning of Chapter 4). Be sure to state clearly your conclusion (who is most responsible), your reasons for this conclusion, and evidence from the case study to support your reasons. For example, your journal might begin, *I think the person most responsible for the group's grade of D is . . . The first reason I think this is . . . The evidence in the case study shows that . . . A second reason I think this person is most responsible is . . . and so on.*

Learning to Make Course Corrections

 FOCUS QUESTIONS How can you recognize when you are off course? More important, how can you get back on course?

Here's a little problem for you: Draw *one straight line* that touches all three of the stars below:

Notice how your scripts and preferred learning style dictate the way you go about solving this problem:

- **What are you thinking?** Do you think, *This is great, I love intellectual challenges,* or *I was never any good at puzzles,* or *This is impossible,* or *Oh, I already know the answer,* or *Who cares?*

- **What are you feeling?** Do you feel excited by the challenge, or overwhelmed by the difficulty, or irritated by the request, or bored by your disinterest, or depressed by your inability to solve it immediately?

> The capacity to correct course is the capacity to reduce the differences between the path you are on now and the optimal path to your objective . . . .
>
> *Charles Garfield*

- **What are you doing?** Do you immediately begin drawing lines to seek a solution, or sit back trying to think of a solution, or turn the page to look for the answer, or ask a friend, or keep reading without attempting to solve the puzzle?

- **What are your unconscious core beliefs?** This puzzle is easy to solve, but most people have unconscious beliefs that keep them from seeing the answer. What belief is keeping you from solving this simple problem?

If your present habit patterns and beliefs aren't working to solve the puzzle, you'll have to change your approach. The same is true in life. When you face a problem and your present choices aren't working, you need to learn to do, think, feel, or believe something different. In other words, you need to make a course correction.

Change Requires Self-Awareness and Courage

Before we can make a course correction, we need to be aware that we are off course. Luckily, the world bombards us with helpful feedback every day. Sadly, many ignore it. At first, feedback taps us politely on the shoulder. If we pay no heed, feedback shakes us vigorously. If we continue to ignore it, feedback may knock us to our knees, creating havoc in our lives. This havoc might look like failing out of school or getting fired from a job. There's usually plenty of feedback long before the failure or firing if we will only heed its message.

In college, think of yourself as an airplane pilot and your instructors as your personal air traffic controllers. When they correct you in class or write a comment on an assignment or give you a grade on a test, what they are really saying is, *You're on course, on course . . . whoops, now you're off course, off course . . . okay, that's right, now you're back on course.* Airplane pilots appreciate such feedback. Without it they might not get to their destination. They might even crash and burn. Likewise, effective learners welcome their instructors' feedback and use it to stay on course. They heed every suggestion instructors offer on assignments; they understand the message in their test scores; they request clarification of any feedback they don't understand; and they ask for additional feedback. Maybe the idea of paying attention to feedback sounds obvious to you, but I can't tell you how many students I've had who made the same mistakes over and over, ignoring both my feedback and the reality that when you keep doing what you've been doing, you'll keep getting what you've been getting.

Everywhere in life, heeding feedback is critical to creating the life you want. The feedback may be something said by friends, lovers, spouses, parents, children, neighbors, bosses, coworkers, and even strangers. Or it may be more subtle, coming in the form of an unsatisfying relationship, a boring job, or runaway credit card debt. Any areas of discomfort or distress are red flags of

All human beings are periodically tested by the power of the universe . . . how one performs under pressure is the true measure of one's spirit, heart, and desire.

Spike Lee

Life is change. Growth is optional. Choose wisely.

Karen Kaiser Clark

warning: *Hey, wake up! You're headed away from your desired outcomes and experiences. You need to make a change!*

You see, it's one thing to be aware that you are off course. It's quite another to do something about it. Something different. Something uncomfortable. Maybe even something frightening. Course correction is not for the disempowered. It requires courage to admit that what you are doing isn't working, to abandon the familiar, and to walk into the unknown. Victims stay stuck. Creators change.

©TED GOFF

Change and Lifelong Learning

When we make a course correction, we hope the change improves the quality of our lives. Sometimes it does. Sometimes it doesn't. But change *always* presents an opportunity for learning. That's the way the University of Life works, and you're enrolled whether you know it or not. Courses in the University of Life are a little different from those in a regular college. These courses are often offered by the Department of Adversities and they include subjects such as Problems 101, Obstacles 203, Mistakes 305, Failures 410, and, for some, a graduate course called Catastrophes 599. Tests are given often, and there are no answers in the back of the book. In fact, there are no textbooks in these courses, only your experiences from which to learn and, hopefully, grow wiser. Following are some examples of the kind of wisdom that the University of Life can teach.

One of my off-course students was feeling overwhelmed by all she had to do, and then she made a course correction, changing the way she tackled large projects. In her journal she wrote, "When I break a huge task into chunks and do a little bit every day, I can accomplish great things."

Another off-course student discovered he was an expert at blaming his failures in college on other people: his boss, his teachers, his parents, his girlfriend. He decided to change and hold himself more responsible. He learned, "In the past I have spent more energy on getting people to feel sorry for me than I have on accomplishing something worthwhile."

A third off-course student was filled with hate for her father who she felt had abandoned her, and then she decided to change. She forgave him and moved on with her life. She wrote, "Spending all of my time hating someone leaves me little time to love myself."

And one more off-course student realized how little effort and care he put into everything he did, including his college assignments. He discovered, "I'm always

> To me, earth is a school. I view life as my classroom. My approach to the experiences I have every day is that I am a student, and that all my experiences have something they can teach me. I am always asking myself, "What learning is available for me now?"
>
> *Mary Hulnick, vice-president, University of Santa Monica*

> If we don't change direction soon, we'll end up where we're going.
>
> *Professor Irwin Corey*

looking for ways to cut corners, to get out of doing what's necessary. It doesn't work. I have to do my best in order to be successful."

We seldom move toward our goals and dreams in a straight line. With constant course corrections, however, we improve our chances of getting there eventually. And along the way, the University of Life offers us exactly the lessons we need to develop our full potential. We only have to listen and learn as a Creator.

JOURNAL ENTRY | **26**

In this activity, you will explore making course corrections to improve your outcomes and experiences.

Did you figure out how to connect the three stars with one straight line? If you were stumped, what limiting belief kept you from solving this problem? Did you assume that you were restricted to a pen or pencil with a narrow point? You weren't. In fact, the solution is to use a writing implement (such as a large crayon) with a point wide enough to cover all three stars in one straight line. Once you change your limiting belief, solving the problem is easy! How many other problems could you solve in your life if you mastered the creative art of course correction?

1. Write about where you are presently off course in your role as a student and offer a plan for making a course correction. In your journal entry, address the following:

1. Examine each of your college classes to see in which one you are most off course. Write about your desired outcomes and/or experiences for the course and where you actually are in the pursuit of these goals. If you believe that you are on course in all of your college classes, write about where you are off course in another role in your life.

2. Write about any feedback (from inside or outside of you) informing you that you're off course. What does this feedback tell you is the cause of your problem? Is it your present ways of thinking, feeling, doing, or believing? If you need more feedback, ask your instructor or your Inner Guide.

3. Write about new ways of thinking, feeling, doing, and/or believing that will replace your old ways and move you back on course. What will you do differently? Design a concrete plan to change.

4. Explain the lesson that you believe the University of Life wants you to learn from this situation.

One Student's Story

Jessie Maggard
Urbana University, Ohio

The first friends I made in college were my teammates on the soccer team. After practice we started riding around, shopping, and going to parties. We almost never talked about school or personal problems. To them, play time was more important. I wasn't getting much sleep and I was exhausted all the time. I didn't feel like studying and when I went to class, I wasn't learning much. Then a couple of things happened that shook me up. First, my English teacher handed back a paper and told me it wasn't very good. I thought all day about what she said and it really bothered me. I'm the first person in my family to go to college, and I started worrying about whether I was going to make it. If I was doing poorly in a class that I thought was easy, what would happen in more difficult classes? Second, I learned that my parents were getting divorced. I tried talking about my feelings with some of my teammates, but they just listened and didn't say anything. I might as well have been talking to a wall, and I realized they weren't really interested in my problems.

The *On Course* book talks about how easy it is to get off course even when you want to be successful. That is so true. By the time soccer season ended, I was *way* off course and I knew I had to make some serious changes. At first I spent more time by myself. I wrote out a schedule and started to get more organized. Then I slowly began spending more time with people in my dorm, and over time I developed friendships with six amazing people who have really touched me. Doing well in school is important to them, too. We started studying together, and my grades began to improve. I even got comments from my teachers about how I had changed. Still, I felt weighed down by my parents' divorce and it was a huge distraction from my schoolwork. One of my new friends had gone through her parents' divorce, and she gave me tips on how she had gotten through it. She encouraged me to sit down with my parents and talk about my feelings. I did, and it helped so much to talk with them and understand why they had fallen out of love with each other.

Through all of this, I've learned that when you get off course, you have to do something different. My soccer friends had different goals. I'm not trying to put them down. Their goals weren't bad, they just weren't my goals. My goal is to get my degree and teach kindergarten, and when I was hanging out with my soccer friends, I was headed in the wrong direction. I totally changed my peer group, and now I am back on course. I know I'm the only person who can change my life. I just need the courage to stand up for myself. At the time, changing seemed so difficult, but now in the big picture, it seems so easy.

Photo: Courtesy of Jessie Maggard

Creators Wanted!

Candidates must demonstrate a commitment to lifelong learning, strong critical thinking skills, and the ability to adapt to new challenges.

Lifelong Learning AT WORK

The intellectual equipment needed for the job of the future is an ability to define problems, quickly assimilate relevant data, conceptualize and reorganize the information, make deductive and inductive leaps with it, ask hard questions about it, discuss findings with colleagues, work collaboratively to find solutions and then convince others.
Robert B. Reich, former U.S. Secretary of Labor

Some students believe that once they graduate from college they'll finally be finished with studying and learning. In fact, a college diploma is merely a ticket into the huge University of Work. In one year recently, U.S. employers spent more than 55 billion dollars for employee training, according to the American Society for Training and Development.

Continuing education in the workplace includes instruction in hard skills, such as mastering a new product line, a computer system, or government regulations. Companies also offer their employees instruction in many of the same soft skills that you're learning in *On Course,* skills such as listening, setting goals, and managing your time and work projects. In fact, soft skills are in such demand in the workplace today that top training consultants charge many thousands of dollars *per day* to teach these skills to employees of American businesses.

Smart workers take full advantage of the formal classes provided by their employers. They also take full advantage of the informal classes provided by the University of Life. In this university, you have the opportunity to learn from every experience you have, especially those on the job. Lifelong learners aren't devastated by a setback, such as having a project crumble or even losing their job. They learn from their experiences and come back stronger and wiser than ever. A report by the Center for Creative Leadership compared executives whose careers got off course with those who did well. Although both groups had weaknesses, the critical difference was this: Executives who did *not* learn from their mistakes and shortcomings tended to fail at work. By contrast, those executives who *did* learn the hard lessons taught by their mistakes and failures tended to rebound and resume successful careers.

Your work-world learning begins as soon as you get serious about finding your ideal job. Unless you're sure about your career path, you'll have much research to do. Even if you do feel sure about your career choice, further research might lead to something even better. More than 20,000 occupations and 40,000 job titles exist today, and you'll want to identify careers that match the personal talents and interests you identified in your self-assessment.

Your college's library or career center probably has a number of great resources to learn about careers. For example, computerized programs such as DISCOVER, SIGI PLUS, CHOICES, and CIS may be available to explore thousands of career possibilities. Helpful books include the *Dictionary of Occupational Titles* (DOT), which offers brief descriptions of several thousand occupations; *The Guide for Occupational Exploration* (GOE), another source of occupational options; and the latest edition of the *Occupational Outlook Handbook* (OOH), which provides information about the demand for various occupations. With these resources, you can learn important facts

Lifelong Learning
AT WORK

about careers you may never have heard of, including the nature of the work, places of employment, training and qualifications required, earnings, working conditions, and employment outlook. Keep in mind that in today's fast-paced world, occupations will be available when you graduate that don't even exist today.

Ned Herrmann, creator of the Brain Dominance Inventory, wrote, "Experience has shown that alignment of a person's mental preferences with his or her work is predictive of success and satisfaction while nonalignment usually results in poor performance and dissatisfaction." So use your discoveries in this chapter about your preferred thinking styles to help you choose a compatible career. See Figure 7.1 for some examples.

When you have narrowed your career choices, you may want to learn even more before committing yourself. To get the inside scoop on how a career may fit you, get some hands-on experience. Find part-time or temporary work in the field, apply for an internship, or even do volunteer work. At one time I thought I wanted to be a veterinarian, but one summer of working in a veterinary hospital quickly taught me that it was a poor career match for me. I'm sure glad I found out *before* I went through many years of veterinary school!

Now it's time for your job interviews. Keep in mind that most employers are looking for someone who can learn the new position and keep learning new skills for years to come. In fact, a recent U.S. Department of Labor study found that employers of entry-level workers considered specific technical skills less important than the ability to learn on the job. So, how can you present yourself in the interview as a lifelong learner? First, of course, have a transcript with good grades to demonstrate your ability to learn in college. Be ready for questions such as, "How do you keep up with advancements in your field? What workshops

---

A. Thinking Learner: biologist, stock broker, engineer, city manager, science teacher, computer designer/programmer, computer technician, detective, educational administrator, radiologist, electrical engineer, financial planner, lawyer, chemist, mathematician, medical researcher, physician, statistician, veterinarian

B. Doing Learner: reporter, accountant, librarian, bookkeeper, clinical psychologist, credit advisor, historian, environmental scientist, farmer, hotel/motel manager, marketing director, military personnel, police officer, realtor, school principal, technical writer

C. Feeling Learner: actor, social worker, clergy, sociologist, counseling psychologist, human resource manager, public relations specialist, journalist, musician, teacher, nurse, occupational therapist, organizational development consultant, recreational therapist, sales, writer

D. Innovating Learner: dancer, poet, advertising designer, florist, psychiatrist, artist, creative writer, entrepreneur, fashion artist, playwright, filmmaker, graphic designer, humorist, inventor, landscape architect, nutritionist, photographer, editor, program developer

Figure 7.1 ▲ Learning Preferences and Compatible Careers

"Even though you're exceptionally well qualified, Kate, I'd say that 'victim' is not a good career choice."

© The New Yorker Collection, 1996. Edward Koren from cartoonbank.com. All rights reserved.

or seminars have you attended? What kind of reading do you do?" Go to the interview prepared to ask good questions of your own. And demonstrate that one of the things you're looking for in a particular job is its ability to help you keep learning your profession.

Today's work world is marked by downsizing and rightsizing. Companies are operating with leaner staffs, and this means that every employee is critical to the success of the business. It also means that someone who can't keep up with inevitable changes is expendable. One powerful way to give yourself a competitive advantage is to continually learn new skills and knowledge, even before you need them on your job. When your supervisor says, "Does anyone here know how to use a desktop publishing program?" you'll be able to say, "Sure, I can do that." Another way to keep learning on the job is to seek out feedback. Superior performers want to hear what others think of their work, realizing that this is a great way to learn to do it even better.

According to Anthony J. D'Angelo, author of the *College Blue Book,* world knowledge doubles every fourteen months. Suppose he's way off, and knowledge actually doubles only every five years as others claim. That still means we'll have to keep learning a little every day just to keep pace and a lot every day to get ahead. Educator Marshall McLuhan once said, "The future of work consists of *learning* a living (rather than *earning* a living)." His observation becomes truer with each passing day. Future success at work belongs to lifelong learners.

▸ *Believing in Yourself*
Develop Self-Respect

 FOCUS QUESTIONS What is your present level of self-respect? How can you raise your self-respect, and therefore your self-esteem, even higher?

Self-respect is the core belief that I AM AN ADMIRABLE PERSON. If self-confidence is the result of **what** I do, then self-respect is the result of **how** I do it.

Two crucial choices that build up or tear down my self-respect are whether or not I live with integrity and whether or not I keep my commitments.

Live with Integrity

The foundation of integrity is my personal value system. What is important to me? What experiences do I want to have? What experiences do I want others to have? Do I prize outer rewards such as cars, clothes, compliments, travel, fame, or money? Do I cherish inner experiences such as love, respect, excellence, security, honesty, wisdom, or compassion?

Integrity derives from the root word *integer,* meaning "one" or "whole." Thus we create integrity by choosing words and deeds that are one with our values. Many students say they value their education, but their actions indicate otherwise. They leave assignments undone; they do less than their best work; they miss classes; they come late. In short, their choices contradict what they say they value. Choices that lack integrity tear at an aware person's self-respect.

One of my greatest integrity tests occurred years ago when I left teaching to find a more lucrative career. I was excited when hired as a management trainee at a high-powered sales company. Graduates of this company's five-year training program were earning more than thirty times what I had earned as a teacher. I couldn't wait!

My first assignment was to hire new members of the company's sales force. I gave applicants an aptitude test that revealed whether they had what it took to succeed in sales. When the scores came back to the sales manager, he would tell me whether or not the applicants had qualified. If so, I'd offer them a sales position. Lured by dreams of wealth, many of them left the security of a steady salary for the uncertainty of a commission check. Unfortunately, few of them lasted more than a few months. They sold to their friends. They struggled. They disappeared.

Before long, I noticed an unsettling fact: No applicant ever failed the aptitude test. Right after this realization, I interviewed a very shy man who was a lineman for the local telephone company. He was only a year from early retirement, but he was willing to give up his retirement benefits for the promise of big commissions. If ever someone was wrong for sales, I thought, this was the person. I knew he'd be making a terrible mistake to abandon his security for the seductive promise of wealth. Surely here was one person who wouldn't pass the aptitude test. But he did.

"In fact," the sales manager told him in person, "you received one of the highest scores ever. How soon can you start?"

"Errr . . . well, let's see. It's Friday. I guess next week? If that's okay?"

That night, after the sales manager had left, I went into his office and located the lineman's folder. I opened it and found the test results. His score was zero. The man had not even scored!

All weekend, my stomach felt as though I had swallowed acid. My self-respect sank lower and lower. My Inner Defender kept telling me it was the

> Always aim at complete harmony of thought and word and deed.
> *Mohandas K. Gandhi*

> This above all; to thine own
>   self be true
> And it must follow, as the night
>   the day
> Thou canst not then be false
>   to any man.
> *Polonius, in Shakespeare's* Hamlet

lineman's choice, not mine. It was his life. Maybe he'd prove the aptitude test wrong. Maybe he would make a fortune in sales. My Inner Guide just shook his head in disgust.

On Monday, I phoned the lineman and told him his actual score.

He was furious. "Do you realize what I almost did?"

I thought, *Do you realize what I almost did?* Two weeks later I quit. Soon after, my stomach felt fine.

Each time you contradict your own values, you make a withdrawal from your self-respect account. Each time you live true to your values, you make a deposit. Here's a quick way to discover what you value and whether you are living with integrity: Ask yourself, *What qualities and behaviors do I admire in others? Do I ever allow myself to be less than what I admire?*

When you find that your choices are out of alignment with your values, you need to revise your dreams, goals, thoughts, feelings, actions, or beliefs. You can't abandon what you hold sacred and still retain your self-respect.

Keep Commitments

Now let's consider another choice that influences your self-respect. Imagine that someone has made a promise to you but doesn't keep it. Then he makes and breaks a second promise. And then another and another. Wouldn't you lose respect for this person? What do you suppose happens when the person making and breaking all of these promises is YOU?

True, your Inner Defender would quickly send out a smoke screen of excuses. But the truth would not be lost on your Inner Guide. The fact remains: You made commitments and broke them. This violation of your word makes a major withdrawal from your self-respect account.

To make a deposit in your self-respect account, keep commitments, especially to yourself. Here's how:

- **Make your agreements consciously.** Understand exactly what you're committing to. Say "no" to requests that will get you off course; don't commit to more than you can handle just to placate others.
- **Use Creator language.** Don't say, *I'll* try *to do it.* Say, *I* **will** *do it.*
- **Make your agreements important.** Write them down. Tell others about them.
- **Create a plan; then do everything in your power to carry out your plan.** Use your self-management tools to track your promises to yourself and others.
- **If a problem arises or you change your mind, renegotiate** (don't just abandon your promise).

The person we break commitments with the most is, ironically, ourselves. How are you doing in this regard? Here's some evidence: How are you doing with

You will always be in fashion if you are true to yourself, and only if you are true to yourself.

Maya Angelou

Whenever I break an agreement, I pay the price first. It breaks down my self-esteem, my credibility with my self, my self-trust, my self-confidence. It causes me not to be able to trust myself. If I cannot trust myself, whom can I trust?

Patricia J. Munson

the commitment you made to your goals and dream in Journal Entry 9? How are you doing with your 32-Day Commitment from Journal Entry 14?

If you haven't kept these commitments (or others), ask your Inner Guide, *What did I make more important than keeping my commitment to myself?* A part of you wanted to keep your agreement. But another, stronger part of you obviously resisted. Pursue your exploration of this inner conflict with total honesty and you may uncover a self-defeating pattern or limiting core belief that is crying out for a change. After all, our choices reveal what we *really* value.

Keeping commitments often requires overcoming enormous obstacles. That was the case with one of my students. Rosalie had postponed her dream of becoming a nurse for eighteen years while raising her two children alone. Shortly after enrolling in college, her new husband asked her to drop out to take care of his two sons from a former marriage. Rosalie agreed, postponing her dream once more. Now back in college ten years later, she made what she called a "sacred vow" to attend every class on time, to do her very best on all work, and to participate actively. This time she was committed to getting her nursing degree. Finally her time had come.

Then, one night she got a call from one of her sons who was now married and had a two-year-old baby girl. He had a serious problem: His wife was on drugs. Worse, that day she had bought two hundred dollars worth of drugs on credit, and the drug dealers were holding Rosalie's granddaughter until they got paid. Rosalie spent the early evening gathering cash from every source she could, finally delivering the money to her son. Then, all night she lay awake, waiting to hear if her grandchild would be returned safely.

> To me integrity is the bottom line in self-esteem. It begins with the keeping of one's word or doing what you say you will do, when you say you will do it, whether you feel like it or not.
>
> *Betty Hatch, president, National Council for Self-Esteem*

At six in the morning, Rosalie got good news when her son brought the baby to her house. He asked Rosalie to watch the child while he and his wife had a serious talk. Hours passed, and still Rosalie cared for the baby. Closer and closer crept the hour when her college classes would begin. She started to get angrier and angrier as she realized that once again she was allowing others to pull her off course. And then she remembered that she had a choice. She could stay home and feel sorry for herself, or she could do something to get back on course.

At about nine o'clock, Rosalie called her sister who lived on the other side of town. She asked her sister to take a cab to Rosalie's house, promised to pay the cab fare, and even offered to pay her sister a bonus to watch the baby.

"I didn't get to class on time," Rosalie said. "But I got there. And when I did, I just wanted to walk into the middle of the room and yell, 'YEEAAH! I MADE IT!'"

If you could have seen her face when she told the class about her ordeal and her victory, you would have seen a woman who had just learned one of life's great lessons: When we break a commitment to ourselves, something inside of us dies. When we keep a commitment to ourselves, something inside of us thrives. That something is self-respect.

Character, simply stated, is doing what you say you're going to do. A more formal definition is: Character is the ability to carry out a worthy decision after the emotion of making that decision has passed.

Hyrum W. Smith

JOURNAL ENTRY   27

In this activity, you will explore strengthening your self-respect. People with self-respect honor and admire themselves not just for *what* they do but for *how* they do it.

1. **Write about a time when you passed a personal integrity test.** Tell about an experience when you were greatly tempted to abandon one of your important values. Describe how you decided to "do the right thing" instead of giving in to the temptation.

2. **Write about a time when you kept a commitment that was difficult to keep.** Fully explain the commitment you made to yourself or to someone else, and discuss the challenges—both inner and outer—that made it difficult for you to keep this promise. Explain how you were able to keep the commitment despite these challenges.

Asking motivating questions leads to meaningful answers. Anticipate questions a curious reader might ask you about your stories . . . and answer them.

Embracing Change Do One Thing Different This Week

Being a lifelong learner will enhance the quality of your outcomes and experiences through your years in higher education and far beyond. Victims handicap their future success by focusing on "getting out" of college. If they do earn a degree, their learning experience is often so shallow that they haven't created a strong foundation on which to build their success. Creators, on the other hand, participate actively in the learning process, and thus have the information and skills (not to mention the neural networks) that will enhance their success for years to come. Here's your chance to develop one lifelong learning strategy. From the following actions, pick ONE new belief or behavior and experiment.

1. Think: "I learn valuable lessons from every experience I have."
2. Find someone in my class with the same learning preference as my own and ask about his or her most effective learning strategy.
3. Make an educated guess about the learning preference of one of my present instructors, and then determine a new learning strategy I could use to improve my outcomes in that class.
4. Make an effort to persuade someone to think or do something that I believe is important.
5. Ask probing questions about an argument that someone else presents.
6. Identify one piece of feedback received that day and determine what course correction, if any, I will make as a result of that feedback.
7. Identify one choice I am making that does not support my commitment to get a college degree and change it.

Now, write the one you chose under "My Commitment" in the following chart. Then, track yourself for one week, putting a check in the appropriate box when you keep your commitment. After seven days, assess your results. If your outcomes and experiences improve, you now have a tool you can use to improve your self-management for the rest of your life. Psychologist Carl Rogers reminds us that "The only person who is educated is the one who has learned how to learn and change."

My Commitment						
Day 1	**Day 2**	**Day 3**	**Day 4**	**Day 5**	**Day 6**	**Day 7**

During my seven-day experiment, what happened?

As a result of what happened, what did I learn or relearn?

Wise Choices in College WRITING

Along with reading, few academic skills support your success in college more than effective writing. In most college courses, you'll be asked to do at least some—and perhaps much—writing. You'll write compositions, lab reports, term papers, journal entries, and research papers. Additionally, you'll take many tests and exams that contain essay questions. Obviously, then, writing well increases your ability to earn good grades in college. But this is only one of writing's many benefits.

After you graduate, writing well can help you acquire and advance in the career of your choice. In fact, you'll likely write more in your career than you ever expected. With the growth of the Internet and a global economy, more and more business is transacted through e-mail and websites. The popularity of social networking sites and the explosion of blogging create additional needs for good writing. In both your professional and personal life, writing gives you a means to inform, persuade, or even entertain people. And writing helps you maintain relationships, especially with people who are far away. While these benefits may be evident, here is one that may be less obvious: **Writing well enhances learning.**

Consider what experienced writers say:

- *We do not write in order to be understood; we write in order to understand.*
  –Robert Cecil Day-Lewis

- *Writing became such a process of discovery that I couldn't wait to get to work in the morning . . . .*
  –Sharon O'Brien

- *The best way to become acquainted with a subject is to write a book about it.*
  –Benjamin Disraeli

- *Writing is making sense of life.*
  –Nadine Gordimer

- *Learn as much by writing as by reading.*
  –Lord Acton

Among other reasons, writing enhances learning because the process raises questions that require answers. For instance, if you were writing an essay about self-awareness, you might anticipate a question your reader will want answered: *What childhood experience caused the author to adopt a negative script about her math skills?* Or, more academically, you might find yourself wondering, *How does the activity of neurons contribute to self-awareness?* Your effort to **Collect**, **Organize**, and write answers to these questions (and others) expands your understanding of yourself, other people, and the world. And that is the essence of learning!

Here's another reason why writing enhances learning: Like learning, writing is a process. Most experts recognize four components in the writing process: prewriting, writing, revising, and editing. As you'll see, these four have much in common with the four components of the CORE Learning System. In fact, knowing the CORE Learning System gives you a real advantage when it comes to writing.

- **Prewriting** (also called *invention*) includes any preparation you do before actually writing. Guiding this process is an awareness of your audience and your purpose for writing. Prewriting activities include **Collecting** ideas and supporting details, then **Organizing** these raw material into a possible structure. Prewriting is a step that many novice writers unwisely skip.

- **Writing** (also called *drafting*) is the act of creation—turning your raw materials into a document that achieves your defined purpose. As you write, your mind both **Rehearses** the ideas you want to express and **Evaluates** your understanding of them. Thus, while writing you may realize that you need to **Collect** more information, re-**Organize** the information you already have, or both. When the first draft is complete, novice writers often pat themselves on the back and declare themselves done. Experienced writers know they have only just begun.

- **Revising** (also called *rewriting*) means "seeing again." When revising, you "re-see" in order to **Evaluate** your present draft. Does it say what you mean? Will it achieve your purpose for writing? If you have a poor understanding of your subject, your writing will likely be muddy and unclear. Revising, which is a kind of **Rehearsing**, helps identify what you don't understand and encourages you to think more critically about the subject. With this effort come both a deeper understanding and the ability to express that understanding more effectively in writing. That's why experienced writers often spend as much (or even more) time revising as they took planning and writing the first draft.

- **Editing** (also called *proofreading*) eliminates surface problems (e.g., errors in grammar, sentence structure, and spelling). When writing is littered with errors, your readers may wonder if your thinking is as careless as your proofreading. Worse, they may not understand what you mean. Either way, surface errors undermine the achievement of your purpose. Editing is your final **Evaluation** of how well you think your writing will achieve its purpose.

Perhaps now you understand why so many instructors require writing. To write well requires you to be the most active of learners, developing deep and lasting learning. And that, after all, is the goal of all good teaching.

Writing: The Big Picture

So, experiment with the many writing strategies that follow and, as you do, keep in mind the big picture of writing: **The goal of the four steps of the writing process is to inform, persuade, or entertain your intended audience. Thus, writing requires that you anticipate and answer the questions that engaged readers will have about your subject. In the act of asking and answering these questions, you will implement all of the steps of the CORE Learning System. That's why good writing is not only an important means of** communication; it is also one of the most powerful ways to create deep and lasting learning.

Before Writing

1. Create a positive affirmation about writing. Create an affirming statement such as, *I use all steps of the writing process to express my ideas clearly and effectively.* Use this affirmation to develop a "growth mind-set" about writing. Remember, a "growth mind-set" is a core belief that you can improve your academic outcomes by employing effective strategies and hard work. (The opposite belief is that there is nothing you can do to improve your academic results, which is a Victim stance.)

2. If you get to choose the topic, select one that truly interests you. You'll enjoy researching and writing about something meaningful to you, and your grades will probably improve as well. Even if your instructor assigns the topic, look for an approach to the topic that appeals to you.

3. Carry index cards for Collecting ideas. Once you begin thinking about a subject, ideas will pop into your mind at the strangest times. You might be ordering French fries in the cafeteria when a great idea hits you. Don't think you'll remember the idea later. Pull out an index card and write yourself a note. Keep the cards rubber-banded together for **Organizing** later.

4. Create focus questions. Make a list of questions to guide your **Collection** of information. Choose questions that arouse your curiosity. If you want to know the answers yourself, you'll be more motivated to find answers that you can shape into a successful writing assignment. For example, suppose you're going to write about financial aid. You might be very interested to know:

- What are the secrets for getting the most scholarship money?

- What mistakes keep students from getting all of the financial aid available to them?

- Is there a legal way to avoid repaying student loans?

Write each question on a separate index card or type a list of questions into your computer file.

5. Discuss your topic with others. Engage as many people as possible in a conversation about your topic. Start by asking your focus questions and follow where they lead. If possible, interview experts. For example, think how much you could learn about financial aid by talking with the head of your college's financial aid office. Having a conversation about your topic will get your neurons firing and your creative juices flowing. **Collect** the best ideas and supporting details by writing them on index cards.

6. Group your notes. Once you've **Collected** a stack of note cards on your topic, it's almost time to write . . . but not quite yet. First, group your notes by sorting them into piles, with one pile for each main idea or focus question. Better yet, type your notes into a computer; then, cut and paste them into clusters of related ideas. In our example about financial aid, three of these clusters would contain ideas related to your focus questions:

- Secrets of getting the most in scholarship money

- Mistakes that keep students from getting all of the financial aid available to them

- Legal ways to avoid repaying student loans

It's likely that you'll have gathered additional information as well. Find logical categories for these extra ideas as well. For example, you might group ideas together related to:

- The differences between grants, scholarships, and loans

- Government sources of financial aid

- Private sources of financial aid

- Ways to qualify for low-interest loans

- The consequences of not paying back student loans

7. Identify your audience. Every piece of writing has one or more intended readers. After all, there's no point in writing to no one. In most college writing, you will be informing your instructors about what you have learned. Perhaps you see the challenge: You'll be telling instructors about subjects that they know more about than you do. Usually the best approach is to write to a general audience. Picture a *general audience* as a group of interested, well-educated readers who know little or nothing about the topic. In this way, you will be more likely to provide all of the ideas and supporting details needed to show your instructors that you have mastered their course content. Sometimes instructors will specify your audience (e.g., readers of your college newspaper). If so, use this information to make choices as you write such as: *What tone (formal or informal) to adopt? What information to include or exclude? How much evidence is needed to overcome resistance?*

8. Define your thesis. A thesis states the most important idea you want to convey to your audience. Everything else you write merely supports this idea by answering questions that an engaged reader might have about your thesis. A thesis is made up of two elements: (1) the **topic** you're writing about and (2) the **claim** you make about the topic. Thus, a thesis statement is usually one sentence and has the following structure:

[Topic] + [Claim].

The two most common kinds of writing in college are informative and persuasive. The thesis of **informative** writing tells your readers something they presumably don't already know. For example:

[*Subprime mortgage loans*] + [*are those made to borrowers with questionable ability to pay back the money they borrow*].

The thesis of **persuasive** writing asks your readers to think or do something that presumably they are not inclined to think or do:

Think: [*Franklin Pierce*] + [*was one of the finest American presidents*].

Do: [*The student government*] + [*is an organization you should join*].

Sometimes you'll know immediately what your thesis is. Other times you may need to think and write for a while before a thesis emerges. Even after you've settled on your thesis, be prepared to change it as the process of writing causes you to learn more about your topic. Eventually, though, you'll need to settle on a clearly stated thesis, because an essay without a thesis is like a body without a spine—nothing holds it together.

9. Organize your ideas and supporting details. In Chapter 3, we looked at linear and graphic ways to **Organize** information. These methods also work well for **Organizing** information during prewriting. Let's revisit two of these strategies and introduce a third. The one you favor is probably explained by your preferred way of learning, as shown on the self-assessment you took at the beginning of this chapter.

  Outline. (For a review of how to create an outline, along with an example, see pages 95–97.) When creating an outline for a writing assignment, place your thesis statement at the top of a page (realizing that it may evolve as you write). Below it and flush to the left margin, add the subject of each of the groups you determined in Strategy 6. These are now your main ideas (Level 1). Next, indent a few spaces and add secondary ideas (Level 2) beneath each main idea. Finally, indent a few more spaces and add supporting ideas (Levels 3 and 4). Most word processing programs have a feature to help you create an outline. In Microsoft Word, for example, you'll find it in the View menu.

  Concept Map. (For a review of how to create a concept map, along with an example, see pages 96–98.) To create a concept map for a writing assignment, write your thesis statement at the top of a page. Then write the key concept in the middle of the page and either underline or circle it. Now draw lines out from the key concept and write the topic of each of the groups you determined in Strategy 6; these will be your main ideas (Level 1). Next,

draw lines out from your main ideas, and write secondary ideas (Level 2). Further out from the center of the concept map, write your supporting details (Levels 3 and 4). If you like organizing with concept maps, you may want to experiment with computer software designed for creating them. To find such software, search for "concept map software" using an Internet search engine.

  Question Outline. Here's a variation of an outline that's easy, quick, and effective. After determining your thesis, choose the most interesting questions from the list you created in Strategy 4. Make sure you have enough information to answer each question thoroughly . . . or **Collect** more. Use one question as the topic of each body paragraph. Thus, if you choose four questions, you'll probably be writing a six-paragraph essay (after adding your introduction and conclusion). It is possible, of course, that you could write two or more paragraphs to answer a question, making your essay longer than six paragraphs. Here's what a Question Outline about scripts might look like:

  – Introduction (including the thesis)

  – What are scripts?

  – How do we write our scripts?

  – Why do some scripts sabotage our success?

  – How can we revise self-sabotaging scripts?

  – Conclusion

While Writing

10. Use an essay blueprint. When you want to assemble something with many parts, a picture can help. For beginning writers, a blueprint showing a good way to assemble the parts of an essay is also a big help. Just as there are many blueprints for building a house, so are there many blueprints for writing an essay. But the one in Figure 7.2 is both effective and easy to understand. When one of my

Paragraph 1: Introduction Hook Thesis Agenda
Paragraph 2: Body Paragraph #1 Transition (presenting Main Idea #1) Secondary Ideas and Supporting Details (4E's)
Paragraph 3: Body Paragraph #2 Transition (presenting Main Idea #2) Secondary Ideas and Supporting Details (4E's)
Paragraph 4: Body Paragraph #3 Transition (presenting Main Idea #3) Secondary Ideas and Supporting Details (4E's)
Paragraph 5: Refutation (included in a persuasive essay) Transition (presenting opponents' argument) Refutation (presenting reasons and evidence to weaken opponent's argument)
Paragraph 6: Conclusion Summary or Echo Restatement of Thesis

Figure 7.2 ▲ Essay Blueprint

students saw this essay blueprint, she exclaimed, "So *that's* what the structure of an essay looks like? I can do *that*!" Each part in the blueprint is explained in the strategies that follow. As you add these parts to the essay blueprint, realize that the structure is flexible and can be modified. For example, the essay blueprint shows a six-paragraph essay; if you have a different number of main ideas, simply add or delete body paragraphs. Also, Paragraph 5 in the essay blueprint presents a feature (refutation) that is useful in a persuasive essay but usually unnecessary in an informative essay. As you become a more skilled writer, you will begin to take more and more liberties with this blueprint. Ultimately you'll be creating your own original ways to organize your main ideas and supporting details.

11. Write a hook. The beginning of your essay should hook your readers' interest. To do so, start with an engaging strategy such as a question, quotation, humor, surprising data, shocking statement, or fascinating story. Even though a *hook* is the first thing your audience reads, you don't have to write it first. In fact, you may think of a good hook only after writing the entire first draft of your essay. If you read the beginning of any essay in this book, you will see my efforts to "hook" your interest. For example, I began the section on "Rewriting Your Outdated Scripts" in Chapter 6 with the story of my student Diana screaming at me in class. My hope was that Diana's dramatic and unexpected outburst would hook your attention and motivate you to read on to find out more.

12. Add your thesis statement. After hooking your reader's attention, present your thesis—the key concept about which you are writing. Your thesis statement may be exactly as you wrote it in Strategy 8, or you may now decide that it needs revision. In fact, it's possible (even probable) that you will revise your thesis statement a number of times as the writing process helps you learn even more deeply about your topic.

13. Write an agenda. An agenda for a meeting lists the main ideas that will be discussed. Similarly, an agenda for an essay states the main ideas that readers can expect to encounter. Although agendas appear more commonly in long essays, articles, or even books, they can be a great help to keep both your readers and you (the author) focused even in a short essay. For example, suppose your thesis is *Students should get involved in campus activities.* Your agenda might give a list of the reasons: *First, getting involved in campus activities will increase your chances of earning a degree. Second, you'll meet people who may become lifelong friends. And finally, involvement in campus activities offers valuable learning experiences that are unavailable in an academic classroom.* This three-part agenda lets your readers know exactly the points you intend to present. Even if you choose not to include an agenda in your essay, having one in your mind helps keep your essay organized.

14. Use transitions. A transition is a bridge between ideas. Transitional words, phrases, or sentences help your readers follow the flow of your ideas. One important place to use a transition is at the beginning of a paragraph. You want to make sure you don't lose your readers as you shift to a new thought (or to answer a new question, if using a Question Outline). A good transition connects the idea just discussed with a new idea . . . and maybe even includes a reminder of the thesis. For example, suppose your thesis intends to persuade your readers to get involved with campus activities. Further, suppose that you have just completed a paragraph about how involvement in campus

activities increases a student's chances of earning a degree. The first sentence of your next paragraph might be: *Not only will getting involved with campus activities increase your chances of earning a degree, you'll also meet people who may very well become lifelong friends.* Notice how the transition does three things:

- It reminds readers of the thesis: *Get involved with campus activities.*

- It reminds readers about the main idea made in the previous paragraph: *Getting involved in campus activities increases your chances of earning a degree.*

- It makes a bridge to the main point of the new paragraph: *By getting involved in campus activities, you'll meet people who may very well become lifelong friends.*

The beginning of paragraphs is only one place in your essay where transitions are helpful. When you offer concrete support for main ideas, you can signal with transitional words such as *for example, as an illustration,* or *for instance.* When you point out similarities, signal with *likewise* or *similarly.* When you point out differences, signal with *by contrast, but, however,* or *on the contrary.* When you summarize or conclude, signal with *in other words, in summary, in conclusion,* or *finally.* Treat your readers like tourists in a strange land. As their guide, you don't want to lose or confuse them.

15. Add support. To generate specific and sufficient support, expand each body paragraph with secondary ideas and supporting details. This is easy to do when you remember to use the 4E's. The 4E's represent four questions that almost always need answering as you develop a paragraph:

- Can you give an EXAMPLE of that?

- Can you give an EXPERIENCE to illustrate that?

- Can you EXPLAIN that further?

- Can you give EVIDENCE to support that?

Answering one or more of the 4E's causes you to dive deeper and makes your writing more complete and fully developed.

16. Offer a refutation in a persuasive essay. When you write to persuade, assume your readers are resistant to what you want them to think or do. (After all, if they already agree with you, there's no need to persuade them.) Put yourself in their place and see if you can empathize with their reasons for resisting. Then dispute those reasons. For example, why might fellow students resist your efforts to persuade them to get involved in campus activities? Maybe they think they are too busy with their classes, assignments, and possibly a job. How could you refute their belief that they are too busy? As another example, in Chapter 1 ("A Few Words of Encouragement" on page 9), I used refutation in my efforts to persuade you to give the strategies in *On Course* a fair chance. Take a look back and see if . . .

A) I empathized with a reason that you may have resisted this course (if you did) and

B) I offered a refutation that reduced or even eliminated your resistance.

17. Write a satisfying conclusion. One easy way to conclude is to summarize the main points you have made (e.g., *So, if you want to become better at self-management, learn to use a calendar, next actions list, tracking form, and thirty-two-day commitment.*). For a more sophisticated conclusion, end with an **echo**. An echo restates all or part of an idea presented early in your essay, perhaps in your hook. For example, suppose your hook said, *Do you realize that college graduates earn nearly a million dollars more in their lives than non-grads?* You might echo this thought in your conclusion by ending with this sentence: *So, if you want to raise your lifetime earnings by nearly a million dollars, make getting your college degree a high priority.*

After Writing

18. Incubate. Set your writing aside and do something else . . . in fact, anything else. That's right—don't even think about what you wrote for at least a couple of hours. Better yet, for a couple of days. When you return to your writing later, you'll see your writing with new eyes. You'll notice problems and possibilities that earlier were invisible to you.

19. Revise. As mentioned earlier, "re-vision" means to "see again." After incubation, you'll be ready to see your writing with new eyes. Look for major changes to improve the quality of your communication. Consider a revised thesis statement, better organization, additional support (4E's: examples, experience, explanation, evidence), improved transitions, a catchier hook, a stronger conclusion. Perhaps most important, make sure that you have answered all important reader questions. Remember, good writing anticipates and answers questions that interested readers might ask. Even if you created questions before writing and answered them as you wrote, be alert for new questions that emerge as you revise. Two questions that almost always need answering are "*Why?*" and "*How do you know?*" Other important questions begin with *What? When? Who? Where? How?* and *What if?*

20. Edit carefully. Writing filled with errors is distracting to readers. At best, errors will cause them to think less of what you have to say (especially college instructors). At worst, your readers may misunderstand. The challenge with proofreading your own writing is that you know what is *supposed* to be there . . . and that is what you will often see instead of what is *actually* there. Here's a proofreading trick that can help: Start with the last sentence. Then proofread the second-to-last sentence. And continue proofreading from the bottom of your writing to the top. In this way, you can focus on the surface details of grammar, spelling, and punctuation without being distracted by the flow of ideas. If writing on a computer, remember that a computer's spell check will not pick up words used incorrectly but spelled correctly (such as using *there* for *their*). Your computer may also help you identify possible grammar errors that need to be corrected. But be careful, because sometimes it will point out "errors" that aren't errors at all.

21. Keep an Error Log. Some instructors, especially for a writing class, will point out your grammar and punctuation errors. When you get a writing assignment back with errors noted, enter them in an Error Log. An Error Log is a record of every sentence in which you had a grammar or punctuation problem. Below the error sentence, rewrite the sentence correctly. Then, write the relevant grammar or punctuation rule(s) so you can learn to correct all errors of the same kind. You'll find this information in the grammar section of a writing handbook, or you can ask a writing tutor to help you identify the rule. Everyone makes errors, but Creators seldom make the same mistake twice. Here's an example:

> **Error Sentence:** I went to the tutoring center, the tutor I was supposed to see wasn't there.

> **Corrected Sentence:** I went to the tutoring center, but the tutor I was supposed to see wasn't there.

> **Rule:** When two complete sentences are joined with only a comma, this error is called a comma splice. There are three ways to correct a comma splice: (1) Replace the comma with a period, thus creating two complete sentences. (2) Replace the comma with a semi-colon. (3) Add a coordinating conjunction (i.e., *and, but, or, nor, for, so,* or *yet*) after the comma.

Keeping an error log is time-consuming at first, but seeing your errors disappear from future papers is a great reward.

22. Rewrite graded papers. Most instructors provide feedback on substantive problems with your writing (e.g., unclear purpose, poor organization, lack of support). Use this feedback to rewrite and improve your assignment. Such a revision is the ultimate **Rehearsal** of your writing skills, and can help you immensely. Impressed with your initiative, most instructors will be glad to meet with you to discuss your revision. Some will even raise your grade if your revision shows improvement. Regardless of how your instructor responds to your rewrites, realize that there is as much, if not more, learning available to you in revising as there was in writing the original.

Writing Exercise

Compare the quality of your writing in Journal Entries 1 and 2 with the quality of your writing in Journal Entries 26 and 27. Be prepared to answer the following questions:

- Has the quality of your writing improved? If so, how? Offer specific examples.

- If your writing has not improved, why do you suppose it hasn't?

- Which of your journal entries do you think is the most well-written?

- What could you do to improve the writing in your remaining journal entries?

- How did you feel about writing when you began this course?

- Have your feelings about writing changed while keeping your journal? If so, how? And why?

Developing Emotional Intelligence

8

Creating worldly success is meaningless if I am unhappy. That means I must accept responsibility for creating the quality of not only my outcomes but also my inner experiences.

I create my own happiness and peace of mind.

Successful Students . . .	Struggling Students . . .
demonstrate emotional intelligence, using feelings as a compass for staying on course to their goals and dreams.	**allow themselves to be hijacked by emotions,** making unwise choices that get them off course.
effectively reduce stress, managing and soothing emotions of upset such as anger, fear, and sadness.	**take no responsibility for managing their emotions,** instead acting irrationally on impulses of the moment.
create flow, feeling fully and positively engaged in college and the rest of their lives.	**frequently experience boredom or anxiety in their lives.**

Case Study in Critical Thinking

After Math

When **Professor Bishop** returned midterm exams, he said, "In twenty years of teaching math, I've never seen such low scores. Can anyone tell me what the problem is?" He ran a hand through his graying hair and waited. No one spoke. "Don't you people even care how you do?" Students fiddled with their test papers. They looked out of the window. No one spoke.

Finally, Professor Bishop said, "Okay, Scott, we'll start with you. What's going on? You got a 35 on the test. Did you even *study?*"

Scott, age eighteen, mumbled, "Yeah, I studied. But I just don't understand math."

Other students in the class nodded their heads. One student muttered, "Amen, brother."

Professor Bishop looked around the classroom. "How about you, Elena? You didn't even show up for the test."

Elena, age thirty-one, sighed. "I'm sorry, but I have a lot of other things besides this class to worry about. My job keeps changing my schedule, I broke a tooth last week, my roommate won't pay me the money she owes me, my car broke down, and I haven't been able to find my math book for three weeks. I think my boyfriend hid it. If one more thing goes wrong in my life, I'm going to scream!"

Professor Bishop shook his head slowly back and forth. "Well, that's quite a story. What about the rest of you?" Silence reigned for a full minute.

Suddenly **Michael,** age twenty-three, stood up and snarled, "You're a damn joke, man. You can't teach, and you want to blame the problem on us. Well, I've had it. I'm dropping this stupid course. Then I'm filing a grievance. You better start looking for a new job!" He stormed out of the room, slamming the door behind him.

"Okay, I can see this isn't going anywhere productive," Professor Bishop said. "I want you all to go home and think about why you're doing so poorly. And don't come back until you're prepared to answer that question honestly." He picked up his books and left the room. Elena checked her watch and then dashed out of the room. She still had time to catch her favorite soap opera in the student lounge.

An hour later, Michael was sitting alone in the cafeteria when his classmates Scott and **Kia,** age twenty, joined him. Scott said, "Geez, Michael, you really went off on Bishop! You're not really going to drop his class, are you?"

"Already did!" Michael snapped as his classmates sat down. "I went right from class to the registrar's office. I'm outta there!"

I might as well drop the class myself, Kia thought. Ever since she was denied entrance to the nursing program, she'd been too depressed to do her homework. Familiar tears blurred her vision.

Scott said, "I don't know what it is about math. I study for hours, but when I get to the test, I get so freaked it's like I never studied at all. My mind just goes blank." Thinking about math, Scott started craving something to eat.

"Where do you file a grievance against a professor around here, anyway?" Michael asked.

"I have no idea," Scott said.

"What?" Kia answered.

Michael stood and stomped off to file a grievance. Scott went to buy some French fries. Kia put her head down on the cafeteria table and tried to swallow the burning sensation in her throat.

Listed below are the five characters in this story. Rank them in order of their emotional intelligence. Give a different score to each character. Be prepared to explain your choices.

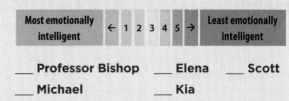

| Most emotionally intelligent | ← 1 2 3 4 5 → | Least emotionally intelligent |

___ **Professor Bishop**   ___ **Elena**   ___ **Scott**

___ **Michael**   ___ **Kia**

DIVING DEEPER Imagine that you have been asked to mentor the person whom you ranked number 5 (least emotionally intelligent). Other than recommending a counselor, how would you suggest that this person handle his or her upset in a more emotionally intelligent manner?

Understanding Emotional Intelligence

FOCUS QUESTIONS What is emotional intelligence? How can you experience the full range of natural human emotions and still stay on course to a rich, fulfilling life?

During final exam period one semester, I heard a shriek from the nursing education office. Seconds later, a student charged out of the office, screaming, scattering papers in the air, and stumbling down the hall. A cluster of concerned classmates caught up to her and desperately tried to offer comfort. "It's all right. You can take the exam again next semester. It's okay. Really." She leaned against the wall, eyes closed. She slid down the wall until she sat in a limp heap, surrounded by sympathetic voices. Later, I heard that she dropped out of school.

At the end of another semester, I had the unpleasant task of telling one of my hardest-working students that she had failed the writing proficiency exams. Her mother had died during the semester, so I was particularly worried about how she would handle more bad news. We had a conference, and upon telling her the news, I began consoling her. For about a minute, she listened quietly and then said, "You're taking my failure pretty hard. Do you need a hug?" Before I could respond, she plucked me out of my chair and gave me a hug. "Don't worry," she said, patting my back. "I'll pass next semester," and sure enough, she did.

For most of us, life presents a bumpy road now and then. We fail a college course. The job we want goes to someone else. The person we love doesn't return our affections. Our health gives way to sickness. How we handle these distressing experiences is critical to the outcomes and experiences of our lives.

Success depends on much more than a high IQ and academic success. Karen Arnold and Terry Denny at the University of Illinois studied eighty-one valedictorians and salutatorians. They found that ten years after graduation, only 25 percent of these academic stars were at the highest level of their professions when compared with others their age. Actually, many were doing poorly. What seems to be missing for them is **emotional intelligence.**

An experiment during the 1960s shows just how important emotional control is to success. Four-year-old children at a preschool were told they could have one marshmallow immediately. Or if they could wait for about twenty minutes, they could have two. More than a dozen years later, experimenters examined the differences in the lives of the one-marshmallow (emotionally impulsive) children and the two-marshmallow (emotionally intelligent) children. The adolescents who as children were able to delay gratification scored an average of 210 points higher on their SATs (Scholastic Aptitude Tests). Additionally, the two-marshmallow teenagers had borne fewer children while unmarried and had experienced fewer problems with the law.

> I know it is hard to accept, but an upset in your life is beneficial, in that it tells you that you are off course in some way and you need to find your way back to your particular path of clarity once again.
>
> *Susan Jeffers*

> In the realm of emotions, many people are functioning at a kindergarten level. There is no need for self-blame. After all, in your formal education, how many courses did you take in dealing with feelings?
>
> *Gay & Kathlyn Hendricks*

Clearly, the ability to endure some emotional discomfort in the present in exchange for greater rewards in the future is a key to success.

Four Components of Emotional Intelligence

As a relatively new field of study, emotional intelligence is still being defined. However, Daniel Goleman, author of the book *Emotional Intelligence,** identifies four components that contribute to emotional effectiveness. The first two qualities are personal and have to do with recognizing and effectively managing one's own emotions. The second two are social and have to do with recognizing and effectively managing emotions in others.

> Every great, successful person I know shares the capacity to remain centered, clear and powerful in the midst of emotional "storms."
>
> *Anthony Robbins*

1. **EMOTIONAL SELF-AWARENESS: Knowing your feelings in the moment.** Self-awareness of one's own feelings as they occur is the foundation of emotional intelligence and is fundamental to effective decision making. Thus, people who are keenly aware of their changing moods are better pilots of their lives. For example, emotional self-awareness helps you deal effectively with feeling overwhelmed instead of using television (or some other distraction) as a temporary escape.

2. **EMOTIONAL SELF-MANAGEMENT: Managing strong feelings.** Emotional self-management enables people to make wise choices despite the pull of powerful emotions. People who excel at this skill avoid making critical decisions during times of high drama. Instead they wait until their inner storm has calmed and then make considered choices that contribute to their desired outcomes and experiences. For example, emotional self-management helps you resist dropping an important class simply because you got angry at the teacher. It also helps you make a choice that offers delayed benefits (e.g., writing a term paper) in place of a choice that promises instant gratification (e.g., attending a party).

> Academic intelligence has little to do with emotional life. The brightest among us can founder on the shoals of unbridled passions and unruly impulses; people with high IQ's can be stunningly poor pilots of their private lives.
>
> *Daniel Goleman*

3. **SOCIAL AWARENESS: Empathizing accurately with other people's emotions.** Empathy is the fundamental "people skill." Those with empathy and compassion are more attuned to the subtle social signals that reveal what others need or want. For example, social awareness helps you notice and offer comfort when someone is consumed by anxiety or sadness.

4. **RELATIONSHIP MANAGEMENT: Handling emotions in relationships with skill and harmony.** The art of relationships depends, in large part, upon the skill of managing emotions in others. People who excel at skills such as listening, resolving conflicts, cooperating, and articulating the pulse of a group do well at anything that relies on interacting smoothly with others. For example, relationship management helps a person resist saying something that might publicly embarrass someone else.

* From Emotional Intelligence by Daniel Goleman, © 1995 by Daniel Goleman. Used by permission of Banton Books, a division of Random House, Inc.

Knowing Your Own Emotions

The foundation of emotional intelligence is a keen awareness of our own emotions as they rise and fall. None of the other abilities can exist without this one. Here are some steps toward becoming more attuned to your own emotions.

BUILD A VOCABULARY OF FEELINGS. Learn the names of emotions you might experience. There are dozens. How many can you name beyond anger, fear, sadness, and happiness?

BE MINDFUL OF EMOTIONS AS THEY ARE HAPPENING. Learn to identify and express emotions in the moment. Be aware of the subtleties of emotion, learning to make fine distinctions between feelings that are similar, such as sadness and depression.

UNDERSTAND WHAT IS CAUSING YOUR EMOTION. Look behind the emotion. See when anger is caused by hurt feelings. Notice when anxiety is caused by irrational thoughts. Realize when sadness is caused by disappointments. Identify when happiness is caused by immediate gratification that gets you off course from your long-term goals.

> In the midst of great joy do not promise to give a man anything; in the midst of great anger do not answer a man's letter.
>
> *Chinese proverb*

RECOGNIZE THE DIFFERENCE BETWEEN A FEELING AND RESULTING ACTIONS. Feeling an emotion is one thing; acting on the emotion is quite another. Emotions and behaviors are separate experiences, one internal, one external. Note when you tend to confuse the two, as a student did who said, "My teacher made me so angry I had to drop the class." You can be angry with a teacher and still remain enrolled in a class that is important to your goals and dreams. A fundamental principle of emotional intelligence is, ***Never make an important decision while experiencing strong emotions***.

You will never reach your full potential without emotional intelligence. No matter how academically bright you may be, emotional illiteracy will limit your achievements. Developing emotional wisdom will fuel your motivation, help you successfully negotiate emotional storms (yours and others'), and enhance your chances of creating your greatest goals and dreams.

JOURNAL ENTRY 28

In this activity, you will explore your ability to understand your own emotions and recognize them as they are occurring. This ability is the foundation for all other emotional intelligence skills.

It made me feel better sometimes to get something down on paper just like I felt it. It brought a kind of relief to be able to describe my pain. It was like, if I could describe it, it lost some of its power over me. I jotted down innermost thoughts I couldn't verbalize to anyone else, recorded what I saw around me, and expressed feelings inspired by things I read.

Nathan McCall

1. **Write about an experience when you felt one of the following emotions: FRUSTRATION or ANGER, FEAR or ANXIETY, SADNESS or DEPRESSION.**

Describe fully what happened and your emotional reaction. Because emotions are difficult to describe, you may want to try a comparison like this: *Anger spread through me like a fire in a pile of dry hay. . .* or *I trembled in fear as though I was the next person to stand before a firing squad,* or *For weeks, depression wrapped me in a profound darkness.* Of course, create your own comparison. Your journal entry might begin, *Last week was one of the most frustrating times of my entire life. It all began when . . . .* Most important, be aware of any emotions that you may feel *as you are writing.*

2. **Write about an experience when you felt HAPPINESS or JOY.** Once again, describe fully what happened and your emotional reaction. A possible comparison: *Joy bubbled like champagne in my soul, and I laughed uncontrollably.* Most important, be aware of any emotions that you may feel *as you are writing.*

3. **Write about any emotional changes you experienced *as you described* each of these two emotions. What did you learn or relearn about how you can affect your emotions?** If you weren't aware of any changes in your present emotions as you described past emotions, see if you can explain why. Were you not experiencing any emotions at all? Or could you have been unaware of the emotions you were feeling?

One Student's Story

Lindsey Beck
Three Rivers Community College, Connecticut

When I started college, I had been in an abusive relationship for almost three years. I was terrified to leave this man (I'll call him Henry) because we have a child together and he had convinced me that I had no worth as a human being without him. At 6'4", Henry is a foot taller and weighs twice as much as I do. He would punch or kick me until I was in so much pain I couldn't go to my classes. When I did go, I'd often leave early because he became convinced I was cheating on him and I didn't want to give him another reason to beat me. I have a fair amount of academic ability and I did well in high school, but I started allowing my emotions to overrun my intelligence. It was like I had a bunch of emotions in a bowl and I'd just pull one out at random when something happened. One day when my mother expressed concern about my bruises, I got furious at her. But instead of get-

ting angry at Henry for beating me, I'd feel afraid, confused, and depressed. Rather than stepping back and thinking logically about what was going on, I allowed my emotions to control me.

Studying became my escape. In my freshman year experience course, I loved expressing myself in my journals. In Chapter 8, I started writing about my emotions, and for the first time in years, I wasn't ashamed of my feelings. I decided to be totally honest, and I wrote down exactly what was going on and how I *really* felt about it (not how Henry told me I felt about it). Writing the journals really made me look at myself and ask, *What am I doing in this relationship?* When I read about all of the positive ways I could manage my emotions, I started looking at things as though I wasn't going to take it any more. I got stronger every

day, and then one day I made the decision to leave Henry.

I've always done well at writing papers, studying, and taking tests, but I've never really taken responsibility for my emotions before. I learned that I need to get my emotional life under control if I want the rest of my life to work. I now realize that how I feel at one moment isn't necessarily how I'll feel ten minutes later. Emotions change. Why let things control me that are so temporary? By growing emotionally, I'm able to control my emotions instead of letting them control me. I am finally starting to picture a positive life for myself without Henry, and I am growing more confident every day. My dream is to earn a degree in microbiology and make a difference by working for the World Health Organization. Enrolling in this course was the best life decision I will probably ever make. If I hadn't, ten years from now, I might not have wanted to change my life. However, I have been able to do that, and now I have my whole life ahead of me.

Photo: Courtesy of Lindsey Beck

Reducing Stress

 FOCUS QUESTION How can you soothe stressful feelings that make life unpleasant and threaten to get you off course?

Changes and challenges are inevitable in our lives; thus, so is the potential for stress. Maybe you waited until the last minute to print your essay for English class and the printer wouldn't work. Stress. Or you bounced a six-dollar check and the bank charged you a $25 penalty. Stress! Or you've got a test coming up in history and you're two chapters behind in your reading. STRESS!

Even life's pleasant events, like a new relationship or a weekend trip, can bring on a positive form of stress called *eustress*. If we're not careful, stress of one kind or another can bump us off course.

What Is Stress?

The American Medical Association defines stress as any interference that disturbs a person's mental or physical well-being. However, most of us know stress simply as the "wear and tear" that our minds and bodies experience as we attempt to cope with the challenges of life. The body's response to a stressor is much the same today as it was for our ancestors thousands of years ago. As soon as we perceive a threat, our brain releases the stress hormones cortisol and epinephrine (also known as adrenaline), and instantly our bodies respond with an increase in heart rate, metabolism, breathing, muscle tension, and blood pressure. We're ready for "fight or flight."

To our ancestors, this stress response literally meant the difference between life and death. After they'd survived a threat (a saber-toothed tiger, perhaps), the stress hormones were gone from their bodies within minutes. In modern life, however, much of our stress comes from worrying about past events, agonizing about present challenges, and fretting about future changes. Instead of stress hormones being active in our bodies for only minutes, they may persist for months or even years. For many of us, then, stress is a constant and toxic companion.

What Happens When Stress Persists?

Ongoing stress is bad news for our health, damaging almost every bodily system. It inhibits digestion, reproduction, growth, tissue repair, and the responses of our immune system. As just one example of the impact of long-term stress on our health, Carnegie Mellon University researchers exposed four hundred volunteers to cold viruses and found that people with high stress in their lives were twice as likely to develop colds as those with low stress.

In fact, the National Institute for Mental Health estimates that 70 to 80 percent of all doctor visits are for stress-related illnesses. Physical symptoms of stress can be as varied as high blood pressure, muscle tension, headaches, backaches, indigestion, irritable bowel, ulcers, chronic constipation or diarrhea, muscle spasms, tics, tremors, sexual dysfunction, fatigue, insomnia, physical weakness, and emotional upsets.

Immediately relevant to college students is the discovery that stress has a negative impact on memory. It also hinders other mental skills such as creativity, concentration, and attention to details. When you're feeling stressed, you can't do your best academic work, let alone enjoy doing it. So, when you feel stressed, what are your choices?

The process of living is the process of reacting to stress.

Stanley J. Sarnoff, M.D.

Every stress leaves an indelible scar, and the organism pays for its survival after a stressful situation by becoming a little older.

Hans Selye, M.D.

Unhealthy Stress Reduction

When stressed, Victims' greatest concern is escaping the discomfort as fast as possible. To do so, they often make unwise choices: drinking alcohol to excess, going numb for hours in front of a television or computer, working obsessively, fighting, taking numbing drugs, going on shopping binges, eating too much or too little, smoking excessively, gulping caffeine, or gambling more than they can afford to lose. When confronted with the damage of their self-sabotaging behavior, they typically blame, complain, and make excuses. *Stress made me do it!*

Like the impulsive children of the marshmallow experiment, Victims seek instant gratification. They give little thought to the impact of these choices on their futures. By making one impulsive and ill-considered choice after another, Victims move farther and farther off course.

Healthy Stress Reduction

Creators find a better way to reduce stress. They realize that managing emotions intelligently means making wise choices that release the grip of stress, not just mask it. Effective at identifying their distressing feelings early, Creators take positive actions to avoid being hijacked by emotional upset. Here's a menu of healthy and effective strategies for managing four of the most common symptoms of stress.

A special note to the highly stressed: Your Inner Defender may take one look at the list of strategies that follows and say something like, "I can't deal with this right now. It's just going to make me even *more* stressed out!" If that's really the case, consider making an appointment at your campus counseling office to get some caring, professional help for your stress.

To reduce your stress on your own, here's a simple, two-step plan. First, read the following section that addresses your most pressing symptoms of stress: overwhelm, anger, depression, or anxiety. In that section, pick one stress reduction strategy and make a thirty-two-day commitment (page 121) to do it. In little more than a month, you'll likely feel less stressed. Better yet, you'll have proven that *you,* and not stress, are in charge of your life.

OVERWHELM. Overwhelm is probably the most common stressor for college students. Its message, if heeded, is valuable: Your life has gotten too complicated, your commitments too many. Overwhelm warns us that we've lost control of our lives. Creators often notice overwhelm when it shows up as a tightness or pain in their jaw, shoulders, or lower back. Or lack of

Of all the drugs and the compulsive behaviors that I have seen in the past twenty-five years, be it cocaine, heroin, alcohol, nicotine, gambling, sexual addiction, food addiction, all have one common thread. That is the covering up, or the masking, or the unwillingness on the part of the human being to confront and be with his or her human feelings.

Richard Miller, M.D.

sleep. Or they may notice themselves thinking, "If one more thing goes wrong, I'm going to scream!" Or, maybe they *do* scream! With this awareness, Creators understand it's time to take action. Many positive strategies exist for rescuing your life from the distress of feeling overwhelmed.

> When you take full responsibility here and now for all of your feelings and for everything that happens to you, you never again blame the people and situations in the world outside of you for any unhappy feelings that you have.
>
> *Ken Keyes*

Choose new behaviors: Here are some actions you can take when you feel that your life is stretched a mile wide and an inch thin. As you'll see, many of them are variations of self-management strategies you learned in Chapter 4:

- *Separate from an external stressor.* Perhaps the external stressor is a neighbor's loud music or a demanding job. You can choose to study in the library where it's quiet and find a new job with fewer demands.

- *List and prioritize everything you need to do.* Using a next actions list (page 114), record all of your incomplete tasks according to life roles. Assign priorities to each task: A = Important & Urgent actions. B = Important & Not Urgent actions. C = All Unimportant actions.

- *Delete C's.* Identify where you are wasting time and cross them off your list.

- *Delegate A's and B's.* Where possible, get another person to complete some of your important tasks. Ask a friend to pick up your dry cleaning. Pay someone to clean your apartment. This choice frees up time to do the tasks that only you can do, like your math homework.

- *Complete remaining A's and B's yourself.* Start with your A priorities, such as a looming term paper or a broken refrigerator. Handle them immediately: Visit the library and take out three books to begin researching your term paper topic. Call an appliance repair shop and schedule a service call. Spend time doing only A and B priorities and watch your overwhelm subside.

- *Discover time-savers.* Consciously make better use of your time. For example, keep an errand list so you can do them all in one trip. Or study flash cards during the hour between classes.

- *Eliminate time-wasters.* Identify and eliminate Quadrants III and IV activities. For example, reduce the time you spend on Facebook. Cut down on watching television. Stop playing video games.

- *Say "no."* Admit that your plate is full, and politely refuse requests that add to your commitments. If you do agree to take on something new, say "no" to

THE FAR SIDE® By GARY LARSON

© 1982 FarWorks, Inc. All Rights Reserved/Dist. by Creators Syndicate

"You know, we're just not reaching that guy."

The Far Side® by Gary Larson © 1982 FarWorks, Inc.
All Rights Reserved. Used with permission.

something already on your plate. If saying "no" is difficult for you, do role plays with a friend to practice. Or put it in writing.

- *Keep your finances organized.* A survey of 11,000 adults by *Prevention* magazine revealed that their number one source of stress is worry over personal finances. So curtail unnecessary spending, pay bills when due, balance your checkbook. Use the money-management strategies later in this chapter for stress relief as well as debt relief.

- *Exercise.* Aerobic exercise increases the blood levels of endorphins, and these hormones block pain, create a feeling of euphoria (the exercise high), and reduce stress. One caution: Consult your doctor before dramatically changing your level of exercise.

- *Get enough sleep.* If sleep is a problem, don't eat after seven o'clock and go to bed by ten. If thoughts keep running through your mind, write them down. Breathe deeply and relax. Clear your mind. If sleep eludes you, consider seeing a doctor. You can't learn effectively when deprived of sleep.

Choose new thoughts: Since we create the inner experience of overwhelm in our mind, we can un-create it. Here's how:

- *Elevate.* Rise above the overwhelm and see each problem in the bigger picture of your life. Notice how little importance it really has. From this new perspective, ask, "Will this problem really matter one year from now?" Often the answer is "no."

- *Trust a positive outcome.* How many times have you been upset by something that later turned out to be a blessing in disguise? Since it's possible, expect the blessing.

- *Take a mental vacation.* Picture a place you love (e.g., a white-sand beach, mountain retreat, or forest path) and spend a few minutes visiting it in your mind. Enjoy the peace and rejuvenation of this mini-vacation.

ANGER AND RESENTMENT. Healthy anger declares a threat or injustice against us or someone or something we care about. Perceiving this violation, the brain signals the body to release catecholamines (hormones) that fuel both our strength and our will to fight. Creators become conscious of oncoming anger through changes such as flushed skin, tensed muscles, and increased pulse rates.

With this awareness, Creators can pause and wisely choose what to do next, rather than lashing out impulsively. Emotions don't ask rational questions, so we must. For example, Creators ask, *Will I benefit from releasing my anger, or will it cost me dearly?*

When you perceive a true injustice, use the energy produced by your anger to right the wrong. However, to avoid being hijacked by anger and doing something you will regret later, here are some effective strategies:

> The sign of intelligent people is their ability to control emotions by the application of reason.
>
> *Marya Mannes*

Choose new behaviors: Allow the tidal wave of anger-producing hormones about twenty minutes to recede. Here's how:

- *Separate.* Go off by yourself, allowing enough time to regain your ability to make rational, positive choices.
- *Exercise.* Moving vigorously assists in reducing anger-fueling hormones in your body.
- *Relax.* Slowing down also aids in calming your body, returning control of your decisions to you (as long as you don't spend this time obsessively thinking about the event that angered you).
- *Journal.* Write about your feelings in detail. Rant and rave to your journal. Explore the cause and effect of your anger. Take responsibility for any part you play in creating the anger. Honest expression of emotions can help the dark storm pass and rational thoughts return.
- *Channel your anger into positive actions.* That's what Marie Tursi did when a drunk driver killed her twenty-year-old son and received only a $151 fine and four years of probation. Tursi turned her anger into action and created Mothers Against Drunk Driving (MADD). Now a nationwide organization, MADD strives to end drunk driving and provide support for its victims. After your anger has subsided, the Wise Choice Process can help you decide on positive actions that you might take.

Choose new thoughts: Since thoughts stir emotional responses, revising our anger-producing thoughts can calm us. Here's how:

- *Reframe.* Look at the problem from a different perspective. Search for a benign explanation for the anger-causing event. If you realize you were wronged unknowingly, unintentionally, or even necessarily, you can often see the other person's behavior in a less hostile way.
- *Distract yourself.* Consciously shift your attention to something pleasant, stopping the avalanche of angry thoughts. Involve yourself with uplifting conversations, movies, books, music, video games, puzzles, or similar diversions.
- *Identify the hurt.* Anger is often built upon hurt: Someone doesn't meet me when she said she would. Below my anger I'm hurt that she seems to care about me so little. Shift attention from anger to the deeper hurt. Consider expressing the hurt in writing.
- *Forgive.* Take offending people off the hook for whatever they did, no matter how offensive. Don't concern yourself with whether *they* deserve forgiveness; the question is whether *you* deserve the emotional relief of forgiveness. The reason for forgiveness is primarily to improve *your* life, not theirs. We close the case to free ourselves of the daily self-infliction of poisonous judgments. Of course, forgiveness doesn't mean we forget and allow them to misuse us again.

No one can create anger or stress within you, only you can do that by virtue of how you process your world, or, in other words, how you think.

Wayne Dyer

Living life as an art requires a readiness to forgive.

Maya Angelou

FEAR AND ANXIETY. Healthy fear delivers a message that we are in danger. Our brain then releases hormones that fuel our energy to flee. Many Victims, though, exaggerate dangers, and their healthy fear is replaced by paralyzing anxiety or even terror about what could go wrong.

Creators become conscious of oncoming anxiety through their body's clear signals, including shallow breathing, increased pulse rate, and "butterflies" in the stomach. With this awareness, Creators can pause and wisely choose what to do next rather than fleeing impulsively from or worrying constantly about a non-threatening person or situation.

One of the areas where fear hinders academic performance is test anxiety. Unless you minimize this distress, you will be unable to demonstrate effectively what you know. Many colleges offer workshops or courses that offer instruction in anxiety-reducing strategies. Here are some wise choices to avoid being hijacked by fear, especially fear generated by a test.

Choose new behaviors: As with anger, help the anxiety-producing chemicals to recede. Here's how:

- *Prepare thoroughly.* If your anxiety relates to an upcoming performance (e.g., test or job interview), prepare thoroughly and then prepare some more. Confidence gained through extensive preparation diminishes anxiety. Using your CORE Learning System is a great way to increase your realistic expectations for success on any test.

- *Relax.* Slowing down helps you reclaim mastery of your thoughts and emotions (but don't spend this time obsessing about the cause of your anxiety).

- *Breathe deeply.* Anxiety and fear constrict. Keep oxygen flowing through your body to reverse their physiological impact.

- *Bring a piece of home to tests.* For example, bring a picture of your family.

- *Request accommodations.* Visit your college's disability services to see about making special arrangements, such as a longer time to take tests.

Choose new thoughts: Changing our thoughts can soothe irrational anxieties. Here's how:

- *Detach.* Once you have prepared fully for an upcoming challenge (such as a test), there's no more you can do. Worrying won't help. So do everything you can to ready yourself for the challenge; then trust the outcome to take care of itself.

- *Reframe.* Ask yourself, "If the worst happens, can I live with it?" If you fail a test, for example, you won't like it, but could you live with it? Of course you could! (If not, consider seeking help to regain a healthy perspective.)

- *Visualize success.* Create a mental movie of yourself achieving your ideal outcomes. Play the movie over and over until the picture of success becomes stronger than your fear.

> Anxiety...sabotages academic performance of all kinds: 126 different studies of more than 36,000 people found that the more prone to worries a person is, the poorer their academic performance, no matter how measured—grades on tests, grade-point average, or achievement tests.
>
> *Daniel Goleman*

If your images are positive, they will support you and cheer you on when you get discouraged. Negative pictures rattle around inside of you, affecting you without your knowing it.

Virginia Satir

- *Assume the best.* Victims often create fear through negative assumptions. Suppose your professor says, "I want to talk to you in my office." Resist assuming the conversation concerns something bad. In fact, if you're going to assume, why not assume it's something wonderful?

- *Face the fear.* Do what you fear, in spite of the fear. Most often you will learn that your fear was just a <u>F</u>alse <u>E</u>xpectation <u>A</u>ppearing <u>R</u>eal.

- *Say your affirmation.* When fearful thoughts creep into your mind, replace them with the positive words of your affirmation.

SADNESS AND DEPRESSION. Healthy sadness overtakes us upon the loss of someone or something dear. Fully grieving our loss is essential, for only in this way do we both honor and resolve our loss. Unhealthy sadness, however, becomes a lingering depression, a dark, helpless feeling that anesthetizes us, keeping us from moving on to create a positive experience of life despite our loss.

Creators become conscious of oncoming depression through their body's clear signals of low energy, constant fatigue, and lack of a positive will to perform meaningful tasks. With this awareness, Creators wisely take steps to avoid an extended stay in the dark pit of depression. Here are some positive options:

Choose new behaviors: Help your body produce natural, mood-elevating hormones. Here's how:

- *Do something (anything!) toward your goals.* Get moving and produce a result, no matter how small. Accomplishment combats depression.

- *Exercise.* Moving vigorously helps your body produce endorphins, causing a natural high that combats depression.

- *Listen to uplifting music.* Put on a song that picks up your spirits. Avoid sad songs about lost love and misery.

- *Laugh.* Like exercise, laughter is physiologically incompatible with depression. So rent a funny movie, go to a comedy club, read joke books or cartoons, or visit your funniest friend.

- *Breathe deeply.* Like fear, depression constricts. Keep breathing deeply to offset the physiological impact of depression.

- *Help others in need.* Assisting people less fortunate is uplifting. You experience both the joy of lightening their burden and the reminder that, despite your loss, you still have much to be grateful for.

- *Journal.* Writing about your sadness or depression can help you come to terms with the feelings more quickly and effectively. Often our emotions on paper are much less distressing than those roaming unexamined in our mind and heart.

- *Socialize with friends and loved ones.* Isolation usually intensifies depression. Socializing re-engages you with people who matter and helps you gain a healthier perspective on your loss.

Choose new thoughts: As with other distressing emotions, changing our thoughts soothes depression. Here's how:

- *Dispute pessimistic beliefs.* Depression thrives on pessimism. So challenge negative beliefs that make the loss seem permanent, pervasive, or personal. Think, instead, how life will improve over time, how the loss is limited to only one part of your life, and how the cause is not a personal flaw in you, but something you can remedy with an action.

- *Distract yourself.* As with anger, consciously replacing depressing thoughts with pleasant ones will help stop the anxiety. So involve yourself with engaging activities that will take your thoughts on a pleasant diversion.

- *Focus on the positive.* Identify your blessings and successes. Think of all the things for which you are grateful, perhaps even making a list. Appreciate what you *do* have instead of regretting what you don't.

- *Find the opportunity in the problem.* At the very least, learn the lesson life has brought you and move on. At best, turn your loss into a gain.

- *Remind yourself, "This, too, shall pass."* A year from now, you'll be in an entirely different place in your life, and this depression will be only a memory.

- *Identify others who have much more to be sad or depressed about.* Realize by this comparison how fortunate you actually are, changing your focus from your loss to all that you still have.

> The greater part of our happiness or misery depends on our dispositions and not our circumstances.
>
> *Martha Washington*

Choose Your Attitude

When dealing with stress, the critical issue is, *Do you manage your emotions or do they manage you?* If you have made an honest effort to manage your emotions and they have defied you still, you may want to seek the help of a counselor or therapist. In some cases, persistent emotional distress is the result of a chemical imbalance that can be treated with prescription drugs. But if it's inspiration you seek, consider Viktor E. Frankl, a psychiatrist imprisoned in the Nazi concentration camps during World War II. In his book, *Man's Search for Meaning,* Frankl relates how he and other prisoners rose above their stressful conditions to create a positive inner experience.

In one example, Frankl tells of a particularly bleak day when he was falling into a deep despair. With terrible sores on his feet, he was forced to march many miles in bitter cold weather to a work site, and there, freezing and weak from starvation, he endured constant brutality from the guards. Frankl describes how he "forced" his thoughts to turn to another subject. In his mind he imagined himself "standing on the platform of a well-lit, warm and pleasant lecture room." Before him sat an audience enthralled to hear him lecture on the psychology of the concentration camp. "By this method," Frankl says, "I succeeded somehow in rising above the situation, above the sufferings of the moment, and I observed them as if they were already of the past."

> The greatest discovery of my generation is that human beings, by changing the inner attitudes of their minds, can change the outer aspects of their lives.
>
> *William James*

From his experiences and his observations, Frankl concluded that everything can be taken from us but one thing: "the last of the human freedoms—to choose one's attitude in any given set of circumstances, to choose one's own way."

Creators claim the power to choose their outcomes whenever possible and to choose their inner experiences always. If Victor Frankl could overcome the stress of his inhumane imprisonment in a concentration camp, surely we can find the strength to overcome the stresses of our ordinary lives.

> Emotion comes directly from what we think: Think "I am in danger" and you feel anxiety. Think "I am being trespassed against" and you feel anger. Think "Loss" and you feel sadness.
>
> *Martin Seligman*

JOURNAL ENTRY 29

In this activity you will practice identifying positive methods for reducing the stress in your life.

1. **Write about a recent time when you experienced overwhelm, anger or resentment, sadness or depression, fear or anxiety.** Choose an experience different from the one you described in Journal Entry 28. Fully describe the situation that caused your emotional response; then describe the feelings you experienced; finally, explain what you did (if anything) to manage your emotions in a positive way.

2. **Identify three or more strategies that you could use in the future when you experience this emotion.** Explain each strategy in a separate paragraph, and remember the power of the 4E's—examples, experiences, explanation, and evidence—to improve the quality of your writing. When you're done, notice if simply writing about your stressors and ways to manage them may have reduced your level of stress. It did for students in a study at Southern Methodist University.

One Student's Story

Jaime Sanmiguel
Miami Dade College, Florida

I don't consider myself someone who lives in fear, and very few things in life intimidate me. However, the one fear that I could never overcome was my dread of public speaking. When I had to give a speech or read an essay aloud in junior high or high school, I would develop a shaky voice, get sweaty palms, and turn completely red. When I got to college, I took a fundamentals of speech class in which much of our grade depended on two speeches that we had to give using a PowerPoint presentation. My first speech didn't go very well. I hadn't really learned to use PowerPoint, and the slides didn't seem to fit what I was talking about. I began to feel insecure, and I started going all over the place. My teacher said the speech was okay, but I wasn't happy with it, especially because my

goal is to work in public relations, where I'll need to be able to speak to groups with confidence.

I was taking SLS 1125, Student Support Seminar, at the same time, and I discovered many helpful hints in *On Course* to overcome my fears. The first thing I did for my next speech was to make sure I was thoroughly prepared. This time I wrote out my whole speech first and then put my key points on index cards. I learned how to work PowerPoint and made sure all of the slides went with what I was talking about. I practiced giving my speech a number of times, with my dog as my audience. Another student in my class gave a great speech on the history of watches, and I visualized myself doing some of the things she had done, like using my hands effectively, looking relaxed,

smiling, and being more natural and friendly. I also did some relaxing and deep breathing, and that helped take my mind off my concerns. I used to worry that people would think I didn't know what I was talking about, but I changed these worries by picturing my audience as friends who want to know what I have to say. When I actually gave my speech, I picked out individual students and talked to each of them one at a time. These techniques helped me believe in myself more and not be so self-conscious in front of an audience, and in the end I passed the course with a B.

But just as important, in *On Course* I learned, "If you keep doing what you've been doing, you'll keep getting what you've been getting." I took ownership of that fact that if I want to be successful in a public relations career, I have to face and overcome my fears of giving presentations. I think I'm well on my way to achieving this goal.

Creating Flow

FOCUS QUESTIONS What are you doing when you feel most happy to be alive—when you become so absorbed that time seems to disappear? How can you create more of these peak experiences in college and beyond?

Happiness has been called the goal of all goals, the true destination of all journeys. After all, why do we pursue any goal or dream? Isn't it for the positive inner experience our success will create?

For centuries, explorers of human nature have pondered how we can consciously and naturally create happiness. Psychologist Mihaly Csikszentmihalyi has called highly enjoyable periods of time **flow states.** Flow is characterized by

a total absorption in what one is doing, by a loss of thoughts or concerns about oneself, and by a distorted sense of time (often passing very quickly). His studies offer insights into how we can purposely create such positive inner experiences in college and beyond.

Csikszentmihalyi believes that the key to creating flow lies in the interaction of two factors: the **challenge** a person perceives himself to be facing and the related **skills** he perceives himself to possess. Let's consider examples of three possible relationships of skill level and challenge. First, when a person's perceived skill level is higher than a perceived challenge, the result is *boredom:* Think how bored you'd feel if you took an introductory course in a subject in which you were already an expert.

Second, when a person's perceived skill level is lower than that needed to meet a perceived challenge, the result is *anxiety:* Think how anxious you'd feel if you took an advanced mathematics course before you could add and subtract.

Third, when an individual's perceived skill level is equal to or slightly below the challenge level, the result is often *flow:* Recall one of those extraordinary moments when you lost yourself in the flow—maybe while conversing with a challenging thinker or playing a sport you love with a well-matched opponent. In flow, participation in the activity is its own reward; the outcome doesn't matter. Flow generates the ultimate in intrinsic motivation: We do the activity merely for the positive experience it provides.

Creating Flow

Skill level HIGH and challenge level LOW = Boredom

Skill level LOW and challenge level HIGH = Anxiety

Skill level EQUAL TO or SLIGHTLY BELOW challenge level = Flow

---

> Being able to enter flow is emotional intelligence at its best; flow represents perhaps the ultimate in harnessing the emotions in the service of performance and learning.
>
> *Daniel Goleman*

Nadja Salerno-Sonnenberg, one of the world's great concert violinists, describes her own experience of flow this way: "Playing in the zone is a phrase that I use to describe a certain feeling on stage, a heightened feeling where everything is right. By that I mean everything comes together. Everything is one . . . you, yourself, are not battling yourself. All the technical work and what you want to say with the piece comes together. It's very, very rare but it's what I have worked for all my life. It's just right. It just makes everything right. Nothing can go wrong with this wonderful feeling."

College and Flow

What if you could have this kind of experience in your college courses? Creators do all they can to maximize that possibility, and how you choose your courses and your instructors is a good first step. Victims typically create their course schedule based on convenience: *Give me a class at 10:00 because I don't like to get up early.*

Creators have a very different approach. They realize that it's worth a sacrifice to get a course with an outstanding instructor, one who creates flow in the classroom. As you plan your schedule for next semester, ask other students to recommend instructors who . . .

1. demonstrate a deep knowledge of their subject,
2. show great enthusiasm for the value of their subject,
3. set challenging but reasonable learning objectives for their students,
4. offer engaging learning experiences that appeal to diverse learning preferences, and
5. provide a combination of academic and emotional support that gives their students high expectations of success.

> We tend to experience flow when we become absorbed in something challenging.
>
> *Jere Brophy*

These are the instructors who are going to create flow in their classrooms, support you to achieve academic success, and inspire you to be a lifelong learner.

Work and Flow

It is also important to consider flow when choosing your academic major and your career. You may be surprised by what psychologist Csikszentmihalyi found in his research: Typical working adults report experiencing flow on their jobs three times more often than during free time. When it comes to creating flow, work trumps evenings, weekends, and even vacations. The lesson is clear: If you want to create a positive experience of life, engage in work that appeals to your natural inclinations. When will you have time for boredom if you wake up every morning excited about your day's work?

Carolyn, a twenty-year-old student of mine, was studying to be a nurse, which was the career her mother wanted for her. Carolyn's dream was to dance, but she made keeping the peace at home more important. "If I even mention dancing, my mother goes ballistic," Carolyn confided. "It's not worth the hassle to fight her."

> The best career advice to give the young is "Find out what you like doing best and get someone to pay you for doing it."
>
> *Katherine Whitehorn*

I saw Carolyn some years after our first conversation and asked what she was doing.

"I'm a nurse now," she said.

"Any dancing in your life?"

"I've sort of stopped thinking about that."

As best I could tell, Carolyn had abandoned her dreams.

Have you? Are you headed for a career that represents your passion? Is it the work you would choose if you had absolutely no restrictions, either from outside you or inside you?

For the next couple of decades at least, you'll probably spend many of your waking hours at work. You don't have to settle for just a paycheck. Some people do what they love. Why shouldn't you?

When you study people who are successful as I have over the years, it is abundantly clear that their achievements are directly related to the enjoyment they derived from their work.

Marsha Sinetar

I spent more than a year of my life doing work that wasn't me, and I know how quickly my joy shriveled. I woke up many mornings with a stomachache. I lived for weekends, but by Sunday afternoon I began to dread Monday morning. Finally, I heeded the feedback from my emotional distress and sought work where I was happy. I urge you to follow your bliss. This choice may require self-discipline to get you through the education or training necessary to qualify for your desired career, but it's worth all of the discomfort in the present for all of the rewards in the future.

One more point remains to be made about the benefits of creating flow in college, at work, and everywhere else in your life. Not only does flow improve your inner experience, but it also promotes your professional and personal growth. Each time you create flow by testing your present skills against a new challenge, your skills improve. To create flow the next time, you have to increase the difficulty of the challenge, which in turn offers an opportunity to improve your skills once again. Over time, by creating flow again and again, your skills improve greatly, and this growth adds even more to the success and happiness in your life.

JOURNAL ENTRY **30**

In this activity, you will explore ways to create flow in your life. The more flow you create day to day, the more positive will be your inner experience of life.

1. **Write about a specific past event when you experienced flow in any part of your life.** Remember, flow is characterized by total absorption in what you're doing, an altered awareness of time, and a sense of performing at your very best.

Think back to a time in your childhood when you were doing what you loved to do, and how each day flew by. Hours seemed like minutes. When you love your work, when you love your life, then every day is like that.

Dr. Bernie Siegel

2. **Write about your perfect work of the future, the kind that you believe will create the most flow in your life.** Think about any past or present work experiences. Identify the feelings these jobs generated in you (particularly boredom, anxiety, or flow). Then let your imagination run free. Design your perfect job, its challenges, rewards, fellow workers, hours, location, and environment. Consider everything that will make this work something you would love to do *even if you didn't get paid*. Indulge in some no-limit thinking!

Consider illustrating this journal entry with drawings, stickers, pictures cut from magazines, or clip art.

Emotional Intelligence AT WORK

During nearly twenty years working as a consulting psychologist to dozens of companies and public agencies, I have seen how the lack of emotional intelligence undermines both an individual's and a company's growth and success, and conversely how the use of emotional intelligence leads to productive outcomes at both the individual and the organizational levels. *Hendrie Weisnger, Emotional Intelligence at Work*

Imagine this: The local store manager of a large retail chain sends a one-line email to her department heads: "Quarterly sales figures on my desk by 9:00 A.M. tomorrow!" The head of the menswear department reads the email, feels insulted by the demanding tone, and fires back an angry email response: "I've been working here a hell of a lot longer than you have, and I don't need your nasty reminders about when sales reports are due. You might try treating people more like colleagues and less like servants awaiting your every command." On an impulse, he copies his response to the company president and the five vice-presidents at the store's national headquarters.

How much lost time and productivity do you think will result from this exchange of two emails? How much damage will be done to the employees' professional relationship and their ability to work well together in the future? How might their reputations and careers suffer when others hear rumors of this incident?

Now consider how different this event might have been if the head of the menswear department had followed a fundamental principle of emotional intelligence: ***Never make an important decision while experiencing strong emotions.*** Suppose he'd read the store manager's email, taken a deep breath, and read it again. Feeling angry at what appeared to be the manager's dictatorial tone, what if he had waited about thirty minutes before responding? During that time, maybe he would have done some deep breathing. Maybe he would have recalled that the store manager has been very respectful of him since she took over the store six months before. Having calmed his initial upset, suppose he now went to the store manager's office and asked for a brief meeting. "You know," he says to her in this revised scene, "I just read your email about turning in the third-quarter sales figures, and I got that you're angry or upset. Is there something we need to talk about?" "What? Oh no," she responds, "there's no problem. I meant to send you a reminder last week, but I'm so far behind in my paperwork that I forgot. When I remembered this morning, I wrote the email while I was doing five other things. Sorry if it sounded like I was upset with you. On the contrary, I think you're doing a terrific job!"

Another name for emotional intelligence in the workplace is "professionalism." Professionals are aware of their own emotions, and they've developed methods for managing them. They're also good at perceiving emotions in others, and they know how to communicate effectively, building alliances rather than destroying them. Notice that in the revised scene just described, the department head doesn't reply to his manager with another email. He communicates with her in person. And he does so only after getting his emotions under control. Little

Creators Wanted!

Candidates must demonstrate emotional intelligence, including the ability to manage emotions in themselves and others.

Emotional Intelligence
AT WORK

decisions like these make all the difference when it comes to building a reputation as a business professional. And that reputation can be destroyed with one careless tantrum—or, in the digital age, with one reckless email.

Your emotional intelligence begins to impact your work life as soon as you consider a career path. If you choose work for which you have no passion or emotional commitment, you're starting your career with a huge handicap. Unmotivated by the outcomes or experiences of your work, you'll likely cut corners, doing less than is necessary to propel your career to success. By contrast, when you match your interests and talents to your career choice, you'll find work stimulating and success more likely. As Shoshana Zuboff, a psychiatrist and professor at Harvard Business School put it, "We only will know what to do by realizing what feels right to us."

Emotional intelligence continues to support your success during your job search. Chances are, every applicant invited for an interview has the training to do the job. So, what will distinguish you from the crowd? One answer lies in what employers are looking for beyond job skills. A 1997 survey of major corporations, done by the American Society for Training and Development, discovered that four out of five companies seek emotional intelligence as one of the qualities they look for in new employees. Realizing this, you'll know to communicate not only your academic and job-related skills, but your emotional intelligence competencies as well.

Employers have good reason to seek employees with emotional intelligence. In his book *Working with Emotional Intelligence,* Daniel Goleman writes, "We now have twenty-five years' worth of empirical studies that tell us with a previously unknown precision just how much emotional intelligence matters for success." Goleman presents his analysis of what 121 companies reported as the necessary competencies for success in 181 different career positions. He found that two out of three of the abilities considered essential for effective job performance are emotional competencies. Put another way, according to employers themselves, emotional competence matters *twice* as much as other factors in job effectiveness.

You might think that the soft skills associated with emotional intelligence would be less important for those employed in highly technical and intellectual fields such as engineering, computer science, law, or medicine. Paradoxically, the exact opposite is true. Since academic success and high intelligence are required of all who enter these careers, virtually everyone in these careers is "book smart." However, not everyone is emotionally intelligent. In these professions, there is more variation in the "soft" domain than there is in education and IQ. Therefore, if you're at the top end of the emotional intelligence scale, you have a great advantage over your emotionally illiterate colleagues. As Goleman puts it, "'Soft' skills matter even more for success in 'hard' fields."

While emotional intelligence is important in entry-level positions, as one moves up the ladder into leadership positions, it becomes essential.

Emotional Intelligence
AT WORK

According to Goleman, employers report emotional intelligence as making up 80 to 100 percent of the skills necessary to be an outstanding leader. As just one example of its importance, leaders need to be able to spot and resolve conflicts that happen in their workforce. Otherwise such upsets can get an individual, group, division, or even the whole company off course.

Doug Lennick, executive vice-president at American Express Financial Advisors, sums up the case for emotional intelligence in the workplace: "The aptitudes you need to succeed start with intellectual horsepower—but people need emotional competence, too, to get the full potential of their talents. The reason we don't get people's full potential is emotional incompetence."

▶ *Believing in Yourself*
Develop Self-Love

> **?**   **FOCUS QUESTIONS** How much do you love yourself? What can you do to love yourself even more?

Self-love is the core belief that **I AM LOVABLE.** It's the unwavering trust that, no matter what, I will always love myself and other people will love me as well.

Self-love is vital to success. It empowers us to make wise, self-supporting choices instead of impulsive, self-destructive ones. These wise choices create a rich, full life of outer achievement and inner happiness.

Adults who have difficulty loving themselves typically felt neglected or abandoned as children. Many grew up in families in which they felt unappreciated and unloved. What meager love they did experience was often little more than a short-lived reward for giving in to their parents' expectations and demands. For children who felt unloved, each new day meant a desperate search for something they could say or do to earn approval from others.

A student in my English class once wrote an essay about the outrageous stunts she'd done to become "head rabbit" for her fifth grade's spring festival. As she read her story, everyone laughed loudly. Afterward, someone asked, "Why did you go to all that trouble just to be the head rabbit?"

The student paused. "Simple. The head rabbit got to wear the best costume." Then a serious look came over her face. "The truth is, I thought people would like me more if I was the head rabbit." She paused again. "And, I guess I hoped that *I* would like me more, too."

Like my student, we may believe that self-love depends upon our outer accomplishments and what others think of them. This kind of self-love is conditional: *I'll love myself **after** I earn my degree, **after** I get a great job, **after** I marry the perfect person, **after** I buy my dream house . . . .*

> Ultimately, for most of us, the journey comes down to the same issue: learning to love freely. First ourselves, then other people.
>
> *Melody Beattie*

If the belief that accomplishment creates self-love were accurate, then why do so many people who appear successful on the outside feel so empty on the inside? Worldly success will not fill all the empty places in our souls. But love for ourselves will.

Design a Self-Care Plan

If we felt unloved as children, we may need to learn how to love ourselves as adults and do so without confusing self-love with egotism, arrogance, or self-righteousness.

First, we might ask, *How do we know when other people truly love us?* Isn't it when they treat us well, when they consider our welfare along with their own, concern themselves with our success and happiness, treat us with respect even when our behavior seems least deserving, give us honest feedback, and make sacrifices for the betterment of our lives? Don't we feel loved when others nurture the very best in us with the very best in them?

Our parents' job was to love and nurture us when we were children. Some parents did a great job; some did a terrible job. Most parents probably fell somewhere in between. Now that we are adults, we are responsible for continuing (or beginning) our own nurturing. The more we care for ourselves, the more we feel lovable. And the more we feel lovable, the more overflow of compassion and love we have for others.

Nurturing yourself can begin today with a conscious self-care plan. As you consider the following options for nurturing yourself, look for choices you could adopt to increase your self-love.

NURTURE YOURSELF PHYSICALLY. People who love themselves make wise choices to nurture their bodies for a long, healthy life. How's your diet? The next time you're about to eat or drink something, ask yourself: *Would I be proud to serve this to someone I love?* This question will raise your awareness, encouraging you to make wiser choices about eating and drinking. Visit your college's health office or library for valuable information on improving your diet.

Do you exercise regularly? Even moderate exercise done routinely helps most people stay stronger and healthier. Regular exercise strengthens the immune system and produces hormones that give us a natural sense of well-being. Your physical education department can help you begin a safe, effective, and lifelong exercise program.

Do you have habits that harm your body? Do you drink too much coffee, smoke cigarettes, drink alcohol to excess, take dangerous drugs? If so, consider giving up the immediate pleasure of such substances for the improved health you'll gain. Substance abuse is misnamed. You're not abusing the substance— you're abusing yourself. Would you abuse someone you love? Your college's health office can provide you with information on how to stop these self-destructive habits. Additional community resources include Alcoholics Anonymous (AA),

> Self-esteem is the capacity to experience maximal self-love and joy whether or not you are successful at any point in your life.
>
> *David Burns, M.D.*

> The extent to which we love ourselves determines whether we eat right, get enough sleep, smoke, wear seat belts, exercise, and so on. Each of these choices is a statement of how much we care about living.
>
> *Bernie Siegel, M.D.*

Narcotics Anonymous (NA), Overeaters Anonymous (OA), and other twelve-step programs.

Here are additional ways to nurture your body: Get enough rest. Swing on a swing. Have regular medical checkups. Hug someone dear to you. Laugh until your sides ache. Take a bubble bath. Go dancing. Get a massage. Do nothing for an hour. Stretch like a cat. Breathe deeply. Relax.

NURTURE YOURSELF MENTALLY. How you talk to yourself, especially when you're off course, will greatly influence your sense of self-love. Whenever your Inner Critic begins to condemn you, stop. Replace these negative judgments with positive, supportive comments.

You may find it difficult at first to choose self-loving thoughts rather than self-criticism. To help, try separating the doer from the deed. If you fail a test, your Inner Critic may label you a failure. But your Inner Guide knows you're not. You're a person who, with many other successes in life, got one F on one test. Keep your self-talk focused on facts, not judgments. When you create an undesirable outcome, learn from the experience, forgive yourself for judging your shortcomings, and move on.

Here are additional ways to nurture yourself mentally. Say your affirmation(s) often, read uplifting books (many are listed in the bibliography on pages 287–288), ask a motivating question and seek the answer, learn new words, visualize your success, balance your checkbook, sing or listen to a song with positive lyrics, analyze a difficult situation and make a decision, teach someone something you know how to do.

NURTURE YOURSELF EMOTIONALLY. The times you need self-love the most are often the times you feel self-love the least. You may be feeling shame instead of self-acceptance, helplessness instead of confidence, timidity instead of assertiveness, self-contempt instead of self-respect, self-loathing instead of self-love.

An emotional antidote for toxic self-judgments is *compassion*. Treat yourself with the same kindness you'd offer a loved one who's struggling to make sense of this huge, confusing, and sometimes painful world. Realize that how you treat yourself as you go through difficult times—with judgment or compassion—is what will continue to affect your self-love long after the difficult times have passed.

Here are more ways to nurture yourself emotionally: Feel your feelings, share your feelings with a friend, write about your feelings in your journal, see an uplifting and inspiring movie, spend time with loved ones, listen to inspiring music, do something special for yourself, remind yourself that strong feelings, like storms, will pass.

Deep self-love is the ongoing inner approval of who you are, regardless of your accomplishments. You are not your results. When you learn to love yourself even when you're off course and struggling, your belief in yourself will soar.

> I believe that the black revolution certainly forced me and the majority of black people to begin taking a second look at ourselves. It wasn't that we were all that ashamed of ourselves, we merely started appreciating our natural selves . . . sort of, you know, falling in love with ourselves just as we are.
>
> *Aretha Franklin*

> The First Best-Kept Secret of Total Success is that we must feel love inside ourselves before we can give it to others.
>
> *Denis Waitley*

JOURNAL ENTRY   **31**

In this activity, you will explore ways to develop greater self-love. Typically, people who love themselves achieve many of their goals and dreams and, regardless of the outer circumstances of their lives, often experience positive feelings.

1. On a blank journal page, draw a circle. Within the circle, create a symbolic representation of your most **LOVABLE INNER SELF.** If people could get a glimpse of you without your protective scripts, patterns, and habits, this is what they'd see. Such a picture is a kind of "mandala." Roughly translated from the classical Indian language of Sanskrit, *mandala* means "circle." As a circle represents wholeness, let your mandala symbolize your own personal wholeness. Let it represent your greatest potential as a human being, your ideal self. This picture needs to make sense only to you. Use colors, words, or shapes as appropriate. To create your mandala, feel free to draw, add personal photographs, or clip and paste pictures cut from magazines. This image here is an example of a mandala.

Mandala illustration created by Marcia Backos.

2. Outside of the mandala circle, write different ways that you could take care of yourself **PHYSICALLY, MENTALLY,** and **EMOTIONALLY.** In this way you are creating a self-care plan for the LOVABLE INNER SELF depicted in your mandala. Look back at the text for examples of ways to nurture yourself physically, mentally, and emotionally. If appropriate for you, add ways to nurture yourself spiritually as well.

3. On the next page in your journal, write an explanation of your mandala and the self-care plan that you have created. Think of questions an inquisitive reader would ask you, and let your Inner Guide answer them. For example, what is the significance of the shapes, pictures, words, lines, and colors that you have chosen to represent your full potential as a human being? What personal characteristics have you depicted as representing your best self? Why are these qualities important to you? In what ways have you decided to take care of yourself? And why have you chosen these particular ways to nurture yourself?

> One of the ways I nurture my own soul is by waking every morning around four-thirty and spending two hours by myself—for myself—doing yoga, visualization, meditation, or working on dreams . . . . Another way I nurture my soul is by keeping a daily journal . . . . This is what my two solitary hours in the morning are about—experiencing the core of my soul and discovering the truth that I have to live.
>
> *Marion Woodman*

Embracing Change   Do One Thing Different This Week

Strong emotions are part of the human experience, but what we do with them is up to us. Victims often let strong emotions become their excuse for making choices that promote immediate pleasure or escape from discomfort while sabotaging future goals and dreams. Creators, however, have learned to weather the storms of strong emotions and refuse to be blown off course. From the following actions, pick ONE new belief or behavior.

1. Think: "I create my own happiness and peace of mind."
2. Write a list of eight emotions and add eight more emotions to the list each day. Afterward, circle which of the fifty-six emotions I experienced during that week.
3. Identify and record a "strong emotion" as I experience it. Note at the end of the week if I see a pattern in the kind of strong emotions that I experience.
4. Identify a "strong emotion" as someone else is experiencing it, and note how I respond.
5. Talk to someone about emotions, mine or theirs.
6. Take the following new action to reduce stress in my life: _____ (choose from the list on pages 251–257).
7. Notice when I experience "flow," and observe what I am doing at the time.
8. Show fellow students the list of five instructor qualities on page 261 that create "flow," and ask them to name the instructor they have had who most demonstrates these qualities. I will consider enrolling in a class taught by one of these instructors.
9. Do the following to nurture myself: _____ (choose from the list on pages 266–267).

Now, write the one you chose under "My Commitment" in the following chart. Then, track yourself for one week, putting a check in the appropriate box when you keep your commitment. After seven days, assess your results. If your outcomes and experiences improve, you now have a tool you can use to improve your self-management for the rest of your life. Consider the insight of Confucius, the ancient Chinese philosopher, who said, "They must often change, who would be constant in happiness or wisdom."

My Commitment						
Day 1	Day 2	Day 3	Day 4	Day 5	Day 6	Day 7

During my seven-day experiment, what happened?

As a result of what happened, what did I learn or relearn?

Wise Choices in College   MANAGING MONEY

When asked why they enrolled in college, many students say, "To get a better-paying job." Quite understandably, they want what money can buy: a nice house, quality medical care, good food, reliable transportation, nice clothing, and time for recreation, to name just a few. They also want the peace of mind that financial security can offer. In a nutshell, they want the good life for themselves and for those they love.

These students are correct that a college degree correlates with greater abundance. Check out Figure 8.1 to see how level of education affects the earnings and unemployment rate of people aged twenty-five and older.

Clearly, earning a degree increases the likelihood of abundance. Sadly, however, many students' inability to manage money keeps them from completing the very degree that would help them earn the money they desire. Managing money is a skill as important and challenging as reading and writing. And, just as poor reading or writing skills are barriers to college success, so, too, are poor money management skills. To earn money, many students

work so many hours that their learning and grades suffer. Still others drop out of college because they decide they just can't afford it. Creators, however, treat a money problem as they would any other. They identify their goal, analyze their options, make a plan, carry it out, and, finally, assess its level of success. They will not be denied.

In this chapter, you will learn some of the basics of money management. There is, of course, much more to know. But if you apply these basic skills effectively, you can look forward to building a bank account that will provide you with many of the things that money can provide, including a college education.

Managing Money: The Big Picture

When I was a young college instructor, a colleague and I were complaining one day about how little money we were making. Both of us had young families, and our salaries barely got us from paycheck to paycheck. One day we decided to stop complaining and do something about it. We decided to award ourselves a raise. To do so, we brainstormed

Level of Education	Median Earnings	Unemployment Rate
Less than a high school diploma	$22,256	7.1%
High school diploma, no college	$31,408	4.4%
Some college, no degree	$35,516	3.8%
Associate degree	$38,480	3.0%
Bachelor's degree	$51,324	2.2%
Master's degree	$60,580	1.8%
Doctoral degree	$77,844	1.4%
Professional degree	$74,204	1.3%

Figure 8.1 ▲ Yearly Salaries and Unemployment Rates by Levels of Education
Source: U.S. Bureau of Labor Statistics, Current Population Survey, 2008.

how we could save or earn more money. Our first discovery was that we were both paying about six dollars a month for our checking accounts. We switched to free checking and gave ourselves an instant raise of $72 a year. By itself, no big thing. But we also thought of twenty-one other ways to make or save money. All told, our self-awarded raises amounted to more than a thousand dollars a year. And that was just the beginning of our realization that we had more control over our money than we had thought.

So, be a Creator when it comes to money. As you examine the following strategies, keep in mind the big picture of managing money. D**o everything legal to increase the flow of money into your personal treasury and decrease the flow of money leaking** *out*. **The better you become at these two complementary skills, the more abundance you will create to enhance your life and the lives of the people you love**.

Increasing Money Flowing In

1. Create a positive affirmation about money. Many people hold negative beliefs about money and their ability to accumulate it. These doubts keep them from making wise choices that would cause more money to flow in their direction, or reduce the amount of money flowing away from them. Create an affirming statement about money, such as, *I am creating unlimited abundance in my life.* Along with your personal affirmation, repeat this financial affirmation to revise your choices about money. There is great abundance on our planet, and there is no reason why you shouldn't enjoy your share of it.

2. Create a financial plan. Like a life plan, a financial plan helps you define and achieve your goals. It helps you make important decisions about the dollars flowing in and out of your bank account. Beginning your financial plan is as simple as filling out the form on the next page of this section. As a guideline, some financial experts suggest that expenditures in a healthy financial plan should be close to the following percentages of your net

income (i.e., the money remaining after all required federal, state, and local tax deductions):

31% Housing	7% Entertainment
20% Transportation	7% Savings
16% Food	6% Clothing
8% Miscellaneous	5% Health

Obviously, after subtracting all of your expenses from your income, your goal is to have a positive and growing balance. If you have a negative balance, with each passing month you'll slide deeper into debt. To avoid debt, you need to increase your income, decrease your expenses, or both.

3. Find a bank or credit union. A bank or credit union helps you manage your money with services such as checking accounts, savings accounts, and easy access to cash through automated teller machines (ATMs). Your ideal financial institution offers a free checking account that requires no minimum balance and pays interest. Further, it offers a savings account with competitive interest rates. And, finally, your ideal financial institution offers free use of its ATMs and those belonging to other banks or credit unions as well. If you need to pay for any of these services, seek to minimize the yearly cost. Credit unions typically offer lower rates on these services than banks do. If you don't know of a credit union for which you qualify, contact the Credit Union National Association (800-358-5710) to get the phone number of your state's credit union league, where you'll get help in finding one you may be able to join. Whether your checking account is with a bank or a credit union, be sure to balance your account regularly. This will save you the embarrassment and expense of bounced (rejected) checks because of insufficient funds.

4. Apply for grants and scholarships. A great place to get an overview of financial aid sources is provided on the Internet by the U.S. government at http://www.ed.gov/fund/grants-college.html. The process of applying for financial aid dollars begins

My Financial Plan		
Step A: Monthly Income	**Amount**	**Balance**
Support from parents or others		
Scholarships		
Loans		
Investments		
Earned income		
TOTAL MONTHLY INCOME (A)		
Step B: Necessary Fixed Monthly Expenses		
Housing (mortgage or rent)		
Transportation (car payments, insurance, bus pass, car pool)		
Taxes (federal and state income, Social Security, Medicare)		
Insurance (house, health, and life)		
Child care		
Tuition		
Bank fees		
Debt payment		
Savings and investments		
TOTAL NECESSARY FIXED MONTHLY EXPENSES (B)		
Step C: Necessary Variable Monthly Expenses		
Food and personal care items		
Clothing		
Telephone		
Gas and electric		
Water		
Transportation (car repairs, maintenance, gasoline)		
Laundry and dry cleaning		
Doctor and medicine		
Child care		
Books and software		
Computer/Internet access		
TOTAL NECESSARY VARIABLE MONTHLY EXPENSES (C)		
Step D: Optional Fixed and Variable Monthly Expenses		
Eating out (including coffee, snacks, lunches)		
Entertainment (movies, theater, night life)		
Travel		
Hobbies		
Gifts		
Charitable contributions		
Miscellaneous (CDs, magazines, newspapers, etc.)		
TOTAL OPTIONAL VARIABLE MONTHLY EXPENSES (D)		
Money Remaining or Owed at End of Month (A − B − C − D = ?)		

with the FAFSA: Free Application for Federal Student Aid. Using information you report on this form, the government decides what you or your family can afford to pay toward your education and what you may need in the way of financial assistance. Get copies of the form from your college's financial aid office or online at http://www.fafsa.ed.gov. There is also a "forecaster" at this site that will help you estimate the amount of financial aid you can expect to receive. The deadline for completing the FAFSA form is early July; however, some colleges use the information from the FAFSA form to determine their own financial aid, so be sure to check your school's deadline or you could be out of luck (and money) for that year. The benefit of qualifying for grants and scholarships is that, unlike loans, you don't need to pay them back. Federal Pell Grants provide financial support to students with family incomes up to $55,000; however, most Pell awards go to students with family incomes below $20,000. In 2008–2009, the grants ranged from $523 to $4,731, with an average grant in 2006–2007 of approximately $2,500. You can get comprehensive information from the Federal Student Aid Information Center in Washington at 800-433-3243 (http://www.studentaid.ed.gov). Here you can order a free copy of *The Student Guide,* and learn about programs that make up nearly three-fourths of all financial aid awarded to students. You can also search without cost for scholarships at Internet sites such as http://apps.collegeboard.com/cbsearch_ss/welcome.jsp, http://collegeanswer.com, and http://www.fastweb.com (so, don't waste money paying a private service to find you scholarships). Perhaps most important, spend time with a counselor in your college's financial aid office and let him or her help you get your share of the financial support available for a college education. Ron Smith, head of financial aid at Baltimore City Community College, offers this advice: "Students should apply early, provide accurate information, and follow up until an award has been received."

5. Apply for low-cost loans. Stafford loans are guaranteed by the federal government, so they generally offer the lowest interest rates. For dependent students, subsidized Stafford loans of up to $5,500 per year for first-year students, $6,500 for sophomores, and $7,500 for juniors and seniors are awarded on the basis of financial need. The U.S. government pays interest until repayment begins, usually after graduation. For independent students, loan maximums are significantly higher. Unsubsidized Stafford loans do not depend on financial need, but the interest accumulates while you are in college. You can apply for them through the Federal Direct Loan Program at 800-848-0979 (http://www.ed.gov/offices/OSFAP/DirectLoan/index.html) or through a private lender such as a bank. Other federally guaranteed student loans include PLUS loans (made to students' parents) and Perkins loans (for lower-income students). You may be approved for more loan money than you actually need and be tempted to borrow it all; just remember that what you take now, you'll need to repay later. You don't want to finish your education with the burden of an unnecessarily large debt. The standard repayment plan for student loans is equal monthly payment for ten years. That's a long time to pay for an earlier bad choice.

6. Work. Even with grants, scholarships, and low-cost loans, many college students need employment to make ends meet. If this is your situation, figure out how much money you need each month beyond any financial aid, and set a goal to earn that amount while also adding work experience in your future field of employment. In other words, your purpose for working is both to make money *and* to accumulate valuable employment experience and recommendations. In this way, you make it easier to find employment after college and perhaps even negotiate a higher starting salary. One place that may help you achieve this double goal is your campus job center. Additionally, on some campuses, instructors are able to hire student assistants to help them with their research. If you try but can't find employment that provides valuable work experience (or you're not sure what your future employment plans are), then seek work that allows you to earn your needed income in the fewest hours (saving you time to excel in your studies). Since many jobs you'll encounter in the newspaper pay little more than minimum wage, you may do better to create a high-paying job for yourself by using skills you already possess (or could easily learn). For example, one student noticed that each autumn the rain gutters of houses near his college became clogged with falling leaves. With a gasoline-powered leaf blower and a ladder in hand, he knocked on doors and offered to clean gutters for only $20. Few homeowners could resist such a bargain, and averaging two houses per hour, he earned nearly $700 each fall weekend.

7. Save and invest. If you haven't done so already, open a savings account and begin making regular deposits, even if it's only $20 per month (about what you'd pay for a pizza and a movie). Set a goal to accumulate a financial reserve for emergencies equal to three months' living expenses. After that, begin regular deposits in higher-income investments such as stocks, bonds, and mutual funds, topics beyond the scope of this book, but well worth your effort to research. (For a brief overview, visit http://www.fool.com/60second/indexfund .htm?ref=prmpgid.) To gain practical experience and guidance, consider joining (or starting) an investment club on your campus. You don't have to be an economics major to realize that by investing money regularly and benefiting from compound interest (earning interest on interest), even people with modest incomes can accumulate significant wealth. A way to make your savings grow even faster is to invest in a tax-deferred retirement account in which the money you deposit is not taxed until you withdraw it many years later, increasing the amount you can potentially save by many thousands of dollars. You can open such an account through your employer (who may even make additional contributions) or by opening an IRA (Individual Retirement Account) on your own. Some experts even suggest that you invest in such a tax-deferred retirement account before making deposits in a savings account. Your safety net in this approach is your credit cards, which you use

only in an emergency (as you would use your savings account, if you had one). Of course, this latter approach depends on your responsible use of credit cards and isn't for everyone, but it is another choice to consider.

Decreasing the Flow of Money Out

8. Lower transportation expenses: Cars are expensive. Beyond car payments, there's also the cost for insurance, registration, regular maintenance, gasoline, repairs, tolls, and parking. And if you're under twenty-five, you'll pay more for insurance than someone over twenty-five (especially young men, whose rates are double or triple those of older men). So, if money is tight, consider whether you can get along without a car for now. If you live on campus, this option should be fairly easy; if you commute, you could use public transportation or offer gas money to a classmate for rides to school. If you decide that you do need to buy a car, one expert suggests the following strategy for getting a good purchase price: After determining the model and options you want, call or email a number of dealers (preferably on the last day of the month when they are more likely to be anxious to make sales quotas), saying, "I'm going to buy this car today from the dealer who gives me the best price, so what's your lowest offer?" After receiving responses from at least six to eight dealers, contact the one with the second-to-lowest bid, reveal your lowest bid, and ask if they'll beat it. If so, buy their car. If not, purchase the one with the lowest bid. You can confirm that you're getting a fair price on a new or used car by visiting Kelley Blue Book (http://www.kbb.com) or Edmund's (http://www .edmunds.com).

9. Shop for car loans and insurance. *Before* you shop for your car, check interest rates for car loans with at least two banks and a credit union, and check insurance rates with at least three insurance companies. Knowing available interest rates will protect you from being pressured into signing a high-interest loan contract with the car dealer. On a car purchase, a lower interest rate can mean hundreds (even thousands) of dollars in savings over the life of the loan. You can also check for low interest rates on the Internet at http://www .Bankrate.com or http://www.Lendingtree.com. Likewise, automobile insurance rates for the same coverage can vary significantly from company to company. If you have good grades, tell the agent. A high GPA can reduce your premium by up to 25 percent with some companies! Oh, and think twice before allowing friends to drive your car; if they get in an accident, it's *your* insurance record and premiums that suffer, not your friend's.

10. Use credit cards wisely. You'll very likely be swamped with invitations to open credit card accounts. You're not alone. From 1990 to 2000, the average credit card debt of college students jumped 305 percent, from $900 to $2,748, and nearly 10 percent of college students owe greater than $7,000 on their credit cards, according to a 2000 survey by Sallie Mae, a major national handler of student loans. "These credit card issuers circle the campus like sharks circling a fish," says Elizabeth Warren, a Harvard Law School professor. So, first, consider whether you should even *have* a credit card. Visa, Master Card, and other credit cards provide you with short-term loans to purchase anything you want up to your credit limit. These companies are counting on you to postpone paying off the loan beyond the grace period (the time during which the loan is free), and thus to accumulate interest at their high rates. The consequences to your finances can be staggering. Suppose you're twenty years old and owe $3,500 on a credit card that charges 17 percent interest and you regularly pay the minimum charge. You won't pay off that debt until you're fifty-three years old, and the amount you will ultimately pay is nearly $11,000! And if you ever miss a payment, you'll incur a triple penalty. First, you'll be charged a late fee that can be as much as $35 for being even one day overdue. Next, some banks punish late payers by raising their interest rates to "penalty rates" of 20 percent or more. Finally, late payments can show up on your credit report, making it difficult for you to get

loans later for a house or car. Additional penalties will be assessed if you go over your credit limit. How serious is the problem of credit card misuse by college students? One widely quoted statement attributed to an administrator at the University of Indiana noted, "We lose more students to credit card debt than to academic failure." So, use a credit card only if you can discipline yourself to pay off most, and preferably all, of your balance every month. If you can't, a wiser choice would be to cut up your credit cards (or not even apply for one in the first place). To understand the true cost of buying with credit cards, try the exercise "The Cost of Credit" on the *On Course* website at: www.cengage .com/success/Downing/OnCourse6e.

11. Choose credit cards wisely. If you decide that you do have the discipline to use a credit card wisely, realize that all credit cards are not created equal. Compare your options and choose the one with the lowest interest rates, the longest grace period (time you get to use the money before paying interest), and the lowest annual fee (preferably free). Some cards offer a reward for using them, such as rebates for purchases or frequent flyer miles that can be exchanged for airline tickets. To find the best deals on credit cards, visit Internet sites such as http://www.bankrate.com or http://www .cardweb.com.

12. Use debit cards wisely. A debit card is similar to a credit card, except that the funds come not as a loan from the credit card company but as a withdrawal from your own checking account. The danger is that you may not record and track every purchase made on your debit card, as you more likely would if you wrote a check. Consequently, you can easily overdraw your checking account and incur financial penalties for bounced checks (not to mention annoying your creditors). Use a debit card only if you have the discipline to track its every use and keep your checking account balance current.

13. Use ATM cards wisely. An ATM card, like a debit card, draws from your personal account, but here the withdrawal is in cash. ATM cards are so easy to use that some financial experts refer to them as "death cards." Say you withdraw $100 in cash on Monday, and by Thursday the money has dribbled away, so you take out another $100 that disappears by the weekend. After a couple of weeks like this, your money runs out before the month does, and you're slipping ever deeper into debt. Use an ATM card only if you have the self-discipline to record every withdrawal and track what you do with your cash.

14. Pay off high-rate debt. When you pay off a loan (such as a credit card balance) that charges 17 percent, that's the same as investing your money at a guaranteed 17 percent rate of return. Better yet, the 17 percent return is tax free, so you're actually earning a return of more than 20 percent. Compare that to the puny interest rate you'd be earning in a savings account. If you don't have extra money in savings to pay off money you owe, a variation is to transfer debt from high-interest-rate loans to lower-interest-rate loans (but watch carefully for hidden transfer costs on some accounts).

15. Dispute inaccurate charges. Don't assume all of your bills are correct. Inspect your credit card bill, your bank statement, and all of your bills carefully for suspicious charges, such as a purchase you didn't make or an inaccurate late fee. Call the number on your statement and explain pleasantly but assertively why you believe the charge is an error. Usually the person you talk to is empowered to correct such errors. In fact, if you have a good credit history, it may even pay to question legitimate charges. I once forgot to pay my credit card bill on time and got charged more than $100 in late fees and interest; I called the credit card company, asked the representative to look at my excellent record of paying on time, and requested that the penalties be waived this once. She agreed, making my five-minute phone call well worth the effort!

16. Avoid credit blunders. There are serious consequences for being financially irresponsible. Every time you create a debt, national credit agencies are keeping detailed records. When you later apply for credit, potential lenders will have access to how much you owe, whom you owe, and how well you pay your debts. In fact, they'll learn your credit history for at least the past seven years, including late payments, underpayments, and lack of payments. This financial record tells lenders whether you are a good or bad risk, and, if you're seen as a bad risk, your application for a house or car loan may be turned down or only offered to you with extremely high interest rates. Your credit report might even wind up in the hands of a potential landlord or employer, affecting your ability to rent an apartment or even get your dream job. So, unwise financial choices in the present will follow you for years into the future, affecting the quality of your life and the life of your family. To see your present credit report and verify its accuracy, order a copy from Equifax at 800-685-1111 (http://www.equifax.com), Experian at 888-397-3742 (http://www.experian.com), or Trans Union at 800-888-4213 (http://www.tuc.com). Depending on where you live, the report will range in cost from free to about $8. If you make a credit blunder, immediately contact the company you owe and work out a payment schedule. The sooner you clean up your credit report, the sooner your past mistakes will stop sabotaging your future success. If you need help with debt, contact the National Foundation for Credit Counseling (NFCC) for low- or no-cost credit assistance at 800-388-2227 (http://www.nfcc.org).

17. Use tax credits. Tax credits are expenses you can subtract directly from your federal income tax. If you're paying for college yourself, you may be eligible for a Hope Credit of up to $1,800 in your first two years. For details on the Hope Credit (as well as the Lifetime Learning Credit), get a copy of IRS (Internal Revenue Service) Publication 970, *Tax Benefits for Higher Education,* or go to http://www.irs.gov/publications/p970/ch02.html#en_US_publink100020759.

18. Avoid the "Let's Go Out" trap. You or a friend says, "Let's go out." You go for food or drinks and spend $20 . . . or more. Do this a couple times a week and you'll wind up dropping hundreds of dollars a month into a deep, dark hole. One student reported that even after she ran out of money for the month, friends would say, "Oh, c'mon out with us. I'll loan you the money." That meant she was already spending next month's income. By all means, put entertainment money into your monthly financial plan, but, when it's gone, have the self-discipline to stop going out. Instead, invite friends over and make it BYO—Bring Your Own. Or, you could make a great financial choice by staying home and studying. Studying costs you nothing now and makes a great investment in your future income.

19. Track your expenditures. To plug a leak, you have to know where it is. So, carry a note pad with you and record every penny you spend for at least a week, preferably longer. (Of course your Inner Defender will probably say, "This is stupid and boring." Okay, it is boring, but the benefit is worth it!) Examine your recorded expenses and look for financial leaks that don't show up in your financial plan. One student was shocked to discover that he was averaging $21 per week ($1,144 per year!) on fast-food lunches; he started packing his lunch and saved a bundle.

20. Examine each expense line in your financial plan for possible reductions. Here are some of the money-saving options my students have come up with: Find a roommate to reduce housing costs. Exchange babysitting with fellow students to minimize child-care expenses. Car pool to share commuting costs. Cut up credit cards. Change banks to lower or eliminate monthly checking fees. Exchange music CDs with friends instead of buying new ones. Shop at discount clubs and buy nonperishables (such as toilet paper and laundry detergent) in bulk. Read magazines and newspapers at the library, instead of buying them. Pay creditors on time to avoid penalty charges. Delay purchases until the item goes on sale (such as right after Christmas). Find other money saving ideas on the Internet at http://www.lowermybills.com.

Money Management Exercise

To help *increase* your flow of money in, make a list of skills you have that you could possibly turn into a high-hourly-wage self-employment opportunity. To help *decrease* your flow of money out, make a list of choices you could make that would each save you $25 or more per year. If you need help, try an Internet search for "saving money" or "budget tips." Compare your two lists with those of classmates to see if you can find additional choices you didn't think of. Add up all of the items on your list (income and outflow) and see how much you could improve your financial picture in one year by making these choices.

Staying On Course to Your Success

9

Successful Students . . .	Struggling Students . . .
gain self-awareness, consciously employing behaviors, beliefs, and attitudes that keep them on course.	**make important choices unconsciously,** being directed by self-sabotaging habits and outdated life scripts.
adopt lifelong learning, finding valuable lessons and wisdom in nearly every experience they have.	**resist learning new ideas and skills,** viewing learning as fearful or boring rather than as mental play.
develop emotional intelligence, effectively managing their emotions in support of their goals and dreams.	**live at the mercy of strong emotions** such as anger, depression, anxiety, or a need for instant gratification.
believe in themselves, seeing themselves as capable, lovable, and unconditionally worthy human beings.	**doubt their competence and personal value,** feeling inadequate to create their desired outcomes and experiences.

Planning Your Next Steps

 FOCUS QUESTIONS How have you changed while keeping your journal? What changes do you still want to make?

Although our travels together are coming to an end, your journey has really just begun. Look out there to your future. What do you want to have, do, or be? What actions do you need to take to achieve your desired outcomes and experiences? Make a plan and go for it!

Sure, you'll get off course at times. But now you have the strategies—both outer and inner—to get back on course. Before heading out toward your goals and dreams, take a moment to review those strategies. Anytime you want, you can look over the table of contents of this book for an overview of what you've learned. Scan the chapter-opening charts to review the choices of successful and struggling people. Revisit the Embracing Change activities for a list of the empowering beliefs and behaviors you've learned. Reread a strategy as a reminder. Review the study skills you chose to create your CORE Learning System. Perhaps most important of all, reread your journal. At any time you can return to *On Course* and to your journal to remind yourself of anything you forget. And, believe me, you *will* forget. But you have the power to remember . . . and to make wise choices . . . and to achieve the life of your dreams.

> Destiny is not a matter of chance; it is a matter of choice. It is not a thing to be waited for; it is a thing to be achieved.
>
> *William Jennings Bryant*

Assess Yourself, Again

On the next page is a duplicate of the self-assessment you took in Chapter 1. Take it again. (Don't look back at your previous answers yet.) In Journal Entry 32, you will compare your first scores with your scores today, and you'll consider the changes you have made. Acknowledge yourself for your courage to grow. Look, also, at the changes you still need to make to become your best self.

You now have much of what you need to stay on course to the life of your dreams. The rest you can learn on your journey. Be bold! Begin today!

Onward!

> It isn't where you came from; it's where you're going that counts.
>
> *Ella Fitzgerald*

Self-Assessment

You can take this self-assessment on the Internet by visiting the On Course website at www.cengage.com/success/Downing/OnCourse6e.

Read the following statements and score each one according to how true or false you believe it is about you. To get an accurate picture of yourself, consider what IS true about you (not what you want to be true). Remember, there are no right or wrong answers. Assign each statement a number from 0 to 10, as follows:

Totally false　0　1　2　3　4　5　6　7　8　9　10　Totally true

1. _____　I control how successful I will be.
2. _____　I'm not sure why I'm in college.
3. _____　I spend most of my time doing important things.
4. _____　When I encounter a challenging problem, I try to solve it by myself.
5. _____　When I get off course from my goals and dreams, I realize it right away.
6. _____　I'm not sure how I learn best.
7. _____　Whether I'm happy or not depends mostly on me.
8. _____　I'll truly accept myself only after I eliminate my faults and weaknesses.
9. _____　Forces out of my control (such as poor teaching) are the cause of low grades I receive in school.
10. _____　I place great value on getting my college degree.
11. _____　I don't need to write things down because I can remember what I need to do.
12. _____　I have a network of people in my life that I can count on for help.
13. _____　If I have habits that hinder my success, I'm not sure what they are.
14. _____　When I don't like the way an instructor teaches, I know how to learn the subject anyway.
15. _____　When I get very angry, sad, or afraid, I do or say things that create a problem for me.
16. _____　When I think about performing an upcoming challenge (such as taking a test), I usually see myself doing well.
17. _____　When I have a problem, I take positive actions to find a solution.
18. _____　I don't know how to set effective short-term and long-term goals.
19. _____　I am organized.
20. _____　When I take a difficult course in school, I study alone.
21. _____　I'm aware of beliefs I have that hinder my success.
22. _____　I'm not sure how to think critically and analytically about complex topics.
23. _____　When choosing between doing an important school assignment or something really fun, I do the school assignment.
24. _____　I break promises that I make to myself or to others.
25. _____　I make poor choices that keep me from getting what I really want in life.
26. _____　I expect to do well in my college classes.
27. _____　I lack self-discipline.
28. _____　I listen carefully when other people are talking.
29. _____　I'm stuck with any habits of mine that hinder my success.

(continued)

30. _____ When I face a disappointment (such as failing a test), I ask myself, "What lesson can I learn here?"
31. _____ I often feel bored, anxious, or depressed.
32. _____ I feel just as worthwhile as any other person.
33. _____ Forces outside of me (such as luck or other people) control how successful I will be.
34. _____ College is an important step on the way to accomplishing my goals and dreams.
35. _____ I spend most of my time doing unimportant things.
36. _____ When I encounter a challenging problem, I ask for help.
37. _____ I can be off course from my goals and dreams for quite a while without realizing it.
38. _____ I know how I learn best.
39. _____ My happiness depends mostly on what's happened to me lately.
40. _____ I accept myself just as I am, even with my faults and weaknesses.
41. _____ I am the cause of low grades I receive in school.
42. _____ If I lose my motivation in college, I don't know how I'll get it back.
43. _____ I have a written self-management system that helps me get important things done on time.
44. _____ I know very few people whom I can count on for help.
45. _____ I'm aware of the habits I have that hinder my success.
46. _____ If I don't like the way an instructor teaches, I'll probably do poorly in the course.
47. _____ When I'm very angry, sad, or afraid, I know how to manage my emotions so I don't do anything I'll regret later.
48. _____ When I think about performing an upcoming challenge (such as taking a test), I usually see myself doing poorly.
49. _____ When I have a problem, I complain, blame others, or make excuses.
50. _____ I know how to set effective short-term and long-term goals.
51. _____ I am disorganized.
52. _____ When I take a difficult course in school, I find a study partner or join a study group.
53. _____ I'm unaware of beliefs I have that hinder my success.
54. _____ I know how to think critically and analytically about complex topics.
55. _____ I often feel happy and fully alive.
56. _____ I keep promises that I make to myself or to others.
57. _____ When I have an important choice to make, I use a decision-making process that analyzes possible options and their likely outcomes.
58. _____ I don't expect to do well in my college classes.
59. _____ I am a self-disciplined person.
60. _____ I get distracted easily when other people are talking.
61. _____ I know how to change habits of mine that hinder my success.
62. _____ When I face a disappointment (such as failing a test), I feel pretty helpless.
63. _____ When choosing between doing an important school assignment or something really fun, I usually do something fun.
64. _____ I feel less worthy than other people.

Transfer your scores to the scoring sheets on the next page. For each of the eight areas, total your scores in columns A and B. Then total your final scores as shown in the sample on the next page.

SELF-ASSESSMENT SCORING SHEET

Sample

A		B	
6. _8_		29. _3_	
14. _5_		35. _3_	
21. _6_		50. _6_	
73. _9_		56. _2_	
_28_ + 40 − _14_ = _54_			

SCORE #1: Accepting Personal Responsibility

A	B
1. ___	9. ___
17. ___	25. ___
41. ___	33. ___
57. ___	49. ___
___ + 40 − ___ = ___	

SCORE #2: Discovering Self-Motivation

A	B
10. ___	2. ___
26. ___	18. ___
34. ___	42. ___
50. ___	58. ___
___ + 40 − ___ = ___	

SCORE #3: Mastering Self-Management

A	B
3. ___	11. ___
19. ___	27. ___
43. ___	35. ___
59. ___	51. ___
___ + 40 − ___ = ___	

SCORE #4: Employing Interdependence

A	B
12. ___	4. ___
28. ___	20. ___
36. ___	44. ___
52. ___	60. ___
___ + 40 − ___ = ___	

SCORE #5: Gaining Self-Awareness

A	B
5. ___	13. ___
21. ___	29. ___
45. ___	37. ___
61. ___	53. ___
___ + 40 − ___ = ___	

SCORE #6: Adopting Lifelong Learning

A	B
14. ___	6. ___
30. ___	22. ___
38. ___	46. ___
54. ___	62. ___
___ + 40 − ___ = ___	

SCORE #7: Developing Emotional Intelligence

A	B
7. ___	15. ___
23. ___	31. ___
47. ___	39. ___
55. ___	63. ___
___ + 40 − ___ = ___	

SCORE #8: Believing in Myself

A	B
16. ___	8. ___
32. ___	24. ___
40. ___	48. ___
56. ___	64. ___
___ + 40 − ___ = ___	

CHOICES OF SUCCESSFUL STUDENTS

Successful Students . . .	Struggling Students . . .
accept personal responsibility, seeing themselves as the primary cause of their outcomes and experiences.	**see themselves as victims,** believing that what happens to them is determined primarily by external forces such as fate, luck, and powerful others.
discover self-motivation, finding purpose in their lives by discovering personally meaningful goals and dreams.	**have difficulty sustaining motivation,** often feeling depressed, frustrated, and/or resentful about a lack of direction in their lives.
master self-management, consistently planning and taking purposeful actions in pursuit of their goals and dreams.	**seldom identify specific actions needed to accomplish a desired outcome,** and when they do, they tend to procrastinate.
employ interdependence, building mutually supportive relationships that help them achieve their goals and dreams (while helping others do the same).	**are solitary,** seldom requesting, even rejecting, offers of assistance from those who could help.
gain self-awareness, consciously employing behaviors, beliefs, and attitudes that keep them on course.	**make important choices unconsciously,** being directed by self-sabotaging habits and outdated life scripts.
adopt lifelong learning, finding valuable lessons and wisdom in nearly every experience they have.	**resist learning new ideas and skills,** viewing learning as fearful or boring rather than as mental play.
develop emotional intelligence, effectively managing their emotions in support of their goals and dreams.	**live at the mercy of strong emotions such as anger,** depression, anxiety, or a need for instant gratification.
believe in themselves, seeing themselves as capable, lovable, and unconditionally worthy human beings.	**doubt their competence and personal value,** feeling inadequate to create their desired outcomes and experiences.

INTERPRETING YOUR SCORES

A score of . . .

0–39	Indicates an area where your choices will **seldom** keep you on course.
40–63	Indicates an area where your choices will **sometimes** keep you on course.
64–80	Indicates an area where your choices will **usually** keep you on course.

JOURNAL ENTRY 32

In this activity, you will examine the changes you have made since the beginning of this course, and you'll plan your next steps toward success in college and in life.

1. In your journal, write the eight areas of the self-assessment and transfer your two scores from the scoring chart on page 8 (first score) and the scoring chart on page 283 (second score), as follows:

First Score   Second Score

____	____	1. Accepting personal responsibility
____	____	2. Discovering self-motivation
____	____	3. Mastering self-management
____	____	4. Employing interdependence
____	____	5. Gaining self-awareness
____	____	6. Adopting lifelong learning
____	____	7. Developing emotional intelligence
____	____	8. Believing in myself

And the end of all our exploring
Will be to arrive where we started
And know the place for the first
time.

T. S. Eliot

2. **Comparing the results from the two self-assessment questionnaires, write in depth about the area(s) in which you have raised your score.** Remember to answer questions that a thoughtful reader would have about what you are writing, diving deep by using the 4E's (examples, explanations, experiences, and evidence)!

3. **Further comparing the results from the two self-assessment questionnaires, write in depth about the area(s) in which you most want to continue improving.** Remember the saying "If you keep doing what you've been doing, you'll keep getting what you've been getting." With this idea in mind, identify the specific changes you'd like to make in your behaviors, thoughts, emotions, and beliefs in the months and years to come.

By the way, if one of your scores went down over the semester, consider that this result may not indicate that you became less effective; rather, it may be that you are now more honest with yourself or more aware of what's necessary to excel in this area.

4. **Write one last entry in which you sum up the most important discoveries that you have made about yourself while keeping your journal so far.** Dive deep!

One Student's Story

Stephan J. Montgomery
Washtenaw Community College, Michigan

In 2002, I hit rock bottom when I moved into a homeless shelter. For the next four years, I cycled in and out of one shelter after another. There, I saw how people can become passive and numb, with no life or hope left in their eyes. They smell bad, walk with their heads down, and are filled with negativity. Their only goal in life is getting a handout. I knew I couldn't allow a sheltered life to become my life.

I was a Detroit police officer from 1985 to 1998. In 1996 I lost my mother and not long after that my 17-year-old son died of an asthma attack. In my mind, crying on someone's shoulder was a sign of weakness, so I kept it all inside. I had been drinking before, but now I started drinking even more. I left the police force in 1998 and started a limo service. Four years later, I was arrested for drunk driving and lost my license. When I couldn't pay rent, the woman I was living with put me out, and I lived in my car for two months. That's when I turned to a homeless shelter for help.

My first concern was to become self-supporting, but I wasn't sure where to start. I went to a state employment service and told a counselor, "I want a college degree; not one of those low paying jobs listed in the job bank." She told me about scholarships at the local community college, and with her help, I registered for classes in 2007. I hadn't been a student for thirty-plus years, and the thought of attending college scared me. But I had a goal. I wanted to become a computer systems security analyst, a career that starts at about $48,000. The money sure sounded good.

In my English Fundamentals class I encountered *On Course*. The book gave me insights into my past failures and successes and provided specific strategies for achieving success in college and in my life. I realized that many of my past problems were rooted in victim language. When I was on the police force, I felt that some of the supervisors picked on me. I'd say they didn't like me because I wasn't in the right group. The truth was, I was missing a lot of work, but I always shifted the blame. After reading about Victim/Creator, I told myself, *You have to rebuild yourself. No one else is going to do it for you.* I even started telling people back at the shelter about what I was learning in this class.

My greatest concern about attending college was how to organize my time. The newly discovered creator in me used the Four Quadrant Chart to prioritize my daily tasks. As I used the self-management tools in the book, I developed self-confidence that I would do well in college. I showed the Next Actions List to others and told them how important it is to have a list to keep you focused. If someone tells you they have tickets to the Detroit Pistons game, you have to say no and do what is important for your goals.

Along with how to organize my time, I discovered the beauty of interdependence. Two of my English classmates and I decided to meet in the Writing Center after each class and work on our assignments together. We encouraged each other and became teachers as well as students. Our newfound interdependence made us feel valuable and gave us increased confidence and feelings of self-worth. This confidence translated into academic success as well. I earned a 3.88 GPA, high honors, for my first semester.

In the next semester I got a part-time job in the writing center. I love to see a twinkle in students' eyes when I help them do well on a paper. I also started volunteering at the Washtenaw Literacy program. I continue to use *On Course* principles in my daily life, and I share them at the tutoring center, in my volunteer work and at the shelter. These principles provide the best hope for people to lead successful, happy, and unsheltered lives. Two of the men from the shelter are now enrolled at the college, and they come to me when they have a problem. One guy still has a victim mentality. I tell him, "Why do you blame your woe-is-me on everyone else and not look in the mirror and see yourself as the cause? If I can help you, I will. But you have to help yourself first."

People have to learn to stand on their own two feet, and I now have the skills to help others do that. I've even changed my career goal. I plan to teach elementary school. For me it's no longer about the money. It's about sharing myself. After experiencing the lessons in *On Course*, I feel I have something to share. My fear of failure is gone. Being a creator, I believe in myself and feel confident that I can solve any problems I face. Now I want to share that feeling with others.

Photo: Courtesy of Stephan J. Montgomery

Bibliography

Adams, Kathleen. *Journal to the Self: Twenty-Two Paths to Personal Growth.* Warner Books, 1990.

Allen, David. *Getting Things Done.* Viking, 2001.

———. *Making It All Work.* Viking. 2009.

Brandon, Nathaniel. *The Psychology of Self-Esteem.* Jossey-Bass, 2001.

Burka, Jane B., and Lenora M. Yuen. *Procrastination.* DeCapo, 2008.

Burns, David, M.D. *Feeling Good.* William Morrow & Company, 1980.

Buzan, Tony. *Make the Most of Your Mind.* Simon and Schuster, 1977.

Cappacchione, Lucia. *The Creative Journal.* Newcastle, 1989.

Ciarrochi, Joseph. *Emotional Intelligence in Everyday Life.* Psychology Press, 2001.

Covey, Stephen R. *7 Habits of Highly Effective People.* Simon and Schuster, 1989.

Csikszentmihalyi, Mihaly. *Flow: The Psychology of Optimal Experience.* Harper & Row, 1990.

Davis, Martha, Elizabeth Robbins Eshelman, and Matthew McKay. *The Relaxation and Stress Reduction Workbook.* New Harbinger, 2000.

deBono, Edward. *deBono's Thinking Course.* Facts on File, 1982.

Doidge, Norman. *The Brain That Changes Itself.* Penguin, 2007.

Dweck, Carol. *Mindset: The New Psychology of Success.* Random House, 2006.

Dyer, Wayne. *Excuses Begone.* Hay House, 2009.

Fieori, Neil. *The Now Habit.* Tarcher, 2007.

Firestone, Robert W., Lisa Firestone, Joyce Catlett, and Pat Love. *Conquer Your Critical Inner Voice.* New Harbinger, 2002.

Frankl, Viktor E., M.D. *Man's Search for Meaning.* Washington Square Press, 1959.

Garfield, Charles. *Peak Performers.* Avon Books, 1986.

Glasser, William. *Reality Therapy.* Harper & Row, 1978.

Goleman, Daniel. *Emotional Intelligence.* Bantam Books, 1995.

———. *Working with Emotional Intelligence.* Bantam Books, 2000.

Griessman, B. Eugene. *The Achievement Factors.* Dodd, Mead, 1987.

Harmon, Willis, and Howard Rheingold. *Higher Creativity.* J.P. Tarcher, 1984.

Harris, Thomas. *I'm OK, You're OK.* Harper & Row, 1967.

Helmstetter, Shad. *Choices.* Simon and Schuster, 1989.

Herrmann, Ned. *The Creative Brain.* Brain Books, 1989.

Holden, Robert. *Success Intelligence.* Hay House, 2009.

Howard, Pierce J. *The Owner's Manual for the Brain.* Bard Press, 2006.

James, Muriel, and Dorothy Jongeward. *Born to Win.* Addison-Wesley, 1978.

Jensen, Eric. *Enriching the Brain.* Jossey-Bass, 2008.

Keirsey, D., and M. Bates. *Please Understand Me.* Prometheus Nemesis Books, 1978.

Kernis, Michael. *Self-Esteem: Issues and Answers.* Psychology Press, 2006.

Lehrer, Jonah. *How We Decide.* Houghton Mifflin Harcourt, 2009.

Leyden-Rubenstein, Lori. *The Stress Management Handbook.* Keats Publishing, 1998.

Mandino, Og. *A Better Way to Live.* Bantam Books, 1990.

Mazlow, Abraham H. *Toward a Psychology of Being.* Van Nostrand Reinhold, 1968.

McKay, Matthew, Patrick Fanning, Carole Honeychurch, and Catherine Sutker. *The Self-Esteem Companion.* MJF Books, 2001.

Merlevede, Patrick E., Denis Bridoux, and Rudy Vandamme. *7 Steps to Emotional Intelligence.* Crown House, 2001.

Merrill, A. Roger. *Connections: Quadrant II Time Management.* Publishers Press, 1987.

Myers, David G. *The Pursuit of Happiness.* Avon Books, 1992.

Myers, Isabelle. *The Myers-Briggs Type Indicator.* Consulting Psychological Press, 1962.

Ostrander, Sheila, and Lynn Schroeder. *Super-learning.* Dell, 1979.

Peck, M. Scott, M.D. *The Road Less Traveled.* Simon and Schuster, 1978.

Progroff, Ira. *At a Journal Workshop.* Dialogue House Library, 1975.

Restak, Richard, M.D. *The Mind.* Bantam Books, 1988.

Richardson, Cheryl. *Turning Inward: A Private Journal for Self-Reflection.* Hay House, 2003.

Satir, Virginia. *The New People-making.* Science and Behavior Books, 1988.

Schiraldi, Glen R., Patrick Fanning, and Matthew McKay. *The Self-Esteem Workbook.* New Harbinger, 2001.

Segal, Jeanne. *Raising Your Emotional Intelligence.* Henry Holt, 1997.

Seligman, Martin. *Learned Optimism.* Alfred A. Knopf, 1991.

Smith, Hyrum W. *The 10 Natural Laws of Successful Time and Life Management.* Warner Books, 1994.

Sousa, David A. *How the Brain Learns.* Corwin Press, 2006.

Steiner, Claude M. *Scripts People Live.* Bantam Books, 1974.

Stone, Hal, and Sidra Stone. *Embracing Your Inner Critic.* HarperCollins, 1993.

Tobias, Sheila. *Overcoming Math Anxiety.* W.W. Norton & Co., 1993.

vonOech, Roger. *A Whack on the Side of the Head.* Warner Books, 1983.

Ward, Francine. *Esteemable Acts: 10 Actions for Building Real Self-Esteem.* Broadway Books, 2003.

Index